Islamism and Democracy in India

PRINCETON STUDIES IN MUSLIM POLITICS

DALE F. EICKELMAN AND AUGUSTUS RICHARD NORTON, *EDITORS*

Diane Singerman, *Avenues of Participation: Family, Politics, and Networks in Urban Quarters of Cairo*

Tone Bringa, *Being Muslim the Bosnian Way: Identity and Community in a Central Bosnian Village*

Dale F. Eickelman and James Piscatori, *Muslim Politics*

Bruce B. Lawrence, *Shattering the Myth: Islam beyond Violence*

Ziba Mir-Hosseini, *Islam and Gender: The Religious Debate in Contemporary Iran*

Robert W. Hefner, *Civil Islam: Muslims and Democratization in Indonesia*

Muhammad Qasim Zaman, *The Ulama in Contemporary Islam: Custodians of Change*

Michael G. Peletz, *Islamic Modern: Religious Courts and Cultural Politics in Malaysia*

Oskar Verkaaik, *Migrants and Militants:* Fun, *Islam, and Urban Violence in Pakistan*

Laetitia Bucaille, *Growing up Palestinian: Israeli Occupation and the Intifada Generation*

Robert W. Hefner, editor, *Remaking Muslim Politics: Pluralism, Contestation, Democratization*

Lara Deeb, *An Enchanted Modern: Gender and Public Piety in Shi`I Lebanon*

Roxanne L. Euben, *Journeys to the Other Shore: Muslim and Western Travelers in Search of Knowledge*

Robert W. Hefner and Muhammad Qasim Zaman, eds., *Schooling Islam: The Culture and Politics of Modern Muslim Education*

Loren D. Lybarger, *Identity and Religion in Palestine: The Struggle between Islamism and Secularism in the Occupied Territories*

Augustus Richard Norton, *Hezbollah: A Short History*

Bruce K. Rutherford, *Egypt after Mubarak: Liberalism, Islam, and Democracy in the Arab World*

Irfan Ahmad, *Islamism and Democracy in India: The Transformation of Jamaat-e-Islami*

Islamism and Democracy in India

THE TRANSFORMATION OF JAMAAT-E-ISLAMI

Irfan Ahmad

PRINCETON UNIVERSITY PRESS
PRINCETON AND OXFORD

Published by Princeton University Press, 41 William Street, Princeton, New Jersey 08540
In the United Kingdom: Princeton University Press, 6 Oxford Street, Woodstock, Oxfordshire OX20 1TW

Library of Congress Cataloging-in-Publication Data

Ahmad, Irfan, 1974–
Islamism and democracy in India : the transformation of Jamaat-e-Islami / Irfan Ahmad.
p. cm. — (Princeton studies in Muslim politics)
Includes bibliographical references and index.
ISBN 978-0-691-13919-7 (hardcover : alk. paper) — ISBN 978-0-691-13920-3 (pbk. : alk. paper) 1. Jama'at-i Islami (India) 2. Jama'at-i Islami (India)—Political activity. 3. Islam and politics—India. 4. Islam and secularism—India. 5. India—Politics and government. 6. Democracy—Religious aspects—Islam. I. Title.
BP10.J343A46 2009
324.254'082—dc22 2009011056

British Library Cataloging-in-Publication Data is available

This book has been composed in Sabon

Printed on acid-free paper. ∞
press.princeton.edu

Printed in the United States of America

10 9 8 7 6 5 4 3 2 1

TO

Ammī (Najma Khatoon)

Abbī jī (Fazil Ahmad)

&

Bẖikhāri bẖāī (Bhikhari Paswan)

The simple truth is that whenever religion gets into society's driving seat, tyranny results.

SALMAN RUSHDIE, *The Guardian*,
March 18, 2005

Religion is like a candle that can illuminate one's cottage; it can also set it on fire: the choice is one's own, what use is made of it.

Persian adage, in Partha S. Ghosh,
BJP and the Evolution of Hindu Nationalism

Contents

Illustrations and Tables

Maps

Figures

Graph

Tables

Preface and Acknowledgments

In 2002 the Bharatiya Janata Party (BJP) was at the helm of power in Delhi, and the agenda of Hindu Nationalism, or Hindutva, was barely hidden. In an interview with an Urdu weekly, the minister for human resource development Murli Manohar Joshi, remarked that if the Jamaat-e-Islami Hind (hereafter, the Jamaat) could talk of establishing an Islamic state, *islāmī shāsan*, in India, what was wrong if the Rāsḥtriya Swayamsevak Sangh (RSS), the ideological fountainhead of the BJP, desired a Hindu state, *hindū shāsan* (*Friday Special* 2002 [November 1-15]: 11). Strangely enough Joshi's statement came at a time when, having long abandoned the agenda of an Islamic state, the Jamaat had been fervently campaigning to defend and strengthen secularism and democracy. Joshi's statement, it seems, was aimed at legitimizing his own project of Hindutva. In so doing he appeared to lavishly canonize the Jamaat, a small organization or movement that as late as 2000 had fewer than five thousand members and three hundred thousand sympathizers (see Appendix 1). Even if we combine the number of members and sympathizers, what percentage would it constitute of the more than 130 million Indian Muslims?

This book is a historical ethnography of the *ideological* transformation or moderation of the Jamaat from its formation in 1941 to the present. It demonstrates how the Jamaat, which, before the Partition of India, invoked the Qur'an and *hadīth* (Prophet's sayings) to argue that secularism and democracy were *haram* (forbidden), later came to accept, even embrace them. It shows the remarkable transformation of Islamism and the conflicts and contestations that accompanied that transformation. In arguing against the putative fixity of Islamism, I stress the commonality of processes, structures, and argumentations that it shares with other religious or secular movements, and vice versa. Along with moderation of the Jamaat and its constitutional student wing, the Student Islamic Organization of India (SIO), the book also deals with the radicalization of the Student Islamic Movement of India (SIMI), a breakaway young group of the Jamaat.

The themes and processes of moderation and radicalization are fundamental to postcolonial Indian modernity. Their salience is not limited to India, however. My attempt here is to think through the complex interrelationships among Islamism, Muslim minority identity, and the politics of secularism and democracy. Combining the tools and insights drawn from anthropology, Islamic studies, and social movement studies, the book seeks to raise a number of questions about the state, religion, modernity, authenticity, pluralism, secularism, minority identity, and what has come to be called Islamic radicalism or terrorism. Raising productive (and unpalatable) questions, I believe, is far more valuable than rushing for simple answers.

I was awarded a Ph.D. scholarship by the Amsterdam School for Social Science Research (ASSR), University of Amsterdam, where I completed my dissertation. The book in your hand is a revised version of my dissertation. It is based on sixteen months of intensive fieldwork, ethnographic as well as archival. I conducted the first phase of the fieldwork from October 2001 to October 2002, and the second from January to May 2004, with a grant from the Netherlands Organization for Scientific Research. I selected Aligarh, a town some 125 kilometers southeast of Delhi and known worldwide as the seat of the Aligarh Muslim University, the site of my fieldwork. The dynamics of my research, however, pushed me to adopt a multi-sited ethnographic approach. Azamgarh, Rampur, both in the state of Uttar Pradesh and Patna, the capital of the state of Bihar, became other sites of my fieldwork, as did New Delhi where the Jamaat headquarters is based.

I first began working on the Jamaat for my M.Phil. degree at Jawaharlal Nehru University (JNU), New Delhi, in 1996. During these years I have accumulated enormous debt to the Jamaat community, colleagues, teachers-mentors, friends, and my family. First I thank the current and former activists of the Jamaat, the SIO and the SIMI. Though initially suspicious of my research, later their trust evolved and they spared their precious time to talk with me. They offered valuable insights into the dynamics of the Jamaat, introduced me to relevant persons, and lent me important documents of the movement. I am grateful to them all for their time and warm hospitality (and, yes, the dinner, *daʿvat*). The list is far too long to name every individual, but deserving mention is Nabi Muhammad, the former *amīr* of the Jamaat in *shahr*, Aligarh, and previously a communist activist. He wanted his name to appear in print, but, sadly, he died before the book's publication.

Most of the archival-historical research was done in libraries at the Jamaat's headquarters in New Delhi, its former headquarters in Rampur, and its research institute in Aligarh. I am indebted to Aslam, Manzoor Fakhir, and Razi-ul Islam *ṣāḥibs* for making the materials available to me. Muzaffar Alam *ṣāḥib* of the Khuda Bakhsh Oriental Public Library, Patna, directed me to rare documents about or by the Jamaat. Part of the archival work was done at Maulana Abulkalam Azad Library, Aligarh Muslim University (AMU), Aligarh and Reza Library, Rampur. I thank the staff of these libraries.

At JNU's Center for the Study of Social Systems (CSSS), where this project took off, I thank my M.Phil. supervisor, R. K. Jain. To Avijit Pathak, I am eternally indebted for his love, encouragement, and firm faith in me. In various ways, Maitreyee Chaudhary, J. S. Gandhi, Dipankar Gupta, Anand Kumar, T. K. Oommen and Susan Visvanathan took an interest in the project, offering guidance and encouragement. I am also grateful to Imtiaz Ahmed of JNU for his many suggestions. Neshat Quaiser of Jamia Millia Islamia (JMI), New Delhi, where I received my undergraduate training in sociology, offered insights into the trajectory of the Jamaat. My thanks also go to Mohini Anjum, Tulsi Patel, and Mohammad Talib of the JMI for their interest in my work.

In the new atmosphere of Dutch-European academia, I greatly benefited from my association with a number of individuals. I thank Jan Breman, Abram de Swaan, Peter Geschiere, Thomas Blom Hansen, Christophe Jaffrelot, Marcel Van der Linden, Jamal Malik, Birgit Meyer, Peter Pels, Abdulkader Tayob, and Peter van Rooden. For their comments on different versions of the chapters or conference papers, I am thankful to Gautam Bhadra (CSSS Calcutta), Asef Bayat (ISIM), Veena Das (Johns Hopkins University), Linda Herrera (ISS, The Hague), Stephen Hughes (SOAS, University of London), Patricia Jeffery and Roger Jeffery (University of Edinburgh), Mohammad Khalid Masud (Islamabad), Harbans Mukhia (Delhi), Farish Noor (Singapore), Arvind Rajagopal (New York University), Ghanshyam Shah (Surat), Yogi Sikand (Bangalore), J. P. S. Uberoi (Delhi School of Economics), and Willem van Schendel and Oskar Verkaaik (both at the University of Amsterdam). I am also grateful to Olivier Roy for sharing some of his unpublished materials. For their insightful and critical comments on the manuscript, I thank Kamran Asdar Ali (University of Texas, Austin), Faisal Devji (University of Oxford), Filippo Osella (University of Sussex), Mathijs Pelkmans (London School of Economics), Samuli Schielke (Das Zentrum Moderner Orient, Berlin), Benjamin Soares (Africa Studies Center, Leiden), Vazira Zamindar (Brown University), and my brother Rizwan Ahmad (first at the University of Michigan, Ann Arbor, and now at the American University of Kuwait). Though I did not incorporate each of their suggestions, their input sharpened my position. I am also grateful to Filippo Osella and Benjamin Soares for their general interest in my work. A special thanks to Kamran *bhāī* (Ali), who offered incisive suggestions at critical moments. Austin did not seem distant from Amsterdam and Leiden. I am equally thankful to the reviewers of Princeton University Press for their appreciation and constructive criticisms of the manuscript.

The award of a fellowship by Humboldt Foundation resulting in my participation in the European-American Young Scholars' Summer Institute, "Public Spheres and Muslim Identities," held in 2001 in Berlin, offered a rich venue to interact with colleagues working on different regions of the Muslim world. I am especially thankful to Dale Eickelman and Armando Salvatore, conveners of the Institute. Dale guided me to key works on Islam and offered useful advice. Over the course of writing this book, I had the good fortune to present earlier incarnations before a number of receptive and engaging audiences, including the following professional conferences: the American Anthropological Association (AAA) Conference, San Jose (2006); the Association for Asian Studies (AAS) Conference, San Francisco (2006); and the European Conference for Modern South Asian Studies, Manchester (2008). For the AAS Conference, Elora Shehabuddin, of Rice University, and I organized a panel on the Jamaat-e-Islami in South Asia to which Faisal Devji became an engaging discussant. I also made presentations at the conferences on "Cultures of Voting," Centre d'Études et de Recherché Internationales, Paris; "Islamic Learning in South Asia," Erfurt University; "Islamic Reform Movements in South Asia," SOAS; "Contemporary Islamic Movements: Ideology, Aesthetics, Politics," University of Texas, Austin; "Youth and the Global South," Dakar; and seminars at the Department of Anthropology, University of Sussex; the Center for South Asian Studies, University of Cambridge (thanks to Magnus Marsden); the Public Culture Colloquium, Department of Anthropology, University of Texas, Austin; the Staff Seminar of the International Institute for the Study of Islam in the Modern World (ISIM); the International Institute for Asian Studies Fellows' Seminar, Leiden; and CSSS, JNU, New Delhi.

As part of the Ph.D. committee, Gerd Baumann and Mario Rutten have been extremely helpful in their suggestions, criticism, and encouragement. As members of my doctoral defense committee, stimulating questions and observations were made by Willem Duyvendak, Ruud Peters, Annelies Moors, and Martin Van Bruinessen. Along with Asef Bayat, the latter two became my colleagues at ISIM, Leiden, where I moved to work on a Postdoctoral Fellowship—Rubicon Grant—awarded by the Netherlands Organization for Scientific Research (NWO). I thank all three of them, especially Martin van Bruinessen. ISIM proved an ideal place for such a project.

To my guru, Peter Van der Veer, I owe a special gratitude far surpassing words. He gave me ample freedom to find my own path. Many insights in the book emerged from a critical dialogue with him and his work. As my Ph.D. supervisor, he was intense in his imagination, theoretically challenging in his suggestions, and constructive in his criticism. Without his unfailing encouragement, love, and compassion, this project would not have seen the light of day. The usual disclaimers apply.

In Aligarh, Azim's family was like my own. I am deeply indebted to him and his wife, Maryam, for accepting me as a member of his family. Among friends—some old, some new—I thank Mohammad Amer, Anjana Singh, Anouk de Koning, Ashraf Khan, Barak Kalir, Kausar Mazhari (Ehsan *bẖāī*), Faiyaz Beg, Francio Guadeloupe, Lotte Hoek, Martijn Osoterbaan, Mehtab Alam, Miriyam Aouragh, Mohammad Waked, Murari Dwivedi, Nasim Bhattacharjee, Puspesh Kumar, Pranay Krishna Shrivastava, Rivke Jaffe, Sanjeev Kumar, Satyajit Puhan, Mohammad Shakeel, Shifra Kisch, and Thirunavakkarasu. They all lent their support and encouragement with much enthusiasm and humor.

Words alone cannot express the gratitude I feel toward my family. As always, *bẖaiyā*, my elder brother Rizwan Ahmad, was a joyful source of intellectual exchange and ethical solidarity. Despite his own academic engagements and family obligations, he came to my support in difficult times. My little sister, Shannu (Nusrat Yasmeen), remained enthusiastic throughout, asking "*bẖaiyā*, when is your book coming." Unlike Shannu, my elder sisters, *baṛi bājī* (Shaheena Parveen), and *chẖoti bājī* (Talat Jahan) could not obtain an education. They are unable to read even a single sentence of this book. However, it is their affection and encouragement which significantly inspired me to embark upon a journey such as this. I am eternally indebted to my parents, *ammī* and *abbī*, for their unbounded love, encouragement, and support. Without fully understanding what I was doing, my mother, *ammī*, dreamed of the completion of my Ph.D. and publication of this book. Ammi prayed for me; her palms joined together in *duʿā*. I really don't know how to thank—Can I ever?—*ammī* and my father, *abbī ji*. As parents from an obscure village in Bihar, they chose to educate their son. As someone who could not go to school, my mother's determination to educate us was perhaps stronger. *Abbī* heartily supported what I chose to do. I forgot many lessons from my years at madrasa but always remember a Farsi line *abbī* told us: *kasb-e- kamāl kun ke azīz-e- jahāñ shavī* (strive for perfection so that the world admires you). Both *ammī* and *abbī* suffered hardships, privately, without letting me know. It is because of their firm determination, silent sacrifice, and unexpressed love that I was able to write these pages. And it is primarily to them, and *bhikhāri bhāī*, an enduring family friend in our village, that I dedicate this book.

Minor aspects of the book were previously published in *Global Networks: A Journal of Transnational Affairs*, *Modern Asian Studies*, and the *Journal of the Royal Anthropological Institute*.

My editor at Princeton University Press, Fred Appel, nurtured this book with the utmost care and attention. Special thanks to Fred whose extraordinary enthusiasm, patience, and interest made the publication of this book possible.

Irfan Ahmad
Leiden, August 15, 2008

Notes to the Reader

Unless indicated otherwise, all English translations from Urdu and Hindi are mine. The underlined words or phrases indicate their original usage in English, spoken or written (often in roman script, occasionally also in transliterated forms).

In transliterating Urdu and Hindi words, I follow the Annual of Urdu Studies (AUS) transliteration guidelines 2007 with the exception that I use the symbol "ch" for the first sound in the word "chaman" rather than Č. I do this because the diacritic above the letter "C" is not common among most social scientists. Similarly, I use the symbol "ḳh" for the first sound in the word "ḳhaṭ̤" rather than "kh" and "g̣h," as in "g̣halaṭ̤," rather than "gh." This is to avoid confusion with the Indic sound "kẖ" as in "kẖulā" (meaning "open") and "gẖ" as in "gẖar" (meaning "home").

In representing Arabic or Urdu words that have gained currency in the academic world, I follow the standard transcription convention even if they deviate from the AUS guidelines. For example, I use "sharia" rather than "sharīʿā." Other examples are "fatwa," Islam, and "sunna." These words, as well as "halal," "haram," "fatwa," and "eid," have been incorporated into the *Oxford English Dictionary* (*OED*) and are familiar to readers. Another deviation from the AUS system occurs in the representation of the word "Jamāʿat." The organization itself spells the word "Jamaat" in its English publications, and so I use that spelling here. Likewise, since the Jamaat spells its Urdu organ "Dawat" in English, I retained that spelling as well. However, when this word is used as a common noun to mean "invitation to Islam," I spell it "*daʿvat*." All non-English words are italicized. Exceptions are jihad, madrasa, sharia, and ulema, because of their frequent use in the text. I add the English plural marker suffix –s to the word "madrasa" when referring to its plural form.

A note on bibliography is in order. The primary materials are divided into three categories: (1) pamphlets, reports, proceedings, and documents of the Jamaat, SIO, and SIMI; (2) articles, books (mostly in Urdu), and Web sites on the movement, written by movement activists and their critics; and (3) magazines and newspapers. The secondary materials includes sources other than these three types. The primary and secondary materials are further divided into Urdu and English sources. The few Hindi references I use include "in Hindi" at the end of the reference. I list an edited volume as an independent entry to avoid its repeated mention when referencing multiple articles from the same volume. After the author's name, year of publication, and article title, I simply indicate, for example, *In* Carol A. Breckenridge and Peter Van der Veer (eds.). Finally, an asterisk (*) denotes that the documents were meant only for Jamaat members.

Abbreviations

AMU	Aligarh Muslim University, Aligarh
AMUSU	Aligarh Muslim University Student Union
APB	Arabic and Persian Board, Lucknow
AU	*Amar ujālā*, Agra, Aligarh edition
FA	*Fihrist-e-arkān*, published by the jamāʿat -e-islāmī hind
HN	*Ḥayāt-e-nau*, Urdu organ of Falāḥ's Old Boys' Association
IM	*Islamic Movement*; Urdu and Hindi organs of SIMI
JID	*Jamāʿat kī daʿvat, uskā naṣbul ʿain . . . lāʾeḥa-e-ʿamal, unmēñ tarmīm aur iẓāfē*
JCHSP	*Jamāʿat-e-islāmī hind kā chahār sāla prōgirām*
JMPP	*Jamāʿat-e-islāmī hind kā mīqātī prōgirām aur paulīsī*
JIMI	*Jamāʿat-e-islāmī hind aur masʾala-e-intikḥābāt*
JISS	*Jamāʿat-e-islāmī hind kē satāis sāl*
JMK	*Johd-e-musalsal kē pachīs sāl*, SIMI
ME	*Masʾala-e-elekshan aur markazī majlis-e-shura jamāʿat-e-islāmī hind*
MMR	*Maqālāt-o-mokḥtaṣar rūdād ijtimāʿ bhōpāl, jamāʿat-e-islāmī hind*
MMS	*Markazī majlis-e-shura jamāʿat-e-islāmī hind kī qarārdādēn*, 1961–1997
ODI	*Oxford Dictionary of Islam*
PJ	*Pānch janya*, weekly Hindi organ of the RSS
RIR	*Rūdād-e-ijtimāʿ rāmpūr*, jamāʿat-e-islāmī hind 1951
RAM	*Rafīq-e-manzil*, Urdu organ of SIO
RMS-1	*Rūdād majlis-e-shura, jamāʿat-e-islāmī hind*, August 1948 tā July 1966
RMS-2	*Rūdād majlis-e-shura, jamāʿat-e-islāmī hind*, May 1967 tā May 1989
RSS	Rāshṭriya Swayamsēvak Sangh, ideological fountainhead of Hindutva
Sangh parīvār	Hindi term for a group of organizations committed to the RSS ideology; used interchangeably here as *Sangh parīvār* and Sangh family
SIMI	Student Islamic Movement of India
SIO	Student Islamic Organization of India
TYP	*Three-Year Progress Organizational Report* by the General Secretary

Tarjumān	*Tarjumānul Qur'an*
UP	Uttar Pradesh, the largest state of the Indian Union
VHP	Vishwa Hindu Parishad, an affiliate of the Sangh parīvār

Islamism and Democracy in India

JAMMU & KASHMIR
Srinagar
Pathankot
HIMACHAL PRADESH
Chandigarh
PUNJAB
Shimla
Dehradun
UTTARAKHAND
HARYANA
DELHI
PAKISTAN
CHINA (TIBET)
Muzaffarpur
Darbhanga
NEPAL
SIKKIM
Gangtok
BHUTAN
ARUNACHAL PRADESH
Itangar
ASSAM
Dispur
NAGALAND
Kohima
Imphal
MANIPUR
Aizawl
MIZORAM
MYANMAR
BANGLADESH
RAJASTHAN
Jaipur
UTTAR PRADESH
Lucknow
BIHAR
Patna
JHARKHAND
Ranchi
WEST BENGAL
Kolkata (Calcutta)
GUJARAT
Gandhinagar
Bhopal
MADHYA PRADESH
CHHATISGARH
Raipur
ORISSA
Bhubaneswar
Aurangabad
MAHARASHTRA
Mumbai (Bombay)
ARABIAN SEA
Hyderabad
ANDHRA PRADESH
Panaji
GOA
KARNATAKA
Bangalore
Chennai (Madras)
TAMIL NADU
KERALA
Thiruvananthapuram
LAKSHADWEEP
BAY OF BENGAL
Port Blair
ANDAMAN & NICOBAR ISLANDS
N
▲ Additional locations relevant to this study

Map 1. India

INTRODUCTION

> "Islam," without referring it to the facets of a system of which it is part, does not exist.
>
> —Abdul Hamid El-Zein, *"Beyond Ideology and Theology"*

Having faced acute suspicion from the Jamaat in Aligarh, I was thrilled when Shaheed, an eminent leader of its student wing (the Student Islamic Organization of India, SIO), agreed to a meeting. It was January 2002, and the debate on the February elections for the Uttar Pradesh (UP) Assembly had started. Hearsay had it that to defeat the "communal, fascist" Bharatiya Janata Party (BJP), the Jamaat would canvass for the victory of candidates committed to secularism and democracy. And this precisely was the thorniest debate in the Jamaat circle: Was the Jamaat not departing from its earlier position according to which secularism and democracy were *haram*, forbidden? While talking to Shaheed about this issue, he told me that the Jamaat had "fundamentally changed" and that its acceptance of secularism and democracy was the glaring sign of that change. A week later I met him by chance near a *pān* shop at the busy crossing of Dodhpur. We began talking about the Jamaat, and he reiterated his earlier view. When two of his friends joined our conversation, however, Shaheed, to my surprise reversed his view and said the Jamaat had not changed.

I encountered several such episodes. For example, to my question as to whether the Jamaat had changed considerably, a Jamaat member told me, while doing ablution inside the central mosque of Aligarh *shahr*, that he would go one step further to say it had "completely [*bilkul*] changed." After the prayer, he offered to share with me his rich experience as a Jamaat member since 1961, and we made an appointment to meet. At that meeting, two other Jamaat members were also present. When I brought up the issue of change, he, like Shaheed, also made a turn-around. I learned later that the other two members of the Jamaat were still unfriendly to its embracing democracy and secularism. In Rampur, a national leader of the Jamaat told me that he would accept the "massive" change privately but he would not say the same from a "public platform" (*ijlās*). While the members of the Jamaat themselves acknowledged the "massive" change, many of its Muslim critics—liberal, leftist, as well as ulema (religious experts) of other sects—told me that the Jamaat had not changed, and, if it had, the change was only tactical (see Qadri 1965; and Taban 1994).

Back in Amsterdam I came across a debate that resonated with my field experience. In 1999 the *Middle East Quarterly* carried a debate on the question "Is Islam a Threat?" The participants included Martin Kramer, John Esposito, Daniel Pipes, and Graham Fuller. Based on the writings of Olivier Roy and Abdulkarim Soroush, Kramer indicated a shift in Islamism. Pipes dismissed such a shift, arguing that Islamists continued to be ideologically unwavering. When Esposito stressed the mutation of Islamism, he admitted a minor shift but described it as merely tactical, not real (also see, Sivan 2003).

This book explores the theme of transformation or moderation of the Indian Islamists. Calling the "persistence of Islamism" thesis into question, I show the ideological transformation of the Jamaat and SIO, and the conflicts and ambiguities that accompanied the transformation. Far from being tactical, the transformation of Islamism, I maintain, is deeply ideological. In these pages I show how the trajectory of the Jamaat demonstrates a substantive mutation in the discourse of Islamism. Simply put, I demonstrate how its radical goal changed from establishing Allah's Kingdom to embracing and defending Indian secular democracy. I also explore the issue of the radicalization of the Student Islamic Movement of India (SIMI), a young, breakaway group of the Jamaat founded in 1976. SIMI's radicalization unfolded with the intensification of Hindu nationalism, or Hindutva, from the 1980s on. The twin calls for jihad and caliphate formed the core of SIMI's radicalized agenda.

In accounting for the transformation of Indian Islamists, this book addresses a series of interlocking ideas. What led to the moderation of the Jamaat? Did the secular, democratic nature of the Indian polity and the disavowal of its ideology by the Muslim public shape the Jamaat's moderation? If so, did it act up on the Jamaat only externally? Or did the Jamaat also undergo democratization and secularization from within? If we assume, however, that secular democracy catalyzed the moderation of the Jamaat, how can we comprehend the radicalization of SIMI? Does this suggest, then, an affinity between the altered form of secular democracy during the 1980s and the concomitant radicalization of SIMI? More important, is there a link between SIMI's radicalization and the democratization of the Muslim community? In other words, was SIMI's radicalization a mere staging of the pristine doctrine of jihad, or was it the beginning of the fragmentation of "traditional" Islam? Comparatively, does India's secular democracy—in contrast to the mostly undemocratic regimes in the Middle East—offer a fresh framework to understand the moderation and radicalization of the Islamist phenomena? Can the study of Islamism in a Muslim-minority context such as India shed light on the trajectory of Islamists (and Muslims) living as a minority in the secular, democratic countries of the West and Africa?

To address these issues, I start with the question with which I began my research, and then unpack the concepts of Islamism, moderation, and radicalization. Next I lay out my argument and also outline an alternative genealogy of secularism. Finally, I describe the theoretical framework of this study and I then end with a synoptic account of the chapters.

Research Question

In the course of my research on the Jamaat, I was intrigued by its distinct ideology. Founded by Syed Abul Ala Maududi (1903–1979), in 1941, before the Partition of India, the Constitution of the Jamaat proclaimed as its goal the establishment of *ḥukūmat-e-ilāhiya*, an Islamic state or Allah's Kingdom.[1] Maududi argued that the very declaration of faith—the recitation of *kalima, lā ilāha illallāhu muhammadur rasūlullāh* (there is no God except Allah, and Muhammad is His messenger)—obligated Muslims to establish Allah's Kingdom. Because there was no Islamic state in British India and its Constitution was "infidelic [*kāfirāna*]" (in Tahir undated: 18), he considered it *dar al-kufr*, the land of unbelief. For Muslims to "even breathe," let alone live, "under such an [infidelic] state was not legitimate [*jā'iz*] unless they strove to transform it into *dar al-Islam* [land of Islam]" (ibid.:18; also see Rahmani 1955). The mission of the Jamaat, as Maududi (2003a) defined it, was to transform India into *dar al-Islam*. Secular democracy, according to Maududi, was *haram* because it replaced *divine* sovereignty with *human* sovereignty. In his reading of the *kalima*, its profession also obligated Muslims to boycott what he called "*jāhiliyat*," "*bāṭil*," and "*ṭāghūtī niẓām*"—an anti-Islamic political system. The Constitution of the Jamaat made it compulsory for its members to boycott the following:

- Assemblies that legislate secular as opposed to sharia laws
- An army that kills "in the path of non-God [*qitāl fī ghair sabīl Allāh*]"
- Judiciary based on secular laws, either as plaintiff or defendant, and also banks based on interest
- Teaching or studying in colleges or universities, including Muslim ones, that serve *jāhiliyat* and whose goal is not the pursuit of an Islamic state; Maududi called them "slaughterhouse[s]"
- Government services and jobs in all institutions that are part of the anti-godly system
- Social ties with those who are *fāsiqīn* (transgressors) and neglectful of God (in Maududi 1942:178–82).

With India's Independence and the creation of the separate Muslim state of Pakistan in 1947, the Jamaat was divided into Jamaate-Islami

Hind (India) and Jamaat-e-Islami Pakistan. Maududi himself chose to migrate to Pakistan. Following the Partition, Indian Muslims became a minority, territorially dispersed. It is worth exploring whether the Jamaat still believed in its pre-Partition goal of Allah's Kingdom. Did it continue to boycott the elections to the Assembly, the Indian judiciary, government services, and so on? Did it persist in severing ties with Muslims of different sects or ideologies, which in the past it had characterized as *jāhiliyat*? Did it continue to ban its members from studying or teaching in the "slaughterhouses"? Or did it reconcile itself to secularism and democracy which it had condemned as *haram* and antithetical to Muslims' very belief in *kalima* (monotheism)? In short, did the Jamaat's ideology change? And if so, how?

To answer this question I decided to study a Jamaat school and the SIO, both in Aligarh, a town southeast of Delhi with a sizable Muslim population and known internationally for being the seat of Aligarh Muslim University (AMU). As my research progressed I realized that SIO could hardly be disentangled from SIMI. I also learned that half the SIO members on the AMU campus were from Jāmiʿatul Falāḥ, a Jamaat madrasa in Azamgarh district in UP. This discovery took me to Falāḥ. Similarly, while studying the Jamaat school in the *shahr*, I traveled to Rampur where the first model school of the Jamaat was established (see chapter 1).

Conceptual Terrain

In light of the research question, let us turn to the concepts of Islamism, moderation, and radicalization. An array of concepts is used to refer to Islamic movements, especially their radical variants: "Islamic Resurgence," "Islamic Revivalism," "Islamic Extremism," "Militant Islam," "Political Islam," and "Religious Nationalists." These terms are often ill-defined and used interchangeably. Islamic fundamentalism is the term most used. In fact, without "Islamic," it is a paradigmatic concept in the volumes edited by Marty and Appleby (1991–1995). They use it so loosely, however, that every religious articulation comes under its purview. They include movements as diverse as the Tablīghī Jamaat and the Jamaat-e-Islami in South Asia (Ahmad 1991). Compared to the above terms, "Islamism" is well demarcated. "The Islamist movement," writes Roy (1994:39), "thus conceives of itself explicitly as a sociopolitical movement, founded on an Islam defined as much in terms of a political ideology as in terms of a religion." Roy's definition has two elements: as a movement its prime aim is to establish an Islamic state; and it derives its legitimacy from the Qur'an and the Prophet. The second element echoes Schmitt's idea of political theology that Meier (2002:86) expresses as "a political theory . . .

for which, according to the self-understanding of the political theologian, divine revelation is the supreme authority and the ultimate ground."

Sayyid (1997) finds Roy's definition narrow, as it excludes, inter alia, "neo-fundamentalists" who want to establish a state from the bottom up, that is, by Islamizing the society first. I think Roy's definition is inadequate in other ways as well. To Touraine (1981:81), social movement is "the combination of a principle of identity, a principle of opposition and a principle of totality." Setting aside the centrality he places on the class character of movements (ibid.:77–79) and hence the idea of historicity, we can retain Touraine's principles of identity and opposition, the interrelationship between them, and the goal of actors as four constitutive elements of a movement. From this perspective, Roy's definition does not fully foreground the identity of Islamism. Nor does it identify the adversaries of Islamism. It also falls short of explaining the relationship between Islamism and its adversaries.[2] It is my contention that Islamism, in addition to the properties Roy ascribes to it, expresses itself in two other remarkably interrelated ideas: the notion of purity and the constant maintaining of boundary between itself and its "other." Islamism conceives of itself as "pure" Islam. This, in turn, is based on a novel reading of Islam as a perennial conflict between Islam and *jāhiliyat*, the "other" of Islam. This leads Islamism to disown much of Muslim history. In its discourse, throughout history, most Muslims, including the ulema, appear as impure. When extended outside Muslims and Islam, Islamism's notion of history depicts the West and modernity as new incarnations of *jāhiliyat*; hence its denunciation of secularism, democracy, and communism. It is clear how notions of purity and boundary maintenance go together.

Central to the self-conceptualization of Islamism is also the idea that Islam is an organic system, and the state its nerve center. Likewise, *jāhiliyat* is an organic whole; participation in any of its domains is tantamount to heresy. Thus Islam, as a system, according to Islamism, must dislodge the *jāhiliyat* political system. Its strategy to dislodge it is threefold: first, if possible, remove it by force; second, establish hegemony in civil society and then take hold of the state; and, third, withdraw from and boycott the *jāhiliyat* system. The Jamaat's plan to pursue its goal combined the second and third strategy (Maududi 1942:177). It follows that, as the claimant of pure Islam, Islamism regards practices within Islam other than its own as *fitna*, (sedition) or *jāhiliyat*. Non-Islamic religions or concepts such as secularism or democracy it regards as the opposite of Islam. Islamism is hostile to pluralism (Bayat 1996:45).

This outline of Islamism is obviously heuristic, derived from the specifics of the *Indian* Jamaat. One might ask, for example, if it applies to Islamist movements in Pakistan and in the Middle East. As for Pakistan, the boundary between Islam and *jāhiliyat* that Maududi drew before Partition was revised after the creation of Pakistan. Until 1949 he regarded the Pakistani state as a sign of *jāhiliyat*, because it based itself on popular, as opposed to divine, sovereignty. In 1948 the western Punjab government mandated its employees to pledge an oath to the state. Maududi forbade his party members to do so until the state became Islamic. In March 1949 Pakistan's Constituent Assembly passed the Objectives Resolution acknowledging the sovereignty of God. Only then did Maududi (2003a) no longer regard contesting elections or joining the Pakistani army as *haram* (Nasr 1994:121–24, 246, n. 40; Niazi 1973:106–13). Maududi made many changes in his position by grounding them in this so-called Islamic character of the Pakistani state. Since the state and the Constitution of India were secular, Maududi kept to his old position about India. As for the Middle East, from the 1960s on many streams of the Muslim Brotherhood followed the path initially taken by the Jamaat. These included Takfīr-wa-Hijra and Jihad in Egypt; the Phalanges of Muhammad and Al- mujahidūn in Syria; and Soldiers of the Lord in Lebanon. These groups derived their sustenance from Syed Qutb (Sivan 1990; also see Kepel 2003), who was influenced by Maududi (Shepard 2003). Many positions of the Hizb al Tahrir of Britain (Taji-Farouki 1996) resonate with those of the Indian Jamaat in its early phase. Let us return to the delineation of concepts.

Unlike Islamism,[3] the terms "radicalization" and "moderation" are not limited to the study of Muslim societies; they enjoy wider currency across the social science fields, including in the media. Their meanings remain imprecise, however. In the post–9/11 world, as Islam has become an object of "security," these terms have also become "securitized." From this perspective, the difference between moderates and radicals is *tactical*, not ideological. Moderates seek to achieve their goal by accepting the regime within which they work, whereas the radicals wish to achieve their goal by challenging it. Moderates and radicals thus imply a distinction between those with whom the West can "do business" and those with whom it cannot (International Crisis Group 2005:2) I wish to escape this securitization trap, as it reduces the complex phenomenon of Islamism to the binary distinction between those who are "friendly" and those who are "threatening." I use the terms "moderation" and "radicalization" as each pertains to the content and forms of Islamist ideology in relation to the larger political field in which Islamists participate. I see moderation and radicalization as dynamic, interconnected processes, not as a set of fixed, isolated attributes. They represent two main templates of the Islamist spectrum. More to the point, I disagree with the dualism between tactics and ideology. To me, this dualism is simply false. Tactics spring from and entail a reevaluation of ideology.

I use the term "moderation" to mean the shifting position of a radical movement from a fairly "closed and rigid worldview to one more open and tolerant of alternative perspectives." This definition by Schwedler (2006:4) is useful, but we need to ask: Why does a movement change from a rigid to a more open perspective? It does so, I believe, because it begins to doubt and revise the premises that defined its earlier radical worldview. For example, some key premises of the Jamaat's Islamism were that Islam is a complete system; the West and modernity are *jāhiliyat*; the Jamaat alone is the bearer of pure Islam; and the boundary between Islam and its "other," *jāhiliyat,* is unbridgeable. In the course of its transformation, as this book will show, the Jamaat reexamined its premises. Conceptually, moderation thus signals the transformation of Islamism from an organic system into a process of interpretations, which means that Islamism mutates from an already accomplished system to an evolving process of interactions with its former adversaries. In so doing, the boundaries on which Islamism bases itself become blurred. Moderation, in short, is a discourse marked by the blurring, even dissolution, of Islamism's boundaries, the embracing of its "other," the decentering of the Islamic state from its agenda, and the casting of doubt over its own premises while generating ambiguity and conflict among its practitioners.

Radicalization, in contrast, sharpens the boundary between Islam and its "other," and recenters the Islamic state on its agenda. Conceptually it tends to become rigid and hostile to alternative perspectives, both from within and without (cf. *Oxford Dictionary of Islam* 2003:259). In part, this happens precisely because of the moderating voices of those on what I have called the Islamist spectrum. The motor of radicalization, as well as of moderation, however, is the larger field of politics in which Islamists are one among several actors, and by no means the dominant ones. Here a clarification is in order. Although, historically, the term "radical" connotes a progressive slant, I use it in a neutral sense. Also, I do not use the term "radicalization" to mean acts of violence, even though it has come to signify just that. In my reading, the Jamaat, at the moment of its formation and subsequently, was radical in that it articulated the boundary between Islam and *jāhiliyat*. It maintained this boundary by, for example, boycotting the institutions of *jāhiliyat* such as elections to the secular assembly, government jobs, other Muslim organizations, and so on, clearly a radical approach. The Jamaat's radicalism, however, was *isolationist*. Instead of engaging with the Indian political system and the Muslim society, the Jamaat, in its early phase, mostly withdrew from them. The radicalism of SIMI, in contrast, was *involved*, in that it engaged with the political system in important ways from the late 1980s on.

The Argument

As noted at the outset, a significant transformation has occurred in the ideology of Indian Islamism. I wish to push this transformation to the center of the debate. My main argument about moderation and radicalization of Indian Islamism consists of three interlocking propositions. First, I argue that Islamism is not a static, fossilized entity, immutably locked into a dead end. Instead, it has changed, and the moderation of the Jamaat is a telling illustration of this transformation. Whereas in the past the Jamaat called secularism and democracy *haram*, it now fights to safeguard these principles. Western-style Muslim colleges were previously considered to be "slaughterhouse[s]," but now the Jamaat seeks their minority status. Having its schools affiliated with the government earlier had been seen as an approval of *ṭāġhūt* (idolatry), but now it has no qualms about getting that affiliation. Similarly, whereas earlier it had disregarded other religions, now it accepts them. Previously it had refused to collaborate even with Muslim groups like the Jamiatul Ulema-e-Hind (see below), but now it forges alliances with its former "other"—secular, atheist, even Hindu pontiffs who blow a conch at its meetings. The pursuit of an Islamic state has also ceased to be central on the Jamaat's agenda.

Second, I contend that secular democracy played a key role in the moderation of the Jamaat.[4] This factor markedly distinguished Indian Islamists from their counterparts in the Middle East, where neither non-authoritarian secularism nor democracy has a strong tradition. It was manifest in the Muslim public's disavowal of the Jamaat's ideology, which also played itself out in the realm of secular democratic politics. Critical to this disavowal is what I call an "ideological dissonance" between the Jamaat's agenda and the political subjectivity of the Muslim public. In contrast to the Jamaat, the majority of Muslims, including ulema, did not regard secular democracy as alien to Islam. In fact, they fought for it. For the non-Jamaat Muslims, Islam did not obligate establishing an Islamic state. To make its ideology credible, the Jamaat first had to convince Muslims that a secular democratic state assailed Islamic monotheism. Because the Muslim public disavowed the Jamaat's Islamist version of Islam, the Jamaat had to moderate its position, and in this, the Jamaat leadership played a significant role.

Secular democracy did not only act upon the Jamaat externally but did so internally as well. Indeed, the Jamaat's functioning took on a robust democratic mode. Maududi, as the Jamaat's president (*amīr*) had been the sole decision maker. The task of the consultative body (*shura*) whose members he himself nominated, had been to advise the *amīr*. With the democratization of the Jamaat, *shura* members began to be elected, and the *amīr* had to accept decisions taken by the *shura* in a majority vote.

So crucial had democratic decision making become that even the Islamic creed, the *kalima*, from which, according to Maududi, the ban on voting in the elections of a secular state had been derived, was put to a vote—a practice intractable in history. The Jamaat also underwent secularization. In Maududi's view, Islam necessitated an Islamic state, but in postcolonial India the Jamaat recast its theology to say that an Islamic state was not basic to Islam. Thus it moved away from its position of fusing religion and the state. This differentiation was most glaring when, in 1961, the Jamaat sent a questionnaire to ulema asking if sharia allowed participation in elections. In seeking validation from ulema, the Jamaat differentiated the religious from the nonreligious domain, for it did not regard itself as (sufficiently) religious. When the SIO leadership asked one of its activists if he prayed and why he watched films, the activist was displeased, as he regarded these acts as individual choices. The SIO, he believed, should be concerned with sociopolitical issues and not private religious matters. He also held that the Islamic state had originally been secular and that the West had borrowed secularism from Islam.

Third, I contend that the dramatically changed nature of secular democracy from the 1980s on is what *primarily* led to the radicalization of SIMI. In the 1990s SIMI called for jihad and caliphate, which I contend was a response to the rise of Hindu nationalism that was targeting Muslims. The Ayodhya campaign was not just about a temple but was also a challenge to the secular ethos of the Indian Constitution and the Muslim identity. As Hindutva's assault on secularism grew fiercer—culminating in the destruction of the Babri mosque in 1992, and accompanied by massive violence against Muslims—so did SIMI's call for jihad. By stressing the connection between SIMI's radicalization and the Indian state, I intend to show that the failure of the latter to protect the lives, property, and dignity of its Muslim citizens led SIMI to call for jihad against the Hindutva activists engaged in anti-Muslim riots. It was in the wake of the Babri mosque's demolition and the ensuing large-scale riots across the country that SIMI described secularism as a "fraud" and declared India as *dar al-Islam*. SIMI's call for caliphate was also a response to Hindutva's project of inaugurating a Hindu state.[5]

SIMI's radicalization, I argue, is also related to its activists' yearnings for democratic rights in contrast to the wishes of the older generation of Islamists. A key repertoire of protest employed by SIMI was to stage a strike against the administration of the Falāḥ, a Jamaat madrasa. Historically, strikes are rare in most madrasas, as the dominant discourse there is that of duty and obedience to ulema. SIMI's discourse, in contrast, is that of rights. Coming from what I call the "Islamist class" and possessing a specific type of cultural capital and disposition, the young SIMI activists assert for rights, not duties. Their intellectual dispositions enable them to question Islamic authorities. SIMI's call for jihad and its rejection by all revered Islamic institutions thus gestures demonopolization of religious authority. The discourse of jihad, rather than being a simple replay of Islamic authority, is instead its fragmentation. Like the Jamaat, SIMI also underwent democratization.

These complex processes of moderation and radicalization were shot through with conflicts and contestations over what defines "true" Islam, and here I stress their import. These fierce contestations demonstrate that Islam is not an object "out there" but is continually fashioned and reconfigured in the changing sociopolitical universe that Islamists and Muslims inhabit.

India, Islam, Islamism

No major anthropological or sociological work has been published on Muslim movements in India. A key reason for this neglect is that Westerners identify India with Hindus; is this not an orientalist hubris according to which religion-culture and geography-area converge (Appadurai 1986; Gupta and Ferguson 1992)? Muslims have thus become inconsequential.[6] When Barbara Metcalf (1995:955) told an American professor that she wanted to specialize in Indian Muslims, he spluttered: "Muslims! Why they are no more than 5 percent of the population and they simply do not matter." The reason, as Metcalf observes, was not statistical (that, too, is incorrect). Indian Muslims fall outside the pale of the origin of Islam, the Middle East, the so-called Islamic heartland. Further, given the portrayal of Islam as monolithic, it is assumed that Indian Muslims must also be like those in the "heartland," a shadow of the "universal Muslim" character (Pandey 1993:267). At the hands of Dumont and McKim Marriot, the anthropological-orientalist discourse shared by Hindu nationalism inscribed Muslims either as a foreign other or as an entity subsumed under Hindu culture (Van der Veer 1993, 1994).[7]

That most works on Islamism deal with Muslim-majority countries of the Islamic "heartland," seems itself a good reason to study an Islamist movement in India. A more plausible reason, however, is that India arguably has some distinctiveness that elude the societies of the Islamic "heartland." Historically the latter have largely been undemocratic and nonsecular. Can conclusions drawn from studies of the "heartland" hold up in a secular democracy like India, where Muslims have had a different, complex trajectory? Simply put, I believe that Indian Muslims, in contrast to the view of the distinguished professor noted above, do matter. And they matter, not just because Indian Muslims are the second largest Muslim population in the world, as is novel nowadays to mention in parenthesis. Their salience, I suggest, goes far beyond reducing them to an object of demographic data.

An important debate on Islam in the "heartland" is about Islam's compatibility with modernity. It is often asked: Is Islam compatible with secularism and democracy? There are two major poles in this debate. Fukuyama (1992), Kepel (1994), Bernard Lewis (1988, 1993, 1996, 2002, 2003), Lawrence (1995), Gellner (1994), and Huntington argue, albeit differently, that Islam is incompatible with secularism and democracy.[8] In Gellner's view, Islam presents a "dramatic . . . exception" to the patterns of secularization because "a church/state dualism never emerged in it [Islam]." "It [Islam] *was*," he argues, "the state from the very start" (Gellner 1992:5, 9; also see Gellner 1981: chap. 1). Differentiating between three versions of Islam—namely, religion, civilization, and politics—Lewis states that the last one is surely hostile to democracy (1996:54). The first two, in his view, are also not compatible, for "in Islam . . . there is from the beginning interpenetration of . . . religion and the state" (ibid.:61; also see Lewis 2002). In Huntington's opinion, "The underlying problem for the West is not Islamic fundamentalism. It is Islam" (1996:70, 217).

Bayat (2007), Esposito and Voll (1996), Esposito (2000), Filal-Ansary (1996), El Fadl (2004), and Tamimi (2000) represent the other pole of the debate. They see the possibility of democracy and secularism in Islam. Casanova (2001) predicts that Muslim countries could become democratic in the future, as churches and many Catholic groups became the motor of democracy. Some who don't fit these poles raise a different question. Mahmood (2004), for instance, asks: Should Muslims even want to become better liberal democrats? Should they not instead, she proposes, take "their own resources of the Islamic tradition" to imagine a future different from the one offered by liberal democracy? This proposal, in my view, springs from an assumed authenticity of Islamic tradition as radically different from Western democracy.

Whether or not Islam is compatible with secularism and democracy is not a pertinent question to most Indian Muslims. Secular democracy has been integral to their political life for more than half a century. Founded in 1919 as the largest Muslim organization of ulema in postcolonial India, the Jamiatul Ulema-e-Hind, among others, fought for secular democracy, and the language of its struggle was Islamic (see chapter 2). To the Indian Islamists represented chiefly by the tiny Jamaat—in 1947 it had 999 members (see Appendix 1)—however, secularism and democracy assailed Islamic monotheism.

In the following pages I will make an excursus to outline the conceptions of the secular state formulated and placed in the Constitution after India's independence by the leaders of the Indian National Congress (formed in 1885; hereafter Congress) such as the first prime minister Jawaharlal Nehru (1889–1964) and Abulkalam Azad (1888–1958). I take the reader along to this excursus because to unravel the dynamics of an Islamist party like the Jamaat it is useful to study the ideology, practices, and structure of the state in relation to which a given movement functions (Goldstone 2003; McAdam 1982). More important, because the secular democratic state is central to my argument, we should consider the contours of the political system in which the Jamaat had to play out its politics in postcolonial India. Given the centrality of the state in its ideology, it is crucial to examine how the Jamaat interacted with the secular, democratic state. The state assumes added significance because, for most Muslims in postcolonial India, the ideology of the secular, democratic state became the master framework for almost all mobilizations they undertook, whether it was the issue of Urdu, Aligarh Muslim University, the Babri mosque, the Muslim Personal Law, communal riots, their marginalized presence in government services, and so on. In critical dialogue with recent writings, mainly those of Asad, Casanova, Madan, Mufti, and Nandy, I attempt to present an alternative genealogy of secularism—preliminary, partial, and brief as it is. I broadly agree with Asad's insightful critique of secularism. His genealogy, however, brackets out the perspectives of the religious minorities and dissenters—actors with whom my account is concerned.

Another Genealogy of Secularism

An avalanche of critiques of secularism began in the 1980s. The earliest critiques came from the anthropologist T. N. Madan and the social theorist Ashis Nandy. For Madan, secularism was "an alien cultural ideology," "a gift of Christianity to mankind," and hence "a vacuous word, a phantom concept" (1987:753–54). For Nandy, it was a "borrowed" concept, an "import" from the West, and hence inauthentic to the "indigenous personality" (1985:16, 18; 2002:64). Both argued that the separation of religion from politics was foreign to Indian culture. To bring the Indian state back to the ethos of Indian culture, Madan proposed that it ought to "reflect the character of the society" (1987:749), but he did not spell out what he meant by the society's character—a society, that was religiously diverse. Nor did he state who indeed would define such a character, for what aims and for whom?[9]

This critique of secularism desires to recover the "indigenous tradition" in the name of what Mufti (2000) calls "aura of authenticity." It reifies the diverse trajectories and meanings of secularism within the West (Bader 2007; van der Veer 2001) to posit it against an assumed Indian "indigenous personality." Also contestable is Madan's and Nandy's assumption of a ruthless process of secularization by the state. Do they mean, for example, the passage of the Hindu Code Bill in the 1950s? If so, one may agree with Mehta (2004) that it was less an example of secularism and more an attempt to fashion a "territorially unified body of Hindu law" whereby the state acted as the custodian of Hindus. My point is that I do not see such a ruthless secularization. In the three *mofassil* Bihar government schools I attended in the 1980s, much of the schools' culture was already Hindu and callous to the sensibilities of Muslim students there. In the dining hall of my high school's hostel, Muslim students (only a few) were segregated from Hindu students. Thus, instead of ruthless secularization by the state, what one witnesses is the process of grotesque othering of Muslims presided over by the state. During the genocide against Muslims in 2002, *Newsweek* (April 22, 2002) reported "the chilling message" inscribed on the wall in Gujarat: "This is the Kingdom of lord Ram. No Muslim can stay here. India is for the Hindus."

Furthermore, Madan and Nandy, and also their critics, seldom ask what Muslims thought about secularism. Did they view it as "a vacuous word, a phantom concept"? For example, the Jamiatul Ulema-e-Hind called secularism a "golden principle" (Siddiqi n.d.:2), a "pious objective" and resolved to keep the "candle of secularism alight" (Miftahi 1995:69–70). I suggest that this perspective has been elided, because the context of secularism has not been adequately thought through (but see Bajpai 2002; Jha 2002; Sarkar 2001; Bhargava 1998; and Rudolph and Rudolph 2000). The prime concern of secularism was the "Muslim question" by which I mean the whole issue of religious minority[10]—its culture, language, religion, visibility in public life, and its place in the religiously heterogeneous polity in colonial and future free India.[11] In the political arena, the Muslim question was present since the birth of the Congress. As early as 1886 the Congress used the term "secular" to rally Indians of all faiths for "general interests" (in Mitra 1991:766). The Muslim question, expressed in the idiom of minorities' rights (Austin 1999), was central to the Motilal Nehru Report of 1928, the Congress ministries in 1937, Interim Government formation, and the Cabinet Mission Plan of 1946. Without going into its complex history, let me stress that the Muslim elites had imagined that Pakistan's creation would resolve the Muslim question for good. It did not. Millions of Muslims refused to go to Pakistan, and thus the Muslim question remained a vital issue for free India. Secularism was adopted, amid opposition from its rivals, to address this question. At the heart of the crisis of secularism (Needham and Rajan 2007), therefore, is "the terrorized and terrorizing figures of [the] minority" (Mufti 2007:2).

In speaking of the Muslim question, I am aware of the particularity of India. But I reject the uniqueness of this particularity. Indicated earlier by Tyabji (1971:7), Mufti's (2007) remarkable work is perhaps the first to comparatively situate the minority question—Muslims in India and Jews in the West—in relation to the nation-state in the nineteenth century.

"The crisis of [Indian] Muslim identity," he writes, "can't be understood in isolation from the history of the so-called Jewish question in modern Europe" (ibid.:2). So, what would a genealogy of secularism look like from the perspectives of minorities? This genealogy, I submit, invites us to see secularism as a mechanism of power sharing by and nondiscrimination against religious minorities; and also to maintain and produce their distinctive religious-cultural identity. Such a genealogy clearly goes beyond the dichotomized categories of East versus West. My goal is not to overlook the difference between them. I simply question the uniqueness of each and, in so doing, clear the ground for appreciating the connected forms of this issue in East as well as in the West.

Like Madan and Nandy, Asad's *Formations of the Secular* (chapters 1& 2) treats secularism as a comprehensive philosophy. He sees an organic link between secularism as a political doctrine and the secular as an ontology and epistemology, and he traces the genealogy of the secular through its "shadows." He also goes into the etymology and meanings of the secular, sacer, myth, profane, and so on. "The genealogy of secularism," he argues, "has to be traced through the concept of the secular—in part to the Renaissance doctrine of humanism, in part to the Enlightenment concept of nature, and in part to Hegel's philosophy of history" (2003:192). I recognize the value of this approach, but it is too discourse-oriented to unpack tangible histories and workings of secularism in practice. It is also partly a secularist account; it presumes thoughts of Enlightenment philosophers determining people's actions.[12] The average actors are conspicuously absent from their accounts. I submit that one of the key actors is the religious minorities—Jews and other minorities in the West and Muslims in India—for whom secularism was, however, not an all-encompassing philosophy. Most Indian Muslims viewed it as a political arrangement guaranteeing them the right to be equal citizens and lead their lives—collectively, not just individually, and publicly, not just privately—in accordance with their own religious traditions. If words acquire their meaning in constellation with other words, in India, as is evident, inter alia, from the debates in the Constituent Assembly, secularism is tied to phrases such as minority rights, anti-colonial *united* nationalism, the language and culture of Muslims, their Personal Law, and so on (Bajpai 2002; Madni 2002).[13] In this sense, Muslims' view of secularism echoes one of the three elements of secularization expressed by Casanova (1994:11–39): the differentiation of religion from the state. This principle was important to ward off discrimination against Muslims and to resist the imposition of majoritarian religion and culture on minorities. Mahajan (2003) thus rightly argues that nondiscrimination and citizenship rights are the core of secularism. Is this stance of Indian Muslims toward secularism unique?

In the United States, the call to disengage religion from the state arose because in establishing "dictatorship of the holy" (Archer 2001:276) the Puritans as the dominant sect, persecuted and sought to impose its own version of Christianity on the minority denominations. Those demanding this disengagement were minority sects—Baptists, Methodists, and dissenters in Massachusetts. In Virginia it was non-Anglican minorities that disavowed the imposition of an Anglican Christianity (Gill 2008:chap. 3). This also holds true for the Catholic minority in the nineteenth century, when "Enlightenment liberals and the dominant Protestants came together to oppose Catholic influence . . . to impose their own generalized Protestant establishment on all of society" (Monsma and Soper 1997:44). The minorities resisted the entanglement of religion and the state not because religion was unimportant to them; rather, they regarded it as too important. The position of Jewish and Catholic minorities in Holland tells a similar story. In 1868 *Nieuw Israelietisch Weekblad*, a Jewish weekly, carried a front-page article arguing, "As a rule, they [Catholics] shared common interests with us to be promoted and defended, and therefore they are favorably disposed towards us" (in Ramakers 1996:33). What were the common interests between Jews and Catholics? Both were minorities facing legalized discrimination for centuries in a missionary Republic run by a Protestant majority. It was in such a context that Herman Schaepman (1844–1903), a Catholic activist, demanded that the state act secular by recognizing Catholic educational institutions. The party Schaepman desired, Carlson-Thies summarizes, "would promote freedom of religion, independence of the churches from the state, and equal rights for all citizens and all religious bodies" (in Monsma and Soper 1997:60). In France, whereas Jews and Huguenots stood for *laïcité*, its opponents belonged to the Catholic majority (Roy 2007:19). The resistance by minorities against the imposition of the hegemonic religion, and hence the demand that the state became secular, I argue, should figure in the genealogy of secularism.

What is also unconvincing in Asad's genealogy is the foreignness of modernity or secularism. Like Madan and Nandy, he, too, sees it as an "importation" (2003:215). He views modernity as a project that people in power want to attain by institutionalizing democracy, civil equality, secularism and so on, in the non-Western world (ibid.:13). An important question here is why certain ideas and practices are classified as "importation," whereas others are not? Put differently, why do many in the Middle East consider democracy and secularism as "importation," whereas most Indians no longer regard democracy and secularism as "foreign" or "Western"? Leaving aside the struggle for democracy by the subalternated in the South that Asad fails to address, I sense a dash of authenticity in his premise. In discussing reforms, he disavows the intent of

Egyptian activists to reformulate the existing legal system (sharia) as "an aspiration for a Westernized future rather than a reformed continuity of the recent past" (ibid.:215, 198). Is "continuity" something self-evident, however? Or is it a representational trope and an ideological claim in a given discourse? My discomfort with "continuity" as well as "importation" comes from the ways in which Asad juxtaposes modernity and Islam. This argument, like Madan's and Nandy's, assumes, to cite Van der Veer (forthcoming:19), that "an already finished modular modernity has been shipped from Europe to the rest of the world." However, if we view modernity as a series of interactions between the West and non-West, then both the aspiration for a "Westernized future" and "continuity of the . . . past" are representational tropes emerging precisely as a result of interactions between the West and Islam. From this perspective, Van der Veer (ibid.:19) rightly questions the efficacy of arguments in which "defenders of secularism are branded as 'modern-westernized' and defenders of religion as 'traditional-nativist.'" If Hegel is central to the secular, Islamist ideologues like Maududi, *pace* Asad, are equally beholden to Hegel. As I demonstrate in chapter 2, Maududi's reading of Islamic history indelibly bears the marks of Hegel.

Persuasive and relevant to my argument, however, is Asad's revealing chapter on Muslims in Europe (2003:chap. 5). Like the chapter on the Rushdie affair in *Genealogies of Religion* (1993, chap. 7), it is a dazzling critique of the idea of Europe. Here Asad questions liberalism's monochromatism to carve out a space for a multiplicity of worldviews. While making a case for Muslims' status as equal citizens, he argues for their recognition as bearers of their religious distinctiveness, not just privately but also publicly (2003:180). Clearly this is not the case in Europe. Is it, however, because or in violation of secularism?[14] From Indian Muslims' understanding of secularism, it is a violation of secularism. This view may assail the French self-perception of being secular. But self-perception in itself is not sufficient. Equally important is how minorities see the state. It is instructive to note that although the colonial Indian state regarded itself as secular, Indians viewed it as "fundamentally Christian" (Van der Veer 2001:24). The silencing of Muslim voices in the *ḥijāb* controversy under the flag of "universal" indeed masks the provincialism of French liberalism (Brown 2006:173). The French secularism needs to be secularized; it has turned into, to cite Balibar (2007), "another religion." Liberalism takes pride in the fact that, unlike religion, it is open to self-examination. In France (and Europe), the reverse seems to be true. While many Muslim intellectuals have revised their postulates, it is liberals who refuse to examine *laïcité*. The French case presents a classic illustration of the state's monism—in law and language alike. In granting equality of rights to Jews, the French National Assembly demanded that they erase every trace of their identity and become assimilated into the mainstream, which seldom was acknowledged as suffused with Christianity. Most important from the perspective of minorities in Europe is the Jews' refusal to assimilate and assert their distinctiveness. While pledging allegiance to the Republic, in 1792, the rabbi Isaac Berr asserted: "Each of us will naturally follow the religion of his father. Thus, we can be loyally attached to the Jewish religion and be at the same time good French citizens" (in Kates 1989:213). Let us now turn to India.

After Independence, when the framework for the future state was being debated, Hindu nationalists sought to cast it along majoritarian lines. The creation of Pakistan gave them more legitimacy to push for this project—Hindu raj. The Congress stalwarts—Sardar Patel, for example—barely concealed their verve for such a project. G. B. Pant, another Congress stalwart, warned Muslims that if they did not support the Congress then the "establishment of a purely Hindu raj was inevitable" (in Brennan 1996:130). It was against this rabid majoritarianism that Nehru called for a secular state. In September 1947 he made it clear that as long as he was "at the helm of affairs, India [would] not become a Hindu state" (in Brennan 1996:128). The obverse of secular was thus not religion *per se*, as Asad,[15] Madan, and Nandy contend, but rather was majoritarianism couched as nationalism and its practice to exclude Muslims. In Mufti's (2000a) reading, Edward Said's secularism stemmed from a similar concern. For Said, the opposite of secularism was not religion but majoritarianism. In the context of the Arab world, Said viewed secularism as an idiom to think about the predicament of its minorities. Mufti situates this Saidian meaning of secularism in relation to Christians in the Arab world. It was probably in this context that, in the Constituent Assembly, Brajeshwar Prasad urged for the inclusion of secularism in the Preamble of the Indian Constitution, arguing that it would boost the morale of minorities (Jha 2002).

Also crucial here was the climate in which the Constituent Assembly (1946 to 1948) debated the future state. It was an atmosphere rife with grotesque religious violence. Delhi itself, where the Constituent Assembly met, witnessed the convulsion of mass violence. In one estimate, half a million people—Hindus, Muslims, and Sikhs—were killed. In response to violence against Hindus by the Muslims of west Punjab, especially the massive influx of humiliated Hindus and Sikhs from Pakistan, Indian Muslims came under attack in many places—Uttar Pradesh, Rajasthan, and Delhi. They stepped into free India in the midst of discrimination. The Evacuee Property Law was one such agency. Thousands of Muslims who went to Pakistan simply to visit their relatives were denied citizenship on their return to India. Their properties and businesses were confiscated. The Evacuee Law empowered authorities to take over the property of anyone whom they suspected of intending to migrate to Pakistan. In fact, many Congress leaders, including G. B. Pant and Mohanlal Sukhadia, chief ministers of UP and Rajasthan respectively, forced Muslims to leave for Pakistan (Copland 1998; Zakaria 1995; Zamindar 2007; also see Friedmann 1976). Worse, Muslims became suspect. Regarded as fifth columnists, they were required to prove their loyalty to the Indian nation-state. At the high noon of the British Empire, Hunter (1871) had raised the issue of Muslims' loyalty to the state. Now the postcolonial state did the same. Muslims' "disloyalty" became the ground for their exclusion and expulsion by the authorities. When Gandhi asked the government to treat the Muslims with justice, the Hindu nationalists ignored him. A Hindi paper reported that it would be a "political blunder of high order" were every Muslim granted the same privileges as a Hindu (in Pandey 1999:615). Even "Nationalist Muslims"—so called because as Congress activists they had opposed Pakistan—became suspect.[16] As Sardar Patel put it: "There is only one *genuinely* nationalist Muslim in India—Jawaharlal [Nehru]" (in Balasubramanian 1980:100; emphasis added). Note that, to Patel, a Muslim can never be loyal.

In such a climate Nehru made secularism a state ideology. On this point the opposition between "indigenous" Gandhi and "Westernized" Nehru, as Nandy suggests, is false (Tambiah 1998:420–24). Nehru used secularism to ensure equal rights to all, especially Muslims and other minorities, and to include them in the democratic processes. To Amartya Sen (1998:479), secularism was an ideology of "symmetric treatment of different religious communities in politics and in the affairs of the state." The Constitution embodied this spirit of secularism, as it did away with discriminations based on ascriptive identities, including religion, and granted equal rights to all citizens. In this sense the Constitution was a book of classic liberalism; it was not, however, a book of diversity—or culture-blind liberalism, what Parekh calls "assimilationist liberalism" (1998:205; 2000). The Constitution made provisions to ensure the cultural, linguistic rights and identity of Muslims; they were free to profess, practice, and propagate their religion (Article 25). Likewise, they had the freedom to manage their "religious affairs" (Article 26). To protect the "interest of minorities," the Constitution granted citizens the right to conserve their "distinct language, script or culture" (Article 29) and "establish and administer educational institutions of their choice" (Article 30). All these articles pertain to Part III, titled "Fundamental Rights" of the Constitution.

It should be clear that, unlike the monistic French *laïcité* (Bowen 2007), the Indian Constitution did not regard the headscarf as a violation of secularism. Sikhs had the liberty to carry a sword (*kirpān*) and many tribal communities and minorities—both Christians and Muslims—had the right to retain their personal laws. Muslims had their own law: the Muslim Personal Law (MPL). Given this blend of individual and community rights, Parekh (1995:41) calls the state that the Constitution envisioned "both an association of individuals and a community of communities." Recognizably this blend is not bereft of tension. Madan (1993) sees conflict between Article 25 to 30 and Article 44 requiring all citizens to have a Uniform Civil Code. He cites the 1986 Muslim Women Bill that overruled the Supreme Court's judgment in the Shah Bano case, which upheld the right of a divorcee to receive maintenance from her ex-husband, as a "contradiction." To him, this is the *locus classicus* of the crisis of secularism. Nehru saw it differently. Although he saw the need for reform in the MPL, he argued that the initiative came from within. He stressed for fashioning the conditions for such reform (Balasubramanian 1980). In my view, as an issue of gender equality, at stake is not what Madan calls *contradiction* but rather *condition*. The question is: has the postcolonial state created such a condition; or, Why do Muslims oppose reforming the MPL?[17]

The Language of Muslim Politics

It may seem, from the above discussion, that the choice for secularism was an act of generosity on the part of the majority (Friedman 1976; Tambiah 1998). This appears credible, given the tiny presence of Muslims in the Constituent Assembly. However, it would be a mistake to endorse the generosity thesis. Abulkalam Azad and Maulana Hifzur Rahman (d. 1962)—both from the Congress-Jamiatul Ulema-e-Hind alliance—played key roles in shaping the Constitution. Furthermore, as noted, secularism and democracy did not emerge suddenly; their roots lay in the shared Independence struggle that began in the nineteenth century (Austin 1999). Most important, secular democracy was equally pivotal to Muslim politics.[18] With several other organizations,[19] the Jamiatul Ulema-e-Hind (hereafter, Jamiatul Ulema) was the bearer of this Muslim politics, which in postcolonial India became nearly hegemonic. As a party of ulema, it also enjoyed religious legitimacy from Muslims (Adrawi 1988).

The leaders of the Jamiatul Ulema came from Darul Uloom Deoband, a madrasa founded in 1867. Qasim Nanotwi, the madrasa founder, issued a *fatwa* (signed by three hundred ulema) urging Muslims to join the Congress (Al-jamʿiyat 1995:59; Engineer 2006). The role of ulema, however, remained marginal until the Khilafat campaign began in 1919 and they founded the Jamiatul Ulema. This phase of the anticolonial struggle also witnessed the onset of mass politics led by Gandhi, when a distinct language of Muslim politics began to evolve. Employing Islam, the Jamiatul Ulema argued that Hindus and Muslims formed a united nation, *muttaḥeda qaumiyat*, based on territory rather than faith. Though religiously different,

Hindus and Muslims, it was thought, should jointly fight against colonial rule for Independence. In 1927, citing Prophet Muhammad's example, the Jamiatul Ulema argued that if the Prophet could make a truce with the Jews against a common enemy at Medina, Muslims and Hindus could likewise come together as one nation against the British. In the tract *Muslims and the United Nationhood* (1938), Husain Ahmad Madni, the Deoband principal, reiterated that Islam and the Qur'an indeed entailed that Muslims support the Congress. He saw no contradiction in being a Muslim and a nationalist at once. He argued that the Qur'an never used the word *qaum* (nation) religiously. Instead it referred to a population with ties based on territory, occupation, or language (Madni 2002).[20]

Abulkalam Azad, a luminary of the Congress, and later the education minister of free India, held a similar view. In 1921 he wrote, "Thus if I say that the Muslims of India can't perform their duty unless they are united with the Hindus, it is in accordance with the tradition of the Prophet who himself wanted to make a nation of Muslims and non-Muslims to meet the challenge of the people of Mecca" (in Huq 1970:118). As president of the Congress, in 1940, he reasserted this position. Given its significance to my point, I quote his speech at length.

> I am a Muslim and proudly conscious of the fact that I have inherited Islam's glorious traditions. . . . As a Muslim I have a special identity within the field of religion and culture and I can't tolerate any undue interference with it. . . . I am equally proud of the fact that I am an Indian, an essential part of the indivisible unity of Indian nationhood, a vital factor in its total makeup, without which this noble edifice will remain incomplete.
>
> It was India's historic destiny that its soil should become the destiny of many different caravans of races, cultures and religions. . . . The last of these caravans was that of the followers of Islam. . . . This was the meeting point of two different currents of culture. . . . We had brought our treasures with us to this land which was rich with its own great cultural heritage. We handed over our wealth to her and she unlocked for us the door of her own riches. We presented her with something that she needed urgently, the most precious gift in Islam's treasury, its message of democracy . . . equality and brotherhood.
>
> Eleven hundred years of common history have enriched India with our common . . . achievements. Our language, our poetry, our literature, our culture, our art, our dress, our manners and customs all bear the stamp of this common life.
>
> Our shared life of a thousand years has forged a common nationality. . . . Whether we like it or not, we have now become an Indian nation, united and indivisible. (in Noorani 2003:32–33)[21]

The conceptualization of a "united and indivisible" nation clearly entailed a differentiation between religion and the state. According to Madni, Islamness (*Islāmiyat*) belonged to the domain of religion where Islam was supreme; in worldly affairs, Indianness (*hindustāniyat*) reigned high. For military, economic, and political pursuits Islam permitted Muslims to make common cause with Hindus. Such a separation between religion and the state, he noted, was already in practice and Islam legitimized it. "Islam is a flexible religion," was Madni's motto. Dismissing the view that democracy was European, he called upon Muslims to embrace it. Islam, Madni held, had laid the foundation of democracy (2002:36–46). The separation between Islam and state meant stressing that Muslims qua Muslims could flourish under a secular state. It was not a smooth task given the nineteenth-century jihad by ulema to found an Islamic state after Delhi's takeover by the British.[22] In the viewpoint of the Jamiatul Ulema, the aim of the jihad movement was to expel the British, and ulema did not care if Hindus or Muslims formed the state (Friedmann 1976).

Although the Jamiatul Ulema worked with the Congress, it did not merge itself with the Congress but retained its autonomy vis-à-vis Muslim issues (Faruqi 1963). Some important issues were the preservation of civil sharia laws, for example, the freedom to practice Islam, advancement of Urdu, nondiscrimination against Muslims in various services, and so on. Given Muslims' minority status, the Jamiatul Ulema urged the Congress not to adopt any majoritarian policy (*Al-jamʿiyat* 1995:91; Rahman 1995). Dismissing assimilation, Madni, in the tract cited above, made it clear that Muslims desired guarantee not just of their individual belief but of their "culture." He further argued that for Muslims religion was not a "private" affair (2002:41–42). The 1931 Fundamental Rights resolution of the Congress addressed these concerns. According to S. Gopal (1996), Nehru's biographer, this resolution formed the core of secularism in the Constitution. After Independence, secular democracy became the idiom of Muslim politics. The Congress made Hindi in Devanagiri script as the official language. Arguing that Urdu was not the language of Muslims alone, in 1949 the Jamiatul Ulema lamented that this decision was a betrayal of secularism. Hifzur Rahman observed: "In my opinion, it is the worst event in the history of the . . . Congress. Despite the claim of secular state and one nation, the mother tongue of millions of people of the Indian Union . . . is being trampled upon with hatred and contempt" (in Freidmann 1976:207).

In 1941 Maududi had founded the Jamaat precisely to contest the secular, democratic language of Muslim politics. To make itself prevail, the Jamaat had to convince both Muslims and non-Muslims of its ideology. Winning Muslims to its cause was indeed far more crucial, as they constituted the primary constituency of the Jamaat. Given that India was a democracy, the Jamaat enjoyed freedom to persuade citizens in favor of it. Notwithstanding its limited resources, the Jamaat strove to enlarge its influence, but it did not meet with success. As I argue in this book, the disavowal of the Jamaat's ideology by the Muslim public impelled it to the path of moderation. The Jamaat argued that secular democracy negated Muslims' belief in *kalima*, and, based on this reasoning, they should boycott elections. Common Muslims and organizations like the Jamiatul Ulema, on the contrary, believed that Islam sanctioned secular democracy. Disregarding the Jamaat's call, Muslims actively participated in elections in the 1950s, triggering a debate within the Jamaat. As a result, in 1967, the Jamaat agreed, in principle, to participate in elections, but the debate continued through the 1970s and 1980s. Because of mounting pressure from the Muslim public, as well as from its own members, the Jamaat, in 1985, eventually decided to participate in democratic politics.

Precisely at a time when the Jamaat had undergone moderation, Hindu nationalism ascended on the horizon. During the 1980s and thereafter Hindutva grew stronger to become India's rulers. The virulence of Hindu nationalism was accompanied by massive anti-Muslim violence throughout India. Its aim was to fashion a unitary Hindu identity by erasing the plural identities that Nehru envisioned. In short, it sought to erode secularism. It was this erosion of secular democracy that led to the radicalization of SIMI. The project of a Hindu state had occupied the center stage of politics. I do not mean to imply that Hindu nationalism did not exist in the Nehruvian era or before. It did. But it remained on the margin. My contention that the erosion of secular democracy led to SIMI's radicalization, however, does not only mean that from the 1980s the state increasingly became anti-pluralistic and discriminated against Muslims. Drawing on the works of Iris Young (2000) and Lijphart (1996), my argument also calls for our attention to the failure of democracy, as evident in the abysmally low presence of Muslims in important arenas of public life: education, economy, police, civil services, and so on. In the midst and because of such marginalization of Muslims, SIMI's radicalism unfurled.

The radicalization of SIMI was also symbolic of a complex dynamics of democratization within Muslim society. Until the 1960s democracy worked along the lines of "command politics" (Rudolph and Rudolph 1987). The elites commanded the "masses" to act in a certain way. Anthropologically, this was facilitated by a patron-client relationship. The Congress cultivated ties with the Jamiatul Ulema. Hifzur Rahman was a Congress Member of Parliament from Independence till his death in 1962. After his death, the Congress elected Syed Asad Madni, son of Husain Ahmad Madni, to Parliament, which he served for eighteen long years (*Al-jamʿiyat* 1995:455). The shift from command to demand politics, or what Hansen (1999) calls the "plebeianization" of democracy, occurred with the rise of new social strata from below. SIMI activists belonged to one such stratum, which I call the "Islamist class," that democratization had unleashed. Unlike the students of most madrasas, SIMI activists had a distinct cultural capital and disposition that enabled them to question rather than obey the authorities of elders. It was these democratic urges for rights that empowered SIMI activists to stage a strike in Falāḥ. SIMI's call for jihad thus reflects the demonopolization and democratization of Islam. Historically institutions such as Deoband, Nadwa in Lucknow, Jāmiʿā Salafīya in Varansi (for Ahl-e-hadīth), and Jāmiʿā Ashrafiya in Azamgarh (for Barēlvīs) were centers defining Islam for their respective followers. None endorsed SIMI's jihad. Yet SIMI claimed that its call for jihad was Islamic. Indeed, it accused ulema of being ignorant of "true" Islam. The claim for true Islam did not emanate from a painstaking study of Islam. SIMI members were quite young, as their Constitution required that they retire on reaching the age of thirty. Under the flag of "true" Islam, SIMI indeed subverted the authority of ulema who had spent their entire lives studying Islam. SIMI's contestation of Islamic authorities testifies to Devji's (2005) telling observation that the discourse of jihad is the fragmentation of such authorities and the democratization of Islam.

The Framework

An attempt such as this to understand the dynamics of moderation and radicalization of Indian Islamism calls for a nuanced, critical framework. Many premises that animate the readings of Islamist politics in general, and Indian Muslims in particular, need to be rethought. The scholarship on Indian Muslim politics in the past two decades or so has mostly dealt with, for example, the "Muslim vote bank," conversion, the Shah Bano case, communal riots, and the Babri mosque. Scarcely anthropological, it takes the whole Muslim community as subject of inquiry. An in-depth, longitudinal, ethnographic study of Muslim collective actions is rare. Located at the intersection of three traditions—political anthropology, Islamic studies, and social movement studies—this book seeks to go beyond the predominant themes of Muslim politics. My aim, in so doing, is to present an ethnography of the changing ideological contours of the Jamaat and SIMI. In this section I outline the broader framework that informs the description of my material and my argument.

Beyond "East" and "West"

Eickelman and Piscatori, in their important book *Muslim Politics* (1996), urge for a nuanced, non-alarmist approach to Islamic politics, pointing to the multiplicity of contexts in which Islamic politics plays itself out. Sensitive to theology, however, these authors caution against its canonization. They argue that theology, its meaning seldom stable, is only one among many factors shaping Muslim politics. Criticizing the texts-centered approach, Van der Veer (1988; 1994) argues for a historicized, anthropological framework to study the South Asian religious formations. In this respect, Eickelman's (1982) critique of the dichotomies of "Little" and "Great" traditions is compelling and persuasive, as is Asad's (1986) call to view Islam as a discursive tradition. This book tries to build on this stream of literature on religious politics and, I hope, take it a step further. I accord primacy to the political dynamics, especially the contours and role of the secular-democratic state, as key to comprehending the changing discourse of Islamism. The shifts in the Jamaat and SIMI have as much to do with the larger political terrain they inhabit as they do with the internal dynamics. Thus seen, the Islamic tradition is far from "indigenous" and its very ambition for "coherence" (ibid.:17) reflects and produces disjunctions within it.

Despite Said's critique of Orientalism, it continues to be dominant. According to Said (1995), the unbridgeable difference between the Orient and the West and the textualization of the Orient are important elements of Orientalism. A recent example of the latter is David Cook's *Understanding Jihad*, where he makes an inevitable link between the Qur'an and jihad. In his judgment, Islam is a religion "rooted in . . . domination and violence" (2005:166). In the first chapter of his book, titled "Quran and Conquest," he argues that the doctrine of jihad galvanized its readers to conquer one territory after another. He presents a timeline of jihad, which begins with Muhammad and ends with 9/11. This approach, in many ways, also informs writings on Indian Islam. Laced with citations from Bernard Lewis, Grunebaum, Montgomery Watt, and others, Krishna (1972) argues how the doctrinarian character of Islam poses a crisis for Indian Muslims to live in a democratic polity. In the same vein, Francis Robinson avers that Muslim separatism sprang from the faith of Islam itself (1979; also see Majumdar 1960; and Qureshi 1962). The analysis of Hindu-Muslim animosity by Gaborieau (1985), a French anthropologist, proceeds along a similar path. Dismissing the views that locate the root of religious rivalry in the recent past, he argues that it should be traced back to the writings of the eleventh-century traveler Al-beruni. Madan's (1997; 1998) writings also carry these assumptions. In his survey of one thousand years of Islam in "an alien socio-cultural environment" (south Asia), he traces the root of fundamentalism, inter alia, to Islam's doctrine of fusing religion and politics (1997:108).

This book calls into question such an approach to Islamic politics. To take the issue of state, a doctrine-driven explanation is flawed. The contention by Madan, Gellner, and others that the state is intrinsic to Islam helps us understand neither state nor Islam. The nature of the premodern state was different from what it came to acquire in modernity. It was not theology that caused the state to become central to Islam; it was the unusual expansion of the early-twentieth-century state in almost every domain of life that made Islamists like Maududi see the state as central to theology.[23] Similarly, I argue that it is not the seamless culture or sacred text of Islam that fosters radicalism; on the contrary, it is the dynamics of politics that sets the discourse of jihad in motion. In stressing the contingent nature of radicalism by severing its almost naturalized link with Islam as "religion" or "culture," my aim is not to bid adieu to culture. Instead, I seek to unsettle the notion of what James Ferguson, in a different context, describes as "a unitary, univocal, cultural system that unequivocally determines *the* meaning of every signification" (1999:228). Words such as jihad derive their meanings not simply because they belong to authoritative texts; they gain salience, even new meanings, in the wider sociopolitical landscape which the mobilizers of these words inhabit. SIMI's call for jihad did not stem from its members' reading the Qur'an but from Hindutva's violent, anti-minority mobilization and the state's failure to ensure the lives and dignity of its Muslim citizens. Clearly, what I critique is the dominant understanding of culture that squarely equates Muslim culture(s) with a unitary theology.

Along with the theological-textual approach, the notion of an eternal difference between the "traditional" Orient and the "modern" West is equally powerful. Commenting on Weber, Said writes that his sociology based on the essential difference between Eastern and Western cultures led him to the "very territory originally charted and claimed by the Orientalists" (1995:259). In Weber's sociology of religion, Islam appears as a series of innate lacks (Turner 1984, 1984a, 2002a). Yet the Weberian-Orientalist framework dominates the study of Islam and Islamic movements (Burke 1988). Even Foucault, whose insights Said harnessed to criticize Orientalism, displayed many of its facets in his welcoming writings on the Iranian Revolution (Foucault 1999). He saw the Revolution as an authentic expression of the spiritual Orient untouched by the West (Stauth 1991; Almond 2004). Advancing this mode of argumentation, Bruce Lawrence says that Islamism is not only "anti-modernist" but also "anti-intellectual" (1995:17; 1987:31; also see Sivan 1990). From an anti-foundationalist approach, Sayyid (1997) states that the success of Islamism lies precisely in its anti-modernism. He takes Sami Zubaida to task for suggesting that Khomeini's Islamism is not outside modernity. In this suggestion he detects that Western hegemony disavows the voice outside of the West by appropriating it. According to Davutoglu (1994), Islamic *weltanschauung* and *selbstverstandnis* are polar opposites of Western ideas, and the difference between them is irreconcilable. Tibi (1995) similarly contends that Islamism is "semi-modern."

Social movement studies also reproduced this East-West divide. It is important to ask why studies on Islamism have only recently embraced a social movement approach (Tilly 2004; Wiktorowicz 2004) or, following Kurzman (2004:293ff.), why there is a "chasm" between the two? Kurzman explains this in a "core democratic bias" of social movement theories, which neglected movements outside of the West (also see McAdam et al. 1996; Smith 1996). The exclusion of Muslim societies, in my view, stems from a larger premise. A social movement, says Tarrow, is "an invention of modern age and an accompaniment to the rise of the modern state" (1998:2). Tilly adds that electoral politics and civil associations are its preconditions (2002; 1984). Because most Muslim societies, the assumption goes, apparently have not experienced modernity, lack modern states, and barely have electoral politics, they can only have a premodern-style rebellion but not a social movement, as the latter is a gift of modernity (Ahmad 2005).[24] After all, the absence of civil society and democracy were pet tropes of Orientalism (Turner 1984).

Several works have questioned the divide between East and West, Islam and modernity. Van der Veer's *Imperial Encounters* shows the ways in which the British political formations shaped Indian nationalist thought.[25] Euben (1999) questions the uniqueness of Islamism by situating the discourse of Egypt's Syed Qutb within the precinct of political theory and showing how it resonates with the critiques of modernity within the West by communitarians, postmodernists and Christian fundamentalists. From this framework, the quest for and assertion of tradition is an ideological move that significantly changes past discursive practices. The assumption that Islamism is a sovereign, anti-Western terrain is hard to sustain if we carefully read the writings of Islamists themselves. Maududi criticized ulema for their apathy to the West. Why did they not send, he asked, a delegation of Muslims to the West to learn its knowledge? He lamented that Muslims could not produce thinkers like Hegel, Comte, Adam Smith, and Voltaire. Delicately twisting Marx's dictum, Maududi declared that Sufism was opium. He did not cling to tradition but rather launched assault on it and in so doing also invented it (see chapter 2).

Plan of the Book

Many monographs only sketchily mention fieldwork sites and the fieldworker's interface with interlocutors. Pushing the process of fieldwork to the border is unsatisfactory, in my view. In chapter 1 I show how America's bombing of Afghanistan and the banning of SIMI after 9/11 made me suspect in the Jamaat community. Thus I question the anthropological premise of "native" versus "outsider," "one's own culture" versus "the other culture." I demonstrate that the source of otherness lies *primarily* in a political rather than a cultural matrix. I also describe how my research evolved from a single- to a multi-sited ethnography. I end with an overview of the Jamaat's evolution in Aligarh.

In chapter 2 I offer the historical-ethnographic context of the Jamaat's formation and ideology. I focus on Maududi's life to show how he evolved into an Islamist and came to support the Muslim League's demand for Pakistan. But, unlike the League, he wanted a sharia state for which he founded the Jamaat. I then tease out Maududi's political theology to depict its resonance with European ideologies. Finally, I delineate what the Jamaat's ideology entailed in practice and describe how the Jamaat boycotted the key institutions of the state, including Muslim institutions like AMU. I give an account of its educational practices, including its decision not to affiliate its schools with the government. I end by discussing Maududi's plan of action for the Jamaat members who remained in India.

The chapters in part 2 show the ideological transformation of the Jamaat, and the conflict and ambiguity it has generated. Chapter 3 deals with the educational project of the Jamaat and the ways that it functions in a school in Aligarh. I demonstrate how the Jamaat has departed from its earlier position and adjusted to the changing context, both local and national, focusing on the school's affiliation with the government, the changing criteria of appointing teachers, and conflict in the school's management body. Because of the Jamaat's mutation, there is a conflict over what indeed was the school's original aim. I also discuss how the desires of students and their parents—different as they were from those of the Jamaat—forced the Jamaat to change its ideology.

Chapter 4 describes the functioning of the SIO at AMU. Here I show that it followed the Jamaat's line of moderation. I focus on SIO's responses to the Babri mosque, the minority status of AMU, and moral indecency on the campus. The SIO, believing in secularism, appealed to the government and political parties to be truly secular so as to restore the mosque to Muslims and retain AMU's minority status. Regarding moral indecency, the SIO persuaded students, for example, not to dance rather than forcibly stopping them. Here I also describe SIO's depiction of the Prophet Muhammad as a symbol of love and compassion. In the final section, I present the contesting worldviews of two SIO activists to argue that, far from cohesion, ambiguity and conflict best defines the everyday practices of activists.

Moving form AMU to the Jāmiʿatul Falāḥ in Azamgarh, chapter 5 shows the raging conflict *within* Islamism. The conflict, implicated in a complex matrix heightened by an aggressive Hindutva, manifests itself in two models of Islam represented by SIO and SIMI. This contention,

I argue, reflects a process of democratization, and I illustrate how principles of democracy, representation, and critical debate inform the conflict between SIMI and SIO. Central to democratization is the language of rights voiced by the young Islamists coming from what I call the "Islamist class." The young Islamist activists are radical not only against Hindutva but also against the older Islamists whom they see as denying to them their rights.

The two chapters in part 3 trace the radicalization of SIMI and the moderation of the Jamaat in postcolonial India. By zooming in on the 1992 student union elections of AMU, chapter 6 examines the whys and hows of SIMI's radicalization. Next I move away from the AMU campus to illustrate its radicalism in response to national politics. I show that SIMI's radicalization unfolded parallel to Hindutva's anti-Muslim campaign to install a Hindu state. I conclude by discussing the theological justifications it offered for its radical turn. I show how SIMI's depiction of Muhammad as a commander resonated with Hindutva's portrayal of Ram as a combative god.

Chapter 7 charts the transformation of the Jamaat since Partition until today. I show how the Jamaat, which once held that true Muslims must establish Allah's Kingdom and regarded any other form of government as an idol, came to defend secular democracy. In postcolonial India the Jamaat redefined its ideology, which was also remarkably different from that of SIMI. In conclusion, I draw out my argument, and discuss the political condition, especially the role of the secular, democratic state. I show how the changing forms of secular democracy crucially acted upon the moderation of the Jamaat, on the one hand, and the radicalization of SIMI, on the other. Understanding the interactions between the Jamaat as a movement and the practices of the secular state entails a new way of thinking through the complex interrelationships between Islamism, minority identity, and the secular-democratic state.

PART ONE

Fieldwork and Historical Context

CHAPTER 1

Doing Fieldwork in Times of War

> Culture is important to anthropology because the anthropological distinction between self and other rests on it. Culture is the essential tool for making other. As a professional discourse that elaborates on the meaning of culture in order to account for . . . and understand cultural difference anthropology also helps . . . produce, and maintain it.
>
> —LILA ABU-LUGHOD, "*Writing against Culture*"

I reached Aligarh in the third week of October 2001. I met Azim, a friend teaching English in a school of Aligarh Muslim University (AMU). He generously allowed me to live with his family until I found my own accommodation. Aligarh was new to me, having only been there once before. To familiarize myself with the place, I visited the AMU campus and met a few individuals whose contacts I had acquired in Delhi. After a few days I went to Muzaffarpur (in Bihar) to see my parents, and returned to Aligarh the first week of November.

On my return I tried to arrange meetings with SIO, SIMI, and Jamaat activists. Some who agreed to meet me became deeply suspicious when I explained my research. My letter of introduction, signed by my supervisor, only amplified their suspicion. Meanwhile, Ramadan, the month of fasting, began, changing routine life in the Civil Line area (see below). My friends advised me to continue my efforts after the Eid holiday, on December 16. When I renewed my efforts in January, again suspicion greeted me.[1] I was not accepted even socially. On January 18, 2002, I visited the SIO office, whose caretaker (also an SIO member) ignored my greetings and did not even acknowledge my presence. After almost half an hour had passed, during which time he was busy chewing *pān* and arranging the office table, he told me there was no connection between the Jamaat and the SIO. Because my research was about the Jamaat, he suggested that I go to its headquarters in Delhi.

The Islamists' suspicion was expressed in a barrage of questions and responses directed at me. A collage of them would read as follows:

Why did your supervisor ask you to do research on the Jamaat?

He did not ask me. It is my own choice.

He is a Christian. Does he know Arabic or Urdu? Can he read and understand the Qur'an?

No. He can't.

How can he supervise your research unless he knows Arabic or Urdu? Why did you not do your research with an Islamic scholar? Where are you doing your research? . . . Thailand?

. . . Holland.

Yes, after the New York incident [9/11], America is after Muslims. They [the U.S.] want to know about Muslims. That is why they have sent their people everywhere to collect information about Muslim organizations and madrasas. The other day somebody told me that a London-based Indian was visiting madrasas to write a book about them. . . . They have already gathered details about Deoband and published a book . . . [a reference to Metcalf's book on Deoband]. Similarly, they have published a book on the Barēlvīs . . . [a reference to Sanyal's book]. Since they did not have one on the Jamaat, they have sent you.

Well, I am not doing research from an American university. As I told you, I am based in Holland. And my research has nothing to do with September 11. I had written my M.Phil. dissertation on the Jamaat in 1998. Then, there was nothing like September 11. I am simply extending my earlier research on the Jamaat.

Holland and America are the same. Is not Holland a Western country? With the help of the Jews, both want to destroy Muslims. Look at Afghanistan! They are dropping bombs on the poor Muslims. Now the Brahmanical forces have aligned themselves with Jews and Christians. The BJP is having meetings with Israel. They [the BJP] want to learn from Israel how to enslave Muslims.

I believe there is a difference between the Western governments and universities. . . . Scores of students in several universities in the U.S. and Europe have also protested against the war on Afghanistan.

- - -

Were you or your family associated with the Islamic movement, *taḥrīk-e-Islami* [the Jamaat]?

In a sense, my father was. While we were in Patna, he used to visit the Jamaat library and also knew some Jamaat members. He subscribed to Dawat [Jamaat's Urdu organ] and urged us to read it. That is how I know the Jamaat.

What is his name and what does he do? Where did you live in Patna?

His name is . . . He was an employee in a government bank. Now he is retired. We lived in Sultanganj. He read Maududi's books and had a collection of them.

What about you? Were you ever associated with the SIO?

No. I have a few distant friends who were active in the SIO [in Patna].

Have you read Maududi's books? Which of his books have you read?

Most.

Why did you not, then, join the Jamaat, or the SIO? I read just one of his pamphlets and became a Jamaat member. Since then I have devoted my whole life to the Jamaat. Having read his books, how could you remain uninfluenced as a true Muslim?

- - -

How old are you, and are you married?

Twenty-seven. I am not married as yet.

You should have gotten married long ago. This is un-Islamic [*ghair Islami*]. . . . Do you pray?

According to the anthropological doxa, I was studying my "own culture," because, as an Indian, I was studying an Indian Muslim movement. The notion of one's "own culture" implies receptivity and trust. Yet, as evident from my experience at the SIO office and the barrage of questions, my initial three months in the field were fraught with suspicion. I looked "other" to the Jamaat, even though I belonged to the putative Muslim community. Can the otherness I faced be explained in the serene arena of the timeless, homogeneous culture or the tumultuous field of the shifting, historically embedded politics? Why did I encounter "otherness" even though I belonged to the culture I was examining? Can the anthropological premise of one's "own culture" versus the "other culture" be sustained?

This chapter addresses these questions in ways that bear on the argument of the book. In the first section I contend that one needs to write *against* culture. I show that the notion of otherness or difference on which anthropology is built and which it continues to produce has less to do with the "other culture" and more to do with the *politics* of culture. The otherness I encountered was enmeshed in not so much in the "Muslim culture" as in the matrix of local, national, and global politics. Extending this argument, I suggest that it is wrong to assume that Muslims have a uniary, stable culture or that, by virtue of a common faith whose understanding is so diverse and contested, other forms of their affiliations simply disappear. Indeed, in Aligarh, class, caste, regional, and sectarian identities superseded religious one. When looking for a house, my being a Muslim mattered little, but my regional heritage, my "baggage," was of great import. I conclude the first section with a discussion of the ways I negotiated otherness to win trust. Here I also discuss my different interlocutors' contending expectations of me. The second section explains why I chose Aligarh for my fieldwork and later extended my research to locations as distant as Azamgarh, Delhi, Patna, and Rampur. I end with an account of the Jamaat's expansion in Aligarh.

Sources of Otherness: Culture or Politics?

Historically culture has been the subject of anthropology but not simply culture. The subject has been "other culture(s)," as affirmed in the title of Beattie's (1964) textbook, *Other Cultures*. This notion of "other culture," which often meant "another culture," presupposed "own culture." In either case, culture was regarded as a unitary, stable, coherent whole. The dualist distinction between "other culture" and "own culture" referred, respectively, to the one anthropologists studied and the culture anthropologists belonged to. Historically, again, "other culture" was non-Western and remote from the "own culture" of anthropologists who were invariably from the West. It was not geographical distance, however, that rendered a culture "other culture"; it was primarily the *difference* in *cultures* between that of anthropologists and that of the people they studied that made it other and exotic. Simple as this account may appear,[2] it has the following premise: non-Western culture is essentially *different* from Western culture. Further, the difference between cultures is the fountainhead of otherness. Based on this assumption, it is only logical that the canonical works verily showed irreconcilable difference between cultures. Dumont's *Homo Hierarchicus* (1988) is a classic example. Geertz's *Negara* (1980) similarly purports to show that notions of time and politics are radically different in Bali and in the West.

A number of works have critiqued the reification of culture and notions of otherness, and the difference anthropology helped to fashion (Abu-Lughod 1991; Baumann 1996; di Leonardo 1998; Friedman 1987; Gupta and Ferguson 1992; Kean 2003; Pels and Salemink 1994; Swidler 1986; Thomas 1991). Describing anthropology as a "discourse of alterity," Thomas (1991: 310), pleads for "disposing of" ethnography. Similarly Abu-Lughod has argued for "writing against culture." Here my intention is neither to dispose of ethnography (for this book is ethnographic) nor to reproduce these critiques. My aim is modest. Drawing on these critiques, I show how the culture-centric theories fail to explain my experience in the field. Despite the critiques, notions of "difference" and "otherness" between cultures persist. In calling for a dialogic interaction with an "other," Marcus and Fischer continue to assume differences in cultures, and therefore the aim of cultural critique is to "apply both the substantive results and epistemological lessons learned from ethnography *abroad* to a renewal of the critical function of anthropology as it is pursued . . . *at home*" (1986:117, emphasis added). Even Bourdieu (2003:282–83) implies this difference when he uses the terms "foreign land" and "foreign milieu" (also see Abu-Lughod 1991:141). The perception of difference between Islam and the West or other religions is perhaps most enduring.

War on Terror, Terror of War

So, did the "otherness" I faced lie in "culture"? Following Crehan (2002), di Leonardo (1998), and Gupta and Ferguson (1992), below I describe how the political factors of the time provided conditions for the articulation of otherness. The U.S. war on terror, its bombing of Afghanistan, and the Indian government's ban on SIMI had fostered an unusual climate of fear in Aligarh. Further, everyday life in Aligarh defied preconceptions that there was a monochromatic culture.

That I was perceived as other is a corrective to the idea that something called "own culture" exists and that it facilitates familiarity, receptivity, and trust. When I reached Aligarh, the war by the mighty U.S. on poor Afghanistan, dubbed operation "infinite justice" and "enduring freedom" by the American media (see Ahmad 2002), was in full swing. As elsewhere, this was a topic of hot talk in Aligarh. Though most people were against the war, there was no public protest. They were angry, but also fearful because of a number of recent episodes. Only two weeks after 9/11, the Government of India, led by the right-wing BJP, had banned SIMI for fomenting "communal disharmony" and "sedition" (*Hindustan Times* [*HT*] 2001), declaring SIMI a "fundamentalist" organization having links with "Pakistan's ISI [intelligence service], terrorist groups" in Kashmir (*The Pioneer* 2001a), and also "Osama bin Laden's terrorist outfit Al Qaeda" (*HT* 2001a, also see *Frontline* 2001, October. 15; *Afkār-e-millī* 2002, April 16–18). Earlier L. K. Advani, the home minister at the time, had anticipated the ban, describing SIMI's activities as "anti India"

(*The Pioneer* 2001).[3] The war on terror had given the BJP an excuse to ban SIMI. The changed global scenario seemed to promote a competition for victimhood. The BJP sought to impress upon the U.S. that it had been facing "Islamic terrorism" long before America became its target. Operation "infinite justice" had thus found echoes in the Indian government's hunt for terrorists, namely, Muslims.

Following the ban on September 27, a crackdown on SIMI ensued. Although SIMI activists were arrested all over the country, Aligarh was a special target, as SIMI had been formed in Aligarh and was headquartered there until the mid-1980s. Further, nany of its leaders came from Aligarh. At the time of the ban, the SIMI president was an alumnus of AMU. Moreover, its national library, which was also confiscated, was still in Aligarh. The press had also begun to portray AMU as a breeding ground for terrorism, and the finger of suspicion was pointed, in particular, at SIMI. In 2000 the police secretly arrested Mobin, a former SIMI member enrolled at AMU, at his hostel, charged by the government with having ties with the ISI and Kashmiri militants. In the government's version, he also had a part in exploding bombs in Agra prior to Bill Clinton's visit in 2000 (Maheshwari 2001:187–88). In prison, I was told, he was tortured to the point where he became unconscious. Before Mobin's arrest, the AMU vice chancellor had remarked that AMU was "bristling with ISI agents," and his statement was quoted in a pamphlet, dated October 22, 1998 (in my possession), of the Leftist student organization Forum for Democratic Rights (FDR). In the late 1990s local newspapers had indeed taken to running rabidly communal headlines such as "Terrorist nabbed on AMU campus," "AMU Becoming Hub of Terrorist Activities," and "ISI Racket Busted in AMU" (in Maheshwari 2001:188).

Madrasas had also come under the government's surveillance. Since the rise of the Taliban, the media had begun to portray madrasas as sheltering the enemies of India—namely, Pakistanis—or producing an anti-India mind-set or both (Saran 2002). During my fieldwork in the Jamaat school in the shahr, intelligence officials, known as Local Intelligence Officials (LIO), visited the school to conduct an enquiry, which coincided with my own research on the school's functioning and syllabus. Talking to my interlocutors was difficult, as I knew their suspicions would resurface. One incident, worth noting, shows that even after months of winning their trust, they still suspected my research. When I visited a SIMI activist in May, he acted indifferently toward me. Warning me not to act like an ignoramus, he asked had I not read the newspaper (which I hadn't). On that very day the former president of the UP unit of SIMI, was arrested in Lucknow (*AU* 2002, May 6; *Rāshṭriya Sahārā* 2002, May 6). A month earlier another SIMI activist had been arrested in the Bhadohi district of UP (*AU* 2002, April 11).

It was in this political context, crisscrossing the local, national, and global matrix, that I encountered otherness.

Beyond Faith: Geography, Class, and Culture

The otherness I faced because of the distinctive politics of the time was peculiar to me. However, among Aligrah Muslims, forms of otherness existed along various lines: class, caste/*birādrī*, region, sect, and the notion of being "un-cultured." Which divide gained salience depended on the context. Different forms of otherness often dovetailed one another, but a defining divide among Muslims concerned the geography of their dwelling.

Aligarh is located some 125 kilometers southeast of Delhi.[4] In 1991 Muslims comprised 37.41 percent of the population (Brass 2003:47), which, in 1981, stood at 320,781 (Mann 1992:27). The railway line laid by the British in 1864 divided Aligarh into two areas: the old part, called *shahr* (town), and the new part called the Civil Line or University. The two were separated by 6–7 kilometers. The Civil Line was a colonial invention. Prior to the British, it was uninhabited (Siddiqi 1981:27 n. 4). When the British arrived, they built cantonments and bungalows. The Civil Line saw further growth when Sir Syed Ahmad Khan founded the Mohammedan Anglo-Oriental (MAO) College (see chapter 2) there. Much later, in 1920, the MAO College flowered into Aligarh Muslim University. As such, the Civil Line emerged as what Mann, following C. A. Bayly, calls a *qasba* town, because it also attracted Muslim gentry from elsewhere. The imposing *ḥavēlīs* of nawabs (local princes) proved this. The Civil Line symbolized colonial-aristocratic modernity. The district administration, court, railway station, post office, and so on, were all in the Civil Line. In the twentieth century the Civil Line area of Aligarh became famous worldwide for its university, and the *shahr* for its locks.

The flyover—called *kaṭhpullā* (wooden bridge)—on the railway line both connected and separated the Civil Line and the *shahr*. It didn't merely symbolize a physical divide but also signaled a monumental class division. The *shahr*, with its dense population and congested streets, wore a medieval look. Most *mohalla* (neighborhood) streets were too narrow even for rickshaws to pass. The sewage system was abysmal: drains were left open, and the filth collected from them remained on the streets for days, fowling the air. In the summer pigs roamed the streets after bathing in the drains. During my second period of fieldwork, for ten weeks I lived at Turkaman Gate, a working-class neighborhood. From morning until evening the neighborhood was noisy because of work in the lock factories. Dust, smoke, mosquitoes, and flies filled the crowded streets. The water supply was available only for an hour or so each morning and

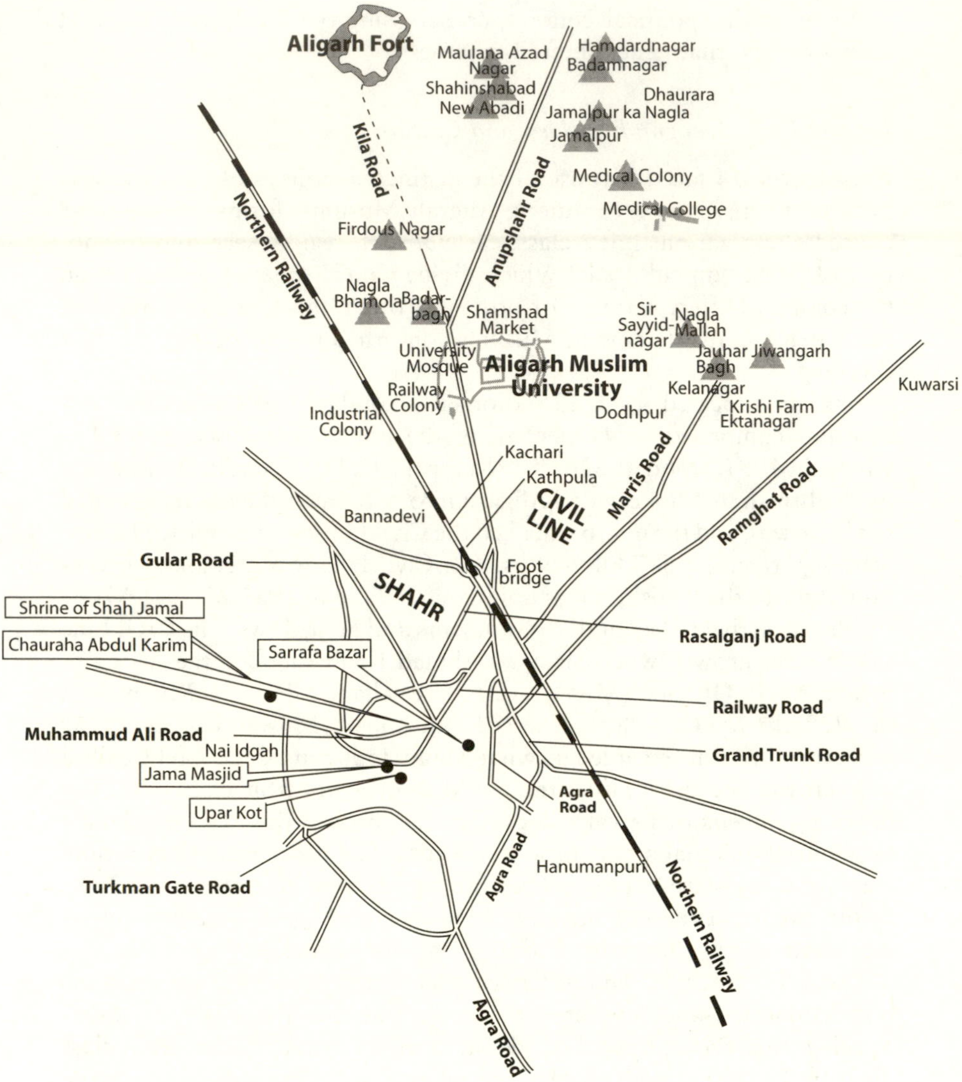

Map 2. Aligarh showing the *shahr* and the Civil Line

evening. The houses were congested and dilapidated, and in one estimate at least 15 percent of the *shahr* population had no toilet facilities. The majority of the poor multitude lived in the most pitiable conditions. Asif, a dropout from the Jamaat school, was a neighbor of mine. He ran a small shop of soft drinks, and eight members of his father's family lived in a two-room house.

The literacy rate among Muslims in the *shahr* was as low as 10 percent (Maheshwari 2001:275). One student told me that in the past twenty years he was the first Muslim from the *shahr* to have passed the test for admission to study medicine at AMU. Twenty-eight percent of the population lived below the poverty line, the income varying between Rs. 500 and 1,500 a month (1 Euro equaled just over 50 Indian Rupees in 2001). An additional 34 percent of the population lived close to the poverty line; their monthly income fluctuated between Rs. 1,500 and 2,500 (ibid.:279).[5] Over 90 percent of Muslims belonged to the low ranks of Ajlaf castes/*birādrīs*.[6] Most of them were Quershi, Anṣārī, Saifi, Abbasi, Salmānī, and Alvi[7]—traditionally butchers, weavers, blacksmith, water carriers, barbers, and beggars, respectively. Congruence no longer existed between caste and occupation. Except for the majority of the minority, high-ranking Ashraf castes such as Syed, Shaikh, and Khan, most Muslims belonging to the Ajlaf castes worked as laborers in the lock factories, sold vegetables or fruits, or owned petty businesses. The *birādrī* identity was supreme. Although Muslims and Hindus lived together in some *mohallas*, most localities were segregated. Muslim *mohallas* were known by the preponderance of a given caste living there.

Most people in the Civil Line, in contrast, were educated. In January, when I rented a house near Jāmiʿā Urdu (in the Civil Line area), my landlord proudly told me that I was lucky to live in the most educated colony. He claimed that every household had at least one Ph.D. The Civil Line was modern, its streets clean and wide. Because a sizable number of Muslims migrated to to the Gulf, the U.S., and elsewhere since the 1970s, the Civil Line saw a rapid growth of middle-class colonies. Many houses were air-conditioned. Some residents drank only mineral water. Close to AMU at the Dodhpur roundabout was the Amīr-e-nishān shopping center. The Center Point, an area near the railway station, represented the globalized face of Aligarh. Besides having pricey restaurants, ice-cream parlors, fancy garment outlets with the latest international designs, and Internet cafes, it also had ATM counters of a number of international banks. It was *the* place for Civil Line residents to visit and consume modernity.

The geography of class was so strong a factor in conditioning intracommunity relations that seldom did their mutual faith bring Muslims from the *shahr* and the Civil Line together. They did so only against external threat: communal riots and the Babri mosque were two extraordinary events that brought them together. In ordinary times the *shahr* and the Civil Line were not only two different worlds, they were nearly unbridgeable. The residents of the latter looked down on those of the former. For them, the *shahr* symbolized backwardness, filth, noise, poverty, laziness, and, above all, gloom. For the Civil Line, the *shahr* was the other, unruly and historically stuck. If the image of southern Italy was

Orientalist for the rest of the country (Schneider 1998), the *shahr* was so for the Civil Line; it exampified what I call "domestic orientalism." A typical "uncultured" person was a figure from the *shahr*, particularly of the Qureshi caste. Many people who had lived in the Civil Line for decades never visited the *shahr*. On the rare occasion when they did, their visit was big news among their friends. The few residents of the *shahr* who managed to be accepted into the university found it hard to have friends from the Civil Line. Nazar, the principal of the Green school in the *shahr* (see chapter 3), told me that her daughter had a friend from the Civil Line who said that had she known Nazar's daughter was from the *shahr*, she never would have befriended her in the first place. Many of my friends from the Civil Line said that my idea to live in the *shahr* was "crazy," and once I had lived there, they congratulated me for my "courage."

Mainly the dynamics of class separated the Civil Line from the *shahr*. Civil Line residents, however, described their otherness toward the *shahr* in a cultural vocabulary. People in the *shahr* were regarded as lacking *salīqa* or *tahẕīb*; that is, they were "uncultured." Indeed, many Civil Line residents used the English term "culture" to say that Muslims in the *shahr* either lacked it or had it wrong.

Belonging, "Birādrī," and the Orientalization of Bihar

Caste, or *birādrī*, was another axis of identity. In both parts of Aligarh, caste mattered. Marriages, for instace, rarely took place outside the caste fold unless they were love marriages, and these were uncommon. Elsewhere I have discussed the significance of caste in Aligarh (Ahmad 2003a). Suffice it to note here that it mattered even for Jamaat members. One Jamaat member, a professor at AMU living in the Civil Line, described the difficulty in finding a groom for his sister outside the Anṣārī caste that they came from. Many men from the Ashraf castes readily agreed to marry his sister, but they turned down the proposal once they learned that the professor was an Anṣārī. Also among those refusing the proposal were Jamaat members. Like caste, sects mattered in marriage. People from the Ahl-e-hadīth, the Doeband, and Ahl-e-sunna-o-Jamaat (popularly called Barēlvī) usually had marital alliances within their own sects. For his sister's marriage, a Delhi-based friend asked me to find out details about three AMU bachelors. I later discovered that all three were Barēlvīs, as was my friend. Sect mattered in another context. Most AMU students of the Barēlvīs sect preferred not to say their prayers, especially the Friday prayer, rather than offer them behind a non-Barēlvī imam. It follows that many mosques were sect-based.

The outsider-insider divide was another feature of Muslim life. In the *shahr*, an outsider (*bāhrī*) was one not born in the *shahr*; hence he did not belong to it. Claim to belonging to the *shahr* howver, was not sufficient to become an insider. Ikram Beg, a Jamaat member, told me that in the 2003 elections of the Jamaat he was not elected as its *amīr* (president) even though he had won the majority of votes (6 out of 9). A local (*maqāmī*) person was "unjustly" chosen in his place, he claimed, because Beg was seen as an "outsider." Though born in Hyderabad, Beg had lived in the *shahr* for decades and considered the *shahr* his "own" because his mother was from there.

In the Civil Line, too, the insider-outsider divide was dominant, expressed mostly in relation to the people of Bihar, the second largest state of India that had become a metaphor for ransom, abduction, violence, backwardness, and "uncluturedness." Much like southern Italy, Bihar had come to be Orientalized in the national imagination as the other. People from UP, especially the adjoining districts of Aligarh, considered Biharis as "outsiders." They also regarded AMU as "their own." The presence of Biharis on the AMU campus—they were the largest segment next only to the students from UP—thus disrupted their sense of AMU being their own. For the people from UP, Biharis were objects of ridicule, jokes, and sarcasm. A student from Aligarh told me that if he wished to abuse someone, he no longer called him a bastard but called him a Biahri instead. Such was the feeling of otherness among UP Muslims against their co-religionists from Bihar.

Given the pervasiveness of the "Bihar phenomenon," if we can call it that, nearly everything at AMU revolved around this divide, perhaps most importantly student politics. This was also a crucial factor in the appointment of teachers. Just as the Bihar phenomenon affected the affairs at AMU, so, too, did it reach into everyday life. Friendships, for example, were based largely on state affiliation. Nothing illustrated this better than my failure to rent a house. Soon after my arrival, I started looking for a house. One day Azim and I met some seven landlords, a few of them retired professors. As my friend and guide, Azim initiated the deal, speaking in English, which mattered in the Civil Line, and impressing the landlords who eyed him with awe and respect. They also displayed pride that I, as someone from the *quam* (Muslim community), had made it to JNU and eventually to a Western university. The rent was even settled with some landlords. But all this was peripheral to renting a house. Ultimately the deal rested on which state I came from. Upon learning that I came from Bihar, all the landlords declined to rent their houses on one pretext or another. It made no difference that I had lived almost half my life outside Bihar or that I had studied for ten years in Delhi. Apparently "once a Bihari, always a Bihari." Despite its claim to unite Muslims on the basis of faith, the Jamaat was also not immune to the Bihar phenomenon. In the thorny debate over the issue of voting in the elections (see chapter 7), a pro-voting Jamaat member from Hyderabad ridiculed the opposition to voting by Ziaulhoda, another Jamaat member from Bihar, by saying that it was "an exact proof of his [Ziaulhoda's] Bihariness [*bihārīpanē*]" (*Rahguzar* 1986 [March]: 40).

Negotiating Otherness

The perception that my research was part of a Western conspiracy[8] continually aroused suspicion, leaving me feeling lost and frustrated. One way that I demonstrated my academic autonomy was through personal interactions based primarily on the questions my interlocutors always asked me about my life: Which state did I come from? Where had I studied? Did I have a political affiliation? What did my father and brother (never my mother or sisters) do? And was I ever associated with the Jamaat? My having been educated in a madrasa and earning a B.A. degree from Jamia Millia Islamia, New Delhi, heightened their trust in me. A breakthrough came, however, when a relative of one of my distant friends, who was then a top Jamaat leader in Delhi, assured them of my credentials; he then asked the SIO president to telephone the SIO activists in Aligarh to help me. Another Jamaat leader, based in Aligarh and educated in the U.S., appreciated my research and introduced me to the Jamaat circle in Aligarh. Once introduced, I approached the former SIMI members first, as they were much less fearful compared to the current members. Through them I contacted the current members who gradually began to trust me. Although these contacts proved valuable, most important ultimately were my personal ties with the people I worked with.

The principal of the Jamaat school in the *shahr* and the Jamaat *amīr* in the Civil Line asked to see my research proposal. Once having read it, they took an interest in my project. As time went on, suspicion gave way to trust, and I began to receive dinner invitations. Toward the end of my first fieldwork trip, I became friends with most of those who had been deeply suspicious of my research. During the second fieldwork trip, all the suspicion fell away. Many, including the SIO office caretaker, apologized for their treatment of me in the past.

But winning their trust also created challenges. Whereas the Jamaat leaders wanted me only to highlight their positive contributions, SIMI activists expected me to be "objective [*ghair jānibdār*]." The SIMI president, whom we meet in chapter 6, urged me to add a chapter stating that the Jamaat had abandoned its original ideology. He wanted me to validate his claim that SIMI members were the true followers of Maududi, indeed of Islam itself. While stressing the massive changes in the trajectory of the Jamaat, he dismissed any such changes in his own organization (see the conclusion).

Choice of Site

My fieldwork began with the assumption that I would do a community-based study of the Jamaat in Aligarh, but the dynamics of my fieldwork soon pushed me to revise my plan. As my fieldwork progressed, it became increasingly clear that a community study would not serve my research purposes well and that more suitable to research was the network- or chain-oriented, multi-sited, ethnographic approach (Marcus 1995). Consequently I reached out to four additional sites—Azamgarh, Delhi, Patna, and Rampur.

Why Aligarh and Beyond?

I first heard of AMU when I was a student in a village madrasa. The madrasa administration had asked us students to get "Aligarhī" pajamas and *kurta* (an upper garment) to wear at an upcoming function. Later, after moving to a government school, I heard more about the university from some of my rich relatives who studied there. As students of AMU, they felt superior to me, who studied in a government school of Bihar. Studying at AMU meant not only getting a degree but also embodying "Muslim culture." Such was AMU's place in the Muslim imagination! Its dress served as a model of Muslim identity in north India.

K. B. Sinha echoed this sentiment when, in a debate in the Parliament, in 1965, he observed that "Aligarh [Muslim University] is the microcosm of the great Muslim community of this country" (in Maheshwari 2001:1). This was why I selected AMU as my fieldwork site. In postcolonial India, AMU had emerged as a prime symbol of Muslim identity (Graff 1990). Given AMU's distinct placement in the Muslim community, the Jamaat sought to establish its hegemony there, and it was at AMU that the Jamaat, soon after its formation, first began its student activism. Again, it was at AMU that SIMI was established in 1976, and it remained headquartered there for several years. Demographically, Aligarh was one of the few towns in north India with a sizable Muslim population. Counter to the official statistics of 37.41 percent, Muslims believed that they constituted half the population. My purpose was to see how the Islamist activists functioned in a setting like Aligarh and to what extent they exercised influence over the "microcosm." Did they change the microcosm, or did the microcosm change them?

In analyzing the social profile of the SIO members on the AMU campus, my curiosity was piqued when I learned that more than half its members came from Jāmiʿatul Falāḥ (hereafter, Falāḥ), a Jamaat madrasa. Falāḥ was situated in a Muslim-dominated small town, Bilariaganj, with a population of 11,891 in 2001, in the Azamgarh[9] district of eastern UP.

Hence my decision to extend my fieldwork to Azamgarh. I learned later that many of the top SIMI leaders were also alumni of Falāḥ. Moreover, both the SIO and SIMI were more active at Falāḥ than on the AMU campus. The Falāḥ factor concerned not only the SIO and SIMI but also AMU at large. In the AMU student union elections, Falāḥ had emerged as a "vote bank," because its alumni numbered around four hundred (see chapter 6). If Falāḥ influenced AMU, the reverse was also true. In the elections of the Old Boys' Association of Falāḥ, AMU was a significant factor (see chapter 5). The two times I visited Falāḥ for my fieldwork I stayed in the Falāḥ guesthouse situated on its campus.

I included Rampur in northwestern UP (see Map 3) in my research because of its centrality in the life of the Jamaat. When working in the Jamaat school in the *shahr* I was advised to visit Rampur, where the Jamaat had established its first model primary school, Darsgāh. A historical understanding of the Jamaat's educational project required meeting the people associated with it. Becase Rampur was also the Jamaat headquarters before it shifted to Delhi, some old members living there knew more about the early phase of the Jamaat. The Jamaat library there also had rare documents that I had been unable to procure elsewhere. I made a week-long visit to Rampur during my second fieldwork trip.

On the campus of the Jamaat headquarters at Abul Fazal in Okhla, located in southeastern New Delhi, the national offices of both the Jamaat and SIO were based. I first went there to surmount the initial difficulties I had faced in Aligarh. Subsequently I made numerous visits. The headquarters had all the figures, statistics, and documentary materials of the Jamaat, the SIO, and the school in Aligarh. Some of the Jamaat's most influential members lived on the campus of the headquarters. Interviews with them provided valuable data for my research. Many former and current members of the Jamaat, the SIO, and the SIMI were also based in Delhi, though not in the headquarters. I met them as well during my visits. The headquarters also housed the central library[10] of the Jamaat where I worked for weeks.

The inclusion of Patna as yet another site of fieldwork came about for many reasons. The Khuda Bakhsh Oriental Public Library of Patna held the unaltered documents of the Jamaat from pre-Partition times. The most severe opposition to the Jamaat's decision to allow its members to vote in the elections came from Patna, and it was important that I visit Patna to meet them. Finally, of the local student organizations that came together to form the SIO, the Patna-based organization, Ḥalqa-e-ṭalaba-e-Islami (HTI), was crucial. Many HTI leaders were based in Patna, and they provided me with information about how the SIO was formed and also lent me important documents.

Map 3. Uttar Pradesh, and its districts

Though my fieldwork changed from single to multiple sites, I *anchored* myself in Aligarh, branching out from there to the other sites. During my first period of fieldwork, I stayed in a rented house (made possible through a Bihari friend) on the Medical road near Jamia Urdu, located at the edge of the AMU campus. When I gained access to the school in the *shahr*, I visited it regularly. I soon realized that to appreciate the workings of the school in relation to the neighborhood I had to live there, and so I stayed in the *shahr* for ten weeks during the second phase of my fieldwork.

In taking field notes I mostly used a notebook computer. My electronic notes were always in English, with important words transliterated in Urdu. Because power failure was frequent in Aligarh, I also handwrote notes, most of them in Urdu. The notes taken outside Aligarh were handwritten in Urdu. Telephone calls and e-mails sometimes proved valuable, especially in establishing contact with the diasporic Jamaat activists. I also extensively use the published materials of the Jamaat, the SIO, and the SIMI, particularly the reports of their activities, proceedings of internal meetings, and their key resolutions and decisions. I draw on several of their organs: *Tarjumānul Qur'an*, *Zindgī*, *Zindgī-e-nau*, *Radiance*, *Rafīq-e-manzil*, and *Islamic Movement*. A significant portion of the written materials I use deals with the historical evolution of the Jamaat, and these I collected in various libraries (see the preface). Finally, to ensure anonymity, I have changed the names of my interlocutors.

Islamists in Aligarh

In closing this chapter I offer a historical-ethnographic account of the introduction and expansion of the Jamaat in Aligarh. Reproducing the divide of geography and class discussed above, the Jamaat had two separate organizational units for the Civil Line and the *shahr*.

Soon after Maududi's graduation to Islamism, his writings in *Tarjumānul Qur'an* came to influence a tiny section of the AMU community. However, no one from AMU took part in the foundational meeting of 1941, when Maududi formed the Jamaat (based on the profiles of the founding members; see the Pakistani Jamaat's Web site 2001). Nor is there evidence that anyone at AMU became a member of the Jamaat before Partition. In 1948, when it was reconstituted as the "Jamaat-e-Islami Hind, at AMU," the Jamaat's organizational report noted, it had only two workers (*kārkun*),[11] and no members. The report further noted that there was not much scope for expanding the Jamaat, as most students and teachers were Communists immersed in "irreligoisty" (*dahriyat*). The two Jamaat workers in 1948 were Jalil Ahmad, a lecturer in the English department, and Anwar Ali Khan Soz, a student (Nadwi 1990:142). In an interview with me, Mahbuburrahman, a student in the English department during the late 1940s and a retired professor at the time of my fieldwork, recalled that Ahmad was not influential at the university. Some years after Partition, Ahmad left for Pakistan. The task of organizing the Jamaat fell to Soz.[12] During the mid-1950s, with the return to Aligarh of the four students who, under Maududi's influence, had boycotted an AMU education and gone instead to the Jamaat's Ṡānvī Darsgāh, an institution built as an alternative to AMU's anti-Islamic education (see chapter 2), the Jamaat expanded as they had already become members at the Ṡānvī. One such student was Qazi Ashfaq Ahmad. Previously a worker of the Congress and the Muslim League, he joined the Jamaat after Partition. In 1957 he became the *amīr* of the Jamaat in the Civil Line (IFEW Web site 2002).

In the absence of reliable data, the number of Jamaat members in the AMU after the Partition is difficult to know precisely. However, based on the available data from the early 1970s on, a reasonable guess might be that the number never exceeded fifteen. In 1974 the AMU unit of the Jamaat had nine members (FA 1974:27–28). The number rose to nineteen in 1981 (FA 1981:32–33). In 1989 it declined to eighteen (FA 1989:71). During my fieldwork (2001–2004) the total number stood at eighteen, of which only two (out of 2,530 AMU teachers) were current faculty at AMU (FA 2001:47). Five of them lived abroad.

The Jamaat in the *shahr* had a different trajectory. As noted, the literacy rate in the *shahr* was far below that in the Civil Line area, as was the economic condition of most Muslims. Of all castes, the Qureshis were the largest and most influential. It was through a Qureshi, Haji Sultan (1916–1996), that the Jamaat made inroads in the *shahr*. Sultan belonged to the Ahl-e-hadīth sect that came to the *shahr* at the end of the nineteenth century and whose followers numbered few—even today they are a minority.[13] Sultan was educated up to the eighth grade. In 1949 his son (an associate professor at AMU) told me that Sultan had been taken to a Jamaat meeting in the Civil Line and that its rational (*modallal*) approach had impressed Sultan. Later he met the Jamaat's *amīr*, Abullais Nadwi, whose simplicity further drew him in. That same year he joined the Jamaat.

After becoming a member, Sultan sought to expand the Jamaat. Though he distributed Jamaat pamphlets wherever he went, he achieved only limited success. His brother joined the Jamaat, and three others became its sympathizers. Sultan was unable to expand the Jamaat largely because of his affiliation with the Ahl-e-hadīth sect. Because most Muslims of the *shahr* were illiterate, practitioners of Sufism of one kind or another, they rejected the puritan, anti-Sufi Islam of the Ahl-e-hadīth sect. Undeterred, Sultan devised a plan. To convert the local Muslims to his version of Islam, he invited the Jamaat members from outside to settle in the *shahr*. In the mid-1950s, he invited Amin Asri, an Ahl-e-hadīth *ʿālim*-member of the Jamaat, who, having been expelled as the imam of a mosque in Malirkotla (Punjab), was then based in the Jamaat headquarters.[14] He made Asri the imam of a mosque for which he was the caretaker. Because Sultan was a wealthy potato merchant, an *ālū wālē*, he enjoyed a high social status and was the caretaker of other mosques as well. But despite his dedication, he could not win many activists for the Jamaat.

No reliable data about Jamaat members in *shahr* exist up to the early 1970s. In 1974 there were seven members (*FA* 1974:28). Five years later their number rose to ten (*FA* 1981:32). In 1989 their number stood at thirteen (*FA* 1989:70–71). In 2001 it had declined to eight (*FA* 2002:47). Most current members are in their late sixties or early seventies. After a gap of some twenty-two years, a former SIO activist, aged thirty-five, became a Jamaat member in 2001.

CHAPTER 2

Contextualizing the Formation and Ideology of Islamism

> The storm of the west made Muslim, Muslim.
>
> —MOHAMMAD IQBAL

> In order to keep everything as it is, we have to change everything.
>
> —GIUSEPPE DI LAMPEDUSA, *The Leopard*

This chapter explores the Jamaat's ideology and practices as they evolved before India's Partition, focusing on the life of Maududi as founder of the movement and central to the Jamaat. I discuss how a cross-current of Western philosophy, Marxism, and a modern Islam shaped his outlook. I then describe the context of the Jamaat's formation, discussing Maududi's move from secular nationalism to communalism and eventually to Islamism. With his turn to Islamism, he came to support the demand for a separate state for Muslims, namely, Pakistan. But he wanted a sharia state based on "pure Islam" for which he founded his own party, Jamaat-e-Islami. I next lay bare his Islamist ideology, which, following Carl Schmitt, I call a "political theology." I tease out the conceptual structure of Islamism to depict its resonance with the European ideologies of the time. Finally, I set down the practices of the Jamaat. Based on historical and fieldwork data, I discuss how ideology played out in practice, concluding with Maududi's plan of action to bring about an Islamic revolution in India before he left for Pakistan.

Far from being "pure" and "sovereign," I argue, Maududi's construction of Islam—conceived here as Islamism–departs from traditions. His ideology is a manifestation of what Therborn (1980:vii–viii) calls "the cacophony of sounds and signs of a big city street" rather than the symphony of a narrow lane dotted only with signs of an un-ruptured Islam. Like the poet Mohammad Iqbal (Puri 2003), Maududi also became Muslim precisely because of the "western storm." As I hope to demonstrate, the corpus of writings by Maududi—never schooled in a traditional *madrasa*—indeed mounts an assault on the lived traditions (Bhatt 1997) and, in so doing, invents them in the name of reclaiming "purity." Just as the invention of tradition is modern (Hobsbawm 1983; Eickelman and

Piscatori 1996), so, too, is Maududi's oeuvre of Islam. Thus, rather than antithetical to or, a revolt against modernity (Davutoglu 1994; Kelidar 1981; Lawrence 1987, 1995; Moghissi 1999; Sayyid 1997; Sivan 1990), Maududi's ideology bears the indelible signature of modernity.

Nasr's (1996) and Adams's (1966) writings show the novelty of Maududi's ideology, and I wish to push their argument further. Equally novel was Maududi's reading of history as a binary battle between Islam and *jāhiliyat* (the "other" of Islam) and the conceptualization of the Jamaat-e-Islami as the sole bearer of Truth, Islam. I stress these points because they are crucial to my argument. Maududi's portrayal of Islam as a perennial battle between Islam and *jāhiliyat* led him to boycott all the prime institutions of the secular polity—the judiciary, army, assembly or parliament, bureaucracy, and so on. For him, even Aligarh Muslim University was an institution of *jāhiliyat*. Likewise, because he considered Muslim organizations other than his own party un-Islamic, he forbade the Jamaat to have any alliance with them. Both Nasr and Adams ignore these aspects of Maududi's ideology, perhaps because their works deal with Pakistan's Jamaat for which the issue of boycotting *jāhiliyat* soon faded. However, the boycott of *jāhiliyat* remained central to the Indian Jamaat.

Modernity, Collective Action, and Biography

Institutional matrixes of modernity facilitated various collective actions from the nineteenth century on, and it is against the backdrop of these novel forms of collective actions that the Jamaat movement arose. Though my intent is not to reduce Jamaat's ideology to the biography of Maududi, I also don't share the explanations of social movement's emergence (Tarrow 1994; Kurzman 2003; Goodwin and Jasper 1999; and Jasper 1997) where biography is reduced to the invisible logic of structure. Indeed, Maududi's role is particularly central to the intellectualist movement that the Jamaat was and it still is in India.[1] Before Maududi's turn to Islamism, he was deeply influenced by Western thought. This influence was not merely intellectual but was also evident in his quotidian life, which ran counter to accepted Islamic norms. These early influences determined Maududi's outlook when he entered politics to propound Islamism.

Social Movements and Islamic Activism

A major consequence of colonial modernity was a newfound consciousness that society was no longer "natural" or "divine." The doctrine of karma, or *taqdīr*, came under question (Kaviraj 1999). In that sense, colonial modernity made a rupture in the traditional order (Aloysius 1997;

Rizvi 1970), as a multiplicity of collectivities began to institute movements to question the naturalness of the social order. For Bourdieu (1979), the break with tradition occurs when societies attempt to take hold of the future by human intervention. This is not to say that movements did not exist in the precolonial era, but, as Touraine (1985:778) contends, they were constrained by the "metasocial principle" such as "order of things, divine rule, natural law." Colonial modernity heralded an epoch where the human capacity for "self-production, self-transformation, and self destruction" grew boundless. Moreover, the *forms* of social movements were novel. In colonial India *associational politics* emerged. The *repertoire* of movements was also new. As in Europe (Tilly 1984), the notion of strikes, demonstrations, public meetings, resolutions, petitions, newspapers, and so on, was largely nonexistent in precolonial India. Another novelty of collective action was its state-centeredness. Again, like the state in Europe in the Middle Ages (Giddens 1985; Tarrow 1998; Tilly 1984, 1995, 2002; Foucault 1982, 1996), the state in precolonial India was marginal to everyday life (Kaviraj 1999). By contrast, the colonial state was unusually interventionist. Precisely because of this, all collective actions in the nineteenth century and later pertained to the state (see Ahmad 2009).

By the mid-nineteenth century an array of associations ascended all over India.[2] My focus is on those relating to Muslims. In 1856 Nawab Amir Ali (d. 1879) formed the National Mohammedan Association in Calcutta. In Bombay Badruddin Tyabji (d. 1906) established Anjuman-e-islām to encourage the spread of modern education, especially among women (Rizvi 1970). Many more associations were formed in Amritsar, Brailly, Lucknow, and Lahore (Hardy 1972). In 1864 Syed Ahmad Khan (1817–1898), the renowned "modernist" reformer, founded Scientific Society. Crafting a theology in line with European rationalism, he believed that Muslims could enter a mosque wearing shoes and that the ideas of heaven, hell, and angels were merely metaphors. "Sir Syed," as he is known, held that Western science was "natural." Critics declared him and his followers *nēcharī*, one who follows "nature," and also heretics (Lelyveld 1978; Rahman 1958). To provide Muslims with a modern education, in 1875 Sir Syed founded a "Muslim Cambridge," the Mohammedan Anglo-Oriental (MAO) College in Aligarh. In 1920 MAO became Aligarh Muslim University (AMU).

These associations and movements created a public sphere, like the one Habermas (1989) argues occurred in Europe. But this public sphere did not revolve around a secular "critical-rational public debate" (Ahmad 2004; Neg and Klug 1993); instead, religion was its central focus. Pandey (1990; 1998) has shown that in precolonial India identity was local, based on one's village or occupation. With the introduction of railways, the telegraph, education, bureaucracy, and so on, Urdu print became key to forging a supra local Muslim identity.[3] The first Urdu newspaper was launched in 1822 (Khurshid 1963), and by 1852 the number had increased to thirty-four (Zaidi 1993:216). Urdu facilitated the participation of a wider population because, unlike Persian, it was a popular language and not exclusively for Muslims. In fact, "the majority of the Urdu organs of the north were edited by Hindus" (Ghosh 1998:127).

Maududi, Islam, and the West

The politics of Islamism emerged against the maze of institutional dynamics described above. Let us now turn to Maududi's life. Given Nasr's (1996) fine biography of Maududi, I do not rehash every aspect of his life but focus only on those that bear on this book. Maududi was born in a Syed family in 1903 at Aurangabad. His forefathers had an aristocratic connection to Mughal royalty and to the princely state of Hyderabad, the Nizams.[4] Maududi's paternal grandmother was related to Sir Syed, the founder of MAO College. Against Maududi's grandfather's wishes Sir Syed persuaded Maududi's father, Ahmad Hasan (d. 1920) to study at his college. However, Maududi's grandfather recalled Hasan from the college because he was "wearing kāfir [infidel] dress and playing cricket" (Maududi 1979:30). His father was, in Maududi's own words, overwhelmed by "western thought and life style." In 1896 Maududi's father went to Aurangabad to practice law; after the collapse of Mughal power in 1857, Hyderabad became the largest "princely"[5] Muslim state and Aurangabad was its second largest town. Under the influence of a Sufi, "all the impact of westernism (*firangiyat*)," Hasan had disappeared and "Islamicness" had taken over. He embraced Sufism and renounced the world (ibid.:31).

Hasan resolved not to give his son a Western education, nor did he want him to study in a madrasa for fear of "bad company." Till the age of nine, Maududi received his education in Urdu, Persian, Arabic, *fiqh*, Islamic laws, and *hadīth* through private tutors. At eleven he went to Aurangabad's Madrasa Fauqāniya Mashriqiya (Oriental high school), founded on the recommendation of the British educationist Mr. Mhew[6] (Ahmad 1981:258) to synthesize Islam and modernity. Shibli Nomani (d. 1914) and his disciple, Hamiduddin Farahi (d. 1930), designed its syllabus. Both were influenced by Syed Ahmad's modernist project and had learned Western philosophy in Aligarh, particularly from a British professor, Thomas Arnold (Nadwi 1999; Zilli 1992). Both regarded the traditional syllabus, *dars-e-niẓāmī*, stultifying (McDonough 1991; Ghazali 1992).[7] Given his modernist approach, Nomani was called a *kāfir* (Nadwi 1999:659). The school's syllabus included natural sciences,

English and math, all subjects that Maududi learned. He acknowledged that the school "widened his horizon of thought" (Maududi 1979:33). Meanwhile, Maududi's father chose to settle in Hyderabad, where he enrolled in Darul Uloom, whose principal was Farahi. Maududi could not continue his education there but had to rush to Bhopal where his father had gone for treatment, and thereafter he did not resume formal studies. At Bhopal Maududi developed a "friendly relationship" with Niaz Fatehpuri, a noted Urdu litterateur. Accused of "heresy," Fatehpuri never concealed his atheism (Sambhali 1993; Zaidi 1993). Like Durkheim, he believed that "the reality is that humans have created God" (in Alqasmi undated:9). Fatehpuri encouraged Maududi (1979) to pursue a writing career.

In 1919 Maududi left for Delhi, where he keenly read the works of Sir Syed (Nasr 1996). Having chosen to pursue a writing career, he became sufficiently competent in the English language to read books in English. He also tried to learn German. According to Abdulhaq Ansari (2003:522), the intellectual leader of the Indian Jamaat, on learning English, Maududi "turned to Western thought, and devoted a full five years to the study of major works in philosophy, political science, history and sociology." He bought the entire set of *Encyclopedia Britannica* (Maherulqadri 1990).

After his turn to Islamism, Maududi reflected on the failure of the nineteenth-century jihad movement.[8] To him, the jihad leaders disregarded the value of Western sciences that had made the British powerful. He wondered why Shah Waliullah (d. 1762) and his son, Shah Abdulaziz (d. 1824), two key revivalist scholars of their times, did not send a delegation of ulema to Europe to discover the "secret of its power" and to learn what "we lacked in comparison to it [Europe]" (Maududi 1940:345). He offered a long list of philosophers whose contribution had made Europe a world power: Fichte, Hegel, Comte, Mill, Quesnay, Turgot, Adam Smith, Malthus, Rousseau, Voltaire, Montesquieu, Thomas Paine, Darwin, Goethe, Herder, Lessing, and so on. Comparing their contribution to that of Muslims, he concluded that the latter had not even contributed 1 percent. Maududi's call to Muslims was to master the Western sciences. A year before he founded the Jamaat and denounced his past as *jāhiliyat*, he wrote:

> In the age of *jāhiliyat* I have read a lot on ancient and modern philosophy, science, history, economics, politics, etc. I have digested a whole library. But when I read the Qur'an with open eyes then I realized, by God, that whatever I had read was insignificant. Now I got the root of knowledge. Kant, Hegel, Fichte, Marx and all other great philosophers of the world now appear to me as kids (in Ali 2000:305–6).

Maududi was also drawn to Marxism. Inspired by the Russian Revolution, many Muslims had become communists (Habib 1998; Nomani

1998). Maududi read the works of progressive writers. In the early 1930s a group of writers, led by Sajjad Zaheer, formed the All-India Progressive Writers Association (AIPWA) to support "the forces of enlightenment and progress" (in Samad 1995:22).[9] Maududi was also impressed by Abdul Sattar Khairi, an influential figure in Delhi's intelligentsia in the 1920s. Khairi worked with the Bolshevik Propaganda Bureau in Moscow, where he came in contact with Lenin. Later he went to Berlin where he married a German woman (Muhammad 1973). Maududi's more direct contact with Marxism came from his in-laws' family. Shahid Zamdi, a Delhi-based university teacher and the son of a senior Jamaat leader, told me that one of Maududi's in-laws had been an active Communist and had translated a book by Marx into Urdu.[10] A friend of Maududi, Maherulqadri (1990:242), recalled that when he met him in Delhi he saw "a thick, latest book on Communism" lying beside his bed. In Hyderabad, Maududi became friends with Syed Abdul Latif, a Ph.D. from London University (Sayeed 1998), and Josh Malihabadi (Alqasmi undated:9). The latter, called "the poet of revolution," renounced his religiosity during his stay in Hyderabad (1924–34) and took to alcohol, which he never gave up (Zaidi 1993).

These associations not only informed Maududi's thoughts but also his quotidian life. As late as 1936 he remained clean-shaven. Later, when he grew a beard, it was so short that it appeared more fashionable than religious. In 1938, when Manzoor Nomani, a Deoband *ʿālim*, first met Maududi in Delhi he was "jolted" to see an Islamic figure with too short a beard. He was also aghast at his "Western (*angrēzī*) hair." When the Jamaat was formed in 1941, Nomani joined, hoping that Maududi would make his appearance Islamic. He did not. Because of what Nomani perceived as a lack of "true religiosity" in Maududi, Nomani (1998) resigned from the Jamaat in 1943. Against the dominant *fiqh* position, Maududi justified his short beard by saying that Muhammad did not specify its length (1999 [1945]:119–24). For ulema, to be called Islamic a beard in itself was not sufficient unless it was also the size of a fist. In Maududi's argument they detected a conspiracy against Islam (Qadri 1965). Maududi also wore a tie (see Figure 1). During the early 1930s he watched films and attended a program of music and singing (Maherulqadri 1990). After his turn to Islamism, Maududi said that wearing a tie (1999a), watching films (1963:438), and listening to or playing music (1999:135–36) was anti-Islamic.

Maududi's fascination with Western life was reflected, above all, in the choice of his wife, Mahmuda Begum, the daughter of a merchant and, in the words of his elder brother, "the biggest Muslim usurer" of Delhi (Nasr 1996:152 n. 45). Begum was educated at Queen Mary School and at the time was "quite liberated and modern in her ways" (Sayeed 1998). She also rode a bicycle and never observed *parda,* the wearing of a veil. For

Figure 1. The many faces of Maududi; clean-shaven Maududi in suit and tie in the center. Photo on the back cover of Sayeed 1997.

Nomani (1998), who lived with Maududi for months, the nonobservance of *parda* was an important reason why he resigned from the Jamaat. It is worth noting that outside Sir Syed's modernist circle, an English education, certainly for women, was considered *kufr* (Islahi 1992:39). Ashraf Ali Thanvi (d. 1943), a Deoband theologian and author of *bahishtī zēvar* (Metcalf 1990), for instance, considered Western education so poisonous that he advised Muslims to send their daughters to brothels rather than let them marry Western educated men (undated:530).

Context of Formation and Maududi's Political Involvement

This section focuses on Maududi's public life to show that his political involvement, which began in the early 1920s, coincided with the era of mass politics inaugurated by the Congress. During this period Maududi's Western approach went hand in hand with his support of the Congress.

But after the 1937 elections he began to criticize the Congress and then later turned to Islamism. To situate Maududi's political involvement, let us first examine the political field he entered and look at its master ideologies.[11]

Master Ideologies

In the 1920s the two master ideologies on the political scene were represented by the Congress and the Muslim League (henceforth, the League). The Congress was the largest of the two, and the League, formed in 1906, was elitist. The Congress claimed to represent the whole of India and spoke of "an Indian nation . . . and national aspirations" (in Hasan 1979:29). S. N. Banerjee, the Congress President in 1895, said: "It is the Congress of United India, of Hindus and Mohammedans, of Christians, of Parsees and of Sikhs" (ibid.:29–30). The Congress resolved "to create a nation by unifying and integrating the different . . . elements which form the Indian population" (in Madni undated:38). Muslims were assured that no subject would be discussed to which "the Hindu or Muslim delegates as a body object" (in Hasan 1979:32; also see McLane 1988). Muslims took part in the Congress from the beginning (Hasan 1991; Vohra 1997).

The Congress, in Allama Mashriqi's words, was a "feminine debating club" (in Makki 2003:171); independence was not its agenda. From 1915 on it entered mass politics. Participation of Muslims in the Congress reached its apogee in 1919 when ulema launched *ḳhilāfat* agitation for the restoration of Caliphate in Turkey, and the Congress under Gandhi supported it. Ulema, mostly from the Deoband, formed Jamiatul Ulema-e-Hind (henceforth, Jamiatul Ulema) in 1919 and plunged into the independence movement. Ulema formed the *ḳhilāfat* Committee to urge the British to retain Turkey's sultan as the caliph and also the custodian of Islam's holy places in Mecca and Medina (Minault 1982). The *ḳhilāfat* mobilization became a mass phenomenon, with Mohammad Ali Jauhar, a graduate of MAO College, its star campaigner. From 1919 to 1922 the Khilafat Committee and the Congress worked as sister organizations. Based on *satyagrah* (civil disobedience), Gandhi aligned the *ḳhilāfat* agitation with the noncooperation movement against the British. Never before was there such a united Hindu-Muslim solidarity against the British (Ahmad 1970). A stunning example of this solidarity was the appearance of the Arya Samaj-Shuddhi leader Swami Shradhanand, in 1919, on the pulpit of Delhi's *jāmeʿ masjid*, to speak for a united resistance against the British (Copland 2001).

In Jamiatul Ulema's reading, the Prophet's teachings and the Qur'an justified its cooperation with the Congress. Though different, Hindus and

Muslims could come together for the common cause of independence. Husain Ahmad Madni and Abulkalam Azad argued that Islam entailed that Muslims supported the Congress. They had full faith in the commitment of the Congress, reiterated in its Karachi session of 1931 (Chandra et al. 1989), that it would guarantee Muslims the right to live their religion. Called "Nationalist Muslims," they espoused religious pluralism and a secular state (Madni 2002; Hameed 1998; see the introduction).

The Congress incorporated divergent elements: liberals, Communists, socialists, and revivalists. Jawaharlal Nehru (1889–1964), second only to Gandhi in the Congress hierarchy, had communist leanings. Hindu revivalism, older than the Congress, was equally part of the Congress (Shakir 1983). The nineteenth-century Bengal renaissance itself was largely anti-Muslim (Sen 1994; Chatterjee 1995). The Shuddhi campaign, an offshoot of the Arya Samaj, formed in 1875 to revive the "golden Vedic age," grew stronger in the 1920s. Its objective was to convert Muslims to Hinduism, since "originally" they were Hindus (Kanaungo 2002). In 1900 Anthony McDonnel replaced Urdu with Hindi as the official language. To Muslims' dismay, Hindus supported McDonnel's move, which strengthened Hindu revivalism synoptically evident in the slogan "Hindi, Hindu, Hindustan" (Pandey 1990; Ahmad 2008). Outside the Congress, Hindu revivalism with anti-Muslim proclivities—or at least Muslims' perception of them—later permeated the Congress (Hasan 1979). The revivalist streak within the Congress grew stronger with the birth of the Hindu Mahasbha in 1915. In north India Pandit Madanmohan Malaviya (1861–1956), also a top Congress leader, was its protagonist. Later he founded Banaras Hindu University. In the following years the Mahasabha adopted an agenda of forging a Hindu nation and, by the 1930s, the early liberalism and secularism of the Congress had become fairly diluted (Copland 2001; Jones 1991; Shakir 1983; Van der Veer 1994; Vohra 1997).

Unlike "Nationalist Muslims," the League regarded Muslim interest as supreme. Anticipating the introduction of reforms to enlarge the Legislative Council, in 1906 a group of English-speaking, land-owning Muslims met the viceroy Lord Minto to present an address (Smith 1946). Apprehending that electoral politics would make Muslims hostage to the Hindu majority, the address pleaded that a share in government services be reserved for Muslims. Also, it asked for a separate Muslim Electoral College to elect Muslims to the Councils. The British agreed to the demand, as it ensured the "pulling back of sixty-two million people [Muslims] from joining the ranks of the seditious opposition [the Congress]" (in Vohra 1997:123). Weeks later this group formed the League.

Dominated by elites from the Muslim-minority provinces, the League had little, if any, backing of Muslims until the mid-1930s (Barlas 1995). However, it scored a victory in 1916 through the Lucknow Pact, when the Congress recognized a separate electorate, introduced by the British in 1909, for Muslims in legislative bodies. The Congress recognized this separate electorate in lieu of the League's commitment to self-government. In 1913, when he was assured that, like the Congress, the League would also stand for self-government, Mohammad Ali Jinnah (d. 1948), a believer in Hindu-Muslim unity, joined the League. While committing to "self-government," the League clarified that "loyalty to the British crown" and "the protection of the rights of Mohammedans" would be its priority (in Smith 1946:298). This master ideology remained central to the League until 1947.

Turn to Politics

Maududi took part in the *khilāfat* and *Satyagrah* campaigns led by Gandhi and worked to involve Muslims in the Congress. He wrote a panegyric biography of Gandhi,[12] which was confiscated (1979:34). In 1919 he published a biography of Madanmohan Malaviya whom he admired for devoting his life to the "services of community [*qaum*] and country [*mulk*]"; he called him "the sailor of India's boat." Urging Muslims to emulate him, Maududi wrote, "today all respect him [Malaviya] and he is venerable not only in the eyes of Hindus but he is also a great figure for us [Muslims] to follow" (1992:13). Wedded as he was to the Jamiatul Ulema–Congress ideology, Maududi assumed the editorship of the Jamiautul Ulema's organ, *Muslim*. In 1924 he became the editor of the Jamiautul Ulema's new organ, *Al-jamʿiyat*, which he edited until 1928.

Maududi later grew disenchanted with the Congress and began to see its nationalism colored with Hindu interests and symbols. He alleged that the Congress did not give influential positions to its Muslim leaders (*Tarjumān* 1938 [March]: 165). Another reason for his distrust of nationalism stemmed from the breakup of the Ottoman Empire along nationalist lines. Dismayed, Maududi quit the Jamiatul Ulema–Congress alliance. In 1928 he left Delhi for Hyderabad, and for the next few years devoted himself to writing about Islamic history, hoping to discover what had gone wrong with Muslims. Madududi (1979) wrote the history of the Seljuq dynasty, as well as a biography of the founder of the Nizams and translated parts of Ibn-e-Khalkan's history of the Fatimid dynasty from Arabic into Urdu. From his readings of Islam and the precarious fate of the Nizams, Maududi concluded that the Muslims had declined because they abandoned "pure" Islam, which became corrupted through their un-Islamic customs and practices. To stem their decline, Maududi presented a scheme to the Nizams which included a radical overhaul of the educational system and the dissemination of "pure" Islam. To Maududi's dismay, the Nizams showed no interest in his ideas (Nasr 1994a). In

1932 Maududi launched an Urdu journal, *Tarjumānul Qur'an* (hereafter, *Tarjumān*), the logo of which proclaimed to offer a modern, rational Islam: "its special subject is to critique from a Qur'anic perspective the thoughts of . . . civilization spreading in the world, to interpret the principles of the Qur'an and *sunna* in every domain such as philosophy, science, politics, economics, civil and social life and to apply them to the *circumstances of the modern age*" (in Azmi 1999:25, my emphasis). Current politics was scarcely debated in the journal (Nomani 1998). In 1937, when the provincial elections were held, Maududi turned *Tarjumān* into what Lenin described as a "pair of smith's bellows."

Realizing that the future of Muslim politics would be decided in the Muslim-majority provinces like Punjab (Khalidi 2003), Maududi, in 1938, moved to the village of Pathankot, in the Gurdaspur district of Punjab, to establish a miniature *dar al-Islam*. Chaudhry Niaz Ali, a landlord, wanted to establish a *waqf* (endowment) at Pathankot for the study on Islam. The poet Iqbal, impressed by *Tarjumān,* wanted to set up a similar center combining Western and Islamic sciences. On Iqbal's advice, Ali invited Maududi to oversee the endowment, which Maududi happily accepted. However, ignoring the intention of both Iqbal and Ali, he surreptitiously turned the scholarly enterprise into a political one, bringing on conflict between himself and Ali. As a result, in 1939 Maududi left the *dar al-Islam* for Lahore (Nomani 1998).

Graduation to Islamism

Based on the Government of India Act of 1935, elections were held in 1937 to form provincial governments. The League fared poorly in the elections. The Congress, on the other hand, gained a majority in six of the eleven provinces, including the nearby all-Muslim North West Frontier Province (NWFP), and formed ministries in those provinces. At Nehru's initiative, the Congress launched a Muslim Mass Contact Program (MMCP), with the aim of puncturing the League's claim that the Congress did not represent Muslims. Nehru saw hidden class interests in the League's claim that Muslims were different from Hindus. In his view peasants and workers, Muslim or otherwise, were both exploited. The only differences between them, Nehru held, was an imperialist invention the League used for its own interests (Hasan 1988).

As the Congress launched the MMCP, Maududi ran a series of articles in *Tarjumān* attacking the Congress. Titled *Musalman aur Maujuda Seyāsi Kashmakash* (Muslims and the Contemporary Political Predicament; henceforth *Kashmakash*), he later published them as three separate volumes. Anticipating that India was on the threshold of a revolution, Maududi began the first volume of *Kashmakash* by stating that he was writing as both a Hindustani and a Muslim. As a Hindustani he wanted to see India become independent as much as anyone else did, but, as a Muslim, he worried about the Muslims' fate, namely, about the "protection of national [*qaumī*] identity and their [Muslims'] culture" (1937:20, 33). To this end, he urged Muslims to form an organization; to inculcate "pure" Islam; and to shun the "hypocritical," Westernized Muslims and ulema committed to the Congress. Maududi devoted the first and second volumes of *Kashmakash* to attack the Congress, especially Nehru. In the MMCP Maududi saw a conspiracy to wipe out Muslim identity. He feared that because Hindus were a majority the identity of Muslims would be annihilated under the democratic state. He wanted to know why the Congress contacted peasants rather than educated, religious Muslims. Drawing a dreary picture of the future Congress rule, he contended that, for Muslims, the independence movement was indeed a movement of political Shuddhi (1938:57), with the intention of converting Muslims to Hinduism.

Questioning the Congress's claim to be secular, Maududi argued that it was only so in words, and he gave numerous examples to prove how several leaders of the Hindu Mahasabha, who were also Congress members, participated in anti-Muslim riots. The ultimate objective of the Congress and Mahasabha, Maududi declared, was to establish a "Hindu Raj" (1938:61, 148–52). To convince his readers of this, Maududi went on to show how the Congress's provincial ministries imposed Hindu culture on Muslims. According to Maududi, the educational plan, the Wardha Scheme,[13] was devised to forge "Hindu nationalism by eliminating Islamic nationalism" (1938:168). To demonstrate his claim, he argued that schools under the said scheme were named Vidya Mandir (literally, "temple"), which "smelled of Hindu religion" (ibid.:174), and Muslim students there were wearing *dhoti* (a garment mostly worn by Hindu men) and singing *vande mātaram*[14] with their hands folded. Maududi (1938:172) described Zakir Hussain, the architect of the Wardha Scheme, as worse than Macaulay, the British official who despised Oriental knowledge. With the imposition of Sanskritized Hindi on Muslims as well as the elimination of Urdu, Maududi saw the coming of the "Hindu Raj." With the demise of Urdu, he saw the elimination of Muslim culture (ibid.:162–90).

Maududi's ire, however, was reserved for Madni, the leader of the Jamiatul Ulema. By invoking Islam, Madni had justified the Muslims' solidarity with the Congress and the Hindus. Calling the Jamiatul Ulema and other Muslim supporters of the Congress "loyal soldiers of the non-Muslim leaders engaged in the mission of 'Shuddhi,'" Maududi (1938:73–77) accused Madni of distorting the Qur'an. He likened the idea of "united nationhood" to "sin" (1962:91) and *jāhiliyat*. Contra Madni, he argued that religion was the cornerstone of the nation, and hence Muslims were a nation separate from Hindu (ibid.:112; 1981:325). In Maududi's view,

India was a cluster of many nations including Muslims, Sikhs, and the untouchables. In the second volume of *Kashmakash* (December 1938), Maududi proposed three formulas for the resolution of the Muslim question. The crux of his formulas was that India should opt for a federal polity and Muslims should be given "cultural autonomy" to live by their religious principles and run educational schemes of their own (1938:204–23). Until then, Maududi did not advocate a separate state.[15] He wrote, "we definitely desire that our [Muslims'] and their [Hindus'] future generations have beautiful . . . relations between each other so that they would jointly work for the welfare of Hindustan" (1938:207). His concern, then, was that under the future democratic order Hindus would eliminate Muslims' identity.

Jinnah also feared that the Congress ministries would herald a "Hindu Raj" (Akbar 1985). Thus, in Maududi, the League found a soldier for its own cause. During its sessions, between 1937 and 1939, the League distributed the second volume of *Kashmakash* (Nasr 1994). Its impact was such that many Muslims, wrote Ishtiaq Hasan Qureshi (2001), grew disenchanted with the Congress and joined the League. The League badly needed an Islamic scholar like Maududi to legitimize its cause, because the whole class of ulema led by Madni and Abulkalam Azad had opposed it (Alavi 1988). The League described Maududi as "our own Abul Kalam [Azad]" (in Nasr 1994:105).

Following Maududi's justification for a Muslim nation, in 1940 the League advanced the theory of Hindus and Muslims forming two separate nations and called for a Muslim state, a call that boosted Maududi's own ambition. He no longer desired accommodation within the Indian state. In the April 1940 issue of *Tarjumān*, he proposed the formation of a "pious party" to establish Allah's Kingdom. Seventy-five people responded to his proposal. On 31 August 1941, at Lahore, Maududi formed Jamaat-e-Islami, with himself as its leader, or *amīr*, and stated as its goal the pursuit of *ḥukūmat-e-ilāhiya*, an Islamic state (*Tarjumān* 1941 [May]:179).

From this point on, the relationship between the League and Maududi became complex. The League and Maududi cooperated with each other to the extent that both wanted to escape a "Hindu Raj" (Nasr 1994:112–13), but the cooperation was limited to opposing the Congress. Maududi and the League seriously conflicted over the content of the future Muslim state. Whereas the League imagined it as a secular-liberal state, as shown later in Jinnah's speech in Pakistan's Constituent Assembly in 1947 (Bose and Jalal 1997), Maududi wanted a sharia state. After the formation of the Jamaat, Maududi toned down his attack on the Congress–Jamiatul Ulema alliance and shifted it onto the League. As the League's popularity grew starting in 1941 so, too, did Madudi's attacks grow fiercer.

That the League's claims were not grounded in the Qur'an sparked the Jamaat's criticism. To Maududi, the leadership of the League was "trained wholly on the Western pattern" and bereft of "even an iota of Islamic feeling" (1942:105, 30) and he viewed the League as "*Jamāʿat-e-jāhiliyat* [a party of the pagans]" (1942:63–69). To show the extent to which the League was Westernized and irreligious, Maududi referred to the statement of one of its leaders who complained that Muslims visited "Anglo-Indian prostitutes" when Muslim prostitutes were available. Maududi continued:

> It is sad that from the *qāid-e-āẓam* ["the great leader," which Jinnah was called] to the ordinary followers [of the League] there is not even a single person who has an Islamic outlook and sees the affairs [of politics] from an Islamic viewpoint. *These people do not know at all the meaning of being a Muslim and his special status.* (1942:30; my emphasis)

Maududi saw in the League a replica of the Congress, believing that its leaders were as opposed to "Islamic culture" as the Congress leaders were. The only antagonism between them, Maududi felt, was whether "Islamic culture" should be killed by means of a *jhaṭkā*, a non-Islamic way of slaughtering an animal (by the Congress) or through *halal* (by the League). Muslim women were "the candles of the party" in the League's meetings in the same way that Hindu women were in the meetings of the Congress. Both believed in a Western, secular form of government. According to Maududi, the League opposed the Congress for its "worldly interests" and wanted a proportional share of Muslims in the Assembly and army to run an "anti-godly system [*ghair-ilāhī niẓām*]" (1942:26). It was inconsequential to Maududi if "a Ram Das [a Hindu] or an Abdullah [a Muslim] ran a state" so long as it was not based on sharia (1942:78–79). In his view, Pakistan would truly be Pakistan (literally, "a sacred land") only when its state was based on sharia. Because the League had no agenda for an Islamic state, Maududi announced that future Pakistan would be *nāpākistān*, a profane land. He even described it as an "infidelic [*kāfirana*] state of Muslims" (ibid.:78, 109).

Maududi's policy vis-à-vis the Pakistan movement was to "watch and wait" and meanwhile empower the Jamaat so as to snatch the leadership away from the League. If a Westernized, English-speaking Jinnah could become a great leader, Maududi thought, as a bearded, Urdu-speaking theologian, then he could become a far greater leader than Jinnah. Between 1941 and 1946 he devoted his energy to exposing the League's anti-Islamic character. Maududi forbade Muslims to vote for the League in the 1945–46 Assembly elections, arguing that to vote in the elections of a secular Assembly violated Muslims' "faith in monotheism" (1999: 304–6).[16] Despite Maududi's decree, the League secured a majority in the Muslim constituencies, and his dream of overtaking the League was never realized. In the bipolar politics between the Congress and the League, the Jamaat, with only 486 members in 1946, was insignificant (Nasr 1994:24). Maududi then jumped on the League's bandwagon. So when the Pakistani demand looked real in the referendum of July 1947 to decide if the NWFP should choose India or Pakistan, he asked Muslims to vote for the League. True to his ideology, he asserted that voting for the League did not mean endorsing its vision of Pakistan. Maududi resolved to fashion it into Allah's Kingdom (1999 [July 5, 1947]:295). Two weeks after Pakistan was created, Maududi bid adieu to India and left for Lahore (Baghpati 1979).

The Ideology of Islamism

Was Maududi's employment of Islam instrumental? His discourse sprang from a conviction that Islam was more than merely a vehicle for articulating interests; it was a system of life. His criticism of the League was epic, not episodic, set in motion by the Mughal Empire's demise and the challenge of the West for the recovery of "pure Islam."

In the introduction I take Islamism to mean a sociopolitical movement founded on an Islam defined as much in terms of a political ideology as of a religion (the Qur'an and the Sunna). In this respect, Islamism resembles Schmitt's political theology (Meier 2002; Turner 2002; Wolin 1990). Unhappy with Maududi's mixing of politics with theology, the Islamic scholar Azmi is not ready to concede that Maududi was a "religious thinker"; "fundamentally, he was a political . . . thinker," according to Azmi (1999:25). In the words of another Islamic scholar, Sufi Nazir Kashmiri, Maududi was a "Muslim Machiavelli," "a hypocrite" who had "affinities with the atheist philosophers [of Europe] of the present age" and hence the "acceptance of Maududism is no less than apostasy" (1979:57–58, 27–29). From his critique of Nehru and the League as secular and Westernized, one may construe that Maududi's own ideology was "Eastern" or "Islamic." I question this view to point out that Maududi's ideology was equally "Western" and shaped by the traditions of Western philosophy, German idealism, and Marxism, in particular. By inventing an "authentic Islam," Maududi transformed Islamic beliefs into political concepts of the then dominant ideologies. The idea of an Islamic state was the product.

The Islamic State and Its Theological Structure

Since the early twentieth century the goal of the Congress was to secure self-rule (*svarāj*) or control of the state. So, too, was the aim of the League to secure a Muslim state. Just as the state had become the master idiom of twentieth-century politics, it also became pivotal to Maududi. Fully aware of its significance, he wrote:

> The conceptualization of the state by the nineteenth-century scholars of politics is now utterly outdated. . . . Gone are the days when if the state presented its economic, educational, industrial or social scheme people made fun of it by calling it grandmotherly legislation. The situation has completely changed. Now the state's arena has almost become as all-encompassing as that of religion. Now it also decides what to wear or what not to wear; who to marry and at what age; what to teach your kids and what mode of life to choose; . . . what language and script to adopt. So, the state has not left even the most peripheral issues of life independent of its ultimate right to intervene. (*Tarjumān* 1938 [March]: 5)

He further observed that "the state is beginning to acquire the same status God has in religion" (ibid.:6). It was this significance of the modern state that found expression in Maududi's reading of the Qur'an. He resorted to the Qur'an to seek legitimacy from ulema who did not consider him an *ʿālim* (*Tarjumān* 1941 [May]: 216). He offered a similar justification for writing the commentary on the Qur'an, titled *Tafhīmul Qur'an* (see Dogar 1980).[17]

The key text of Maududi's political theology is the tract *Qur'an kī chār bunyādī iṣṭelāḥēn* (Four Fundamental Concepts of the Qur'an; hereafter, *Iṣṭelāḥēn*), first serialized in *Tarjumān* in May 1941. In it he argued that to know the "authentic [*aṣl*] objective" of the Qur'an it was "inevitable" to comprehend the "real [*ṣaḥīḥ*] and total" meaning of the four words *ilah* (Allah), *rabb* (Allah), *ʿibādat* (worship), and *dīn* (religion). He claimed that soon after the Qur'an's revelation the real meaning of these words were lost (1979a:7–9). His claim implied that no one in the vast Muslim world understood the "real and total" meaning of those words until he discovered them (see note 18). Upon close reading, however, Maududi's claim reveals that he searched for *authenticity* in an ideal time when "everyone knew" their real meaning. This quest for authenticity was based on the notion of *rupture* from the ideal time. The purpose of *Iṣṭelāḥēn* was to reclaim *authenticity* and overcome the *rupture* by establishing *continuity* with an ideal time. This he did through what Hobsbawm (1983) calls the "invention of tradition." Like the invention of tradition, Lee (1997:3, 16) argues that the quest for authenticity, beginning with Rousseau up to Charles Taylor, is a sign of modernity and that it "can't arise in a traditional society" for it requires "stripping away customs and conventions." This indeed was the case, as with a single stroke of the pen Maududi dismissed the millennium-old tradition of scholarship as defective and partial.[18]

Of the four Qur'anic words, Maududi considered "Allah" the most important one, because one becomes Muslim by reciting the *kalima* and the crucial word in the *kalima* is Allah; unless one understands its real meaning, the very declaration of one's faith is in doubt. Maududi's exposition on Allah is premised on a distinction between the "metaphysical" life and the "worldly political" life which together constitute an indivisible organic whole. To be a Muslim is to worship *Allah alone* not just in the metaphysical realm but also in the political realm because He is the master of both. Accordingly, Maududi contended that Allah must also be the "Ruler, Dictator (*āmir*), and Legislator" of the political domain (1979a:28). Consequently, if someone claimed to be the ruler of a country, then his statement would be equivalent to claiming to be God in the metaphysical realm. Thus, to share political power with someone who disregards the laws of Allah, Maududi declared, would be polytheism in the same sense as someone who worships an idol (ibid.:29). Elaborating on the meaning of *rabb*, a cognate term for Allah, he wrote that it was "synonymous with sovereignty [*sultāni*]" (ibid.:79). Since he viewed sovereignty in political terms, he argued that Allah is also a "political *rabb*" (ibid.:73). Thus *ṯāġhūt*, another Qur'anic word, does not just mean Satan or idol but also means a political order not based on Allah's sovereignty. Maududi chided the ulema for reducing the meaning of *ṯāġhūt* to mean, literally, an idol. For Maududi, the Qur'anic injunction to worship Allah and shun *ṯāġhūt* meant securing a sharia state and rejecting a non-Islamic polity (ibid.:9, 90–92; also see 1980). Like "Allah," *ʿibādat* (worship) also meant obeying political authority. In a sermon in Punjab, Maududi equated rituals like prayer with military training:

> The prayer, fasting . . . provide preparation and training for the assumption of just power. Just as governments train their armies, police forces . . . before employing them to do their job, so does Islam. . . . It [Islam] first trains all those who volunteer for the services to God before allowing them to undertake jihad and install God's rule on earth. (1987 [1940]: 291)

In 1931 Allama Mashriqi (d. 1963), a Cambridge-educated Muslim, founded the Khaksar. Inspired by Hitler and communism, he believed that the British could be driven out only by force. He had a modernized and militarized[19] vision of Islam, whose mission he described as domination (Muhammad 1973). He likened the drill and armed training to religious rituals and made them compulsory for Khaksar activists (most influential in Punjab) who wore khaki uniforms and carried shovels on their shoulders. When the government banned the drill, the Khaksar activists sought their substitute in prayer in the mosque (Makki 2003; Smith 1946). It is unthinkable that Maududi's Punjab sermon was not influenced by the Khaksar's vocabulary.[20]

Maududi interpreted religion politically. "The word of the contemporary age 'state' has . . . approximated it [the meaning of *dīn*]" (1979b:108). Elsewhere he wrote, "in reality, the word *dīn* has approximately the same meaning as the word state has in the contemporary age" (*Tarjumān* 1941 [February–March]: 13; 1987:297–99).[21] The "real objective" of the Qur'an was to establish an Islamic state (1979a:73–80). There was an affinity between Hegel's conception of the state as the sign of the Divine (Hassner 1987) and Maududi's notion of the Islamic state as the embodiment of the Truth. In Kashmiri's (1979) view, *Iṣtelāḥēn* was a justification—an absolutely wrong one, as his book argues—for the establishment of a totalitarian state derived from Hegel.

According to Maududi, Allah sent all his prophets to establish an Islamic state (1979a, 1940). Describing the prophets as "leader[s]" (1941:69),[22] he likened the mission of Yusuf (Joseph) with the "*dictatorship*" of Mussolini (1999b:122). To put it in context, fascism in Europe had impacted Indian politics as well. The office bearers of the Congress were called "dictator."[23] And for Khaksar activists, Mashriqi was like a dictator (Muhammad 1973; Makki 2003). By the late 1930s communism had become influential in places like AMU, as was the slogan "dictatorship of the proletariat." The idiom of the time influenced Maududi's likening of the prophet Yusuf to Mussolini. Maududi further argued that because there would be no prophet after Muhammad, (1981a:57–60), humans would work as Allah's deputy or vice regent[24] to fulfill His will (1977; 1941).

New Philosophy, New Politics

As Schmitt's (1996) political theology had its "foe," so had Maududi's. The "other" of Maududi's Islam was what he called *jāhiliyat*. He conceived of Islam as an organic totality and its history as a reformulated dialectic between Islam and *jāhiliyat*. Expressed in two articles, "Renewal and Reform of Religion" (1940) and "Islam and *Jāhiliyat*"[25] (1941a), Maududi defined *jāhiliyat* as a perspective to run the world based on senses and superstition. The ultimate sign of the first perspective, which he called "pure [*ḳhāliṣ*] *jāhiliyat*" (1941b), was the atheistic West. Politically it expressed itself in human sovereignty. He described "secular states" as the obverse of "true" Islamic ideology (1941:53).

Maududi termed the superstition-based perspective "polytheistic [*mushrikāna*] *jāhiliyat*" because, like the ancient civilizations of Babylon,

India, and Greece it held that several Gods existed. Many beliefs and practices, mainly those of Sufism associated with the Ahl-e-sunna-o-Jamaat sect (henceforth, Ahl-e-sunna) were polytheistic.[26] He likened the Sufi notion of *qutb*, *abdāl*, and *ghauṡ* with idols. He also described visiting tombs of saints and a host of other practices as polytheistic. He believed, however, that under Western influence polytheistic *jāhiliyat* would disappear. Novel in Maududi's ideology was not only the political reading of Islam and *jāhiliyat* but also their formulation as a rehearsed dialectic à la Hegel. Recall his critique of ulema for ignoring Western philosophers. In 1939 he wrote a long article titled "The Philosophy of History of Hegel and Marx."[27] I contend that he borrowed his views of history from Hegel and Marx and applied it to Islam. The following summarizes Maududi's understanding of Hegel and Marx.

According to Hegel, human civilization evolves with the battle, and synthesis, of opposites. Each historic age is an integrated totality like an organism that reflects the *spirit*. When the spirit of an age, the "thesis," reaches its zenith it gives birth to a new spirit, the "antithesis," which begins to battle the old one. Later God or the "world spirit"[28] strikes a new synthesis between the old and the new, leading to a new age of history. Humans are merely instruments of God in this "dialectical process" in which God is also evolving. To Maududi, Marx borrowed the "dialectical process" from Hegel but replaced "spirit" with materialism and called it "dialectical materialism." In Marx, there is no eternal principle for religion. It is the result of a system of "production relations" where the clash of economic interests shapes the evolution of history. When the "system of production" changes, so, too, does religion, morality, law, and so on, change (Maududi 1999a:262–69).[29]

Maududi faulted both Hegel and Marx for denying the role of Islam in the evolution of history. For Hegel, prophets such as Muhammad offered an antithesis to the thesis of their age which became mutated into a synthesis that bore a new thesis, and so on. Their message no longer had relevance. Maududi was harsher on Marx, for Marx, unlike Hegel, dismissed religion entirely. Although Maududi acknowledged their contributions, he believed that because they had not read the Qur'an, they could discover "only one part of the Truth" which was that "throughout history there has been a battle between opposites," namely, truth (*ḥaq*) versus falsehood (*bāṭil*) (ibid.:271). The truth, which was the "original human nature" Maududi called the "straight line" (*ṣirāṭ-e-mustaqīm*). Referring to *sura ar-ra'd* 17, *sura al-baqara* 213, he argued that "in the beginning" humanity was on the "straight line" of Islam but later it developed bad tendencies (*bāṭil*) which he called a "crooked line" marked by obscenity, sin, tyranny, and hedonism. This battle between *ḥaq* and *bāṭil* had been going on since time immemorial. Maududi concluded the article as follows: "Hegel and Marx both only saw the crooked line but failed to see the straight line of Islam drawn since eternity" (ibid.:275).

Clearly Maududi's discourse was deeply influenced by Hegel and Marx in that he cast the history of Islam as a perennial battle between *ḥaq* and *bāṭil,* or between Islam and *jāhiliyat*.[30] However, his Islamist dialectics differed from Hegel's since the former, despite the synthesis between Islam and *jāhiliyat*, emerged victorious and uncontaminated by the latter. What I call Maududi's Islamist dialectics informs all his writings after he turned to Islamism. A classic example, echoing the *Communist Manifesto*, is the following:

> In principle, the whole human history is in fact the history of the battle between two opposite forces: Islam, which is the real nature of man, and *jāhiliyat*, which is the perverted nature of man. In this battle sometimes Islam rises and *jāhiliyat* is suppressed and sometimes *jāhiliyat* rises and Islam is suppressed. When Islam becomes dominant, then, in reaction, *jāhiliyat* prepares itself against Islam. When *jāhiliyat* rises, then Islam prepares for revolution against it [*jāhiliyat*]. . . . During this long historical battle many a time Islam appeared in its pure form and became the foundation of civilization and society. . . . Under the leadership of Muhammad, Islam appeared in its pure and perfect form and *jāhiliyat* was completely wiped out. (*Tarjumān* 1940 [May–June]: 185–86)[31]

Maududi argued that after Muhammad and during the reign of caliph Usman, *jāhiliyat* reappeared as a "counterrevolutionary force" (ibid.:187) and the caliphate degenerated into monarchy. In a book-length article of ninety-one pages, "Renewal and Reform of Religion," he maintained that the battle between *jāhiliyat* and Islam was the motor of history. From Hegel he borrowed the notion of Islam as an organic unity, an idea central to German idealism (see Armstrong 2003). Like Hegel (Hassner 1987), Maududi also used the metaphor of the inseparability of the organs of the human body to define an Islamic whole. The soul of the organic whole was the state. Like Islam, *jāhiliyat*, too, was an indivisible organic system. Both could never coexist. Like Schmitt, who believed there were no "neutral parties" between God and Satan (Meier 2002:79), Madududi warned, "there is no mid way between *jāhiliyat* and Islam" (1942:34).

In Maududi's formulation, Islam was a movement since the earliest of times and Adam was its first leader (1941). He lamented that rather than considering it a movement, Muslims shorn of a "scientific study of Islam" had reduced it to "a mere sacred heritage of the ancestors" (1942:18). If Muhammad, "as the greatest revolutionary leader" (2001 [1939]:84), led this movement to install a state, he asserted, then it could also be done now if Muslims acted not as a "nation" but as a party. Earlier, we recall, Maududi had argued that Muslims were a separate nation; now he argued that "nation," or *qaum*, was a "term of *jāhiliyat*" (2001 [1939]: 127). The Qur'an used the term *hizb* or *millat* to refer to Muslims, Maududi defined these terms to mean a "party." The Qur'an saw humanity, he wrote, as torn between the party of Allah (*ḥizb Allah*) and the party of Satan (*ḥizb al-shaiṭān*) (ibid.:128).

In describing Islam as a movement and Muslims as a party, Maududi superimposed the nineteenth-century concepts onto the Qur'an, as a social movement and a party are both innovations of the nineteenth century (Martins 2001). Maududi de-historicized the concepts of party and social movement to eternalize them backward, now to seventh-century Arabia, now to the beginning of the world when Allah created Adam. The question is why. Previously I have shown that a break with tradition occurs when societies wish to take hold of the future by human intervention. Social movement is the articulation of that desire as it defies the "metasocial principle" to foreground the human capacity for "self-transformation." In describing Islam as a movement and Muslims as a party, Maududi actually called for *human* action against a metasocial principle. In a lecture at AMU, he asked, "How will the Islamic revolution come about?" And he answered, "I do not believe in the kinds of miracles [*moʿjeza*] that the former French minister believes in.[32] I believe that action determines the outcome" (1941:458). To the jurists, miracles are divine, they are exclusive to the prophets and are binding on Muslims. Humans have *karāmāt*, associated with Sufis; its source is also divine but is not binding on Muslims.[33] Maududi's call for *action* and distrust of *miracles* clearly indicated his modernist yearning that I have alluded to. He distrusted traditional beliefs and practices that derailed his activist Islam. Here I cite two examples.

Contrary to popular belief (Metcalf 1982), Maududi argued that Muhammad was human like the rest of us (Azami 1999). Nor did he have faith in the coming of *dajjāl*, the anti-Christ. "Dajjal etcetera are no more than fiction. Rather, they are his [Muhammad's] guesses about which he himself had doubts. Have not the experiences of the past thirteen and a half centuries proven that his guess was incorrect?" (in Qureshi 1987:214). If belief in *dajjāl* was a fiction, then Sufism was "opium [*afīm*, *chunyā bēgam*]" because it drove Muslims to become fatalistic (1940:340). Notice, again, the Marxist metaphor. While retaining opium, he replaced religion with Sufism. Clearly Maududi disregarded established traditions and popular practices. In an arithmetic calculation that a statistician would envy, he declared:

> Ninety-nine percent of individuals of this *qaum* [Muslims] are ignorant of Islam, 95 percent are deviant, and 90 percent are adamant on deviance, which is to say that they themselves neither wish to follow the

> path of Islam nor to fulfill the objective because of which they have been made Muslim. (1999 [1944]:290)

Maududi used two terms to describe "impure Muslims": "census [*mardumshumārī*] Muslims" or "born [*naslī*] Muslims" (1959:226). He counterposed these two types to "conscious Muslims." Critical of prevalent Islam, he wrote, "If Islam were the religion that now exists among Muslims, then I would have become an atheist." His Islam, then, was not what he inherited but what he discovered on his own. "In reality," he wrote, "I am a born-again Muslim" (1942:15).

The Sole Spokesman of the Truth: Purity and Party

Before founding the Jamaat, Maududi analyzed the agenda of various parties—the League, the Jamiatul Ulema, the Ahrar, the Azad Muslim Conference, and the Khaksar. He argued that, like the British state, the future secular democratic state supported by the Jamiatul Ulema would be "equally *kufr* . . . sinful" (1942:102). Since the Ahrar and the Azad Muslim Conference were similar to the Jamiatul Ulema, Maududi did not view them as Islamic either. As for the Khaksar, he called Mashriqi impious, preparing Muslims to serve an "anti-godly system."[34]

What was anti-Islamic about all the Muslim parties? Maududi's answer was a simple one: the absence of an Islamic state from their agenda. Quoting the same Qur'anic verse, *sura al-ṣaff* 9, that a Deoband theologian had quoted before to legitimate the Communist Revolution,[35] he argued that the Qur'an enjoined upon true believers to make Islam politically dominant over all other religions even if the polytheists did not like it (1942:95ff.). This, he contended, was the goal that "pure Muslims [*aṣlī musalmān*]" had no choice but to pursue. In an article titled "The Need for a Pious Party [*ṣāleḥ Jamāʿat*]," published in April 1940, he stressed the need to form a party—Jamāʿat-e-islāmī—that would have a "pure Islamic goal" as well as "pure Islamic methods." He made the *kalima* the creed of the Jamaat Constitution. A person could become a member (*rukn*; pl., *arkān*) of the Jamaat only if he understood the "full meaning" of the *kalima*. The "census Muslims" would not be admitted simply because they were "Muslim" but would also be required to recite the *kalima*. His emphasis on the "full meaning" of the *kalmia* indicated the novelty Maududi attributed to the *kalima* (as in his work, *Iṣtelāḥēn*). Because he claimed that the Jamaat was the only party to have grasped the full meaning of the *kalima*, Maududi asked Muslims to embrace it or stand condemned like the Jews.

> So long as scattered elements of the Truth [*ḥaq*] continued to be contaminated with falsehood [*bāṭil*], there was a valid reason for Muslims

> not to accept it. . . . But when the whole Truth is completely unveiled and put forward in its pure form [i.e., the goal of the Jamaat] and Muslims, who claim to believe in Islam, are called upon to accept it . . . it becomes inevitable for them either to support it [the Jamaat] or reject it to be in the same position that Jews had previously acquired. In such circumstances, there is no third way . . . Now that this call [for an Islamic state] has been given in India, the dreadful moment for . . . Indian Muslims has arrived [either to accept or reject it]. (1944:14–15)

To most ulema, only a prophet is entitled to make the judgment Maududi made. Thus they warned him not to act like a prophet (Kashmiri 1979). Nomani called this claim "lethal and seditious" and wondered if "at least the 95 percent of ulema who rejected Maududi's call . . . acquired the same position that Jews had" (1998:135).[36] Unmindful of these warnings, Maududi argued that it would be akin to "apostasy" if a Muslim left the Jamaat (*Tarjumān* 1941 [June–August]: 465). When Nomani left the Jamaat, its members indeed called him an apostate (1998:141).

The Jamaat had clear guidelines for its members; they were banned, for example, from drinking alcohol, dancing, gambling, and so on (1942:178). A distinct guideline was the Jamaat's call to its members to sever all ties with "census Muslims" (Maududi 1942:180). They were asked to begin a jihad against *jāhiliyat* first on the "home front" (1944:18–19). In the introduction I outlined the specific institutions that the Jamaat boycotted; secular democracy was the most important one. Maududi (1999:308) argued why it was *haram* to vote for or contest the elections for a "secular, democratic state":

> All the democratic systems that have been developed in the present age, among them the present assemblies of India, are based on the premise that, in worldly affairs, inhabitants of a country themselves possess the right to . . . frame laws. . . . *This ideology is absolutely the opposite of the ideology of Islam.* Integral to the creed of monotheism in Islam is that Allah is the lord and ruler of people and the whole world. Issuing orders and guidance is His job. . . . From this ideological standpoint, the source of law and foundation in all the affairs of life recognizably are the Book of Allah and the tradition [*sunna*] of his Prophet, and *to accept the above mentioned democratic ideology by deviating from this ideological standpoint is tantamount to deviating from the creed of monotheism. We therefore say that membership in such assemblies and parliaments, which are based on the democratic principles of the present age, is haram, and to vote for them is also haram.* Because to vote means that we elect an individual whose job under the present Constitution is to make legislation that stands in

absolute opposition to the creed of monotheism. (1999 [1945]: 304; my emphasis)

As this quote demonstrates, Maududi saw secularism and democracy as one; secularism is a worldview denying Islam, and democracy is a method to install secularism.[37] He argued that in a secular polity "for a Muslim it is not even legitimate [*jā'iz*] to breathe unless he strove to convert it into *dar al-Islam*" (in Tahir undated: 18). The Constitution of the Jamaat stated that to join the government services of an infidel state was also *haram*. Chastising the ulema who did not regard these services as such, he argued that there was no difference between various parts of an infidelic state, however small and innocent they may appear, because they all contributed to the "establishment of a bigger sin," denial of the divine sovereignty (Maududi 1999:305–6).

Maududi claimed that, unlike other parties, he had adopted a structure that was "exactly like that of the party *Muhammad had established in the beginning*" (*Tarjumān* 1941 [July–August]: 462; my emphasis). "Processions . . . flags, slogans, uniforms, resolutions, addresses . . . emotional writings and everything of this kind are the life of those movements but a killing poison for this one [the Jamaat]" (ibid.:486). The disavowal of the repertoire of modern politics notwithstanding, Maududi's idea of a "pious party" comprising the pious selected out of the "useless Muslims" was a replica of Lenin's "vanguard" (1970). From Lenin, Maududi borrowed the idea of a vanguard which he called *jatthā*, *girōh* (1942:84, 160), but he liberated it from its class content and instead imbued it with a degree of Islamic piety. Nasr is to the point in arguing that the Jamaat is modeled on the Leninist parties (1994:13 ff.).[38]

Communism was so central to Maududi that he exhorted Muslims that if the Communists could bring about a revolution with their faith in Marx, why could the Muslims not do so with their faith in Islam (1942:169). Given his modernist approach, ulema called him an Orientalist who, as a sanitary inspector, only saw dirt in the towns of Islam (Yusuf 1991:46). Abul Hasan Ali, who left the Jamaat, detected Westernism in Maududi (2000:314), as did others (e.g., Kashmiri 1979; Qureshi 1987; and Sambhali 1993). In short, Maududi's Islam looked foreign to ulema. Mainly the modern educated Muslims were drawn to him. In Maududi's words, "when the real interpretation of the religion of the truth was presented to the Communists . . . and atheists, it appealed to most of them. . . . However, if the door was found closed for this [Maududi's Islam] it was in the places where the prayer beads of religion . . . are counted day and night (*Tarjumān* 1940, [November–December]: 252).

Consequences and the Post-Partition Action Plan

Social scientists, particularly anthropologists, hold that a gap always exists between ideology and practice. Their focus is therefore on *practices* rather than ideology, which is often regarded as not very "real." This premise surely has merit, but it is based on studies of a different set of social movements. It is inappropriate to movements like the Jamaat that are ideologically purist. Moreover, is ideology itself not practice? The next section presents an ethnographic history of the Jamaat's ideology as it was practiced from its formation in 1941 to the early 1950s. The section ends with Maududi's action plan for an Islamic revolution to be carried out by his followers who remained in India.

Boycott of the Idolatrous System

The Jamaat activists practiced what the Jamaat's Constitution demanded of them. Membership was not granted unless Maududi was confident that the individual knew the distinction between Islam and *jāhiliyat*, and was prepared to incur whatever socioeconomic and political losses that membership would entail. Members were those who 'had burned their boat on cruising to the Jamaat." The members boycotted what came to be called *ṭāghūtī niẓām* (an idolatrous system). Any institution that did not conform to the Jamaat's definition of Islam was idolatrous, whether it was run by Muslims or non-Muslims.

Born in the 1920s and a resident of Farrokhabad, Farhan Qasmi retired as a teacher at the Jammat school in Rampur and settled there. Before 1947 he studied at the Deoband, in a climate rife with the anti-British mobilizations. Because the Deoband was the center of the Jamiatul Ulema, Qasmi became a member. By chance he came to read one of Maududi's articles, and its argument drove him to read all three volumes of *Kashmakash*. Instantly he came to realize that the Jamiatul Ulema, because it did not speak about the "spirit of Islam," was a "*bāṭil* party" and that "Madni [Deoband's principal] had sold himself off to Hindus." He said that the "state is the spirit of Islam," and by supporting the Congress, "the Jamiatul Ulema was murdering Islam and committing *haram*." He particularly attacked Abulkalam Azad for his ecumenism. According to Qasmi, Azad's argument was Gandhi's ecumenism in Islamic garb. He questioned how Islam and Hinduism could be equally true.[39] Under Maududi's influence, he resigned from the Jamiatul Ulema in 1946. As a Deoband graduate he could have obtained a teaching position in any of its branches, but because the Jamiatul Ulema was a *bāṭil* party, he became a teacher only at the Jamaat School in 1952.

Unlike Qasmi, Ikram Beg studied in a secular school in Hyderabad. Later he settled in Aligarh. A member of the Jamaat, he also served as *amīr* of its *shahr* unit. While matriculating in Hyderabad in the 1940s, he read Maududi. Fired up by his "revolutionary writings," he wanted to join the Jamaat. The Jamaat leadership, however, told Beg that he would not be accepted as a member unless he separated his kitchen from his father who was a lawyer of a secular court. Beg then launched a jihad, in Maududi's words, on the "home front." In Beg's words:

> I thought that my father was committing a sin by practicing in a secular court. He was strengthening the idolatrous system [*ṭāghūtī niẓām*] and thus rebelling against Allah. The money he earned was *haram*. And so was the food made in the kitchen. I was very young then. . . . How can a true Muslim serve an idolatrous secular court and eat *haram* food? . . . I rebelled against the whole family for the sake of Islam. I grew a beard, which my sister-in-law did not like. . . . Once she told me that she would shave it while I was asleep. This made me even more determined to grow the beard.

Beg's and Qasmi's accounts show the magnitude of rebellion against the idolatrous system, a rebellion both voluntary and imposed by the party. Qasmi told me of several cases in Rampur. Three members resigned from their jobs in the excise department because they considered it *haram* to be employees of a non-sharia state. Another member working as an employee in the agricultural department also resigned from his job. Still another, a worker with the Lipton Company, also left his position. When Qasmi tried to persuade him to keep his job since the company was not a government body, he responded that although it might not be under government control, it was nonetheless part of *ṭāghūtī niẓām* as it worked indirectly against Allah's sovereignty. Like Beg, Ziaulhoda, born in 1918 and a matriculate from an Anglo-Arabic School in Patna, also was fired up for a revolution and joined the Jamaat. He then considered his job as an employee with the postal department *haram*, and he resigned (Ahmad 2003:ii–iii).

If the boycott of excise and agricultural departments, and even a private company like Lipton, was so ferocious, one can imagine the intensity against departments involved in flouting sharia such as the secular courts and assemblies. Mohammad Yusuf (1908–1991), whom we will meet in chapter 7, was a reader to the judge of the Court of Allahabad. In 1946, when he became a member of the Jamaat, he resigned his job because he considered it *haram* (*Dawat* 1991 [November 7]: 160). There was no question for a Jamaat member to vote in the elections for a secular assembly. True to Maududi's credo, the Jamaat boycotted the first elections of free India (see chapter 7).

Against the Slaughterhouses

The educational system was another key arena of the Jamaat's boycott. Elsewhere I have discussed the Jamaat's educational ideology (Ahmad 2008); suffice to note here that education was not an autonomous terrain divorced from the Jamaat's political project. To rehabilitate lost power, Maududi proposed establishing a pure Islamic educational system, a ruthless criticism of the madrasa system as well as modern education. Maududi asked ulema to conduct *ijtihād* and give up blind imitation (*andhī taqlīd*) (1991:13–14). He argued that the madrasa system must undergo a "total revolutionary reform" in order to adopt all the elements of Western education, which, according to him, had the following aspects: sources of knowledge, methods of imparting knowledge, facts of knowledge, and the religious values accompanying them. Western education was *amrit* (the elixir of life), although its religious values were "poison." On these grounds he attacked the university and the colleges that Muslims had established—for example, AMU. To Maududi, rather than only borrowing the facts from Western education, they had also blindly borrowed its values. These institutions therefore, were producing "black Englishman" (1991:16). Maududi sadly noted that AMU served Western culture rather than his project about Islam. Remember that Maududi's grandfather had recalled Maududi's father from AMU, because he had played cricket there wearing "infidelic dress." In an address delivered in 1940 at Islamia College[40] Amritsar, Maududi articulated his opposition to modern education as follows:

> In fact, I consider your mother college—and not only this college but also all such colleges—*slaughterhouse*[*s*] [*qatlgāh*] rather than houses of education. In my view, you have been slaughtered here and the educational degrees that you are about to receive are indeed *death certificates*. (1991:45; my emphasis)

The metaphors of "slaughterhouses" and "death certificates" were so powerful that many students left AMU and other modern colleges, considering it un-Islamic to study there. When, in 1947, a student asked Abullais Islahi Nadwi—the Jamaat *amīr* in independent India—if he could study at AMU, Nadwi replied, "My heart is so disturbed by the demerits of the present educational system that I do not have the courage to give you permission to study there" (in Siddiqi 2000:69). After he became a Jamaat member in 1953, Kaif Islahi, then a teenager, sought Nadwi's permission to do his post-matriculation at a college in Braily, a town in UP. Islahi told me why he was not allowed: "The institution that you should forbid other Muslims to study at, you yourself want to go there?" Throughout the 1950s the Jamaat forbade its members to study in "slaughterhouses." This rule applied equally to "friends [*rofaqā'*]" of the Jamaat. In 1957, for the first time the Jamaat relaxed the rule concerning the admission of its friends to "slaughterhouses," but the rule continued to be in force for Jamaat members (*Zindgī* 1957 [July–August]: 133).

Nor did the Jamaat consider madrasas Islamic. According to one account related by Qasmi, in 1957 Mohammad Yusuf, later to become *amīr* of the Jamaat (see chapter 7), forbade his son to study at AMU. Yusuf's son wept for three days and implored his father to let him study there, but Yusuf refused, saying that he would not allow his son to study at a "slaughterhouse." At the son's request, Qasmi tried to persuade his father but could not. Qasmi then asked Yusuf to send his son to Nadwa, the madrasa at Lucknow, but, to Yusuf, Nadwa was just a "different kind of slaughterhouse [*dūsrē ṯaraḥ kī qatlgāh*]."

Since no existing institution had the aim of an Islamic state (Maududi 1991:86–87; *Tarjumān* 1941 [June–August]: 477), establishing one was a key goal of the Jamaat after Partition (*RIR* 1952:119; 156; *RMS*-1:10ff.). In its *shura*[41] meeting of August 1948, the Jamaat announced its plan to found a residential school, Darsgāh Jamaat-e-Islami Hind (hereafter, Darsgāh), at Malihabad, in UP. Along with the headquarters, the school later shifted to Rampur in 1949. The Jamaat *shura* also set up a committee to frame the Darsgāh constitution, which laid down the following criteria:

ADMISSION

Children would be admitted only if their guardians not only "fully agree with the Jamaat's ideology but also commit in writing at the time of their admission that they have given their wards to serve Islam according to the ideology of the Jamaat" (Maududi 1991:110).[42]

RESIDENCE AND FUNDS

Students would stay in its hostel for ideological grooming. The Jamaat would accept funds only from those committed to its ideology (*RIR*: 125).

Four other criteria, though not enshrined in the Constitution, were equally binding. According to Qasmi and other older Jamaat members I met, these four did not figure in the Constitution because they were "self-evident."

NON-AFFILIATION WITH THE IDOLATROUS GOVERNMENT

As a policy, Rampur Darsgāh did not seek recognition of its degrees from the government because it was an idolatrous system, *ṯāġhūtī niẕām*. Further, it did not want government interference regarding the appointment of teachers, the syllabus, and so on, as that would affect the mission of Darsgāh. Government officials, including Muslim public figures who did not share the Jamaat's agenda, were not invited to its functions.

TEACHERS HAD TO BE MEMBERS OF THE JAMAAT

Only teachers who agreed to its ideology were recruited by the Jamaat. In 1952 Mael Khairabadi went to Darsgāh to be interviewed for a teaching appointment and was asked to teach a class. As he finished teaching, a Jamaat member embraced him and said: "It is sad that you are not a member [*rukn*]." Khairabadi, a staunch Jamaat sympathizer, was shocked, and the member explained: "Since you are not a member of the Jamaat, the Jamaat secretary has rejected your application" (Khariabadi 1990:94).

COEDUCATION

Dead opposed to coeducation, Maududi described it as "destructive" and "poisonous" (in Islahi 1997:108). This stemmed from his larger position on gender. In his book, *Parda*, he argued that Islam did not permit the intermixing of the sexes (1953 [1940]; for details, see Ahmad 2008a).

MUSIC, FILM, AND DRESS

Like coeducation, Maududi was opposed to music (1999, 1991) and films (1963). He also argued against "Western dress" (1991:120), though it is not clear what he meant by it. But Darsgāh prohibited its students from wearing shirts and trousers because they were Western. Instead, it prescribed a blue-colored *kurta*, white pajamas, and a compulsory Rampuri *tōpī*.

SPORTS

Participating in sports for one's health was viewed as a materialist goal. Islam, proclaimed *Kirnēñ*, the Darsgāh magazine, entailed that students practice sports realizing that they were Allah's deputy and that they had a divine mission (1984:25).[43] Maududi prohibited Western games but did not specify which games were Western. In his view, Islamic games included horse riding, swimming, using weapons, and so on (1991:120). Cricket was undesirable both because it was a Western game and because it distracted students from their Islamic goal (Salim 1991).

Along with Darsgāh, the Jamaat also established, in 1949, an institute for higher education, Ṡānvī Darsgāh (hereafter Ṡānvī). The immediate catalyst for its formation was to provide higher education for students who had left AMU and other Western colleges (Ahmad 1997; Shamsuddin 1990; Monis 2001). They did not attend the Deoband or Nadwa madrasas because, as noted, they were slaughterhouses of a different kind.

At Ṡānvī the Jamaat elders taught the students theology and jurisprudence courses on Islam. The first student body of around ten students were admitted in 1950, and in 1960 Ṡānvī was closed down (Ahmad 1997). With its closure, the Jamaat leadership realized the need for a full-fledged madrasa for higher grades. To this end, in 1962 the Jamaat founded Jāmiʿatul Falāḥ at Bilariaganj, a sleepy village seventeen kilometers away from Azamgarh town in UP.

In short, in the 1940s and 1950 the Jamaat boycotted every institution that was part of the *ṯāghūtī niẓām*, considered a religion in as much as Islam was one. To be a "conscious Muslim" was to boycott the *ṯāghūtī niẓām* or forsake one's loyalty to Islam. A poem, "Unconscious Muslims," in the organ of the Indian Jamaat *Zindgī* (1950 [January]: 42) demonstrated this attitude:

> *dīn-e-bāṯil sē jō qā'em hai vo rishtā tōṛ dē*
> Sever ties with the false religion [non-Islamic polity]
> *varna behtar hai ke pẖir islām hī kō chẖōṛ dē*
> Otherwise you better leave Islam itself

The Post-Partition Action Plan

Maududi briefly nursed the idea of converting the whole of India into a *dar al-Islam*. In an article, "Minority and Majority," he critiqued the League's politics based on a minority and majority premise, calling it un-Islamic. It was a "nationalist" thinking, whereby Islam was conceived as a nation of "census Muslims." However, if one conceived of Islam as a movement and of Muslims as a party, he argued, the minority-majority question would be irrelevant, and he explained why: if the Communist and Nazi parties comprising fewer than a million members could conquer Russia and Germany, then eighty million Muslims could also inaugurate an Islamic revolution (Maududi 1942; Nasr 1994).

When Pakistan became a reality, however, Maududi opted for Pakistan. India, Maududi declared, was a *dar al-kufr* (2001b [1951]), and he asked that Muslims from *dar al-Islam*, Pakistan, not marry Indian Muslims, a judgment that angered Indian ulema (see Mian 1957). In April 1947 he left a blueprint for the Jamaat members who remained in "Hindu India." Known as the "Madras Address," it became the foundation of the Jamaat agenda in post-Partition India. According to Maududi's plan, the chance for an "Islamic revolution" in Pakistan was as real as one in India (1996:20). He predicted that secular democracy would fail, and he told his followers not to worry about the appearance of Hindus as a majority (1996:20). In his view, unity among Hindus had two negative referents: the British and the League; with Independence, both would disappear, leaving a vacuum. The discriminatory caste system, he predicted, would further undermine this unity. He saw the promise of democracy to the lower castes as a coverup by the upper castes to perpetuate their hegemony. As a result, "Indian masses . . . even the deprived people of the high castes" would clamor for a just system (1996:27).

Maududi urged his followers to combat Communists, who were ready to take advantage of the impending frustration, and present Islam as an alternative. Unlike communism, Islam was spiritual and just, and he saw "at least a 60 percent chance for Islam's success" (1996:30). Believing that non-biased Hindus would not reject Islam straightaway, Maududi's plan included the following four steps:

> *First*, eliminate communal conflict whereby Muslims had become Hindus' adversary. Muslims must not, as the League had done, ask to be represented in assemblies and government services or to be granted rights. "Rather, they should develop indifference toward the new . . . political system" (1996:32).
>
> *Second*, Jamaat activists should spread true Islam among Muslims so they could radically transform themselves—morally, socially, and in every other respect—in such a way that non-Muslims would begin to consider Islamic society better than their own.
>
> *Third*, all resources should be harnessed for the propagation of Islam among non-Muslims. Even if 20 percent of the Muslim population (then numbering fifty million) became the embodiment of pure Islam and started preaching it, the Jamaat would have 2.5 million preachers.
>
> *Fourth*, Muslims should learn various languages with which to preach Islam.

The Madras Address presented a long, bottom-up route to *ḥukūmat-e-ilāhiya*. A few weeks after the address, in a speech at Pathankot in May 1947, Maududi found a quick, top-down route to the Islamic revolution. In the Pathankot speech, he implored Hindus not to make India a "secular, democratic, national state," like the "deviant nations" of the West had done (1951:31). He advised them to analyze the Hindu religious scriptures to find guidelines on how to run a modern state. Muslims would have no objections, he declared, to be ruled by such a Hindu state.[44] Maududi continued:

> However, if you do not find any guidelines there [in Hindu scriptures], then it does not mean that God had not sent it to you. It rather only means that in the long history of revolutions you have lost it. . . . We are giving you only that thing sent by God. . . . This is your own lost thing, which has come back to you through another means [Islam]. (1951:31–32)

Against the "evil" principles of secularism, nationalism, and democracy, Maududi's guidelines included the "pious" principles of submission to God, humanism, and sovereignty of God. In the Pathankot speech, his strategy was to encourage the Hindu leaders to base the future state on Hinduism. The likely assumption behind it was that once they accepted the need for a religious state, they would choose Islam for two reasons. First, the Jamaat would convince them by "arguments" that only Islam was capable of running a modern state. Hindus would accept an Islamic state, for if they had already accepted, without prejudice, the idea of secular democracy from the British, then they would also accept an Islamic state if given good arguments (1951:28–29). In other words, if convinced of the merits of an Islamic state, Hindus would themselves install it. Second, if they did not, the Jamaat would then encourage them to install a Hindu state and wait for it to fail. Maududi predicted that it would indeed fail, because Hinduism lacked a "permanent worldview," and was rife with "hierarchy." Upon its failure, Islam would fill up the vacuum. Maududi did not explain how.

How did the Jamaat's ideology play itself out in practice in post-Partition India? It is to this question that we turn in the next part of the book.

PART TWO

Zigzags to Allah's Kingdom

CHAPTER 3

Educating the Children

> And the whole environment [in the Jamaat's educational system] would be created in such a way that it transforms every individual into *mujāhid* in the path of Allah.
>
> —MAUDUDI, *Taʿlīmāt*

On a bright morning in May 2002 I reached the Green School. Nazar, its principal, was waiting for me. Unlike my earlier visits, this one was special. I was to have a much-awaited interview with schoolteachers. Nazar took me to the hall to the right of his office, and he asked me to sit in a chair facing rows of benches and desks. About ten teachers had gathered there. Nazar introduced me to the teachers and went to his office.

The teachers wanted me to tell them more about the purpose of my visit, so I explained that I wished to study how the Jamaat ran its school and how it imparted its ideology (*fikr*) to the students. In what ways had the school benefited the Muslim community? Nahid, a middle-aged, beardless teacher dressed in shirt and trousers, rose to say that it had produced three doctors and several lecturers, and that thirty of its students were admitted to AMU in grade 6 last year. While still enumerating the school's achievements, he was interrupted by Khalid, who had a flowing beard and was dressed in a long *kurta* pajama: "His topic of research is the ideology of the Jamaat and how it is imparted in school." From this perspective, Khalid continued, hardly anything was being done in the school. Anzar, a colleague of Khalid and the son of a Jamaat member, intervened to endorse him. He said, rather loudly:

> Which ideology? The principal is interested in collecting fees rather than running it along the Jamaat's ideology. And the school manager! He is not just a Jamaat member; he has also been its *amīr*. But he is hardly interested in the school. He works as an accountant at three different places. What for? For money! When does he have time for the school?

Cutting Anzar short, Khalid jumped in again.

> You want to know how the Jamaat is propagating its ideology through this school . . . don't you? It is doing almost nothing, I tell you. Where

> is the Jamaat's ideology in the school? . . . I have been teaching here for the last twenty-eight years. I know everything about it. And I see that the Jamaat's ideology is being flouted flagrantly here.

By then Khalid had become fairly excited. Ikram Beg, a Jamaat member and the school's accountant, asked Khalid to stop. "You don't know how a school is run. Whatever it is doing is a benediction [*ghanīmat*]." Beg's intervention only heightened Khalid's temper. "I am in this school for the last twenty-eight years; did anyone ever ask why I did not become a Jamaat member?" Beg retorted, "This is why the Jamaat is not giving you membership. Emotional you are; understand the situation." The exchange of fiery words between Khalid and Beg put me in an awkward situation, and I suggested dissolving the meeting. Beg and Khalid walked with me to the principal's office. Soon Khalid shook hands, only with me, and left the school. Thereafter Nazar, who had kept an uneasy silence throughout, said, "I am not backbiting, but it is a fact that Khalid *ṣāḥib* is an emotional [*jaẕbātī*] man." Beg nodded his head in approval. To wrap up the incident for my comprehension, Nazar said that it did not concern my research.

As this incident illustrates, there was a fierce conflict at the Green School about its adherence to the Jamaat's ideology. In this chapter I first show the content and magnitude of the transformation of the Jamaat's educational ideology concerning moderation as it played out in practice in the Green School. I describe how the school underwent a change by seeking affiliation with the UP government, a decision that symbolized the shift in the Jamaat's approach from the boycott of the *ṭāg̣hūtī* system to cooperation with it. Next, I depict the transformation of the school syllabus and show that most of the Jamaat textbooks have been removed from the syllabus. Of those that have been retained, their contents are modified. An important change in the syllabus has been the acceptance of religious pluralism. As a result of the transformation, I argue that the very objective of the school changed. I also show the new criteria for appointing teachers. Because the moderation of the Jamaat's ideology was mediated through the school's principal, I dwell on his role. I also discuss changes in the name of the school, the uniform color, and the mode of greeting, as well as the use of the school as an ideological space and the participation of non-Jamaat figures in its functions.

Second, I discuss the factors responsible for the school's transformation. The most important factor was the "ideological dissonance" (see below) between the Jamaat's agenda and the desires of the Muslim public. Consequently the Jamaat transformed itself; that is, the disavowal of the Jamaat by Muslims worked as the chief catalyst. The sum of the transformation, I argue, was that the Green School nearly failed to meet the aim set by Maududi. Instead of transforming the society, the school was transformed by the society.

In order to contextualize these changes, I begin by detailing the school's practices and the reasons the school was established for. Then I discuss different faces of the school's transformation. The final section considers the factors that led to the moderation of the Jamaat's ideology.

Objective and Practices of the School

In chapter 1 I noted that Haji Sultan, who introduced the Jamaat to the *shahr*, belonged to a wealthy Ahl-e-hadīth family. Owing largely to his high status, he was recognized as a leader of the local Muslims. He was the caretaker of many mosques, and with his conversion to the Jamaat in 1949 he became a dedicated activist. He believed in and practiced every word Maududi had penned, and he had a missionary zeal to expand the Jamaat. However, because most Muslims being believers in various shades of Sufism, they rejected Sultan's call to the Jamaat due to his affiliation with the puritan Ahl-e-hadīth sect. Determined, Sultan thought out a plan. He invited Jamaat activists from outside to settle in the *shahr* to convert local Muslims to the Jamaat.

Foundational Vision

Sultan chose the mosque where he was the caretaker for this purpose. In the mid-1950s he invited Amin Asri—an Ahl-e-hadīth *ʿālim* and a Jamaat member (see chapter 1)—to settle in the *shahr*. He appointed Asri as imam of the mosque, and so Asri led the Friday prayer and delivered sermons. He also became a teacher in the Lutfia school, established in 1968 and named after the father of the *jāmeʿ masjid's* imam, also known as *mufti-e-shahr* (who belonged to the Ahl-e-sunna sect). Asri's arrival did not produce the result Sultan expected. In the early 1960s he invited two more Jamaat members from Azamgarh. They stayed in another mosque where Sultan was also a caretaker. However, only a few months later they left the *shahr*. In 1971 Sultan founded the Green School—then called the Darsgāh-e-Jamaat-e-Islami (the Jamaat-e-Islami School). Though details varied, in all accounts, including that of Ijaz Akbar, one of Sultan's sons and a Reader at AMU, Sultan founded the school to produce worker-activists for the Jamaat, gain credibility among Muslims for the Jamaat, and use it as a space for the Jamaat meetings.

These objectives, however, were not explicitly stated in the school's Constitution. Neither were they asserted in public, particularly after Sultan ceased to be an active Jamaat member because of his deteriorating

Figure 2. Jāmeʿ Masjid in Aligarh *shahr*. Photo by author.

health during the late 1980s. Stating the objectives, the Constitution (in Urdu) of Green School, in force from January 1, 1973, specified that it was established to "provide education to boys and girls in modern style," and to "train boys and girls in an Islamic way." The objectives were further explained in a note as "acquainting boys and girls with the fundamental ideals and beliefs of Islam in simple and heart-touching ways." To achieve the objectives, the Constitution further noted that the school would rely more "on the environment rather than on books."

Criteria and Practices

A number of criteria and practices were introduced for the school to follow. Three stand out. As in the case of Darsgāh, in Rampur (see chapter 2), they were not enshrined in the school's Constitution because they were self-evident. The most important criterion was that the school would not seek recognition of its degrees from the government. Because the government was based on secular democracy, seeking recognition from it would be tantamount to acknowledging the legitimacy of an idol (*ṭāghūt*) and thus would compromise Islam. As documented in chapters 2 and 7, this position was an application of Maududi's ideology that he had outlined in pre-Partition India. In post-Partition India, the Jamaat continued to follow Maududi as exemplified in the establishment, in 1949, of its first school in Rampur (see chapter 2). Given this position, Sultan was sternly opposed to voting in the elections because those elected formed the government in violation of sharia. For the same reason, he had opposed seeking government recognition of the school. Further, the Jamaat believed that seeking recognition would invite government interference in administering the school, especially in the choice of courses. Moreover, the Jamaat followed the policy of nonalignment with Muslims who did not belong to its fold. From its formation until the 1980s, non-Jamaat Muslims were seldom invited as guests or speakers in the school's ceremonies. So were government functionaries, Hindu or Muslim, and politicians from any party, even if they were Muslims.

The second criterion was that teachers must be Jamaat members, or at least sympathizers. Sultan hired Nazar, a research student at AMU, as the principal. Both Nazar and Akbar, Sultan's son, were Islamist activists at AMU. Of his four sons, Sultan liked Akbar the most, as he was the only one to follow his father in joining the Jamaat; his brothers—quite unmusical about, if not hostile to, the Jamaat—opted for business and politics (see below). Along with Nazar, he hired two teachers: Kalim, a Jamaat member from Firozabad, and Hashmat, a local Jamaat sympathizer.

Khalid, who joined the school in 1974, told me about the criteria of teachers' appointments. Born and raised in Bhopal, where his father was a low-ranking government servant, he returned to his ancestral place, Rao Sikandrabad (close to Aligarh). Only a year or two after the establishment of the school, he applied for a teaching position there. Kalim, already a teacher there and a member of the Jamaat, rejected his application because he was not a Jamaat activist. On reapplying a year later, he was given the job, but he had to agree that he would attend the Jamaat's weekly *ijtimāʿ* (meeting), read Maududi's books, and become a sympathizer, if not a member, of the Jamaat. As the school's manager, the most powerful post of the school committee (see below), Sultan was strict about teachers' commitment to the Jamaat. From reading Maududi's writings, Khalid became a sympathizer of the Jamaat and in his own words, a "fan of Maududi."

When Khalid joined the school, there were five teachers, including him (but excluding the principal). The two new teachers were Aurangzeb and Shabbir. Aurangzeb, a native of Saharnpur, was a Jamaat member invited to teach at the school, and Shabbir was a local Jamaat sympathizer. A year after Khalid's appointment, Nasim was hired as another teacher. A native of Basti and a member of the Jamaat since 1962, Nasim, before joining the school, had taught for years at different madrasas. In the late 1990s he also served as *amīr* of the Jamaat in the *shahr*. As Khalid told me, when he joined the school all the teachers, as well as the principal, regularly attended the Jamaat's *ijtimāʿ*. Sultan also made it obligatory for the teachers to hold *ijtimāʿ* in their homes to educate their children and wives. The teachers indeed followed Sultan and held *ijtimāʿ* in their homes. So ideological was Sultan that he wanted the Jamaat sympathizers to marry within the Jamaat community. He persuaded Khalid to marry a woman who came from a Jamaat family, but Khalid declined Sultan's proposal because she belonged to the Ahl-e-hadīth sect. As a staunch Deobandi, he disliked the Ahl-e-hadīth for their "extremism" in regarding other Muslims as akin to polytheists.

The compulsory teaching of the Jamaat textbooks or syllabus was a third criterion. From its establishment until the mid-1980s, the school taught the Jamaat textbooks, which were considered necessary to infuse Islamic spirit in the students and produce future worker-activists for the Jamaat. As we will see below, those textbooks later came under minute criticism. It is important to note that by the early 1960s the Jamaat had prepared a full syllabus of all subjects, from nursery to standard 5, and the subjects were being taught in all the Jamaat schools, including Darsgāh at Rampur (Mahmood 1994; Ahmad 1990).[1]

When founded, the school was called Darsgāh-e-Jamaat-e-Islami. In one account, there was also a signboard with that name. One of the rooms of the school also housed the office of the Jamaat, and another was used as a Jamaat library. Part of the school premises was also used as a residence. One of the teachers, a Jamaat member not from Aligarh, stayed there and he looked after the Jamaat office and library. The Jamaat held its weekly *ijtimāʿ* on school premises. After classes ended each day, the school served as a social center in the evening. People inducted into or close to the party circle came there to read the Jamaat literature as well as forge and renew their ties.

The students' uniforms and code of conduct were informed by what the Jamaat then regarded as Islamic. The boys' uniform was white shirts and green shorts. Ties were not allowed. Upon the teacher's entrance into the classroom, students were prohibited from standing up, as this mode of greeting was considered un-Islamic. In particular, the teachers who were also Jamaat members considered it against *sunna*. One such teacher told me that Muslims bent their head down or stood up only in front of Allah. To do so in front of a teacher, he said, was a "*mushrikāna* [polytheistic]" practice. The way the Prophet did it was to say, aloud "Assalam Alaikum [peace be on you]."

Two other criteria basic to the Jamaat in the 1950s (see chapter 2) were conspicuously absent. Neither in the school's Constitution nor in practice was it stressed that at the time of students' admission to the school, their parents should state in writing that "they fully agree with the Jamaat's ideology" and that they gave their wards "to serve Islam according to the ideology of the Jamaat." Also absent was opposition to students' admission into AMU, a "slaughterhouse," in the unforgettable word of Maududi. Let us recall that the Jamaat had banned its members and sympathizers to study or teach at AMU. Although the ban on sympathizers was lifted in 1957, it remained in force for members well into the 1960s. By the early 1970s, when the Green School was established, for various reasons (discussed in chapters 4 and 7) the Jamaat had revised its stand on AMU and came to defend its "Muslim character." Some Jamaat members, however, still opposed this revision.

Ideological Management

The Jamaat established a Management Committee to oversee the running of the school, choice of syllabus, appointment of teachers, and mobilization of funds. All the committee members were also Jamaat members, except for the principal, a Jamaat sympathizer.

According to the school's Constitution, the school administration included a manager, and the Managing Committee. The manager had the most power and was also president of the Managing Committee. He was responsible for the overall conduct of the school, and he determined if the school was meeting its stated aims. He had the right to change the curriculum, prescribe rules for students and staff, and terminate the services of employees. He was also responsible for finances and laying out development schemes. From its establishment till the mid-1980s, Sultan remained the manager. With the manager serving as president, the Managing Committee consisted of two groups. One group included members nominated by the manager and the second included members suggested by the Committee. The manager could accept or reject the Committee's suggestion. The principal, appointed by the manager, was, ex officio, its member-secretary. The maximum number of Committee members, manager and principal included, was fixed at nine.

When the school was established, the Committee had eight members. Barring the principal, all were members of the Jamaat, four from the Civil Line area of Aligarh and two from Agra and Meerutt, both madrasa -educated. Those from the Civil Line were Rahmat Bedar, Saqlain, Imran Khan, and Obaid Anwar, all young faculty members at AMU. The first two taught in the Department of Economics, and Khan and Anwar were in the Departments of Philosophy and English, respectively. During the late 1970s all Committee members from the Civil Line went abroad, and so did Akbar, Sultan's son. He went to the U.S. to obtain his Ph.D. in philosophy. Khan also migrated to the U.S., and the other three went to Saudi Arabia. During my fieldwork I learned that Khan was settled in the U.S. and that Bedar had moved from Saudi Arabia to the U.S. Having spent some ten years or so abroad, the other two returned to Aligarh.

Including the principal, the Committee members from AMU and the Civil Line were a majority for the following reasons. Sultan did not have a university education, nor were the other Jamaat members in the *shahr* highly educated. Sultan inducted AMU members into the Committee because of their high qualification, and the names of the AMU Jamaat members served as an advertisement to parents to send their children to the Green School. In chapter 1 I outlined how, based on the logic of "domestic Orientalism," the so-called educated, cultured, and prosperous Muslims from AMU and the Civil Line looked down on other Muslims. In some ways Muslims in the *shahr*—largely backward and predominantly illiterate—had internalized the logic of domestic Orientalism, and so they often looked up to Muslims in the Civil Line and the AMU as models to emulate. Moreover, although the number of students from the *shahr* in AMU could be counted on one's fingers, most people always dreamed of sending their children there. Most important, they were not ordinary members. Unlike the two Committee members from Agra and Meerut, they were reckoned as national leaders–intellectuals in the Jamaat. In fact, Bedar and Saqlain were members of the Jamaat's national *shura*.

Faces of Transformation

The Green School went through monumental changes on a number of issues. I argue that the initial success of the school was indeed responsible for the ideological defeat (transformation) of the Jamaat. The transformation included renaming the school, affiliation with the government, gradual removal of the most Jamaat-oriented textbooks from the syllabus (and modification of some matters in these textbooks), and a change of criteria in the appointment of teachers. Changes also occurred in the color of the uniform, the mode of greeting, and the use of the school as an ideological space. Because the Principal had such a central role in the school, this section closes with a discussion of crucial transformative moments in his biography.

Success as Failure

The school initially succeeded primarily because its degrees were recognized by AMU, and thus many of its students were admitted there. Since most Muslims in the *shahr* dreamed of sending their children to AMU, upon AMU's recognition of the degrees those Muslims flocked to the Green School to get their children admitted. This success, I contend, resulted from a revision of the Jamaat's position on AMU. No longer was AMU a "slaughterhouse"; instead, it had become desirable. Obviously, the Jamaat's ban on its members studying at AMU was lifted once and for all even as some Jamaat members resented the move.

With Nazar as principal and Kalim and Hashmat as teachers, the school began to function in July 1971. Nazar took up a house-to-house campaign to persuade local Muslims to send their children to the school, as did Sultan. Despite his Ahl-e-hadīth affiliation, he was accepted as an "insider." By contrast, Nazar's words carried much less weight because of his outsider status. His source of authority was that he was a researcher at AMU and came from across *kaṭḫpullā*, the symbol separating the Civil Line from the *shahr*. As noted in chapter 1, the outsider-insider divide mattered in the cosmology of the *shahr*. Precisely because of the divide, the local population was receptive to Nazar. The school started with twenty-five students and two grades, nursery and kindergarten. The annual fee was 5 Rupees (presently, 10 Euro cents).

In 1972 the number of students rose to 95, and grade 1 was added. In the subsequent year, the student body shot up to 105 and grade 2 was added. With the continued increase in the number of students—115 in 1974—grade 3 was introduced the same year. In 1975 the school scored a major victory, as it was included in the list of institutions approved by AMU. The approval led to AMU's recognition of its degrees. Now Green

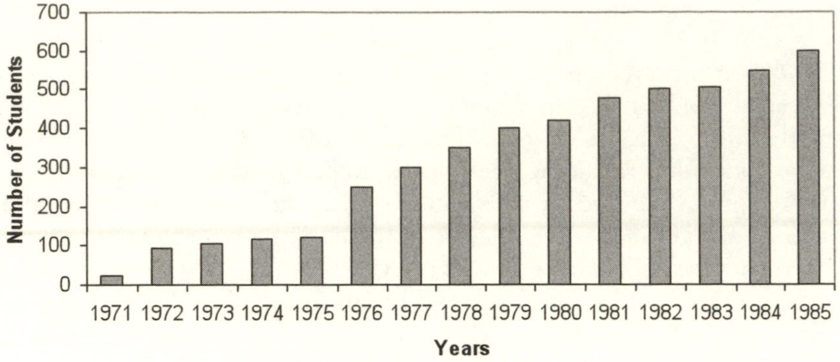

Graph 1. Number of students at the Green School from 1971 to 1986
Source: Data provided by the Green School Office.

School students were eligible for admission to AMU, if they passed the entrance test.[2] AMU allowed grade 3 students from the Green School to take the entrance test for grade 6, and in 1975 Green School students took that entrance test. Thirty-five percent (of thirty) of its students qualified for admission to AMU. AMU's recognition of its degree and the success of Green School students in getting admission to AMU in 1975 led to more than doubling its enrollment the next year (see Graph 1).

The success of the school was partly a result of growing aspirations among Muslims to educate their children so they could become government servants or acquire skills to manage a modern business. In the early 1970s only two schools imparted modern education; the Lutfia and Saifi schools formed in 1965 and run by the Saifi *birādrī*. Many traditional *maktabs*, mainly mosque-based, offered an elementary education in Islam, focusing on prayer, fasting, and a working knowledge of Arabic to read and recite Qur'anic verses. By "traditional," I mean that these schools did not have a syllabus, nor did they have student uniforms or a system of examinations. Above all, they did not teach modern subjects such as math, geography, or physics. For local Muslims, the formation of the Green School was a welcome initiative. They were, however, least interested in the ideological aim of the school. They used it as a ladder to reach AMU.

The principal described the recognition of the school's degrees by AMU as a "great achievement." When I asked him, was AMU not a "slaughterhouse," he told me that Maududi's writings were "emotional." What about the Jamaat's ban on its members from studying there? He dismissed the ban as emotional, too. In seeking the recognition of its degrees from AMU and sending its students there, clearly the Green School was catering to the aspirations of the *shahr* Muslims, rather than transforming them according to the Jamaat's ideology. Because AMU was a dream house for the *shahr* Muslims, it could not have been something else for the Jamaat. It therefore stopped calling AMU a "slaughterhouse." Indeed, AMU became a reference in shaping the development of the Green School. Only a few years after AMU had allowed grade 3 students to take the test for grade 6, it annulled the permission and stated that only grade 5 students would be eligible for the test in the future. For this reason, the Green School added grades 4 and 5 in the early 1980s. As would become apparent, some Jamaat members and teachers regarded the school's efforts to secure eligibility to enter AMU as a conspiracy by their "secularist" colleagues to destroy the Jamaat, and, *mutatis mutandis*, Islam.

As the start of this chapter illustrates, conflict was at the heart of the Jamaat's transformation. An early conflict emerged over deletion of the suffix "Jamaat-e-Islami" from the school's name. Names, badges, slogans, or flags are pivotal to an ideology. Black cultures have used bodies as insignia of identity or as "canvasses of representation" (Hall 1983:27; also see Gilroy 2000). If images and visual icons are central to the iconography of a movement, so is its name. Recall that Maududi had named his party "Jamaat-e-Islami," arguing that it was the only party that stood for "pure" Islam. If so, the deletion of "Jamaat-e-Islami" from the school's name signified an ideological transformation which, I argue, was not superficial but substantial.

True to its ideology, all Jamaat institutions established after Partition carried the suffix "Jamaat-e-Islami." The first school established by the Jamaat, in 1949, was called Darsgāh-e-Jamaat-e-Islami, Rampur. Likewise, the research wing of the Jamaat, established in 1956 in Rampur, carried the suffix "Jamaat-e-Islami." It was called Idāra-e-taṣnīf Jamaat-e-Islami Hind. In 1970 it moved to Aligarh but retained its previous name (*Idāra-e-taṣnīf* . . . 1981). Initially the Green School was named Darsgāh-e-Jamaat-e-Islami, but only a year later the principal proposed a name change. In his view, while the word "darsgāh" sounded like a "madrasa" and had a "conservative [*qadāmatpasand*]" ring to it, "Jamaat-e-Islami" connoted a party school, not an institution for the Muslim public. Further, he wanted the school to be "modern," not a madrasa. When the issue was taken to the Managing Committee, Sultan and two other Jamaat members (not from Aligarh) opposed it, saying that because it was a Jamaat school it must retain the suffix "Jamaat-e-Islami." However, the Committee members from the Civil Line, who, with the principal, formed a majority, endorsed the principal's proposal. The new name chosen was English.[3]

Idolic State: Affiliate or Not Affiliate?

Central to the transformation of the Green School was the thorniest conflict over whether it should secure affiliation with the UP government. Other changes revolved around this. A critical conflict was between "modernist/secularist/materialist" and "conservative/Islamic" streams *within* the Jamaat over its ideology. The pro-affiliation stream called itself "modernist [*jadīd*]" and its rival "conservative [*qadāmatparast*]"; the anti-affiliation stream called itself "Islamic" and true followers of Maududi, and accused its rival as being "secularist and materialist [*māddāparast*]."

What does it mean for a school to become affiliated? It means that the state government recognizes its degrees, as a result of which the degree holders are eligible for admission to any government institution. Put differently, students of a school not affiliated with the government legally cannot apply for admission to an affiliated or government institution because its degrees are not legally valid. Nor are they eligible for jobs in the government or in the private sector. An affiliated school is usually a private institution without government funding (though it may receive partial funding). The government grants recognition to degrees of a given institution if it fulfills criteria such as the teaching of a given syllabus, minimal qualifications of its teachers, and availability of basic infrastructure (space, classrooms, furniture, etc.).

The affiliation of the Green School with the government was a necessity for the future career of its students. This necessity was partially fulfilled when AMU, in 1975, recognized its degrees, but the future remained uncertain for those who did not qualify for admission to AMU. The Green School arranged with other affiliated schools for its students to simultaneously enroll in the latter so as to use their certificates to gain admission to government institutions.[4] From the early 1980s, however, the state strictly prohibited this practice. Consequently the demand for affiliation intensified, unleashing a debate within the Managing Committee and among the teachers, as well as the Jamaat members, of the school. Whereas the "conservative" stream, that included Sultan, Kalim, Nasim, Aurangzeb[5] and two Committee members from Agra and Meerut were dead set against affiliation, the "modernist" stream, consisting of the principal and four Jamaat members from the Civil Line pushed for affiliation.

It should be clear why the modernists wanted to have government affiliation. They wanted to make it a "modern" institution, not a madrasa, as was evident in the conflict over the renaming of the school. By "modern," they meant that the graduates of the school should be eligible to study in a college or university and compete for jobs in the public and private sectors. The modernists wanted to make the graduates bureaucrats, government employees, doctors, engineers, and so on. For this to happen, affiliation with the government was necessary. In contrast to a modern institution, the madrasa graduates usually became *mu'azzin*, madrasa teachers, or imams. They were not eligible for study in a university,[6] or for government jobs, because they were not taught modern subjects such as physics, biology, math, and political science. But why did the modernists want to make the Green School a "modern" institution? Was it simply their own desire or was it for other reasons? As already noted, Muslims wanted to send their children to AMU and make them government employees (see below). Thus the modernists were articulating the desire of the Muslim public.

When modernists advanced the proposal for affiliation in the Committee, the conservatives opposed it. Claiming to be Maududi's true followers, they argued that seeking affiliation with the government was equivalent to obeying the *ṭāghūt*, that is, the Indian state. Recall that this position was a reassertion of Maududi's argument that to serve a non-Islamic government was to obey an idol (1942:178–82). In line with this position, Jamaat members working in various government departments had already resigned. In chapter 2 I discussed case studies of those who resigned from the government considering the jobs to be *haram*. However, conservatives later stopped making this argument under pressure from Muslims at the local and national levels, including the ulema of the Deoband who did not consider the Indian state anti-Islamic.

The conservatives' next argument was that affiliation would invite interference by the state, and, as a result, the Green School would loose its autonomy. This would mean that the Jamaat syllabus would be replaced by the government syllabus, which the Jamaat described as anti-Islamic.[7] Although some of the government's books contained materials about idol worship, most other books were "secular" in that they did not teach, for example, the religious origin of the universe. Teaching such a syllabus, the conservatives—and particularly Aurangzeb—argued would make students "apostates [*mulḥid*]." More important, if the Jamaat syllabus was replaced, how could students be schooled to become Jamaat activists? Another fear was that government interference would entail observance of rituals like Independence Day and Republic Day (August 15 and January 26, respectively). At those times the Jamaat regarded saluting flags and singing the anthem (see chapter 9) as undesirable.

The modernists countered that the changed circumstances in postcolonial India required the Jamaat to recast itself. "It would be an injustice [*ẓulm*]," the modernists contended, "to destroy the career of students by not enabling them to pursue further education and seek jobs." As for the conservatives' claim to be true followers of Maududi, the modernists argued that the conservatives were a "frog in the well," as they only read Maududi's books, interpreted them literally, and moved in the closed circle of the Jamaat, but they did not know how to interact with the wider society. Both streams often told me to interview Saqlain, the most influential member of the modernist stream living in the Civil Line. I went to see him in Sir Syed colony, an affluent are in the Civil Line. He was busy getting his air conditioning fixed. When I asked him if the anti-affiliation stream was right in opposing affiliation with the government because it was *ṭāghūt*, he replied:

> If the government and all its institutions were *ṭāghūt*, why do they [the anti-affiliation Jamaat members] travel in the train, use the postal department to send their letters, go to the hospitals for treatment? Why do they use electricity?. . . The government provides electricity for the thousands of mosques. . . . Are not all these institutions of the government as well?

To Saqlain, Maududi's declaration of the whole polity as *ṭāghūt* was wrong. So was Maududi's call to Muslims to boycott the government. In his reading, Maududi got carried away by "emotions" rather than "reason [*dalā'el*]." Because Gandhi advocated boycotting British goods, Saqlain held, Maududi argued that Muslims must boycott the institutions of a non-Islamic state. When I asked if Maududi's position was not Islamic, he told me, rather angrily, that it was not. The problem with the conservatives, he said, was that "they treated Maududi, God forbid, like a God"; "As Muslims, we are bound to follow the Qur'an and *hadīth*, not him [Maududi]." Clearly Saqlain's was a revisionist reading of Maududi, but he was not alone. Nazar told me that in a private meeting Bedar once remarked that he found it hard to stick to Maududi's tirade against secularism. On the AMU campus Nazar quoted Bedar as saying that he "felt ashamed" speaking against secularism. He asked his colleagues in the Jamaat, "If not secularism, then what?"

The modernists' revisionist reading of Maududi affected the future of students, and for the students' sake the conservatives had no alternative. The conservatives were losing ground, and their position began to weaken further when a significant change occurred in the Committee. Around 1985 Sultan's son, Akbar, was appointed as the new school Manager. The appointment was made because Sultan had become ill, and of his four sons Akbar was deemed the most suitable replacement because he was the only one active in the Jamaat. But when Akbar took charge, he was a changed man. Having returned from the U.S., where he had lived for some five years while studying for his Ph.D., he had become "Westernized [*angrēz*]" and skeptical even about basic ideology of the Jamaat. He wanted the school to be professional, not ideological. His concern was to see the *shahr* Muslims prosper; he did not care about ideology. Akbar demanded that teachers were punctual, did their homework, and performed their duties well. He made no concessions to the teachers who were Jamaat members, as had been the practice. In 1986 grades 6, 7, and 8 were added, and new teachers were appointed. In hiring teachers, Akbar gave no consideration to whether the candidates were Jamaat sympathizers or members. He urged the principal to obtain government affiliation immediately and assured him that he would handle the opposition. On ideological as well as personal grounds (Akbar had withdrawn concessions), Nasim, Kalim, and Aurangzeb opposed Akbar and wanted him ousted as manager. Two years later Akbar was replaced by the then local *amīr* of the Jamaat.

Though Akbar was removed, the conservatives had nearly lost the battle over affiliation. By the mid-1980s, however, the Jamaat itself had undergone a monumental shift nationally. It lifted the ban on its members to vote in elections (see chapter 7). As a result, the school principals who were also Jamaat members started seeking affiliation. The Committee member from Meerut also secured affiliation for the school where he was principal. Nazar did not, despite Akbar's endorsement, because he himself was not a Jamaat member. In the absence of such legitimacy, he expected that the initiative came from the Jamaat members themselves.

Having lost the battle against affiliation, the conservatives came up with a new plan. The Green school should seek affiliation with the Arabic and Persian Board (APB) of Allahabad—a government board to supervise the functioning of madrasas (Anjum 2002)—rather than with the Basic Shiksha Adhikari (BSA), a Lucknow-based government institution that supervised primary education. The reason for insisting on affiliation with the APB was that the Green School was becoming "secular." To make it Islamic, the school first had to become a madrasa and then seek affiliation with the APB. Only a madrasa offered true Islamic education, according to Aurangzeb, Nasim, and the Committee member from Meerut. To support their argument, they asked how many graduates of the Green School became ulema or Jamaat activists. As Nasim told me, during its thirty-year history the school produced no more than fifteen SIO members and just one Jamaat member. The lone Jamaat member, he stressed, became a member not because of the school but because his father was a Jamaat member. Nasim's diagnosis was that the school failed to produce Jamaat activists because something was fundamentally wrong with its education. "It was <u>secular</u> and non-Islamic [*ghair-islāmī*]." It did not teach Arabic, theology, *hadīth*, and the Qur'an at the higher levels; Islam was taught up to class 5, and the general focus was on modern subjects. Did Maududi want, he asked me, an education that produced worldly people rather than ulema? Opposed to modern education and AMU, both he and Aurangzeb held that only madrasas offered a true Islamic education.

The proposal by the Committee member from Meerut to become affiliated with the APB was defeated. A disheartened Nasim opted for other means to achieve his goal. He asked the parents of the ten best students in the school to send their children to a madrasa. Only one student's parents agreed, and Nasim arranaged for the boy to be admitted to a madrasa. On graduation, that student returned to the *shahr*, and for some years he eked out a living as a singer of *na'ṭ* (Islamic hymns). As his voice lost its charm, he was no longer sought after as a singer. With no source of income, he began to work in the lock factory. In Nasim's own words, both the student and his father cursed Nasim for ruining his career.

Notwithstanding the opposition from the likes of Nasim, in 1997 the Green School obtained affiliation with the BSA, and its degrees up to grade 5 became valid. Though still a teacher there, Nasim was perhaps, the unhappiest about the affiliation. I would remain with Nasim for a little longer so that I could present the conservatives' standpoint.

Nasim lived in a dingy, two-room apartment in a poor neighborhood across the Shah Jamal *mazār* (shrine). He had a worn-out, noisy bicycle, his main means of transportation. He held that the soil of Aligarh itself was irreligious and that people born there were "materialist" and "epicurean." Even though Aligarh's soil was corrupted, Nasim believed that people from across the *kaṭhpullā*, the Civil Line, were even more materialist than people from the *shahr*. Unhappy at the Muslims' glorification of AMU as the educational Mecca, he held that AMU was responsible for the downfall of Muslims as it kept producing generations of irreligious, materialist people. On joining AMU, even religious persons became "this-worldly [*dunyādār*]" and disinterested in Islam. In his view, the four Jamaat members from the Civil Line on the school's Committee were no exception, as they had initiated the process of de-Islamizing the school by gaining AMU's recognition.

> You know the Committee people. They are materialist and pleasure-loving [*māddāparast aur 'aishparast*]. Have you seen their houses? . . . Money and religion do not go together. . . . They did not have much interest in Islam because they did not have its true knowledge. They did not study in a madrasa. They were secular and worldly [*dunyāparast*]. So they also de-Islamized [*ghair-islāmī banā diyā*] the school. They have betrayed Maududi. . . . The principal was no different. He followed them. They also supported him though he was in reality anti-Jamaat.

As the quote shows, Nasim held the principal responsible for the downfall of the school. He saw the relationship of a principal to a school as similar to that of a king to his subjects. In his view, Nazar was a sympathizer in public, but in private he worked against the Jamaat. In the late 1970s Nazar mobilized Hashmat against the Jamaat. Shocked at this, Hashmat issued a written complaint to Sultan, who responded by asking for an explanation. Nazar denied the charge and tendered his resignation, but Akbar asked Nazar to rescind it. Sultan, however, did not want Nazar to continue. The issue went to the Chicago-based Imran Khan, an influential Committee member, who then prevailed upon Sultan to retain Nazar as principal. Finally, Nasim explained the de-Islamization of the school in terms of pervasive materialism, because of which Muslims ran after money, not Islam. As an example he cited his own failure to get ten students to seek a madrasa education. People could have been persuaded in favor of Islam, he held, had the principal and the Committee members from the Civil Line made the appropriate efforts.

Change in the Syllabus and Criteria of Teachers' Appointment

The debate over affiliation was linked to the very objective of the Green School. Once the modernists had clinched affiliation, changes also occurred in other arenas—the syllabus, the uniform, the mode of greeting, criteria for appointing teachers, the use of the school as an ideological space, and the appearance of photos of living beings in the Jamaat textbooks.

In its initial years the Green School taught the full Jamaat syllabus. The need to change it arose when the AMU recognized the school's degrees and the school's students started appearing for the AMU entrance test (for grade 6). The textbooks prescribed at AMU were different from Jamaat textbooks, and thus the Jamaat textbooks became a hindrance, not only for entry to AMU but also for other affiliated and government schools. The modernists slowly began to change the textbooks. The need to change, once again, stemmed from the aspiration of local Muslims who wanted their children to have a modern education to become government employees, or acquire sufficient skills to enter the business world. A debate similar to the one on affiliation also arose about changes in the curriculum.

A number of arguments were presented in favor of changing the Jamaat textbooks. According to Nazar, madrasa students were the original audience of the Jamaat textbooks, which were written in chaste Urdu and were incomprehensible to students whose parents were not educated in madrasa. Moreover, the Jamaat textbooks had very small lettering, and they had no illustrations related to lesson contents. During the 1970s and 1980s the Jamaat did not publish photographs of living beings—human or animal—as they were considered *haram*.[8] Book covers were also unattractive, and children were not drawn to them. Moreover, Islam permeated all subjects, even lessons where it was unnecessary. Nazar quoted Saqlain, who once remarked that the Urdu textbooks of the Jamaat appeared more like theology books than literature texts.

In contrast to the Jamaat textbooks, those prepared by the National Council for Educational and Research Training (NCERT), a government institution, were psychologically friendly. For this reason, Nazar had the school adopt them almost wholesale. At the time of my fieldwork, most textbooks for grades 3 through 8 were from the NCERT. Nazar regarded the NCERT textbooks as secular but not anti-Muslim, as were those prepared under the BJP's dispensation during 2001–2004. The Jamaat textbooks that remained in use were only for Urdu, Islam (theology), and history, although from grade 5 on Urdu classes were taught with the NCERT textbooks. The contents of even these subjects were substantially modified, however. For example, the lesson "The Fair," from the Urdu book *Our Book* (*Hamārī Kitāb*), part 1, originally written in 1953, showed the bewilderment of the child Munno at the unreasonable practice of idol worship. In the revised 1995 edition of the book, the portion dealing with idol worship was deleted. Now the two brothers, Munno and Chunno, simply went to the fair to buy sweets for themselves and their family.

The change to NCERT textbooks also entailed a change in the criteria for teachers' appointments. As already stated, teachers in the beginning were appointed based on their commitment to the Jamaat, and most teachers were madrasa-educated. The shift to modern educational methods required teachers who had different qualities. During his tenure as the school manager, Akbar appointed teachers based on their professionalism and teaching skills, not their ideology. In subsequent years, most new appointments of teachers were done along the lines Akbar had outlined. At the time of my fieldwork, out of twenty-five teachers (all male; see below) only one was a Jamaat member. Among the six nonteaching staff, two were Jamaat members: the accountant and a peon. Four teachers described themselves as Jamaat sympathizers. The rest were professional teachers, not ideologues.[9]

Ideology became so peripheral that even teachers belonging to "polytheistic" sects such as the Ahl-e-sunna (Barēlvī) were also appointed. Out of twenty-five teachers, three were devout practitioners of Sufism. (One of the Sufis took me to the shrine of Shāh Jamāl, which he regularly visited.) Another teacher was a staunch Tablīghī Jamaat follower. Three others belonged to the Ahl-e-hadīth sect. The rest were Deobandi. Nasim told me that two teachers were even openly anti-Jamaat. It was not simply the plurality of ideologies among teachers that defined the transformed face of the Green School. Teachers were no longer required to attend the Jamaat *ijtimā*ʿ. Only three teachers who were not Jamaat members voluntarily attended it, and only irregularly. No teacher held the *ijtimā*ʿ at home.

Another significant change was in the school uniform—the shirt remained white, but the color of the pants changed from green to blue. The style of greeting also changed. Now when a teacher entered the classroom, the students stood up. Although Nasim still opposed this greeting, it had become intrinsic to the school culture. It also became acceptable for students to wear a tie. Moreover, the school ceased to be the venue

Figure 3. Children at the Green School offering the morning prayer. Photo by author.

for the Jamaat *ijtimāʿ*. The principal asserted that school was a place for education, not a battleground for politics.

Still another important change concerned the participation of a guest of honor at school functions. During the second leg of my fieldwork, a farewell party was organized for final-year students, and the chief guest of honor was the local Member of the Legislative Assembly (MLA), a Hindu and a member of the Congress Party. It was news in the school that the MLA had agreed to attend the function. A graduate of AMU, the MLA spoke chaste Urdu and used the Islamic terminology for his greeting. He also wore *gulāl*, red powder, on his forehead, an ostensibly religious symbol. To the audience's applause, he concluded his speech with a simultaneous "*ḳhudā ḥāfiẓ* [May Allah protect you]" and "*jai hind* (Victory to India)."

The Principal

In many ways, the principal's biography symbolized the changes in the Green School over the years. Born during the late 1940s in the erstwhile

Princely Muslim State of Rampur, Nazar's father was a state employee. With the abolition of the Princely States in 1948, his father became an overseer with the Public Welfare Department of the government of India. Nazar's early education was in Rampur, and at a fairly young age he was drawn to the Jamaat. The Rampur Jamaat *amīr*, a well-known homeopathic doctor, introduced him to Maududi, whose writings fired up Nazar's imagination. He began to dream of an Islamic revolution. In the mid-1960s, when Jamaat students were activating their fellow students to form an organization, he became one of the leaders of the movement (see chapter 4). By then he had moved to Kanpur, which became his second home, as many of his relatives lived there. The center of the young Islamists was AMU, which Nazar visited as an activist. He was close to Imran Khan (later to become a member of the school's Committee), calling him a friend and patron (*sarparast*).

Maududi's influence on Nazar was so gripping that Nazar considered the Jamaat to be the only organization upholding the truth of Islam. He did not even think of taking up a government job. Doing so would be no less than strengthening the *ṭāghūtī niẓām,* which the Jamaat wished to eliminate. Similarly he considered it anti-Islamic to vote or participate in elections of a secular polity. Like others, he, too, was passionate about an Islamic revolution. Recalling his days of activism, he told me:

> I read Maududi's literature when I was young. It radically changed my whole outlook. I then decided not to go for any government job except teaching. Those days we used to say that to be part of the Indian government in any form was to perpetuate the *ṭāghūtī niẓām*. My friends also thought the same. Everyone believed it. . . . Then we used to think that the Islamic revolution was about to come. It is just a matter of some years. So firm was our belief (*Laugh*) . . . What should I tell you! (*Pause*). I also stopped watching films.

The last feature film he had seen was in 1960, the K. Asif's epic *mughl-e-āʿẓam* (The Great Mughal). Since then he had not gone to any cinemas. Nor did he allow his family members to watch films. In 1986, when his sister-in-law was married in Kanpur, one of his relatives wanted to play a video. When Nazar found out, he chastised him. The video had not been screened despite repeated requests and invocations of the occasion. Some years later, when his in-laws offered him a TV set, he refused. Because his wife wanted it, however, he accepted the gift but did not allow it to be used.

Later he started watching television, and I saw the TV playing in his house. A changed Nazar was now critical of the Taliban, which opposed both TV and audio music. By banning TV and music, he remarked, the Taliban were muffling people's freedom. With a smile, he recalled having listened to the famous ghazal—*abẖī tō main javān hūn̄* (I am still young)—

sung by the female singer Malika Pukhraj when he recently traveled in a car with Sufyan, one of Sultan's four sons. Sufyan was an important figure in *shahr* life, and during the early 1990s he contested elections to the UP Assembly for three consecutive terms. The Qurshi *birādrī* he belonged to supported him wholeheartedly, but he lost. He fought the elections from the Janata Dal, a party formed in the 1980s with the agenda of social justice. As a friend, Nazar was a key campaigner for his elections, but Sultan was firmly opposed to his son's participation in the elections. Sultan also opposed Sufyan's and his brother's involvement in business and "worldly affairs." "Toward the end of his life," a Jamaat member told me, praising Sultan's firm belief, "he even refused drinking water from his sons." He believed that his sons had rebelled against Allah by contesting elections and conducting un-Islamic business (one of his sons owned a TV shop). In fact, Sultan and his wife lived separately from their sons.

Like Sufyan, in 1989 Nazar contested the municipal elections for the ward councilor post, and like Sufyan, he lost. A cyclo-styled poster, with Nazar's black and white photo affixed on the right and his voting symbol of a wristwatch on the left, introduced him as a "well-known personality" of the ward and principal of the Green School. The poster made several promises to voters, such as a clean, electrically lit ward with running drinking water at home and a reduced housing tax. In short, announced the poster, if elected he would strive to make his ward a civic paradise. Nowhere did it mention an Islamic cause, nor was there an exclusive appeal to Muslims. On the contrary, a couplet at the top read: "Carry the life and universe along / when you move, move with the whole world." Explaining his defeat, he told me that because Muslims in the *shahr* saw him as an outsider they voted for the local (*maqāmī*) candidates. They also voted along caste lines. As someone from the Ḳhān, an upper caste, he did not receive votes from the lower castes such as ʿAbbāsīs, Anṣārīs, and Saifīs. The Ḳhāns were a rather small community, with few voters. Among the lower castes, he received the largest number of votes from the Quraishīs because of his friendship with Sufyan.

That Nazar contested the ward election shows the activist urge he acquired as a young Islamist. He continued his activism, and from the 1980s on he participated in a number of organizations except the Jamaat. He became one of the founding members of the All-India Millī Council (AIMC), a Delhi-based organization founded in 1992.[10] He had also been a member of the All-India Babri Masjid Action Committee now nearly defunct (see chapter 6). In 1991 he joined the Rābṭā Committee, which was formed in Aligarh to coordinate organizations working for the educational development of Muslims (Abrar 1997).The diversity of his organizational affiliations shows that, for Nazar, the Jamaat had ceased to be the sole spokesman of Islam.

Ideological Dissonance

In the final section of this chapter, I ask: Why did the school undergo such a momentous change? I argue that the main factor was, borrowing with some modification from Benford and Snow, "ideological dissonance." Benford and Snow use the term "frame resonance" (2000:619; also see Snow et al. 1986) as a variable to explain the effectiveness or otherwise of collective action frames. The greater the resonance, the more successful or effective a social movement (Benford and Snow 2000:620ff.). Logically, lack of resonance would mean that a social movement is less effective. Because that precisely is the larger argument of that book, I use "dissonance" as the opposite of "resonance," and I use "ideology" in place of "frame" for the reason stated in chapter 1. By ideological dissonance, I mean a radical incongruence between the aspirations of the Jamaat on the one hand, and those of the Muslim public, on the other. Although the Jamaat wanted through the school, to produce activists for its organization, the Muslim public wanted their children to become government servants and be economically successful, skilled enough, for example, to manage a business. In showing this ideological dissonance, I move away from the school campus to the neighborhood to ask the parents of its alumni why they chose the Green School and what they expected from its education.

To answer this question, I asked the principal to make a list of the school's alumni, twenty-five males and ten females (girls studied up to grade 5; through grade 4 the school was co-educationed, and in grade 5 girls and boys were segregated). The school had no records of its alumni, so he made the list based on memory and included only those who were then available in Aligarh. I believe that the principal selected "the best" of the alumni. Of the thirty-five alumni, I was able to meet twenty-one of them: fifteen males and six females. I also spoke to four other alumni whom I met incidentally in the course of my interviews with those on the list. The total number of respondents for alumni was thus twenty-five, nineteen males and six females.[11] Of the twenty-five alumni, I spoke to the parents of twenty of them: eighteen fathers and two mothers (in the case of female students).

Mundane, Not Ideological

Based on interviews with the parents of alumni, I learned that the parents sent their children to the Green School for more mundane reasons than ideological ones. In fact, 40 percent of the parents did not even know that the school belonged to the Jamaat. Likewise, 48 percent of the alumni did not know that the Jamaat ran the school that they themselves had attended. In response to my question—why did they choose the Green School for their children—the parents always referred to other schools in the *shahr* as well as in the Civil Line. To contextualize their responses, it is useful to be familiar with other schools, and it is helpful to know these parents' backgrounds.

When the Green School was founded, apart from the mosque-based *makātib*, the *shahr* had only two primary schools, the Luṭfiya and Saifī schools. Both had secured affiliation with the government. Beginning in the early 1980s a number of primary schools were established, most of them run by *birādrī*-based associations (see Mann 1992). In 1981, for example, the Salmānī *birādrī* association established Salmania Primary School, and four years later the Anṣārīs founded Al-anṣār Public School. The 'Abbasīs were the late starter. In 1996 they founded 'Abbasī Model Public School. Though run by respective *birādrī* associations, all the schools were open to students of every *birādrī*. The school that was a recurring reference point (especially for the female alumni and their parents) during the interviews was Sirājul 'ulūm Nisvāñ College (henceforth, Nisvāñ). Established by one Mrs. Bilqis, she handed it over to Sultan before her migration to Pakistan in 1978. Since then it had come under Jamaat control. Though "college" figured in its name, it was a women's madrasa[12] affiliated with the APB and it received aid from the UP government. Aurangzeb, who taught for some years in the Green School, later on became the administrator of the Nisvāñ.

Dozens of other schools could be found in the *shahr*, and hardly a street was without the signboard of a school (often with an English name). This was true for the Civil Line area as well. In addition to the AMU schools, two were quite popular: Lady Fatima High School, run by a Christian mission, and Aligarh Public School, run by Muslims. Lady Fatima was an elite school; its medium was English and its fees were staggeringly high, beyond the reach of the lower middle class. Only in the past five years or so had it allowed Muslim girls to wear *shalvār-qamīz* a traditional dress consisting of loose pajama-like trousers and a loose, long shirt or tunic. Earlier skirts were obligatory. As its students came from various religious backgrounds, it did not teach Islam to its Muslim students. There were many convent schools in the *shahr* as well. Blue Birds School and St. Fidelis were two such well-known schools. Unlike the Lady Fatima, which later introduced the teaching of Urdu, Blue Birds and St. Fidelis taught neither Urdu nor Islam.

Modern educated Muslims (as well as Hindus) from the middle class or rich business families, both in the *shahr* and in the Civil Line, preferred to send their children to convent or other English-medium schools. The students studying in the *birādrī* schools or the Green School came from lower-middle or working-class families. Though it is difficult to give exact statistics, it would not be inaccurate to say that about half the students in the Green School came from working-class families whose fathers worked in lock factories or owned petty businesses selling vegetables or fruits. The rest belonged to the lower middle class, where fathers were lower-level government servants, employees in the private sector, or small businessmen. Parents who opted for the government schools, locally called *chungī* schools, were poor, as they did not expect their children to develop a career from their education. Though they charged only nominal fees, *chungī* schools had the poorest quality of education.

Afsana, aged twenty-nine, lived in Tandonpara, a *mohalla* close to the Green School. Having studied in the Green School since nursery, in 1984 she passed the grade 5 examination and later joined AMU. Her elder brother and two younger sisters also studied there. She worked as a temporary Urdu teacher in an AMU school, and her brother was a medical representative and her younger sister a computer teacher. When I asked her mother (her father had died) why she chose the Green School, she told me:

> Do you mean I should have sent my daughters to the Nisvāñ [college]? . . . Parents send their daughters there only to get married. They flash their degrees to grooms' families to show that their daughters are educated. Otherwise what is the relevance of Nisvāñ's education? Its students hardly get any job. For them, only one line is open, the madrasa line. The door for another line—modern education and job—is closed. I wanted my children to move ahead (*āgē baṛhānā chahtī thī*). The age is changing. The Nisvāñ is not suitable for this. There is religious orthodoxy (*daqyānūsī*) there. Young girls are forced to wear the veil (*burqa*). Except one, I sent all my children to the Green School because it gave a modern education and helped students seek jobs.

Afsana's mother further explained that she wanted to give her children a convent education but could not afford it. She chose the Green School because its fee was lower than that of the convent schools. The Nisvāñ, on the other hand, did not fulfill her desires because it was a madrasa and by going there her daughters could not have been educated to earn a living. For similar reasons, she sent her son to the Green School. Although other schools, especially those run by various *birādrīs*, also offered a modern education, it was not as good as a Green School education. Students of a *birādrī* school were far less likely to gain admission to AMU compared to the Green School students. Shahana's father, a lock maker, also did not send her to the Nisvāñ because its education had no "relevance [*pūchh*]." He wanted her to get an "English education," and he was happy that the Green School had fulfilled his aim. Shahana had finished her Ph.D. at AMU and worked for a computer company.

Zahid of the Sheikhan *mohalla* sent his daughters, Gulshan and Roshan, to the Green School because he, too, could not afford a convent education. He chose the Green School because it offered the best "modern education." Having studied there, Gulshan was in the final year of working toward her master's degree in zoology, and Roshan was about to complete her bachelor's degree in psychology (both from AMU). Both sisters wanted to earn a bachelor's degree in education and become teachers. In the *shahr* Zahid was perhaps the only Muslim who called himself a BJP man. As president of the BJP's local minority cell, he stood opposed to the Jamaat and accused it of having an agenda of establishing a "Muslim raj."[13] But he lauded its educational efforts; the Green School was committed to giving Muslims a modern education, and it was not "commercial."

Nazir of the Teela *mohalla*, who worked in a lock factory, also wanted to give his son a convent education, but his income was insufficient. He chose the Green School because it was modern and its education was the best in the *shahr*. He praised its teachers, particularly the science faculty, who, unlike their counterparts in the Saifī or Al-anṣār schools, were better qualified (holding bachelor's degrees; the Urdu teacher was a Ph.D. student at AMU). He did not expect his sons to become government employees but hoped that at least they would learn mathematics so that, in the future, if he established his own factory, they would be competent to handle business.

> See Ṣāḥib! There are two kinds of school here. You know what the *chungī* schools are. They are worse. We also have religious schools [*makātib*] here. But they don't teach students how to progress (*taraqqī*). . . . They don't even know how to fill out a form to get a railway reservation or send a telegram. Knowledge of prayer . . . is necessary but this alone is not sufficient. The times [*zamāna*] have changed. . . . First of all, we have to fill our empty belly. We need the kind of education that can fetch bread. Don't we? I sent my child to Green School. For the present age, it is the best.

These accounts illustrate that, for most parents, the Green School worked as a surrogate to convent education. Seventy percent of parents told me that, by sending their children there, they expected them either to become employees in the public or private sector or gain skills to manage a business. Their minimum expectation was that their children would at least know how to fill out railway reservation forms and send telegrams. It was to meet the aspirations of the Muslim public like these parents that the modernists argued for a transformation of the school, inter alia, over the issue of affiliation.

The second important reason for the choice of the Green School was that it offered a balanced synthesis of Islam and modern education. Thirty percent of parents stated that they chose the Green School because it offered the best teaching of Islam. In most *birādrī* schools, the teaching of Islam was not treated as seriously as in the Green School, which placed far more emphasis on imparting the fundamentals of Islam to its students. An ancillary factor behind the choice of the Green School was its location in the heart of a Muslim *mohalla*. Parents of adjacent *mohallas* chose it because of physical proximity. Parents from the distant Muslim *mohallas* also chose it because its location ensured the safety of their children during communal violence, which was frequent in the *shahr*.[14]

Jamaat's Image: Revolutionary, Welfarist, or Selfish?

Did parents choose to send their children to the Green School because it was a Jamaat school? When I put this question to them, 40 percent did not even know that the Green School was a Jamaat school. Seventy-eight-year-old Wajahat Husain of the *mohalla* Kala Mahal, who sent all four of his children to the Green School, told me that no one from the Jamaat ever asked him to attend its *ijtimā*ʿ. In fact, at the mention of the Jamaat, most of them talked of the Tablīghī Jamaat, which had tremendous visibility in the *shahr*. Many of those who knew the Tablīgh showed their disinterest toward it, as the demands of family life and work were too pressing for them to care about any Muslim organization. This was especially true for lower-class parents (fathers) working in lock factories or even for small contractors (*ṭhīkēdārs*). As the father, a *ṭhīkēdār*, of an alumnus, recently back from Hajj, put it: "I have nothing to do with any organization. I am busy in my business of locks. I do not unnecessarily mix up with people. If you do, you end up backbiting. This is sin. I do my work, pray, and keep a distance with people. Politics is after all dirty."

Of the 60 percent of parents who knew about the Jamaat and its school, most of them knew for markedly different reasons. They were not even familiar with such basic terms of the Jamaat's vocabulary as *iqāmat-e-dīn*. Nor had they participated in its *ijtimā*ʿ. Most knew it as an organization devoted to the "welfare [*bhalāī, hamdardī*]" of Muslims. That was why its school, they said, was far better than others in both discipline and quality. To make a profit, other schools employed teachers who had only passed grade 10, as they were paid less. The Green School, by contrast, had well-qualified teachers. "Compared to all the schools here, it has the best teachers" was the oft-heard refrain. Unlike other schools, the Green School was also concerned with students' careers. The distinction parents made was between a *kārobārī*- (commercial) and *qaumī*[15] (community)-oriented school. They believed that whereas other schools were commercial, the Green School took an interest in the advancement of Muslims and took care of poor students by reducing their fees. Kabir, of Chiragh Chian *mohalla*, was a sewing machine mechanic. One of his sons studied for eight years from nursery through grade 5 (completed in 1992) in the Green School. Later, he joined AMU to become a Unani doctor. Kabir appreciated the Jamaat's welfare orientation. "The Green School is not *kārobārī*. It has sympathy for the community. It also takes care of poor people like us. The principal reduced the fee of my son whenever I requested him to do so."

Afsana's mother, whom we met before, did not share Kabir's view of the Jamaat, however. For her, the Jamaat people were selfish and money-oriented. When I went to meet her at noon, I was told to come back two hours later. I knocked on her door again in the afternoon. Up some dark, narrow, cracked stairs I was taken to a dingy two-room apartment on the first floor. She was beating the scorching heat with a tattered hand fan. Almost drenched in sweat, she apologized for not meeting me on my first visit. They were busy washing clothes. Had I been let in, I would have had to cross the gate of the first room, which was then being used for washing. They did not want to embarrass themselves or me or probably both. After the customary talk, she revealed her story of helplessness and humiliation. Under mounting social pressure to marry off her daughters, she was unable to find grooms for them. Many fathers of probable grooms came to see her daughters, but none of them returned to her house. They appreciated her daughters' beauty, intelligence, and degrees but turned down the marriage proposal. The dilapidated, dingy house, the absence of furniture, and, above all, a gloomy family economy was too unattractive to forge an alliance. Afsana's mother, unlike Kabir's, felt that all Muslim organizations, including the Jamaat, were at best selfish and at worst a fraud. A while later her eldest daughter joined us. With deep poignancy, she said:

> They [the Jamaat] get lots of money from abroad [*bāhar*]. But it circulates only in their closed circle [*band ḥalqa*]. Look at their houses here [the *shahr*] and there [the Civil Line]. If they really cared about the development [*taraqqī*] of Muslims, why did they not act against the AMU vice chancellor? He raised the fees of City Girls High School [in the *shahr*] a few years ago. For poor Muslim girls, it became impossible to study there. They do not think of the welfare of Muslims. They never consider the issue of poor girls marrying. Do they not know that hundreds of girls remain unmarried here? Can there be any sin greater than this?

Among the alumni, 48 percent did not know that their alma mater was a Jamaat school. Those who did know had views similar to those of their parents. Most had barely any knowledge of the Jamaat's ideology, and although some knew it as an organization committed to the welfare of Muslims, others saw it in almost the same fashion as Afsana's mother did.

Moving on from the *shahr* to the Civil Line, we shift our focus in the next chapter from the Jamaat School to its student wing, the SIO. We see how the SIO worked on the AMU campus and the conflict-ridden forms and processes of its moderation.

CHAPTER 4

Mobilizing the Young

> In short, the objective of the Halqa-e-Talba [Islami] . . . is that students strove to establish a truthful system [*niẓām-e-ḥaq*] where . . . leadership and right to rule lay in the hands of pure Muslims [*ṣālehīn*].
>
> —Javed Akhtar, *Ḥalqa-e-ṭalaba islāmī, bihār*

On my arrival in Aligarh, AMU was uneasily quiet. Strong dissent against the US bombing of Afghanistan—dubbed operation "enduring freedom" by the global media—marked the mood. Yet, that mood was not aired publicly. I was told that had the SIMI not been banned, it would have organized a protest march. After the demolition of the Babri mosque in 1992, SIMI organized a protest procession every December to observe the anniversary of the demolition and to demand reconstruction of the mosque. On many occasions, it organized processions against the wish of the AMU administration. Soon after 9/11, and before the Government of India banned it on September 27, the SIMI brought out an anonymous poster calling for jihad. The poster, full of quotations from the Qur'an and *hadīth*, and displaced all over the campus, argued that jihad was obligatory if Muslims came under attack.

The response of the SIO to 9/11 was substantially different. On September 14, it brought out a handwritten poster, two photocopies of which were pasted on the gates of all AMU hostels. Murshid, the secretary of the SIO, AMU unit, told me what the poster was about.

> In the poster, we had condemned the attack on the twin towers in New York. We had called upon the students to also protest against the possible American assault against Afghanistan.
>
> *Did the SIO mean organizing a protest march against America?*
>
> No! What we meant was that students should write letters to newspapers or e-mail them and thus create a public opinion against the possible attack on Afghanistan. We had also planned a public meeting in which we had invited Kuldip Nayyar and Praful Bidwai [both Delhi-based renowned English journalists].

But the day we stuck the posters, the AMU Proctor asked us to remove them.

What could have been the reasons for it?

The Proctor told us that the District administration had taken strong notice of the posters and feared that they might provoke disturbance on the campus.

What did the SIO do?

We immediately removed the posters and also canceled the public meeting.

As you say, there was nothing objectionable in the poster. Why did you remove them?

See, as the student wing of the Jamaat, we are bound to follow the rules. We don't violate the university rules or national laws [*mulkī qavanīn*]. We are against any activity that may cause disorder on earth [*fasād fil arẓ*]. We are against violence [*tashaddud*]. Islam prohibits it. We believe that we could bring about a change by molding opinion in favor of our demands.

As the conversation with Murshid illustrates, the SIO did not call for jihad. Nor did it go against the AMU administration. In the first part of this chapter I discuss how, unlike the SIMI, the SIO pursued the path of persuasion, exemplified in its adherence to university rules as well as public laws, rather than confrontation to stop what it regarded as immoral practices, such as dance and cyber pornography. The SIO's persuasive approach was also evident in its response to Hindutva. In contrast to the SIMI, the SIO presented Islam and the Prophet Muhammad as symbols of love and peace, which is the subject of the second section of the chapter. In the third section I show that its daily activities have departed from the Jamaat's pre-Partition agenda. Not only has the SIO embraced secularism, but it now invokes secularism to ground its claims and formulate its response to the Babri mosque demolition and the government's decision to bring AMU under the ambit of the centralized Common Admission Test (CAT) for admission to professional courses.

Based on the case studies of the two SIO members, in the final section I describe their contesting worldviews, even though they professed the same ideology. I demonstrate that the diversity of their habitus, educational capital, network of interactions, and personal aspirations shaped their worldviews. On this point I engage with some important theorists of social movements, including Luker, Snow and Benford, and Tilly to deepen our understanding of the interrelationship between ideology, or "frame alignment" and the movement activists. In contrast to theorists of framing who hold that activists within a movement have uniform and coherent worldviews, I show that, in fact, their worldviews are markedly different.[1]

The SIO: A World of Its Own

The SIO was a tiny world within the larger, diverse world of AMU, as well as within the entire nation. In 2001 it had little more than three thousand members nationwide (see appendix 2). Of the twenty-eight thousand students at AMU,[2] around ten thousand boys resided in twelve of its hostels,[3] and only twenty-eight were SIO members and fifty were associates. "Members" were fully committed to the SIO, whereas "associates" broadly agreed with the SIO Constitution. Members and associates were Muslims. Another level of affiliation was exclusively for non-Muslims "willing to practically cooperate" with the SIO (*TYP*:2). They were called "sympathizers." However, the SIO had no sympathizers, even though no fewer than five thousand students were non-Muslims.[4] Although the SIO also had a national wing for women students, the Girls Islamic Organization (GIO), it did not exist at AMU as it had no woman members. This was significant because more than six thousand students at AMU were women (and more than four thousand of them stayed in hostels). Whereas in the faculties of professional courses women and men studied together right from the graduation level, in the faculties of Arts and Social Sciences coeducation was permitted only from the master's level. Before their graduation degrees, women studied in colleges for women only. Further, women had three hostels separate from men's, carefully guarded.

Table 1
Number of Members and Associates of SIO, AMU Unit, 1997 to 2002

Year	*Members*	*Associates*
2002	28	50
2001	32	50
2000	25	75
1999	20	100
1998	15	150
1997	13	200*

Source: SIO Office, AMU Unit.

* In 1997 the SIO launched a special drive to recruit associates.

Why did the SIO have such a low membership? From its inception in 1976 until the early 1990s, the SIMI monopolized the space for Islamist politics on the AMU campus. AMU was the birthplace of the SIMI and it was headquartered there until 1982. From the mid-1990s on, as it was becoming involved in national politics (see chapter 6), its hold on the campus loosened. It was then that the SIO intensified its activism. Yet, because of its religious restrictions its membership did not exceed forty. Its members were obliged to adhere to Islam, praying five times daily, fasting, and abstaining from "major sins" like watching films. Furthermore, as an organization born in 1982 the SIO was still in the making. Until 1995 it did not even have an office. The office of the AMU unit was housed inside the mosque of the Habib hostel. An almirah with books and office papers placed inside the mosque worked as the SIO office.

Of the twenty-eight members, all but two were from the states of UP and Bihar. The two non-northern Indian members were from the same family in Kerala and had been educated in Jamaat schools in Kerala. Two other members had been educated in Jamaat schools in Darbhanga and Rampur. More than half the remaining members had previously studied at the Jamaat madrasa in Azamgarh, Falāḥ. Most members were urban. The few who came from villages were from families living both in villages and towns. Every member's father was educated. Some were teachers, some lower-grade government servants, and some were small businessmen.

As the pre-AMU affiliations of the SIO members show, most were educated in Jamaat schools or madrasas. Thus the fathers or relatives of most SIO members were connected to the Jamaat as members or workers. As for their disciplinary affiliation, five were in Unani medicine, and one each in social work, sociology, communicative English, and architecture. Only one member was in the faculty of engineering. The rest studied Urdu literature, Islamic Studies, and Arabic literature, mostly the latter two.

The members were required to work for the objectives of the SIO's Constitution. On average, if an associate attended three SIO schools, a weeklong training camp, and the leadership felt satisfied with his performance, he would be granted membership after filling out an obligatory form. The form entailed taking a written oath: "With full consciousness and sense of responsibility and in the presence of Allah, I pledge to abide by its [SIO's] Constitution and discipline of the Organization." The oath was renewed orally every year. Any Indian citizen under the age of thirty could become a member if he committed himself to Articles 4, 5, and 6 of the SIO Constitution. Article 4 stated the SIO mission as "the reconstruction of society in the light of the Divine Guidance." To this end, the SIO would work to prepare students for leading their "individual and collective lives in accordance with the Qur'an and sunna" and mobilize them for "promoting Virtues (Maʿruf) and uprooting Evils (Munkar)," present-

Figure 4. Signboard of the SIO's office at Shamshad Market Aligarh Muslim University, Aligarh. Photo by the author.

ing "Islamic Da'wah before students and youth" and thereby make them "useful for the Islamic Movement" (*Constitution of SIO* undated:5–6). Article 5 stated that the SIO would adopt "peaceful . . . lawful means of educating, persuading . . . propagating and shall abstain from all acts . . . which may result into communal hatred, class struggle or Fasad-fil-Ardh (Mischief on the Earth)" (ibid.:6). Article 6 obligated members to be "regular in prayer and fasting, observing other religious obligations and abstain[ing] from Kabai'r (Major Sins)" (ibid.:7). According to the SIO president at AMU, Jalal, major sins included watching films either in cinema halls or on TV in the common room of hostels. Watching TV news was allowed. During my fieldwork, two members were expelled because they stayed in the common room after the news bulletin to watch films and songs. Heterosexual relations outside marriage was a major sin, and, as Jalal told me, even talking to women on campus was a major sin unless there was "a dire need" for the conversation and it did not take place "in seclusion [*ḳhilvat*]."

The SIO's activities were either *maʿmulātī* (routine) or *hangāmī* (special). Routine activities were held weekly, except during vacations or exam times, and were localized and organized at the level of hostels. They included the weekly *dars-e-Qur'an*—the Qur'anic lesson—held in the hostel mosques soon after the evening (*maġhrib*) prayer. Each day of the week was allocated for a given hostel. Because twelve hostels were for men, on a given day more than one Qur'anic lesson at a time could be held in more than one hostel. Appointed *ẕimmedār* (in charge) conducted the Qur'anic lesson. Generally the responsibility was given to a member of the hostel where the Qur'anic lesson took place in its mosque. If there was no member in that hostel, the responsibility for the lessons went to an associate. The lessons were open to all, whether a member or not.

After the *farẕ* (obligatory) prayer was over, the *ẕimmedār* of the hostel, usually standing in the first row right behind the Imam, stood up to announce the lesson. Often the name of the guest speaker, usually a former senior member of the SIO or a Jamaat leader, was mentioned, and certainly mentioned if he had great stature. Roughly five minutes after the *farẕ* prayer, the *ẕimmedār* invited the speaker to begin the lesson. In lotus position, the speaker sat on the prayer mat. The student audience sat in a semicircle facing the speaker. The speaker first read out a passage in Arabic from the Qur'an, which was placed on a wooden lectern in the front, and then interpreted it in Urdu, referring to current affairs—local, national, or international. The copy of the Qur'an used in the lesson was invariably Maududi's abridged translation published by Markazi Maktaba Islami, the publishing house of the Jamaat. Only once did I see someone else's translation used. The lesson often continued for half an hour or so. At the end, the *ẕimmedār* invited the audience to ask questions, but only three or four questions were allowed. Controversial questions were avoided. After the question session, the *ẕimmedār* asked for the *duʿā*, which the guest speaker led. The *duʿā* marked the end of the Qur'anic lesson.

Another routine weekly activity was the *eḥtesāb ijtimāʿ* (EI), or assessment meeting (also called "cadres' meet"), which, unlike the Qur'anic lesson, was for members only. Even SIO associates could not participate. Every Sunday morning the SIO members assembled to assess if and to what extent their behavior was in line with sharia. Each member was supposed to confess if he did anything un-Islamic. The assessment covered the observance of the fundamentals of Islam, such as prayer, fasting, and abstaining from major sins. If someone was found violating sharia, the EI would urge him to rectify his deeds. If he was found transgressing sharia more than thrice, he would be warned. Failure to comply with the warning might lead to expulsion from the SIO.

Unlike the routine, the special activities were irregular and were held as part of the SIO's nationwide campaign, *muhim*, usually a weeklong program. In the past it had organized, for instance, "Eliminate Evil Week," "Educational Awareness Week," and "Anti-Drug Week." These campaigns, organized at the university rather than the hostel level, could also include activities specific to the AMU's calendar, such as those designed to assist prospective students who came to Aligarh to write their entrance exams.

They also included programs to respond to unanticipated situations, such as raising funds for the victims of riots that broke out in Gujarat in February 2002. During the first phase of my fieldwork four such special programs were scheduled, though not all were implemented. They included *Dawat* week (January 16–23), coaching classes for AMU applicants (April 20 to June), assistants to help examinees who were newcomers to AMU (in June), "Students' Solidarity for a Better India" campaign (August 7–15), and the fund raising for the Gujarat riot victims.

As the description of its activities demonstrate, the SIO did not participate in overtly political practices. Its activism was limited to routine activities like the Qur'anic lesson, and only occasionally did it respond to issues such as the Gujarat riots. One of the SIO members from Kerala, where the SIO participated in political issues, told me that on the AMU campus it worked like the Tablīghī Jamaat, which was known for its indifference to politics.

Love and Persuasion All the Way

Unlike the SIMI, which called for jihad (see chapter 6), the SIO pursued a path of persuasion exemplified in the SIO's adherence to public laws. It did not adopt a confrontational approach either to the challenges of Hindutva or what it regarded as acts of immorality. The SIO's persuasive approach is best illustrated in its symbolization of Islam as a religion of love and compassion. This is shown most notably in the SIO's response to the Gujarat riots and in its efforts to stop "evil [*munkar*]" and "immorality," such as dance parties and cyber pornography, on the AMU campus.

Love, Not Jihad

In February 2002, at winter's end, India began to burn in the flames of riot in Gujarat. In one estimate, at least one thousand people were killed, most of them Muslims. What the American attack on Afghanistan could not do, the Gujarat riot did. It galvanized AMU into action. Meetings were held, street plays staged, and press releases issued, all speaking out against the riots. In April the AMU Teachers' Association organized a convention with intellectuals from Delhi participating. The Leftist students—previously with the All-India Students Federation (AISF), the Student Federation of India (SFI), and the All-India Student Association (AISA)[5]—working under the banner of Students against Discrimination and Alienation (SADA), staged several street plays against the communal violence. Apart from collecting funds for the riot victims, the SIO held no meetings. It continued with its Qur'anic lessons, in which riots did not figure. In what follows, I dwell on a contentious Qur'anic lesson where an audience raised the issue of riots and urged the SIO speaker to call for revenge against the rioters. The SIO's response stressed the spreading of love and compassion—the real Islam.

The Qur'anic lesson took place in the newest hostel (with a capacity for 330 students), Nadim Tarin, located in the midst of Sir Syed Colony. Unlike other hostels, Nadim Tarin did not have any SIO members or associates; thus no Qur'anic lesson had previously been held there. When Musarrat, an SIO associate and graduate of the Jamaat school in Darbhanga, Bihar, was admitted to the hostel, the Qur'anic lesson had begun. However, he had faced resistance from the Tablīghī activists who, considering the hostel as their bastion (*gaṛh*), did not allow SIO meetings to take place. As Musarrat told me, they considered the SIO a worldly (*dunyavī*) party, not a religious (*mazhabī*) one. Musarrat took it as a challenge to establish the SIO there. In the first few meetings he organized, only a handful of students turned up, mostly his friends. He organized more Qur'anic lessons but still there were few participants. The low attendance at the lessons, he realized, was because students found it uninteresting. "Students had become bored [*chāt gayē thē*] with the Qur'anic lesson," he felt. So he organized a lecture by Mubarak, a young Jamaat leader from Siddharthnagar (UP), who had come to Aligarh for his personal work. When he asked Mubarak to give the lecture, Mubarak told him, "See, I want a rush in my program. Mobilize as many students as you can." The theme of his talk was "Islamic education."

To Musarrat, the program was a challenge. It was a question of the SIO's establishment in the hostel and, perhaps no less, his own identity. He was also obliged to fulfill the wish of his guest who wanted a "rush" in his program. Musarrat made posters in English and put them up all over the campus. An hour before the evening prayer he went door to door to invite each student to the lecture. He specifically told the students that this time there was a "lecture," not a Qur'anic lesson. Thirty students remained after the prayer to attend the lecture. I was one of them.

After the prayer Mubarak spoke on Islamic education for half an hour. He criticized the Westernized Indian educational systems as "immoral," for it produced "dishonest, corrupt, and criminal" individuals. He enumerated the names of Harshad Mehta and the former prime minister PV Narasimha Rao, both of whom were involved in financial frauds. In contrast, Mubarak argued, Islamic education produced honest, kind, and morally sound individuals. After the lecture Musarrat invited questions. A middle-aged man from the audience, the guardian of one of the residents, remarked that he had heard enough of such lectures. He asked Mubarak to suggest "action" at a time when Muslims were being "massacred in Gujarat and elsewhere." "Will your lecture recover the lives of those killed?" he asked. Without waiting for the response, he suggested that "Muslims must jump into the field with arms to defend themselves and revenge the killing of fellow Muslims." A composed Mubarak listened to him patiently and said that the answer to his question was implicit in his lecture. On hearing this, he grew angry and said that Mubarak had not answered it at all.

Mubarak argued that what the audience member suggested was not correct Islam. He lectured for ten minutes to say that his suggestion went against the Qur'an and the Prophet Muhammad. The Prophet conducted *daʿwat* (propagation) of Islam. He invited non-Muslims to Islam. They tortured him, threw garbage on his face, Mubarak went on, and yet he did not seek revenge. Indeed, he approached them with love. In India, too, he stressed, Muslims must follow Muhammad and do *dāwat*. As followers of Muhammad, who was "the mercy to humanity [*raḥmatul lil ʿālamīn*]," he urged Muslims to "knock on the door of every Hindu" to tell him that Islam stood for love and compassion and that Muslims were not their enemies. Had Muslims done this job before, he said, a situation like that in Gujarat would not have arisen. After Mubarak's long reply, a student raised his hand to ask a question, but Mubarak gestured to Musarrat to end the program.

Muhammad: The Truthful, the Trustworthy

There were no Hindu students in Mubarak's program. The Nadim Tarin hostel had only a few Hindu students, and probably they were neither invited nor came on their own. However, the SIO's model of Islam as a religion of love and compassion was also extended to the Hindu students at AMU. In August the SIO organized a nationwide campaign, "Students Solidarity for a Better India." It was also launched with much enthusiasm at AMU. The SIO national president Rahat Khamni, from Delhi, came to address the students. The objective of the campaign was to invite non-Muslims to Islam, "*daʿvat*." To this end, three meetings were held in the Habib, Iqbal, and Hadi Hasan hostels.

At the meeting in the Iqbal hostel Khamni questioned the portrayal of Islam as a violent religion by both the Western and Indian media. Khamni viewed Fukuyama's celebration of capitalism as bereft of moral principles, and he exhorted the audience to present Islam to both Muslims and non-Muslims as a morally and spiritually superior religion. He stressed the "molding of public opinion" and "mental change [*z̤ehnī tabdīlī*]" in favor of Islam. AMU should lead the Muslim community, he opined, in spreading this message of love and peace.

The meetings in the Habib and Iqbal hostels, with a total of 925 and 781 residents, respectively) were unsuccessful. Barring the SIO members, no more than 40 residents participated. The SIO leaders thus invested their full energy to make their last meeting a success. The campaign was to culminate at the Hadi Hasan hostel—meant for medical students, almost half the residents of the hostel were Hindus. Almost half the students in professional courses like medicine were Hindus (see note 4). The SIO activists went to the rooms of all the Hindu students to invite them to the meeting. Students not in their rooms would find a written invitation on their return. Only three Hindu students came to the meeting. The remaining thirty or so students in the audience were Muslims (the total number of residents were 420). The meeting took place in the common room rather than in the hostel mosque.

Notwithstanding the low turnout of Hindus, the speaker for the meeting, Shahab Jauhar, a lecturer of unani medicine at AMU, said that he would still speak assuming that the audience was non-Muslim. Speaking in fuent English, he stressed the need for "remoralization" of the youth. He began by saying that the modern age started with two slogans: "the human decency of the French Revolution" and the "the progress of the Industrial Revolution." In the last two centuries, however, those slogans had bred only violence and barbarism. He cited the examples of the thousands of deaths in Iraq as a result of the American sanctions and also pointed to the killings in Gujarat. These actions, he said, occurred because America and the rioters were without morality, and hence his call for remoralization. He argued that the Prophet Muhammad was the most shining embodiment of morality, as he continued to invite the infidels and polytheists to Islam even though they tortured him. Jauhar said that the Prophet did not discriminate against people on religious grounds but approached them all with love and affection because he was the "benefactor to all humanity." He urged the audience to read the biography of Muhammad and rationally decide whether his message was relevant.

When the students exited the common room after the lecture, an SIO activist gave everyone a kit of folders, pamphlets, and a small English booklet. The author of the booklet, "Muhammad, the Prophet of Islam," was K. S. Ramakrishna Rao, a "professing Hindu" and Professor Emeritus of philosophy at the University of Mysore. Full of favorable quotations from Bernard Shaw and Thomas Carlyle, much like Jauhar, Rao's booklet highlighted the moral qualities of Muhammad. At the conquest of Mecca, when Muhammed was at the pinnacle of his power, Rao wrote, he could have easily taken revenge against his enemies who had brutally tortured him, but he forgave them because his heart was filled with "the milk of love and kindness" (undated: 6). To Rao, most extraordinary in the biography was that Muhammad was "the trustworthy" and "the truthful."

Belief in Persuasion

The SIO's portrayal of Islam as the epitome of morality and a symbol of love went together with its call for persuasion. As both Murshid and Khamni stressed, molding public opinion was the main agency of persuasion through the SIO sought to stop what it deemed as acts of "immorality" on the campus. This is illustrated by its response to a dance party and its mobilization to stop cyber immorality.

Every year before final exams began, various departments organized farewell parties that began after sunset and went on until about 10:00 P.M. Most such parties that I observed during my fieldword were organized in the faculties of sciences. Given the occasion, girls wore saris, even jeans (*shalvār-qamīz* being the acceptable dress). On February 14, for example, the department of electrical engineering organized a party at which boys and girls danced to Western music. On the day the MBA department held its farewell party, the SIO acting president instructed one of his comrades, Sahir, a graduate of Falāḥ, to request that the proctor stop the party. The proctor showed no interest in stopping what Sahir took to be "obscenity [*faḥāshī*]." Thereupon Sahir approached the organizers of the party, who told him that they would not have organized it had the SIO informed them in advance. When I asked Sahir what he found objectionable, he said:

> Don't you know that dance and music [*nāchnā gānā*] are against Islam? These people openly dance and women wear un-Islamic dress like jeans. They play English [Western] music, that too so loud. What impact such a party would have on the new students? It would destroy the Islamic culture of the university. . . . Even Muslim girls wear jeans and dance there.

Sahir told me that even though women and men danced separately, dance itself was un-Islamic. More horrifying to Sahir was that the party went on till midnight. "You do not know what might have happened between them [boys and girls]." When I asked him how he knew about the timing, he told me that he saw it with his "own bare eyes." Immediately he corrected himself to say that actually one of his friends later informed him (see below).

The persuasive model of the SIO described above was also evident in its mobilization to stop cyber immorality. With the Internet revolution, Aligarh saw a mushrooming of Internet cafés, especially on the Medical and Anupshahar Roads, which ran parallel to the university campus on either side. Most of the cafés were open until midnight, and some were open as late as 2:00 A.M. and played Western music. Invariably all visitors to the cafés were residents of men's hostels. An important reason for the success of those cafés was that students came to chat with women from other countries. Most preferred chatting with Western white women or Indian women who had settled abroad. Visiting pornographic sites was another activity that took place inside the wooden cubes of the cafés, especially late at night. To attract customers on the eve of Valentine's Day, many cafés had advertised fabulous offers. A café on the Medical Road reduced the price from 25 Rupees (less than half a Euro) an hour to 15 Rs, and also provided free coffee. The success of the Internet cafés worried the SIO, because they made the majority of what Jalal, the SIO president at AMU, called "already irreligious" students more irreligious and drove them to "obscenity." To stop them, the SIO organized a tea party with the café owners, all of whom were Muslim. Invoking Muslim culture (*tahzīb*), the SIO leaders persuaded the café owners to block all pornographic sites to save Muslim *tahzīb* from degenerating into immorality. Although the owners agreed in principle with the SIO's concerns, most of them made no efforts to block pornographic sites.

Call for "True" Secularism

Let us now examine the SIO's stand on two important issues: the demolition of the Babri mosque and the central government's move to bring AMU within the ambit of the national entrance test. On both issues SIO's position departed from the Jamaat's pre-Partition ideology. The SIO began to accept, rather embrace, secularism. The demolition of the Babri mosque was, in the SIO's reading, indeed the demolition of Indian secularism. To introduce a national test for admission to AMU was also a breach of secularism, because the SIO believed that in a single stroke, it would undermine the minority character of AMU. The SIO therefore invoked "true" secularism to make its claims about the Babri mosque as well as AMU.

"Demolition of Indian Secularism"

Unlike SIMI, the SIO, on the anniversary of the Babri mosque demolition, did not organize a procession against the demolition or have any public meetings. During my second fieldwork trip, I saw *The Message*, the monthly wall magazine of the SIO, posted at key public places on the campus. Published in English and comprising two pages, *The Message* did not appear regularly. The special December 2003 issue, titled the "Babri Masjid Special," had four pages and its cover carried the photograph of the Babri mosque with three domes.

THE MESSAGE Monthly

BABRI MASJID SPECIAL 1st Dec. – 30th Dec., 2003

Editorial

Controversy of Babri Mosque

For many years, a furious agitation has been organized in this country under Ram Janambhumi-Babri Masjid dispute. The Babri Mosque issue is central to understanding the Hindus militant revivalism and militancy that has left thousand dead in the last 50 year. Babri Msjid has been a source of Hindu extremist mobilization for the last 20 years.

Babri Masjid was a three dome mosque structure in Ayodhya which was built in 1528 by Babar. He is the founder of the Mugal empire which ruled the India for the early 16th to the mid 18th century.

Some fascist claim that the Babri Masjid was built where the Ramjanmabhoomi Temple was located. In 1885, some Hindus field a claim in the country's. British colonial courts that this mosque had been forcibly built by Muslims after demolishing a Hindus temple built on the birth site of their Lord Rama. There request for restoration was denied by the court on the ground that the plaintiff had been unable to substantiate the claim.

But the battle was not yet over, even after India's independence, in 1949, few Hindus entered Babri Masjid at night and installed a deity there... police picket of fifteen persons was on duty at night but did not apparently act.

However, instead of removing the deity and restoring the mosque to its custodians, it was locked. Besides an official receiver, a Hindu, and a priest (also Hindu) were appointed to look after the place. Muslims, filed suit in the court where it is lying still.

Moreover, in December 1985, a Hindu delegation called on the state of Uttar Pradesh's chief Minister, serving him notice that the temple must be handed over to them by March 8, 1986, otherwise they would forcibly occupy it. On February 11, 1986, the Faizabad district opened so as to let the Hindus exercise their "constitutional right" worship. In 1989, the VHP started a country wide movement for collection of consecrated bricks (Ram Shilas) in Ayodhya from all over the country. In 1990 the Rath yatra started from Somnath to Ayodhya to win the support for building temple.

Up to the movement the situation was tense, but no major violence had yet erupted. This was on 6 December 1992, when thousands of Hindu militants, mobilized by Vishwa Hindu Parishad (VHP), and lead by Mr. L.K.Advani and many others stormed Babri Masjid and demolished it. This sparked serious protests by Muslims, police firings, and then Hindu-Muslim riots. Thousand lost their lives in the violence. After the disgraceful demolition of the Babri Mosque, just some months back the Supreme Court ordered for the excavation of the site, que or the Hindu Temple exists there before the construction of Mosuqe in 1528.

Perspective

Demolition of Indian Secularism

This is in reference to the demolition of Babri mosque, the "Demolition of Indian Secularism". December 6th is an ominous day. Exactly 11 years back the world looked the other way as a democracy of millions allowed a few thousand to demolish its most prized possession; a pluralistic and tolerant ethos.

Not a single unit of the country's might military force was called (unlike the prelude of Akshardam temple attack for the safety of which the National commandos were ordered to do or die), no special commandos were rushed to the spot and no effective resistance offered by the police forces present as a group of vandals, encouraged on by their Hindutva-fascist demagagues that include the top officials like L.K.Advani, M.M.Joshi, Umma Bharti and others who pulled down the historic four hundred and fifty years old imposing Babri mosque with axes and scthes in broad daylight.

Dome by dome and wall by wall, Indian secularism was hammered upon until it was nothing but rubble. Each brick was then assiduously removed – some taken home as souvenirs as if the perpetrators or criminals feared that the centuries old pluralistic tradition might somehow arise out of the rubble and stake its claim again.

Just after a day of the demolition of the mosque, the then Prime Minister, Mr. Narasimha Rao, in a nationally televised speech on Dec 7, 1992, made a solemn pledge to the nation, and the whole world that the government will bring the culprits responsible for the violent confusion and disorder, to book and re-build the Babri mosque to the site where it stood for 450 years. He reaffirmed the commitment later in a statement in the parliament.

However even after the passage of more than a decade, the government has not instituted a single court case against any of the culprits responsible for the demolition of the ancient mosque or the killing of over 2000 muslims. The BJP party and its top leaders who organized the demolition of the Babri mosque and the killing of muslim in several Indian cities in 1992, are today the top ministers of the current government.

Event allover the world prove that peace and progress are not possible without peace among religions, and that may remain a pipe dream as long as we refuse to move from conflictual religiously to cooperative spirituality. Religion without spirituality, as the Ayodhya movement has proved beyond doubt, is ever ready to degenerate into communalism majoritarian communalism is only a small step away from fascism.

Figure 5. The SIO's wall magazine on the demolition of the Babri mosque. From author's collection.

While the editorial of *The Message* offered a historical outline of the controversy, the column "Perspective" on the front page spelled out its position. Titled "Demolition of Indian Secularism," it likened the mosque's demolition to the destruction of "its [India's] most prized possession; a pluralistic and tolerant ethos." Holding the "Hindutva fascist demagogues" responsible for the demolition, the column lamented that "dome by dome and wall by wall Indian secularism was hammered upon until it was nothing but rubble." Another article in the issue poignantly noted that, with the demolition of the mosque, "the dreams of many Gandhis, Nehrus, Azads [Abulkalam] and Amdedkars have been falsified." It is instructive to note that by invoking Gandhi, Nehru, and Azad the SIO departed from the Jamaat's previous ideology. Recall from chapter 2 that after his turn to Islamism Maududi saw Gandhi, Nehru, and Azad as nemeses of what he defined as "true" Islam. Also significant was the act of naming. Unlike the SIMI, the SIO did not call the BJP leaders "polytheists" but instead "fascists," a term that belonged to the vocabulary of the Left.

If, for the SIO, the demolition of the mosque was the demolition of India's secularism, so was the central government's decision to bring AMU into line with the Common Admission Test (CAT). In 2003 the University Grants Commission (UGC), a government body to monitor the universities, and the All-India Council of Technical Education (AICTE) jointly issued an order that instead of conducting separate entrance exams for admission to its professional courses (e.g., engineering, medicine, and management), AMU should became part of the all-India level test—CAT—conducted by the AICTE (*Millī Gazette* 2004 [January 1–15]. The implication was that when AMU used the CAT, the number of Muslim students in professional courses would decline. Before the order, AMU conducted the entrance exam only on the university campus; thus students from distant parts of the country could hardly participate, and, as a result, students from AMU managed to obtain around half the seats in professional courses. Under the proposed CAT, exams would be held throughout India, and the successful candidates would be allocated to different universities, AMU included. Under the CAT, then, non-Muslim would outnumber Muslim students.

Almost the entire AMU community condemned the UGC-AICTE order as an invasion of the "minority" character. Per the AMU (Amendment) Act of 1981, Section 5 (2) (C), passed by the Indian Parliament, the AMU enjoyed the unique power to "promote especially the educational and cultural advancement of the Muslims of India" (in Hamid et al. undated: 1). The SIO was not far behind in condemning the CAT. In the final section of this chapter I show that, although monumental differences existed within the SIO on many issues, there was a consensus regarding the CAT. All the

SIO members I spoke to were against it. The January 2004 issue of *The Message* carried many articles opposing the CAT. The then president of the SIO of AMU called the UGC proposal a "sinister agenda" meant "to destroy our minority character." A forceful article in *The Message*, "UGC: Down! Down!," called on Muslim organizations, intellectuals, and "true secular people and forces" to launch a struggle to revoke the UGC order.

The SIO's call to "secular people and forces" to defend "our minority character" was a departure from the Jamaat ideology pursued before and soon after Partition. Readers will recall from chapter 2 that Maududi described secularism as *haram* and urged Indian leaders after Partition to install a Hindu and not a secular state. I also described the sheer hostility Maududi nursed toward AMU and the Muslim Western colleges that he called "slaughterhouse[s]." I also discussed how the students under Maududi's influence boycotted AMU. Given this position, by rule the Jamaat forbade its members, as late as 1957, to study at AMU. Why, then, was the SIO defending the "minority" character of this "slaughterhouse," AMU?

The Character of AMU

In chapter 7 I discuss the larger sociopolitical context that triggered the change in the Jamaat's ideology. Here I only note that, because of the Jamaat's opposition to secular democracy and its boycott of the first two elections to the Assembly and Parliament, it began to lose credibility among Muslims. During the first ten years after Partition it did not even share a dais with other Muslim organizations, because they believed in the "kalima of secularism" rather than that of Allah. The Jamaat thus felt isolated from the Muslim community. To overcome the isolation, in 1964 it became part of the confederation of Muslim organizations, the Muslim Majlis Mushāverat. And for the first time, in 1965, it passed a resolution to defend the "Muslim character" of AMU (RMS-1:250–64). It is worthwhile spending some time to see why the Jamaat did so.

In 1965, during a fracas on the AMU campus, the Vice Chancellor was assaulted. The immediate precipitant of the disturbance was a proposal, somewhat similar to that of 2003, to slash the percentage of admission to science faculties reserved for students with degrees from AMU from 75 to 50 percent. Muslims took the proposal as a threat, as it would lower the percentage of Muslim students in science faculties. In the wake of the fracas led by "communal and reactionary elements," M. C. Chagla, a self-declared "convinced secularist" Muslim from Bombay and at the time the education minister, passed an ordinance that almost disempowered the AMU Court, the AMU's most powerful decision-making body, and instead concentrated authority in the office of the Vice Chancellor and the

Executive Council whose members the University's Visitor, the President of India, had nominated. Put differently, Chagla's aim was to "secularize" AMU by changing the predominantly Muslim composition of the Executive Council; the government also wanted to secularize Banaras Hindu University (BHU), which was regarded as a counterpart of AMU, or vice versa, by deleting the word "Hindu" from its name.[6] For Muslims, the government move was a frontal attack on AMU's "Muslim character." Throughout North India, Muslims launched a protest against the government's decision (Brass 1994; Graff 1990; Wright Jr. 1966).

The Jamaat realized that if it did not support Muslims on that issue, it would stand discredited. Much like its participation in the Mushāverat, the resolution to defend the Muslim character of AMU, otherwise a slaughterhouse in earlier days, was also for fear of being further isolated from the Muslim masses and their leaders. There was also mounting pressure from within. Jamaat members and sympathizers were extremely keen to study at AMU. The 1960s thus saw the Jamaat not only defending AMU but also allowing its members to study there. In 1964 *Radiance* 1964 [June 14], the English organ of the Jamaat, published a notice about admission to AMU.

In 1972 the central government passed the Amendment Act, which extended the changes made in 1965 with the aim of further undermining the "minority character" of AMU. A widespread protest against the Act ensued as Muslims saw the Act as a threat to their community identity (Graff 1990). The Jamaat went a step further to argue that the 1972 Act was not a "communal [i.e., Muslim] issue," and to call on Muslims to be prepared for a long struggle not only for their rights but also for the "secular democratic character of the country" (*RMS*-2:77). The SIO's defense of AMU was a replay of the ideological mutation that the Jamaat had begun to undergo since the 1960s.

One Vision, Many Versions

Shifting from the public activities of the SIO, in the final section, I discuss the divergent worldviews of its members in their personal domains. Even though the SIO members belonged to the same organization and professed the same ideology, a marked difference is found in their worldviews on certain key issues. Their divergent and contesting worldviews is illustrated by a case study of two of its activists. First, a word on why (and if) this theme is significant.

Social movement activists, it is argued, share a common ideology or worldview, and it is this shared cognitive "frame," so the argument goes, that drives them to join the particular movement. Sometimes this shared understanding is developed once individuals join the movement. The participants of a movement thus perceive the world in an identical fashion. Known as a "framing process" (Benford and Snow 2000) or "frame alignment," its proponents have made this point most authoritatively. Snow et al. (1983:464) define "frame alignment" as a linkage whereby the interests, values, and beliefs of the activists get 'congruent' and 'complementary' to the goals and ideology of the organization they belong to. Endorsing this line of argument, Kristin Luker, in her study of pro- and anti- abortion movements in the U.S., concludes that the activists on either side of the debate held a unified worldview:

> In . . . interviews, it became apparent that each side of the abortion debate has an *internally coherent* and *mutually shared* view of the world that is tacit, never fully articulated, and most importantly, completely at odds with the worldview held by their opponents. (Luker 1984:159; my emphasis)

Such an approach animates social movement studies in general. Differentiating an electoral campaign from a social movement, Tilly (2002:88) argues that the latter pays off in the relay of the message that its activists are WUNC—worthy, unified, numerous, and committed. Similarly Bayat (1998:140) suggests that the difference between a movement and an insurrectionary action is that the former has "clarity" whereas the latter has "ambiguity."

I find problematic the idea that activists in a movement have unified and congruent worldviews. Such an approach assumes that activists are cognitively homogeneous regardless of their varied social locations and cultural capital. My view is that because society—Indian or otherwise—itself is differentiated by and divided along multiple lines of class, status, interests, ideology, occupation, and social and cultural capital, these differences are also reflected in the movement and its organization, no matter how cohesive and unified it may portray itself. A movement claiming to be unified does not stand outside the impure, divided society that it seeks to transform. This is not to devalue the apparent consensus among activists but to argue that even the consensus is based on contestation—now silent, now eloquent.

I became aware of the multiple worldviews of the SIO activists as my interaction with them grew. Certainly some shared views that brought them to the SIO. There is no uniform understanding, however, of those views. Moreover, the views were not static but in flux. Each member made sense of the world based on his social background, the kind of network he interacted with, the ideals he cherished, and his cultural and social capital.

Following Maududi

Of all the SIO members, Jalal, aged twenty-nine and a native of a village in the Saharsa district of Bihar, stood out as distinct in several respects. His beard was one. Though the SIO members were allowed to have a trimmed moustache and short beard, he was one of only two members with an untrimmed beard. He never wore trousers and a shirt but was always in a *shervānī* (a long gown-like upper dress symbolic of the traditional elites), and an Islamic cap. His flowing beard and *sherwani* made him look like a *maulānā* (cleric). Indeed he was known as a cleric inside as well as outside the SIO. He himself added *maulānā* as a prefix to his name. The son of a middle-school pass out and a rich *anṣārī* farmer, Jalal's early education was in the village madrasa. He then moved to another madrasa in the Darbhanga district, where he completed his more advanced studies. He then went on to do his master's in Urdu literature at Mithila University, where he learned about the Jamaat from his maternal uncle who was an SIO leader. The uncle took him to some SIO meetings, but later Jalal did not continue to attend them and felt no urge to join the SIO. From Darbhanga he moved to the Deoband madrasa to take a one-year course on *hadīth*, "*daura-e-hadīth*," and there he developed an urge to know "pure Islam [*ḳhāliṣ islām*]." A friend advised him to read Maududi, and in those books he found the pure Islam he had been seeking. Reading *Dawat*, the bi-weekly Jamaat Urdu organ, aided his quest for a pure Islam. By the time Jalal finished the course on *hadīth*, he had come under Maududi's spell and has remained so since then. He told me that during much of Islamic history (*dūr tak*), he found no other scholar who matched Maududi's genius.

On returning to his village Jalal preached Maududi's Islam, and he started organizing the youth and holding meetings in the mosque. He criticized the prevalent beliefs and practices of the villagers, most of whom had not even heard of Maududi, but the villagers opposed his newfound Puritanism. Meanwhile, he had met SIO leaders through his uncle. His friends in the SIO, seeing his disappointment with the villagers' opposition, advised him to go to Aligarh to work with the Jamaat's research institute, the Idāra-e-taḥqīq-o-tasnīf-e-Islāmi (ITTI), the Institute for Research and Publications on Islam. In 1997 he joined the ITTI to work on education in Islam. A year later he entered a Ph.D. program in Urdu. The topic of his dissertation was the Urdu travelogues on Hajj. In Aligarh he joined the SIO.

Jalal's research findings were published in a series of articles in an Islamist journal,[7] where he argued against the distinction between religious and secular education. However, knowledge that fostered doubt about God was *jāhiliyat*. Knowledge was Islamic only if it reinforced the belief in Allah, the Prophet Muhammad, and the afterlife. Thus even a Nobel Laureate of physics was ignorant (*jāhil*) if he did not believe in those three tenets. The objective of education, he wrote, was help the individual recognize Allah and to worship Him. To worship was to strive to establish a caliphate. That was the real meaning of worship in the golden age of Islam. But with the passage of time, he declared, when decline set in among Muslims, the real meaning was lost and worship became ritualistic and narrowly construed as the mere offering of prayers.

Like Maududi, Jalal saw human history as a continual battle between Islam and *jāhiliyat*. As a system of life, Islam was opposed to all other systems based on *jāhiliyat*, old or new. *Jāhiliyat* had been resurfacing in every age, though under a different garb. In its earliest golden era, Islam battled against the *jāhiliyat* of idolatry. In the current age, Jalal said, while addressing the *Students' Solidarity for a Better India* campaign in the Iqbal hostel, it had to fight against *jāhiliyat*'s new incarnations—communism, capitalism, atheistic science, films, and obscenity (*faḥāshī).* In his view, obscenity was a reigning sign of modern *jāhiliyat*, evident, above all, in unveiled women and their freedom. Of all the SIO activists, it was Jalal who was the most concerned that the AMU proctor stop the dance party in the MBA department. Obscenity, for him, was not just bodily but was also literary. The "right" literature (*ṣāleḥ adab*)[8]—was therefore religious and moral. He did not miss any issues of *Peshraft*, an Urdu literary magazine published by the Jamaat to resist the influence of Marxists and promote an alternative Islamic literature. In poetry Iqbal was his ideal—the latter Iqbal who composed poems for the glory of "pure" Islam, not the early Iqbal who sang in praise of Ram, the hero of the Hindu epic *Ramayana*. There has been no great poet in the history of Urdu literature before or after him. Ghalib was a good poet, Jalal admitted, but in his Islamist framework he ranked nowhere near Iqbal.

Given this view of literature, Jalal was not very fond of Urdu stories or novels. Stories dealing with love or sex, where a boy met a girl in a park, were outrageous. Such boy-girl encounters violated sharia and were illegitimate. As president of the SIO, Jalal was opposed to its members meeting girls in seclusion. In the eyes of sharia, an adult man could meet an adult female (if she was veiled) only if there was a dire need for it. Meeting and talking to a girl without this dire need was un-Islamic. Through His laws, Jalal told me, Allah had separated men and women into different worlds. The division was divine and natural. Men were born to rule, women to obey. A Muslim woman could not become head of a state. His opposition to Urdu literature was precisely on the grounds of sharia; most Urdu literature violated the limits of sharia, especially those concerning women. Such literature was obscene (*faḥash*) and sexual (*jinsī*). I saw an issue in his room of *Iste'āra*, an Urdu journal that ran a column,

"Chapter on Body [*bāb-e-badan*]," that was a major topic of discussion in the Urdu circle at the time. In each issue, the columnist, a graduate of Deoband, wrote about a specific part of a woman's body such as the cheek, eye, lip, or eyebrow. He celebrated the body as a site and source of ultimate bliss, but Jalal saw it as pure obscenity and clearly against sharia. He lamented that a madrasa graduate could have spread this obscenity. I asked him if he would remove such literature and the works of Manto and Chughtai (purists called their works "dirty literature") from the syllabi when he became the head of the Urdu department. He replied that he would not because the "system [*niẓām*] would not be Islamic." I then asked him what he would do if the system were Islamic. He replied, without hesitation, that he would "ban" such "dirty literature" and promote "morally right" literature.

Like obscenity in literature, Jalal was also against audio and visual obscenity. Before he joined the SIO, he listened to ghazals and songs. Later on he stopped listening to them, as he regarded music as *haram*. Watching Bollywood films was also against sharia, because they showed only sex and women. His view on films was similar to Maududi's (see chapter 2), and he proudly told me that he did not watch films. Another similarity between them was that, like Maududi, Jalal, before his turn to Islamism, had also watched films during his stay in Darbhanga. To him, watching a film was a major sin.[9] An SIO member who watched a film would be issued a warning, and lack of compliance with the warrant would mean expulsion. He made no distinction between documentary and commercial films. "All are the same," he said, with absolute certainty, an assuredness that also was apparent in his approach to life in general. Seldom was there ambiguity in his responses. Films were not all he abstained from; he rarely joked, and when he did, the jokes were always decent. He also did not laugh freely; at most he only smiled. The nearest figures that he most closely resembled were Calvinist Protestants like Edmund Gosse's parents, who, in late-nineteenth-century Britain, regarded festivals, fiction, smoking, mysticism, humor, and pleasure all as sinful (Gosse 1927).

In the academic complex, Jalal was rarely seen mixing with people. Though president of the SIO, he was not well known, and even in his hostel many of his neighbors did not know him. Friends were few, and all were Muslim. At times he went to lunch in the university canteen. Often he was alone. Only once did I see him with someone, a bearded and *shervānī*-clad student. Jalal preferred to mix only with people like him. It was nearly impossible to engage him in conversation without an un-stated purpose. Once, when I greeted him in the crowded canteen, he dismissively acknowledged me and walked away, fixing his cap. It left me stunned.

Jalal was also secretive. He did not let me meet SIO members independently, even though the Delhi headquarters of the SIO assured me that he had been instructed to do so. He saw to it that I met other members only in his presence. In one meeting with Zamir, an SIO member from Kerala, Jalal remained throughout to supervise our conversation, alhough he did not join in. Jalal could barely speak English, whereas Engligh was the only language that Zamir and I could communicate in. After some twenty minutes Jalal stopped our conversation, although neither Zamir nor I wanted to stop talking. He ordered Zamir to leave. When he found out that I had met some members without his permission, he was irritated and afterward distrusted my intentions. My clarifications that I wanted to know what attracted each member to the SIO did not change his mind. He had one ready-made answer: everyone joined the SIO to serve Islam. I need only have asked, him, and not each member separately. In his words: "I am the president of organization, you should ask me."

Evidently conscious of his power, on many occasions he treated SIO members, especially his juniors, highhandedly, though they seldom took him seriously. He presented himself as a busy and important man, and he would ask me to telephone him at a given time for a meeting. Frequently I would phone only to learn that he was too busy or unavailable to meet. When we would finally meet, he would not apologize but only reassert his presidential stature. He made several promises but kept few, and then only after near begging. Still he never forgot to assert that he had devoted himself to the service of Islam. During my second fieldwork trip, he was somewhat more responsive to me, but he remained reserved, secretive, and boastful of his stature, even though he was no longer the SIO president. He still answered my questions as a teacher would his pupil's. He talked about his personal life only when I asked him about it. In our final meeting that, surprisingly, lasted two hours, he asked me if I could find a job for him teaching Urdu in Holland.

Following Islam

Like Jalal, Jamal was also distinct but in markedly different ways. In his mid-twenties, he was the only clean-shaven SIO member and always dressed in shirt and trousers. Born into a Pathan family in Unnao, UP, his grandfather was a sack carrier and his father, who held a middle school degree, had joined the communist movement in the 1960s. In the 1980s Jamal's father was drawn to Maududi and joined the Jamaat to become one of its leaders in UP. In Jamal's words, his father's dream had shifted from the "red" to the "green." Jamal took his early education in the school his father had established, where there was no Jamaat syllabus. It was a Hindi-language school, where Sanskrit was also taught. Later Jamal matriculated (class 10) from a Hindi-language government school where boys and girls studied together.

Jamal did not know Urdu well, but at Falāḥ he mastered it. He had not chosen to study at Falāḥ; his father sent him there because, as Jamal sarcastically remarked, as a neo-convert to the Jamaat and Islam, his father wanted to secure a place in paradise by giving his son an Islamic education. Jamal did not feel at home there, and criticized his teachers and friends for their "narrow," "orthodox," and "theocratic" views. For example, in a class of *fiqh* (jurisprudence), the teacher instructed the students to follow the Prophet's saying by rolling their pajamas above the ankle, especially during the prayer. Jamal was not convinced of this, and he asked the teacher why God would be displeased just because pajamas were below the ankle. The teacher replied that, since it was a *hadīth*, as a Muslim he must follow the instruction. In another class, a teacher argued that the Qur'an said that women should be under the subordination of men. When Jamal asked for a rationale, the teacher responded that it was a "woman's nature" to be subordinate and remain within the four walls of a home. Jamal argued that there was no such thing as a woman's nature, and that if educated, they could also excel in life. What about women like Razia Sultana (an Indian ruler in the thirteenth century), Rani Laksmi Bai (who fought against the British), and Sarojni Naidu (an anticolonial leader)? Jamal felt that he never received "convincing" and "rational" answers. Though he questioned his teachers, he regarded Maududi as the greatest thinker. "We were taught there to think that, after Allah and the Prophet, Maududi had the highest status and the Jamaat was the only truly Islamic party."

Jamal's rational approach was also reflected in discussions with his father. His father warned that in the utopian Islamic state no opposition party, even an Islamic one, would be allowed. It would be like a communist state. Jamal countered that an Islamic state would be democratic and secular. By "democratic," he meant there would be freedom of thought, because the Qur'an urged its readers to think. Everyone, Muslim or non-Muslim, would be allowed to think freely. The state would also be "secular" in a different sense; it will not discriminate against Muslims on the basis of doctrines, sects, and legal schools of thought. It would be neither Ahl-e-hadīth nor Deobandi nor Barēlvīs; neither Shia nor Sunni. It would be secular. He believed that in its earliest period the Islamic state was secular, and that the West actually borrowed its model of secularism from Islam.

Jamal also became critical of the Jamaat's position on communism. At Falāḥ, his teachers told him that "communism was against Islam" and that it spread "nudity and immorality." He argued this point with a Hindu friend of his father, a communist leader in Unnaon, who suggested that Jamal read the writings of Marx and Engels. On joining AMU (see below), when he had gained knowledge of English, Jamal bought communist literature sold by the Leftist group, SADA. He found nothing in it on "nudity and immorality." Instead, he found a voice against "exploitation" and in favor of a "just" society. With his firsthand knowledge of communism, he began to argue with other SIO activists who mostly thought like his teachers at Falāḥ.

Unlike Jalal, Jamal was familiar with the Jamaat since his childhood, as his entire family was involved with the Jamaat. His sister was married to an SIO leader, and his brother was an SIO activist. Like Jamal, his brother departed from Maududi on some key issues, both believing that a woman could become head of an Islamic state.

Dissatisfied with the ambience at Falāḥ, Jamal applied for admission to AMU to become a doctor of Unani medicine, but he failed the entrance test. Later he gained admission to a bachelor degree program in Communicative English. He chose English to avoid the company of madrasa students, including those from Falāḥ (most madrasa students were in the departments of Arabic, Urdu, and Islamic Studies). He thought the madrasa students were "conservative" and averse to reading non-Jamaat literature; they also did not speak English. Many of Jamal's friends were from countries like Oman, Yemen, Indonesia, and Thailand, and he communicated with them in English. Once, late at night, I met him in the famous Aligarh *numā'ish* (exhibition) with his Omani friends; he was wearing a Western gown and a hat. His interaction with SIO members was thin.

Jamal dreamed of studying for his masters in sociology at the Delhi-based Jawaharlal Nehru University (JNU), a leftist university. He liked its culture of debate and activism, and he was impressed by a report in the *Hindu* that some JNU students had gone to a slum to celebrate India's Independence Day. Even if they did it just for show, he said, it was better than the AMU and SIO students who were not engaged at all in political or social activism. Jamal wanted to orient knowledge to activism, and so he attended meetings of the leftist organization SADA; many of its members, both Muslim and Hindu, were his friends. He was also associated with the Human Rights Forum (HRF), a university-based group that visited jails to observe whether prisoners were treated well by the authorities.

The SIO leadership had an ambiguous attitude toward Jamal. Although the leaders appreciated his academic excellence and knowledge of English—he was far brighter than most members—they were also embarrassed by his nonconformist attitude. An SIO member told me, grudgingly, that Jamal did not grow a beard. When Jamal was asked to give the Qur'anic lesson, he refused, shyly saying that he did not have a beard. The leadership tried to persuade him to grow one, but he refused.

Jamal's opinion was that Islam is not about appearances but about thought (*fikr*). One may have a beard but his thoughts may not be Islamic. Moreover, growing a beard, like wearing a cap or turban, was contextual.

The Prophet asked Muslims to wear caps and put turbans over them, because at the time Christians used turbans and Jews wore caps. The headgear for Muslims was thus set to distinguish them from both Jews and Christians. This was no longer relevant. When I asked him if he should not follow the Prophet as Maududi argued, he said, "Of course." But he stressed that it was impossible to follow the Prophet literally in all respects. He pointed out, for example, that "the Prophet slept on a mat. We do not. He rode a donkey. We travel by bus or train." I asked him further what Maududi and other ulema meant when they said that Muslims must follow Muhammad completely?

> This is an arbitrary definition of *hadīth*. Who says that it means that we must exactly follow Muhammad in every detail of life? I am telling you it is his *fikr* that matters most. However, if you insist on its traditional definition, then the question is who defined *hadīth*? Muhammad himself did not. It is the theologians who defined it so. I am not bound to follow them.

Clearly Jamal's worldview was different from Jalal's. Jamal was not secretive and would often talk of his personal life. He introduced me to his friends. Once, when he saw my scooter parked in front of the McDonald hostel, he left a message on its meter saying that he was waiting for me in his room. Hours later I went to see him and asked if he had any particular reason to speak with me. He said that he simply wanted to have tea with me. At the university *chungī* (tea stall) at the Shamshad market, we would have tea until as late as 3:00 o'clock in the morning. Once he told me that he had seen the film *Devdās*, based on Sharat Chandra's novel by the same name. He had nothing but praise for it.

> I like watching films. Films are about human emotions. I enjoyed watching *Devdas*. Its character Devdas really moved me. I can relate myself to him and empathize with the character of the prostitute cast opposite him, Chandramukhi. Films help me understand human behavior.

That Jamal watched films surprised me, all the more because only a few days earlier Jalal had described it as a major sin. Did the SIO know about it?

In the SIO's assessment meeting, Jamal admitted watching films, and he was given a "show cause notice." The Local Advisory Council (LAC) of the SIO, which included its president, worked as a disciplinary committee keeping watch on members' behavior. According to Jamal, most LAC members were the "conservative" alumni of Falāḥ, concerned with "non-issues" like film and prayer. He thought that the SIO should not be regulating its members' behavior. Watching a film or praying was an "individual choice." He liked the SADA, which did not ask its members to pray or forbid them to watch films. Rather, it raised "concrete issues" like fee hikes or how to fight Hindutva and strengthen secular forces. Responding to the SIO, Jamal wrote a three-page justification for watching films.

Following his father, Jamal argued in the letter that ulema did not know what true Islam was. His father believed that one should think of Islam positively. One should not say, as most ulema did, that Islam permitted only such and such a thing. Instead, one should say that Islam allowed everything except practices such as eating pork and drinking alcohol. From this perspective, the Qur'an did not forbid watching films as it did eating pork. Furthermore, he argued that unless there were alternative Islamic films, it was not proper to forbid watching Bollywood films. He agreed that women were not shown properly in the films, but he would stop watching such films only when alternatives became available.

The SIO leadership was unable to counter Jamal's arguments, so no disciplinary action was taken against him. He was told, however, not to watch films in theaters, as it would tarnish the SIO's image. Jamal had to rely on DVDs. But his nonconforming behavior was not limited to watching films. Against the SIO's directive not to speak to girls unless there was a dire need, he interacted with them regularly. Of twenty-one students in his class, nine were girls, and he socialized with them all. That the girls with whom Jamal interacted were mostly unveiled and in a gender-mixed class was itself a departure from Maududi's position that regarded gender-mixed education un-Islamic. Like his predilection for films, Jamal was also in favor of dancing. When the SIO decided to stop the dance party given by the MBA department, Jamal opposed it, arguing that dance was an entertainment and Islam did not oppose it. "Entertainment is part of Islam," he reasoned. He went to observe the party and clapped along to his favorite musical numbers. According to Jamal, Sahir, who was sent by the SIO to meet the proctor and stop the dancing, also watched the dance party.

Given his radically different worldview, I asked Jamal, while having dinner in a Hindu hotel near the Tasvīr Mahal theater, how he got along with other SIO members. He responded: "I do not go by what people say or believe. They may not be necessarily right. I have my own thinking. Look at Jalal ṣāḥib. His thinking is completely different from mine. He is old and conservative. He has a beard, I do not have [one]." "How do you deal with him then?" I inquired, "He tolerates me, and I tolerate him. Ours is a plural society, we live together."

The day before I left Aligarh, ending my second fieldtrip, Jamal and I, on his initiative, went to watch a new film, *Maiñ hūñ nā* (I Am There). The film depicted friendship between India and Pakistan, and was also popular for the exciting dances performed by Miss Universe-turned-actress Sushmita Sen. During the show, Jamal looked worried that students he knew might spot him in the theater.

In the next chapter, we move to Falāḥ where Jamal and the majority of SIO members came from.

CHAPTER 5

Defining Islam

CONFLICT AND DEMOCRATIZATION

> Where all think alike, no one thinks very much.
>
> —WALTER LIPPMANN, *The Stakes of Diplomacy*

In the wee hours of the last day of my first visit to Falāḥ, the gatekeeper came running to the guesthouse where I was staying. Upset, he asked me if I had called for the police jeep standing at Falāḥ's main gate. I told him, that yes, a friend's relative, the Commissioner of Azamgarh had volunteered to send a jeep to drop me at the railway station, but I had not asked for a police jeep. Dissatisfied with my answer, he took me to the gate where the driver stood by a jeep carrying a plate marked "police" in the front. The driver said that, on the Commissioner's request, he had come to take me to the station. The gatekeeper looked relieved. When I asked him why he was anxious, he explained that last year a police jeep had come exactly at that time to arrest some Falāḥ students.

Only hours after the government banned the SIMI on the night of September 27, 2001, the police came with a list of the eight names[1] of SIMI members studying at Falāḥ. According to the SIMI activists, the police had come to arrest the "traitors of the nation [*dēshdrōh*]" who had made "provocative" speeches. Only three of the eight students were still at Falāḥ: two SIMI activists and a Kashmiri.[2] One of the SIMI activists was an *anṣār* and the president of its Falāḥ unit, and the another was an *ikḥvān*.

A nonviolent confrontation ensued for hours between Falāḥ students led by the SIMI activists on the campus side of the gate and the police standing with their van on the other side. The police insisted that if the Falāḥ administration did not surrender the charged students, they would enter the campus to arrest them. The SIMI activists opposed handing the students over to the police. They believed that the charged students had done no wrong but had only spoken the truth (*ḥaq*) of Islam against the tyranny (*ẓulm*) meted out to Muslims by Hindutva. The standoff continued amid anti-police slogans shouted by the SIMI activists.

Caught between the police, on the one hand, and the SIMI activists, on the other, the Falāḥ administration resolved the issue by assuring the police that it would bring the wanted students to the police station if the latter withdrew from the campus. The only way to calm down the SIMI activists, the administration thought, was to send the police away. But the SIMI viewed the decision as "dishonorable" and "cowardly." The police withdrew, and the SIMI activists' anger subsided, but not for long. When the administration was preparing to take the students in its Armada jeep to the police station, the SIMI activists protested. As the jeep carrying the students left Falāḥ, the SIMI activists angrily followed it on their bare feet, protesting the "dishonorable" handover to "the tyrant." But to no avail.

In this episode the SIO sided with the administration and barely took part in the SIMI's protest. Although some SIO supporters did show solidarity with the SIMI against the police, when the police were out of sight the semblance of solidarity vanished and gave way to a serious conflict between the two groups. In the SIO's view, the SIMI's Islam was not true Islam; only the Islam the SIO upheld was genuine.

Contrary to several currents of argument (e.g., Fukuyama 1992; Huntington 1996; and Tibi 1990, 1999) that highlight perennial conflict between Islam and Western or other religions, I contend that the most significant conflict is *within* Islamism and is enmeshed in a complex matrix of power. The conflict, triggered and intensified by an aggressive anti-Muslim Hindutva, manifests itself in two models of Islam: the moderate model of the SIO versus the radical, jihad-centered SIMI model. Ethnographically, I describe the conflict within Islamism as played out between the SIMI and the SIO on the Falāḥ campus. My second argument, posited against a series of works that stress incompatibility between Islam and democracy (Gellner 1994; Lewis 1988; 1993, 2003; Moghissi 1999; Weiner 1987), is that once we recognize that such a conflict exists, it follows that certain forms of civil society and democracy are at work in the politics of Islamism. The recognition of this conflict, I contend, signals an ongoing process of democratization of Islamist organizations, and indeed of Islam itself (Devji 2005; Eickelman and Piscatori 1996; Esposito and Voll 1996; Hefner 2000). This is evident in the way that principles of democracy, representation, and reasoned discussion inform and condition the conflict between the SIMI and the SIO, as well as the debate over mechanisms to resolve it.[3]

Central to this tendency toward democratization is the awareness of rights among a distinct stratum of the young Islamist activists I call the "Islamist class." Unlike the first and second generations of Islamists, these young activists, predominantly urban and possessing a specific type of cultural capital and disposition (Bourdieu 1997; Field 2003), assert their rights rather than duties. They are radical not only vis-à-vis Hindutva, but are equally radical with regard to the older generation of Islamists who they see as denying them democratic rights. The assertion of rights, I argue, is most pronounced by radical organizations such as the SIMI.

This subject is best analyzed by first understanding how Falāḥ differs from thousands of other Indian madrasas, the social background of its students, and how student politics is played out on the Falāḥ campus. These issues are addressed in the first section of the chapter. In the second section, I describe the nature of the conflict between the SIMI and the SIO and how it is articulated on the Falāḥ campus. Then I demonstrate a link between the conflicts within Islamism and the processes of democratization. I conclude this third section by arguing that the SIMI's radicalism ought to be seen in relation to both the Islamist class's yearning for democratic rights and the process of democratization within the Islamist organizations.

Differentia Specifica of Falāḥ

Falāḥ was established by the Jamaat in 1962 as a madrasa for higher education,[4] where boys and girls studied together up to the primary level. In 1965 an independent girls' wing was formed, and during my fieldwork a separate campus for girls was a kilometer away from the boys' campus.[5] Three yellow busses collected girls from the adjoining villages and dropped them at the boy's campus near the guesthouse, which was the second building after the general store on the right side of the main gate. A narrow path from the guesthouse went to the girl's campus via the canteen and Taiba hostel (for secondary-degree students) situated behind the guesthouse. Early in the morning hundreds of girls stepped off the buses, veiled from head to toe, mostly in black *burqa*. Facing the guesthouse was the playground, with double-storied, white buildings at its edge, one parallel to the guesthouse and another perpendicular to it. Classes took place in the double-storied buildings. The area from guesthouse to classroom was the academic complex.

Two of its three hostels were named after the ideologues of Islamism: Hasan Al-banna (d. 1949), founder of Egypt's Muslim Brotherhood, and Maududi. The hall in the academic complex was named after Maulana Abullais Nadwi, the first *amīr* of the Jamaat after India's independence. The inner campus road from the main gate led to the "Maududi hostel," meant for higher-level students in the tertiary degree. Close to it on the south was the "Hasan Al-banna hostel" for students of lower levels in the tertiary degree. A magnificent mosque facing the canteen lay north of the Maududi hostel. A few furlongs north of the mosque were the Falāḥ library and the Taiba hostel.

Figure 6. Mosque on the campus of Falāḥ. Photo provided by Falāḥ Administration.

At the time of my fieldwork the total number of students was 1,840: 810 at the primary level, 350 at the secondary level, and 610 at the tertiary stage, and another 70 for *ḥifẓ*, (memorization of the Qur'an, see below). The minimum age for admission to class 1 was five years old. Five hundred students lived in the three hostels. All non-local students were required to live in a hostel, but students below class 6 were not admitted to the hostel. Given these conditions, the numbers suggest that all students at the primary level were local, day scholars. At the secondary and tertiary stages, the majority of students (500 out of 960) were non-local hostellers. All hostellers—the youngest was at least thirteen years old[6]—were invariably sons or relatives of Jamaat members. Zahir Madni, the Falāḥ principal, told me that "since Falāḥ was the central madrasa of the Jamaat, the Jamaat members and sympathizers prefer to send their wards there." Most hostellers came from eastern UP, Bihar, Maharashtra, and Nepal. Those from eastern UP were from Gonda, Basti, and Siddharthnagar, a stronghold of the Ahl-e-hadīth sect. Some students were from Kashmir and Andhra Pradesh.

The Jamaat's ideology alone, as Madni observed, did not distinguish Falāḥ and its hostellers from the thousands of other madrasas.[7] The class background of Falāḥ hostellers was also distinct, and significantly affected life and politics at Falāḥ.

Islamist Class

It is well known that most non-Jamaat madrasas are run with resources given to them in cash or in kind as charities, such as *zakāt* and *sadqa* (Agwani 1986; Fahimuddin 1998), or from income of their *waqf* (endowment) properties. The education offered there is free (Fahimuddin 1998), as are food and lodging. The education and hostel are free in almost all madrasas, because the vast majority of their students come from poor families. In his survey of thirty non-Jamaat madrasas in UP, Fahimuddin (1998) concluded that their students were from poor families (see also Sikand 2005).[8] He also found that over 50 percent of students came from rural areas. Analysts have observed that the majority of the fathers of madrasa students are peasants/agriculturalists, often uneducated. Those who are educated have a primary- or at most secondary-level madrasa education.

In contrast, at Falāḥ a day scholar had to pay a monthly tuition fee of 35 Rs. at the primary level, 45 Rs. at the secondary level, and 60 Rs. at the tertiary stages. The cost for a hosteller was higher, at least 900 Indian Rs. (17 Euros): 400 Rs. for food, 200 Rs. for establishment costs (electricity, boarding fee, library, and sports), and 55 Rs. for tuition. Many hostellers told me that they also needed a minimum of 250 Rs. for expenses relating to stationery, toiletry, phone calls, pocket money, and the like. Falāḥ required hostellers to have "at least four pairs of nice dresses" (Jāmiʿatul Falāḥ 2001:7). If a family could spend 900 Rs. a month on their son's education, then clearly that was not a poor family. In 2000, 34.7 percent of India's population lived below the poverty line ($1 a day at 1993 international prices).[9] Another sociological feature of Jamaat members and sympathizers was their urban background. No more than 15 percent of Jamaat members lived in villages. Of the 5,365 members in 2002, 4,300 lived in urban areas, and of these, around 1,100 lived in twenty big cities and metropolises alone.[10]

Parents of sons studying at Falāḥ were invariably educated, and it was rare to meet an illiterate Jamaat member.[11] Fathers of Falāḥ's hostellers had a distinct educational and cultural capital (Bourdieu 1997; Field 2003) in that they had both a madrasa as well as a modern education. In many cases one kind of education was formal and the other informal. Thus what I term "Islamist class" is not just based on monthly income and urban location but, more crucial, the specific cultural capital and disposition toward learning that it fosters.

At home and in the madrasa, Falāḥ hostellers were taught formally and informally to be critical of "traditional" Islam and the madrasa system (as Maududi's corpus of writings indeed does). Whereas the non-Jamaat madrasas taught their students to be loyal to teachers as bearers of Islamic authority, the Falāḥ hostellers were loyal to the ideology of Islamism (*fikr*), not people. Most important to them was not who spoke of Islam but what was said of Islam. In other words, their disposition was toward arguments rather than personalities, as it was, for example, in the cases of Deoband, Nadwa, or Ahl-e-sunna madrasas. Furthermore, the career aspirations of most Falāḥ hostellers was to enter a university such as AMU. Unlike students at non-Jamaat madrasas, who desired to become a *mu'azzin*, *imam*, madrasa teacher, or bookseller, Falāḥ's hostellers almost disdained these career options. They only grudgingly took up such careers if they failed admission to the university. An arresting index of this attitude was the mode of address that Falāḥ graduates used. Call them *maulānā*, the popular title to address madrasa-educated students, and they raised their eyebrows. In the words of Irham, a teacher at Falāḥ and *amīr* of its Jamaat unit, they preferred to be called "mister, not *maulānā*."

University Recognition, Curriculum, and Sect

In accordance with the desire of the Islamist class to enter a university, in 1981 Falāḥ degrees achieved recognition from AMU. Subsequently the degree was recognized by Delhi's Jamia Millia Islamia, Hamdard University, and Hyderabad's Maulana Azad University. In the late 1990s Jaunpur's Poorvanchal University, a regional university near Azamgarh, and Lucknow University also granted their recognition. Whereas Maulana Azad University and AMU recognized *'ālmīyat* and *fazīlat* degrees (see below), other universities recognized only the *'ālmīyat* degree. If a student left Falāḥ before completing *'ālmīyat*, his education was invalid by university standards.

As a result of universities recognizing Falāḥ's degrees, the number of students at Falāḥ increased rapidly. Between 1967 and 1980 108 students completed *'ālmīyat*, and 138 completed *fazīlat*. After 1981, following the universities' recognition of its degrees, the numbers increased dramatically. Between 1981 and 1991 the number of *'ālmīyat* students increased more than three times to 383 and that of *fazīlat* rose to 184. The increase continued in the years between 1992 and 2001 as well (Table 2). Although the number of both *'ālmīyat* and *fazīlat* students rose in absolute terms after Falāḥ's degrees were recognized, the rise of the latter was notably lower than the former, because, upon completing *'ālmīyat*, the degree that all universities recognized, most students left Falāḥ to enter the universities.

TABLE 2
Number of *ʿālmīyat* and *faẓīlat* Students at Falāḥ

Year		*1967–1980*	*1981–1991*	*1992–2001*
Number of students	*ʿālmīyat*	108	383	758
	faẓīlat	138	154	236

Source: Fihrist-e-fāreghīn/fāreghāt 2001.

Recognition by the universities, in the case of AMU, had two implications. First, Falāḥ's *ʿālmīyat* and *faẓīlat* degree holders could be admitted to bachelor's and master's courses in Arabic, Islamic Studies, Theology, Persian, and Urdu. They were also eligible for admission to bachelor degree programs in Unani Medicine and Surgery (BUMS), which was their first priority. Eligibility for admission to those courses was not exclusive to Falāḥ graduates.[12] Second, and this was exclusive to Falāḥ, its students were also eligible for admission to bachelor degree programs in social sciences and English. AMU granted this provision to Falāḥ because those subjects were given comparatively more attention there. Falāḥ's curriculum comprised sixteen years and was divided into three stages: primary (five years), secondary (three years), and tertiary (eight years). The tertiary stage was further subdivided into *ʿālmīyat* and *faẓīlat*. If a student completed five years of education after the secondary stage, he received a degree of *ʿālmīyat*. A further education of three years led to *faẓīlat*, the highest degree.[13] Modern subjects such as mathematics, geography, English, and general knowledge were taught from the primary stage on. At the tertiary level, Arabic gained significance in the curriculum. Yet Urdu, Hindi, English, political science, and economics were taught jointly with Islamic subjects during *ʿālmīyat*.

Both teachers and students of Falāḥ proudly said that, unlike other madrasas, the Falāḥ was nonsecterian and broadminded. Their claim was only partially true. Unlike Deoband, which expelled fifty-five students simply because they belonged to the Ahl-e-hadīth sect (Saif 1996: 306), Falāḥ welcomed students from that sect. Both Ahl-e-hadīth, and Deobandi-Hanafi students studied there, in almost a 50:50 ratio, and both had the liberty to pray in the mosque according to their own creeds. Unlike the Deoband, Nadwa, and Ahl-e-sunna sects, all of whom insisted on following Imam Hanifa, at Falāḥ students were taught the positions of all *imams* and were free to choose. At this point Falāḥ departed from the Ahl-e-hadīth, which considered all sects except itself as *mushrik* (polytheist). In this sense, Falāḥ was nonsectarian. However, it was hostile to sects such as the Ahl-e-sunna. While attending a *faẓīlat* class (Arabi 6) on *fiqh*, I asked the teacher if he would also admit Barēlvī students to

Falāḥ. "We are broadminded but not to the extent that we would accept *shirk* [polytheism]," he replied.

Student Politics

Finally, what set Falāḥ apart from other madrasas was the space it offered to student activism. Because Falāḥ was established as a Jamaat madrasa, from its formation the SIMI worked on its campus under the patronage of the Falāḥ administration. During the early 1980s, when the divide between the SIMI and the Jamaat became unbridgeable, the Jamaat formally broke away from the SIMI and, in 1982, floated its own student wing, the SIO (see chapter 4). Ever since then, the SIO has been functioning on the Falāḥ campus. No other madrasa run by the Deoband, Nadwa, Ahl-e-hadīth, or Ahl-e-sunna sect or ideology legitimated a student organization to work on its campus. Student politics as an institutionalized practice has indeed been foreign to the other madrasas, because none of them had a student organization. Nor did they allow a student organization of their rival sects—if they had one—to work in their campuses. In the early 1990s the SIO tried to establish a branch at Deoband, but the Deoband administration promptly chased the SIO leaders from its campus.[14]

Unique to Falāḥ was the organizational politics of the SIMI and the SIO that was at the heart of the madrasa's life, particularly in its hostels. Both the SIMI and SIO held their meetings separately, and they had their own libraries and wall magazines. Most hostellers were polarized into two camps: SIMI versus SIO. This divide pervaded nearly every domain of life and affected most hostellers. This is not to say that all were members of these organizations, but affiliation of a formal or informal kind to either of them was crucial to most hostellers. Those who shunned an affiliation were looked down upon as dumb. By contrast, leaders of both were generally more studious than the average unaffiliated student.[15] Why did students join the SIMI or the SIO in the first place?

For most newcomers affiliation to an organization and ideology was their first experience out in the world. It gave them a new identity other than the one based on family, age, region, and so on. Moreover, because friendships and social circles were largely built along the SIMI-SIO divide at Falāḥ, newcomers joined or were induced to become part of the already existing social circles. More important, organizational politics was built into Jamaat's ideology. At Falāḥ, unlike the non-Jamaat madrasas, the administration and teachers encouraged students to join the organizations. Given Falāḥ's central role in the Jamaat's ideological scheme, Falāḥ was a source of manpower for the Jamaat. Of thirteen national presidents of the SIMI from its formation to the present, four (all from the 1990s on) were graduates of Falāḥ.[16] As we will see in chapter 6, the SIMI candidate who became AMUSU president was also a Falāḥ graduate. Likewise, Falāḥ had also produced dozens of leaders for both the SIO and the Jamaat. The national SIO president for the 2003–2004 term was a graduate of Falāḥ, as was the president of the Jamaat, UP, eastern zone.

The above description, I hope, is helpful to underscores the *differentia specifica* of the Falāḥ and to illuminate the argument in the following sections. Now I turn to the theme of conflict within Islamism with which I began this chapter. Out of several stories of conflict that defined the relations between the SIMI and the SIO on the Falāḥ campus, I focus on four: conflicting interpretations of what makes a person a hero, how each organization characterizes the other, the banning of the SIMI, and how to face Hindutva's onslaught against Muslims and the demolition of the Babri mosque.

Conflict Unlimited

On visiting Falāḥ I found, to my surprise, that it was in a state of conflict and turmoil. As I stayed on and interacted with a wide variety of people there, what I observed and heard about was not uniformity and unity but never-ending stories of differences and conflict. Falāḥ was a tiny world, but it brimmed with huge differences and mighty conflicts. Almost all conflicts, whatever their causes and whoever were their agents, were articulated as conflicts between the SIO and the SIMI.

Hero or Villain?

The hottest topic of campus talk during my first phase of fieldwork was the imprisonment of the SIMI leaders, particularly those from Falāḥ. SIMI activists portrayed them as heroes, but the SIO activists did not share this view. After the government ban, Samin Patel, a national SIMI leader and former Falāḥ student, was imprisoned. For the SIMI activists, Patel, a Gujarati belonging to a wealthy family and raised in the United States (he was a U.S. national), was a hero. Stories emanated from jail that he was a great, selfless Muslim. The SIMI activists told me that Patel's father, based in New York, offered a bribe of 100,000 Rs. (1,774 Euros) to the jail authorities not to beat him. When Patel learned of it, he was furious, believing that his father should have spent the money on widows and orphans instead. Patel was even angrier that his father had begged the jail authorities to keep him safe. He chastised his father with the following words: "You think the jail authorities would protect my life. But, as a Muslim, I believe that Allah alone is the protector of life."

The SIO activists did not share the SIMI's image of Patel as a benefactor of the downtrodden. To them he was rowdy. The administration had expelled Patel when he was a student for beating the driver of a bus carrying girls to Falāḥ who allegedly had misbehaved with some of the girls. Outraged at this assault on "women's chastity," Patel did not ask the administration to take action against the driver but beat him up instead. When expelled, he refused to abide by Falāḥ's expulsion order and challenged it in court. The court revoked the expulsion order, and legally the Falāḥ administration had no option but to readmit him. When Patel was readmitted, the principal who had expelled him resigned in protest. The SIO activists always told this story (the SIMI activists never did) to discredit Patel and show that his recourse to the court had smeared Falāḥ's image. It was the first time that a student had defied the Falāḥ administration.

The conflict between the SIO and the SIMI was also expressed, somewhat jocularly, through the ways that each characterized the other organization. In an SIO meeting, a young student, when asked what differentiated the SIO from the SIMI, replied: "The SIO has a father [meaning the Jamaat], whereas the SIMI is without a father." While telling me this anecdote, an SIO activist warned me not to take it lightly. The words "without a father" did not simply characterize the SIMI as a bastard but went deeper than that: in every sphere Islam entailed guardianship (*sarparastī*) in the form of a father, and so when the SIMI abandoned the Jamaat's guardianship and called for jihad against the Indian state (see chapter 6), it also turned against Islam. The SIO, on the other hand, was proud that, unlike the SIMI, it had the Jamaat as its guardian. This then became the butt of jokes for the SIMI activists, who characterized their SIO counterparts as infants still needing parental guidance. The SIMI taunted the SIO activists for not acting on their own, for not reacting, even on a small issue, until they had spoken about it to the Jamaat headquarters in Delhi.

Another significant expression of this conflict was the banning of the SIMI. Long before the Indian government did so, the Falāḥ administration had banned the SIMI from the madrasa campus, saying that it had become "extremist" and was tarnishing Islam (*Islam ko badnām kar rahē haiñ*) by calling for jihad. To the SIMI activists, the Falāḥ administration, comprising teachers who were invariably also Jamaat members, was biased in favor of the SIO. In their view the SIO, the Jamaat, and the Falāḥ administration were the same. This does not mean, however, that none in the administration backed the SIMI, just that the SIMI supporters were in the minority. Following the government ban on the SIMI, the administration added a new clause to the pledge form (*ʿahdnāma)*, which all hostellers had to sign: "I hereby declare that I am not associated with any banned organization." The form also stated that if a hosteller broke the pledge, he would accept any punishment. Though nowhere was the

SIMI mentioned in the form, everyone knew that "banned organization" meant the SIMI.

In contrast, the SIO was very active on the campus, holding weekly meetings, pasting posters on the campus walls, and mobilizing student participation. Baqi, a SIMI activist, showed me an SIO poster on the Falāḥ's wall announcing a meeting at Falāḥ to be addressed by the national presidents of the Jamaat and the SIO. Agitated at the administration's ban on the SIMI and its approval of the SIO, Baqi asked me if I would ever expect a fellow Muslim (the administration) to conduct his own activities (SIO's) but ban the activities of another fellow Muslim (SIMI's). He regarded the ban on the SIMI as unjust. The SIO activists, however, as hostellers, felt morally bound to follow Falāḥ's rules. They also justified the government ban on the SIMI, as Islam taught its believers to abide by the rules of whatever land they inhabited. The SIMI did not accept this and, instead, challenged the Indian political order by invoking jihad against the government. SIO activists saw this as violating Islam's basic tenets. For them, therefore, the banning of SIMI was justified. Indeed, they favorably quoted a former SIMI member who said that the government was right in banning the SIMI because the latter was "behaving like the Bajrang Dal [a militant wing of Hindutva]." Where the government was at fault, he added, was in not banning the Bajrang Dal.

Answer to Tyranny: Jihad or Daʿvat?

I asked Baqi why the administration banned the SIMI. Instead of replying, he asked me my opinion. Perhaps the administration feared government action against Falāḥ, I speculated, if it allowed the SIMI to function. He dismissed my speculation.

> No, they were always against us. The [government] ban is merely an excuse to further undermine us. You may not know what happened. . . . Ten years ago [in 1991, when the SIMI called for jihad; see chapter 6] they had banned us. The media and the government did not know us much then. . . . Falāḥ's principal . . . is a big Jamaat leader. He did not allow us to hold our meeting here. When we insisted, he asked us to do it outside the campus.
>
> *Why are they against you?*
>
> Because we tell the truth (*ḥaq)*. We are not cowardly as they are. We openly say that Muslims must be ready for jihad against Hindu forces which are determined to eliminate Islam. Should we not ask Muslims to prepare for jihad, you tell me, when Hindu forces

> are committing genocide [*naṣlkushī*] against Muslims in Gujarat [a reference to anti-Muslim riots in early 2002]. Everywhere. They destroyed the Babri mosque, now they are looting our honor. They are raping our sisters with impunity.

As Baqi said, the urgent task for Muslims was to prepare for jihad against the Hindutva forces which he held responsible for the demolition of the Babri mosque and the "genocide of Muslims." This call from the SIMI dotted the almirah and walls of Falāḥ. In the students' reading hall close to the Maududi hostel, both the SIMI and the SIO had their libraries. On the SIMI's almirah of books, then sealed, was a color sticker in Urdu with the three domes of the demolished Babri mosque. In the center of the two side domes a pair of eyes, dripping tears, was shown, and below this was written: "The greatest jihad is to say the truth in the face of a tyrannical ruler." The slogan was marked with SIM[17] (see chapter 6, Figure 10).[18] Such slogans were also inscribed in blue on the inner walls of the Falāḥ hostel. Once, another SIMI activist invited me to lunch with him at the Maududi hostel. His room had nine beds with no space between them. Behind the rolled mosquito netting on the wall were three slogans, two in Urdu and one in Arabic, and below them was written "SIM"—"Just by hearing the name of battle, *kāfir* runs away," "Love for jihad is but worship," and "Jihad is an obligation for all Muslims."[19]

For the SIMI, the way to face the "Hindu forces" was to exhort Muslims for jihad. The SIO, in contrast, opted for *daʿvat*, the propagation of Islam's message of peace. A short story in the 1999 issue of Falāḥ's annual magazine Al-Falāḥ (which Baqi complained was anti-SIMI because it did not publish articles of "our people") summed up the SIO's approach. The story, "Answer to Tyranny [*javāb-e-sitam*]," begins on the morning of December 7, with Rahim, the protagonist, waking up to learn that the Babri mosque, the "symbol of our greatness," was demolished. He begins to cry. Suddenly three young Muslims approach him: "Today we were destroyed and looted." Assuming they are sad about the demolition of the mosque, Rahim tells them that he, too, is sad. One of them repeats the earlier sentence. Rahim then asks if someone attacked them. He says:

> Yes . . . We have been looted and our houses set on fire. They picked up women and our young daughters. . . . As we heard the news of the martyrdom of the Babri mosque, we got scared. And Jagdish Singh with his loafers entered our village, looted our assets, set our houses on fire, and, the worst, took our daughters away. (*Al-Falāḥ* 1999:147)

Hearing the story of Jagdish's "barbarism" against Muslims, Rahim is furious. He spreads the message to all youth (all Muslims) in the village to gather on his lawn. When they gather, he delivers a speech extolling the bravery of the great victors in Islamic history and exhorts them to take revenge against Jagdish, portrayed as symbolic of barbarism and Hindutva. None, however, responds to his call. Disappointed, he goes to the home of his friend, Parvez, where he also meets Parvez's uncle, Abbas. Rahim narrates his story and asks Abbas: Why should we not "take up swords" against Jagdish? Abbas advises him not to be "emotional" and instead use his "wisdom." In the long conversation that follows between them, Abbas tells Rahim that if Muslims took revenge against Jagdish, even the noncommunal (*samajḫdār*) section of Hindus would turn against them. The story concludes with Abbas's final word: "Today we need to acquaint humanity with the ways of peace and tranquility. . . . Through *daʿvat*, we mold public opinion in favor of Islam." Evidently the character of Abbas symbolizes "wisdom" against the "emotionalism" of Rahim. In the story he appears as a quintessential figure of guardianship (read, the Jamaat) which the SIO, unlike the SIMI, considers integral to Islam.

Myriad other conflicts engaged the SIO and the SIMI, such as how to get one's own candidate nominated to the Union; how to win over a new student to SIO or SIMI; and why a particular candidate, and not another, was appointed to be a Falāḥ teacher. But the thorniest conflict at the time of my fieldwork centered on the split of Falāḥ's Old Boys' Association, Anjuman Talba-e-qadim (hereafter, Anjuman).

New Conflict over Old Boys

During its seventh Session, in 1999, the Anjuman, which was formed in 1977, split, accompanied by accusations, hooting, and even threats between supporters of the SIMI and those of the SIO.[20] The incident took place in the presence of hundreds of alumni gathered to attend the Session. The Jamaat's vice president was also present in his role as Falāḥ's Vice Chancellor (VC). This Session, held every fourth year, was a big event in Falāḥ's life. Alumni from different parts of north India gathered at their alma mater to elect the Anjuman's office bearers. In the wake of the murky scene that marked the first day of the three-day Anjuman Session, the SIO approached the VC to find ways to reconcile with the SIMI. Reconciliation efforts failed, however, and the SIO abstained from participating in the Anjuman's further meetings and on the second night floated a parallel organization, Tanzeem Talba-e-qudim (henceforth, Tanzeem). The Tanzeem elected its office bearers and planned to publish a newsletter, *Ḵhabarnāma*, an alternative to the Anjuman's *Ḥayāt-e-nau*. The next morning posters appeared on Falāḥ's walls announcing the birth of the Tanzeem. Enraged at this development, SIMI supporters shut Falāḥ's gate and threatened the Tanzeem's leaders that they would not be allowed to leave unless they resolved the conflict.

In the SIO's narrative, its supporters formed the Tanzeem because the SIMI had hijacked the Anjuman to spread its "obnoxious [*manḥūs*]" ideology of violence. Maulana Israfil, a key leader of the Tanzeem and a teacher of the Qur'an in the tertiary classes (also a Jamaat member), talked with me about this:

> The main reason to establish the Tanzeem was ideological. The SIMI had hijacked the Anjuman and all its branches throughout the country—Aligarh, Delhi, and Bombay, etcetera—for its own cause. . . . The SIMI believes in extremism [*intihāpasandi*] and violence [*tashaddud*]. It speaks of jihad. We do not share their ideology at all and think that their call for jihad militates against Islam's basic teachings. . . . You may know that the SIMI leaders once also called for autonomy of Indian Muslims.
>
> *I have read about the SIMI's call for* jihad *in its magazine* [*Islamic Movement*]. *But what did the SIMI mean by autonomy?*
>
> In the magazine they used to be milder. You have not heard speeches of their leaders. Have you? . . . They used to vomit fire [*āg ugalte thē*] in their speeches. . . . By autonomy, they meant that only Muslims, not Hindus, should rule over Muslims.
>
> *How is that possible?*
>
> They [the SIMI] themselves did not know it. They simply wanted to provoke the Indian state and the BJP. Anyway, you better ask them. I can tell you only about our positions.
>
> *Ok!*
>
> In the last ten years or so when they grew militant, they also tried to establish their hegemony [*ghalba*] over all the institutions of the Jamaat, including Falāḥ and the Anjuman, and use them for jihad. They got their own man elected as Anjuman's president . . . he has been the president since 1992. They also got their own men in its *shura*. . . . They were taking the Anjuman also along the path of extremism and violence. The outside world came to believe that the Anjuman's was also the Jamaat's and Islam's voice. Because we sharply differ from the SIMI's extremism, we formed the Tanzeem to represent the real voice of Islam and the Jamaat. We stand for peace, not violence.

Curious to know the SIMI's viewpoint, I met Maulana Asim, a hardcore SIMI activist and then an office bearer of the Anjuman. In the first meeting he simply dismissed the reason Israfil offered for the Tanzeem's formation. To him, the real reason was financial embezzlement by the Anjuman treasurer, a Jamaat member and SIMI opponent, during the 1992–96 term. To cover it up, the treasurer and the Jamaat floated the Tanzeem and later gave it an ideological color.

When I asked Irham, another leader of the Tanzeem and the secretary of the Anjuman during the 1992–96 term, if financial embezzlement was the main reason, he denied it and instead charged the SIMI with giving an ideological slant to issues of power. In his view what happened in the 1999 Session of the Anjuman was indeed a culmination of a long battle the SIMI had launched against the Jamaat to take control of Falāḥ and have its own people appointed to key positions. To do so, said Irham, in the mid-1990s the SIMI launched a campaign against the then principal of Falāḥ, Maulana Rahmani (also a Jamaat member). In Irham's view, Rahmani was a genius who had won applause from the ulema of Egypt and Saudi Arabia for his scholarship on Islam. His fault was that he was opposed to the SIMI, and therefore the main obstacle to its scheme to capture Falāḥ.

To discredit Rahmani, continued Irham, the SIMI raised two objections against him. First, Rahmani had published a book arguing that the sharia's provision of *rajam*, stoning to death a married person guilty of adultery, was context-specific and no longer relevant. He had also argued that for adultery and rape[21] sharia entailed just one hundred lashings. Second, in an article in the Anjuma's organ *Ḥayāt-e-nau*, he had argued that the SIMI's call for jihad to rebuild the Babri mosque was un-Islamic. He called it "suicide." *Ḥayāt-e-nau* had also published a favorable review of Rahmani's book while he was Falāḥ's principal, but in the 1996 Session of the Anjuman SIMI supporters, who were a majority, passed a resolution condemning Rahmani's book.

Having heard a different story from Irham, I went to see Asim, who had finished teaching a class. I asked him if he agreed with what Irham told me, especially the SIMI's drive against Rahmani. He smiled and took me to the canteen for tea. He grew passionate as he began a scathing critique of Rahmani, under whose supervision he had done his *takhaṣṣuṣ* (see note 13). Asim was one of two former SIMI members to have written a book discrediting Rahmani.

In Asim's view, Rahmani's argument for the annulment of *rajam* was a new *fitna* to unleash doubts about Islam itself and misguide the entire *millat* (community). Throughout fourteen hundred years of history, he said, the only people who had questioned *rajam*'s sacredness and asked for its annulment were the Kharejites, the Jews, and the Orientalists. By arguing for its annulment, Rahmani had fulfilled the Jews' cherished dream. Asim likened Rahmani's arguments against *rajam* to the "nonsense" about Islam spouted "by Bal Thackeray," a rabidly anti-Muslim leader of Hindutva. Implying that Rahmani was a hypocrite (*munāfiq*), on the cover of his book he quoted the Prophet Muhammad: "In the interest of *ummat*, I fear most that hypocrite who because of his mastery of the Arabic language would create strife through the Qur'anic verses."[22] According to Asim, Rahmani also believed that sharia's order of *qaṣāṣ* (killing a murderer for committing murder) did not apply today and ought to be replaced with *dīt*, a monetary compensation to the victim's nearest kin.

Asim justified the Anjuman's resolution condemning Rahmani's book. Rejecting the Tanzeem's argument that SIMI's jihad was against Islam, he held that SIMI was indeed the true representative of Islam.

> If the SIMI speaks for jihad, what is wrong with it? They are not speaking anything against Islam. If to speak of jihad is against Islam, you go and ask them [the Tanzeem leaders] to scrap, as the Jews and America have been demanding, two hundred verses from the Qur'an that deal with jihad.
>
> *The Tanzeem leaders are also scholars of the Qur'an. They don't see the SIMI's* jihad *in line with its teachings.*
>
> I am not saying that they are not scholars. But they do not correctly interpret the Qur'an. When they teach the Qur'anic verses about jihad, they obfuscate them so that students get confused. They interpret jihad in nonviolent terms like jihad by tongue or jihad by pen. They say that in India doing *daʿvat* itself is jihad. Sometimes, they explain the criteria of jihad by sword so rigidly that its execution becomes impossible. . . . I tell you, they teach the Qur'an in a manner that jihad loses its import.
>
> *You mean the SIMI is right in calling for jihad?*
>
> Yes! The SIMI is not saying anything of its own. The Qur'an says so. . . . I will tell you a story. Once I was explaining to students the merits (*faẓāel*) of jihad. Later, one of their [the Tanzeem's] men told students that if it had so many merits, why was I teaching in the Falāḥ and not displaying a sword in the street. . . . When we speak of jihad they say that the SIMI stands for "gun culture" and they for "peace culture [*aman culture*]." . . . This is the reason I have been removed as teacher of Qur'an in higher classes and Israfil appointed in my place.

I met Israfil to ask him what he thought of jihad and whether he was obfuscating the Qur'anic teachings concerning it, as Asim charged. He shrugged it aside and laughed as if it did not deserve his comment. In his view the SIMI people had read only a few booklets of some half-scholars but pretended that they had mastered Islam. If they really believed in arguments, he said, they should have written a scholarly rebuttal to Rahmani's rejoinder to his critics (Asim never told me that Rahmani had written a rejoinder to his critics). They did not, said Israfil, because they had no arguments. Now they wanted to settle scores with batons (*lāṯhi*). "I told you that they [the SIMI] are emotional [*jaẕbātī*] and do not listen to arguments." In a similar vein, Israfil also dismissed the SIMI's justification for jihad. Had it been an obligation, the ulema of Deoband, Nadwa, or any other madrasa would have issued a *fatwa* for this. "Are these ulema more knowledgeable about Islam," he asked me, "or the SIMI people who pretend to be scholars?" To know more about the Tanzeem's position regarding the SIMI, he recommended that I read its newsletter. In its first issue, the Tanzeem offered advice to Falāḥ alumni: "The brothers of Falāḥ should make it clear to everyone that the SIM's [the SIMI's] policy and method of work is dangerous to country, Muslims, institution [the Falāḥ] and all" (*Ḳhabarnāma* 2001 [January–March]: 5). Without mentioning the SIMI by name, the Tanzeem, in the next issue, described its call for jihad as alcohol and warned the readers of its danger:

> The supporters of the Tanzeem cannot go with the *katta* culture [of the SIMI]. This is our crime. We do not stand for that step and that jihad whose alcohol they [they SIMI] have drunk. We consider that [jihad] lethal for Islam [*dīn*], Muslims (*millat*) and country (*mulk*) and all. (*Ḳhabarnāma* 2001 [April–June]: 5)

Democracy and Conflict

Once we recognize that Islamism as a practice is not monolithic and that it embraces conflicting views, it follows that it is embedded in a pluralistic civil society (cf. Gellner 1994) with multiple associations and contending ideologies. In other words, there is a civil space where the conflict—for instance, between the SIMI and the SIO—is articulated and debated. Tilly (1984) argues that the presence of civil associations is a precondition for social movement. Readers should not take the scuffle I have described between the SIO and the SIMI as an institutionalized reality. Both groups worked normally as vibrant organizations without infringing upon each other's right to work. This demonstrates that a crucial element of democracy, associational politics (see Dahl 2001; Hefner 2000; Putnam 1993, 1995), is at work in the form of activism on the part of the SIMI and the SIO. I argue further that for democracy to flourish it is not necessary that associational networks, as Putnam (1993, 1995, 2000) contends, are based on trust. Just as various types of trust are not all conducive to democracy, all conflicts are not inimical to democracy. Indeed, conflict is healthy for democracy (Warren 1999). The process of democratization at work within

Islamism, I contend, is also manifested in the mechanisms and processes for resolving conflict. Below I depict how both the SIMI and the SIO invoked the principles of rights and debate to resolve the conflict I described above.

Following the split, Falāḥ's VC presented a formula to bridge the conflict between the SIO and the SIMI. He proposed that Anjuman's *shura* should include equal representation of both organizations. He also suggested that if the president of the Anjuman came from the SIMI, its secretary should be from the SIO, or vice versa. The SIMI rejected the formula, arguing that it was "undemocratic." According to the SIMI, because the SIO enjoyed the support of far less than 50 percent of Anjuman members, it would be counter to the spirit of democracy to give it a representational share of 50 percent. It is relevant here to note the qualifications for membership in the Anjuman, the number of members, and the dynamics of elections. According to the Anjuman's Constitution, any student who had obtained an *ʿālmīyat* or *fażīlat* from Falāḥ could become a member of the Anjuman if he completed the membership form and consented to pay the membership fee, and if he agreed with Anjuman's objectives (*Dastūr Anjuman . . .* undated:1).[23] In 1996 one thousand students had completed an *ʿālmīyat* and *fażīlat*, but only between five hundred and six hundred students chose to become Anjuman's members (*HN* 1996 [August–September]: 54).

Anjuman members came from different parts of north India, but those who participated in its elections were mostly local, from Bilariaganj and the adjoining villages in the Azamgarh district. Many of them studied at AMU in Aligarh; on completing the *ʿālmīyat*, they joined universities like AMU. Every fourth year, when the Anjuman held its Session at Falāḥ to elect office bearers, these local alumni comprised the largest number of participants. Participation in the Anjuman's election also gave them an opportunity to visit their homes and meet relatives and friends.

Because the SIMI had more supporters than the SIO among local alumni who participate in Anjuman's elections, the SIMI rejected the VC's formula, contending that Anjuman's members should directly elect officer bearers and *shura* members, as had been the tradition thus far. The reason behind the SIMI's persistence to retain the old method of electing officers was that it had the support of the majority of its members and would thus defeat the SIO and continue to control the Anjuman. The Falāḥ administration then appointed a committee to resolve the conflict and unite the Tanzeem and the SIMI-led Anjuman. The committee invited five representatives from each organization to help restore the Anjuman's unity. The Tanzeem offered a formula calling for a radical change in the electoral procedures: the general members of the Anjuman would first elect a Representative Council, which would then elect a *shura* and the office bearers.

The Tanzeem's proposal aimed to block the chances that SIMI's candidates would be elected to office, as it thought that a Representative

Council would be much easier to manage than a crowd of hundreds of voting members. Notwithstanding its aim, the Tanzeem framed its argument by invoking the idea of a reasoned debate (*modallal baḥas̱*) in the Representative Council in keeping with a deliberative model of democracy (Ferree et al. 2002).[24]

Israfil told me that the Representative Council was necessary for a reasoned debate, whereas a crowd of more than two hundred (the average number of participants) tended to become unreasonable, particularly when the SIMI encouraged it. According to him, most local alumni were not "solidly mature [*nā-poḵhta*]" and "100 percent Muslim," as their behavior was far below the Islamic standard. This was because they only had an *ʿālmīyat* degree, he said, and did not know enough about Islam. They came to Falāḥ not to learn about Islam but to simply get an *ʿālmīyat* degree to enter a university. "SIMI's emotionalism rather than our [SIO's] reasonability," he said, "appeals to them." He hoped that, as a small body, the Representative Council would be more conducive for a reasoned debate than an immature crowd of hundreds.

As it had done with the VC's formula, the SIMI rejected this one, too. In the Tanzeem's proposal, the SIMI saw a scheme of "disenfranchising a large number of alumni" on the flimsy ground that "they were immature" and not "100 percent Muslim." An Anjuman leader told me that to become 100 percent Muslim depended on Allah's will (*taufīq*). As an example, he offered the case of Maulana Majid Daryabadi, who had been a great *ʿālim* of Nadwa but later became a Communist. If the alumni were not 100 percent Muslim, he said, that did not mean that they would be barred from voting in the Anjuman's elections until they achieved that status.

At the end of my fieldwork, these debates were still going on. Efforts at reconciliation, it appeared, had unleashed even more conflicts but also rich debates about Islam.

Rights and Strikes

The remainder of this chapter considers how the SIMI's radicalization and its call for jihad, as the student politics at Falāḥ itself, can be seen as integral to the democratization process that Islamist organizations initiate and are affected by. It is my contention that the SIMI's radicalism should be understood not only as opposed to Hindutva but equally as a radical yearning for rights against the older generation of Islamists themselves and the specific aspirations of the Islamist class from which its members spring.

A SIMI activist casually mentioned an incident concerning the first student strike at Falāḥ. As I listened my interest grew, and I decided to pursue it further. The Falāḥ administration shied away from talking about it, but the SIMI activists proudly told me about it. The response of the SIO activists was mixed; publicly they presented it as an example of students' deviance precisely because the SIMI felt proud of it, whereas privately many SIO members remembered it with pride.

In 1990 students, led by the SIMI, called for the first major strike at the madrasa. It began with an apparently insignificant issue but later on flowered into a serious event. In the SIO's narrative, Mubarak, a new teacher and an SIO member (also a Falāḥ alumnus), found a student (unaffiliated with the SIO or the SIMI) cheating. He took away the student's answer sheet and slapped him. Saleh, who was not a member of the SIMI but had many friends affiliated with it, objected to Mubarak hitting the student. A heated argument ensued between them. The controller of the examination intervened. Saleh argued with him, too, and protested that Mubarak "had the right to expel the student but not beat him." Agitated at Saleh's resistance to Mubarak and to himself as well, the controller beat Saleh. Falāḥ's principal called Saleh into his office and asked him to apologize to both Mubarak and the controller, which he did. The issue was resolved for the time being.

The SIMI activists' narrative differed from the SIO's, however. According to the former, the student was not cheating, though Mubarak had accused him of doing so. Also, in their version Saleh did not apologize. Conflicting accounts notwithstanding, both agreed that, on the very night of the event, the SIMI leaders, Patel and Qasim Omar (whom we meet in the next chapter), launched a campaign in the hostels to boycott the exam the next day. The SIO countered by mobilizing students not to boycott the exam. For the SIMI leaders, striking the student accused of cheating, and hitting Saleh as well, was an example of "outright injustice and tyranny [*sīdḫa nā-inṣāfī aur ẓulm*]" on the part of administration. They demanded that until Mubarak apologized to the student, they would not take their exam.

Despite the SIO's countermobilization, ninety students, mostly at the tertiary stage, did not go to the examination hall the next day. SIMI activists leading the strike gathered in front of the principal's office and chanted slogans against the Falāḥ administration and against Mubarak in particular. In the SIO's account, they also misbehaved with some teachers. An hour passed since the exam had begun, and still the striking students refused to take the exam. A baffled administration then sent some senior teachers to talk to the students, and most of the strikers heeded their appeal. But the key figures—six to ten of them, all top SIMI leaders—persisted with their protest. Because of their defiance, the executive committee of Falāḥ later expelled the SIMI activists who had led the strike. Still defiant, they considered taking legal action against the administration to challenge its expulsion order. Meanwhile, a few teachers sympathetic to the SIMI maneuvered Falāḥ's Administrative Committee, the only body empowered to annul the decision of the Executive Committee, to revoke the expulsions. Eventually the SIMI leaders were readmitted to Falāḥ.

This was the first major episode of student defiance Falāḥ had witnessed, but other acts of protest also occurred. In one such instance, students, again led by the SIMI, refused to eat the food at the hostel mess hall because it was badly cooked. From their pocket money, the SIMI leaders bought food for all the students who participated in the boycot. During the India-Pakistan cricket series in March–April 2004, wardens of different hostels confiscated thirteen radios from students, as hostellers were not allowed to have radios—nor were they permitted to listen to cricket commentaries. Sets were seized from both SIMI and SIO members, but it was a SIMI activist who broke the warden's locked almirah to retrive the radios. At Falāḥ, the SIMI was synonymous with resistance against both the Falāḥ administration and Hindutva.

These SIMI-led acts of defiance demonstrate a gripping awareness of rights. Recall Saleh's assertion that Mubarak had the right "to expel but not to beat him" and the SIMI leaders' framing of the same incident as an example of "outright injustice and tyranny," their subsequent protest, their chanting of slogans in front of the principal's office, and, above all, their boycott of the exam. It seems obvious that both the protest and the strikes belong to what Tilly (1984) calls the "repertoire of collective action" bequeathed by modernity (see also Franzosi 2001; and McAdam et al. 1988:703). Not so obvious is that protests like those the SIMI staged were not defensive but, again to quote Tilly (1984:304), an "offensive pursuit of new rights and advantages." The SIMI's assertion of the right to strike and protest against teachers beating a student, it should be stressed, is novel in the context of Indian madrasas.

The discourse of rights is nearly nonexistent in non-Jamaat madrasas for reasons alluded to in the first section of this chapter. Because most madrasas draw their finances from the community's charity and endowments, they also offer free education, hostel, and food to students who are mostly from poor families. Students accept whatever they are given as Allah's boon. The dominant discourse in these madrasas, therefore, concerns obligation, duties, and obedience. Students are taught to obey their teachers unconditionally. To disobey a teacher's authority is to disobey Islam itself, because teachers embody Islamic authority. Indeed, Islam is recast to mean a series of duties and obligations. There is no concept of protest if a teacher hits a student, a common occurrence in most madrasas. I was perhaps eleven or twelve years old when I studied in a village madrasa. Every Thursday the Farsi teacher asked us students to demonstrate that we had correctly memorized the different forms of Farsi verbs. Once, when I failed to answer correctly, he kept on beating me with a stick until I urinated in my pajamas. There was no way for me to protest except nurse a sense of dislike for him.

The practice of staging a strike is also unusual in most madrasas. Like madrasas elsewhere in Muslim countries, most Indian madrasas have rarely seen students engaged in a strike. Indian Muslims are distinct, however. Unlike most Muslim-majority countries where practices such as elections, strikes, and other democratic processes have weaker traditions, in India they are common occurrences. As a vibrant postcolonial democracy with strong traditions of leftist politics known for strikes, protests, and resistance, Indian Muslims have generally been active carriers of, and participants in, this repertoire of protest. However, in postcolonial India strikes were rare in madrasas until the 1960s.[25] In 1968, when the students of the famous Deoband madrasa called for a strike, the administration declared it "anti-sharia" (Tayyib undated:16). Students opposed to the strike described it—or rather the Deoband administration prevailed upon them to do so—as "*haram*" and "criminal" (ibid.:24, 25).

Unlike students in non-Jamaat madrasas, the SIMI activists felt proud that they had stood against the "injustice and tyranny" of the Falāḥ administration. For them, the strike and defiance of the Falāḥ administration was a true act of Islam. Their understanding of Islam was not that of an Islam of duties, and obedience as is the case in non-Jamaat madrasas, including Deoband. Theirs was an Islam of rights and defiance. The SIMI activists had this different understanding of Islam, because they had a different cultural capital, one that questioned traditional madrasas and their discourse. Their cultural capital disposed them to see Islam not in the personalities of their teachers but in the arguments they made.

The Falāḥ students' protest for rights was, however, also rooted in the economic capital they possessed. As discussed in the first section of this chapter, they belonged to a markedly different class than the non-Jamaat madrasa students. Their aspirations, too, were significantly different. They wanted to enter a university rather than become madrasa teachers, *muezzins*, mosques' *imams*, or booksellers. Unlike students of non-Jamaat madrasas, they did not eat the free food provided by the charity of the Muslim community. They paid for it, and they also paid their tuition fees. This economic independence was at the heart of their assertion of rights and dignity.

In the strike of 1990 Shadab, an SIO activist, defected to the SIMI because he felt that the issue was not the SIO versus the SIMI but rather students versus the "tyrant" administration. "We have our own dignity [*izzat*]. We don't come from illiterate-uncultured [*jāhil-gañvār*] families. Our father did not treat us this way. . . . How can you beat a student?" Shadab told me another story to prove how concerned he and other Falāḥ students were about their sense of dignity. When the SIMI called for the strike, a locally well-known figure came to help the administration resolve it. He asked the SIMI leaders numerous times to call off the strike, but they refused. Angrily, he said: "You guys get free food from the madrasa [Falāḥ], yet work against its interests." On hearing this, the SIMI activists became extremely agitated and almost hit him.

In addition to cultural and economic capital, an important reason why Falāḥ students in general and the SIMI activists in particular protested for rights was their close links with universities, especially AMU. We have already seen why Falāḥ became affiliated with various universities in the early 1980s. With the migration of a large number of Falāḥ students to AMU—in the year 2001 around four hundred of these students were at AMU—they also imbibed the repertoire of protest and student politics so vibrant there. In fact, close interactions developed between the SIMI unit at Falāḥ and that at AMU, where for the first time its candidate was elected president of the AMU Student Union. In the next chapter we turn to the victory of the SIMI's candidate in the AMU elections to see another face of its radicalism: the SIMI's call for jihad against Hindutva.

PART THREE

Opposition and Negotiation

CHAPTER 6

Invoking Jihad

> Great disorders lead to great devotions.
>
> —Emile Zola

> Of course, if progressive liberalism . . . should seriously falter in the country, Hindu communalism in exclusive arrogance should triumph, then it is not perhaps impossible that this revived Islamic communalism [the Jamaat-e-Islami] might well be the form in which the Muslims would participate in India's disintegration.
>
> —Wilfred C. Smith, *Islam in Modern History*

Only a few hours after the Government of India, in the wake of 9/11, banned the SIMI, its national president, Qasim Omar, was arrested in Delhi. Although initially reluctant to speak to me about him, SIMI activists in Aligarh described Omar as a heroic figure. I heard so much about him that I grew curious to meet him, but it was impossible given his imprisonment.

During my second fieldtrip in 2004, my luck changed. When I was at Falāḥ, SIMI activists joyfully told me that Omar had been released and that he had visited his Falāḥ, alma mater, only some days before my arrival there. Like their comrades in Aligarh, SIMI activists at Falāḥ also referred to Omar as a hero. "He was the only Muslim to openly challenge the *Sangẖ parivār* [Hindutva; see below] over the Babri mosque," said Nasir, a SIMI activist. For example, Omar had declared: "If the government wants to test Muslims' strength, let it withdraw its army and then see who stops them from rebuilding [the] Babri mosque." Such speeches, Nasir told me, had contributed to Omar's arrest. On his visit to Falāḥ, Omar received an unusual welcome, as scores of students gathered simply to catch a glimpse of him. At Falāḥ I became even more curious to meet Omar. Wajid, a former SIMI member, told me that it was impossible to meet him because he had countless visitors. The day Omar came out of prison and went to his village 10 kilometers from Falāḥ, a cavalcade of some thirty jeeps accompanied him. Wajid advised me to contact Omar first by phone, and after several tries, I reached him and made an appointment for us to meet. When I reached his village, he again asked me about my personal details and appeared satisfied with my response. I was surprised at his polite treatment of me. He was gracious not only to me but also to the few villagers who had gathered at his house upon seeing the jeep I arrived in. I had not expected this response from the president of a "terrorist" outfit, for the media had portrayed SIMI as anti-India (*dēshdrōh*).[1]

Under a mango tree in front of Omar's house, we sat on a cot for the interview. A theme that dominated the conversation was his invoking of jihad. In a scathing critique of the Jamaat, he said that it had long deviated from the line of its founder, Maududi, and that its shunning of jihad was "the greatest tragedy of the twentieth century." He criticized the entire stratum of ulema who, in his view, had not only given up jihad but presented it as a "condemned [*malʿūn*] word." I asked him why he stressed jihad:

> This is a strange question. Do you not see what the RSS and other militant Hindu organizations have done to Muslims in the last fifty years since [India's] Independence? . . . Don't you know what happened to the Babri mosque? How many Muslims were killed in Bombay, Surat, and elsewhere?

By now Omar had become fairly emotional. I asked him whether his call for jihad would make Muslims more vulnerable to attacks.

> Muslims would become more prone to attack? . . . They [the RSS] are already killing Muslims on a daily basis. They rape our sisters, and we remain a mute spectator. What did we get in the past fifty years? Anti-Muslim riots! They visit tyranny upon Muslims, rape our sisters, and the government remains a spectator. If we do not take up swords and wage jihad, what will we do? Will we regain the lost chastity of our sisters? . . . It is our religious duty to protect their chastity and stop the genocide of Muslims. If we are killed in the course of jihad, we would become martyrs. This death is a thousand times better than the death of humiliation. In Gujarat [referring to the riots of early 2002] we were slaughtered like carrots [*gājar mūli kī ṭaraḥ*].

Omar compared the RSS to the Jamaat, pointing out that whereas the RSS had progressed from a tiny organization to become India's rulers because it gave armed training to Hindus in its *shākhās*, the Jamaat had only declined because it abandoned jihad and deviated from the true path of the Prophet Muhammad. The Jamaat, according to Omar, presented Muhammad as *raḥmatul lil ʿālamīn* (a mercy to mankind), but it purposely did not acknowledge that he was also *nabiʾul malāḥim* (the prophet of wars).

This chapter examines the processes that led to the SIMI's radicalization as articulated in its calls for jihad and caliphate. The SIMI was radicalized in response to Hindutva, and to understand the politics of jihad we need to look at concrete events rather than simply analyze Islamic beliefs. To speak of the SIMI's radicalization, we must also speak of the radicalism of Hindutva and the erosion of Indian secularism. SIMI's radicalization, I contend, was a response to the RSS-led Ayodhya campaign that began in the 1980s, a campaign that was not simply about building a Ram temple but was a direct challenge to the secular spirit of the Indian Constitution (Bhargava 1998; Sen 1993). As the Hindutva assault on secularism grew fiercer—culminating in the destruction of the Babri mosque and massive violence against Muslims—so, too, did the SIMI's call for jihad become stronger.[2]

My argument questions the dominant theories which explain Islamist radicalization in terms of culture or the Qur'an. A classic example is an observation made by the British prime minister Sir William Gladstone in 1913. Holding the Qur'an in his hand, in the House of Commons, he announced: "So long as there is this book, the Qur'an, there will be no peace in this world" (in Azad 1913:17).[3] Gladstone's statement, made over a century ago, may seem anachronistic, but similar positions have been taken in the current debate about Islam. Juergensmeyer (2000:13), for instance, offers a cultural framework to understand religious violence, in which radicalism stems from some kind of "cosmic war . . . conceived in the mind of God" (ibid.:216). More recently he argued that the attack on the World Trade Center was a "religious war" declared by Osama bin Laden (2002:100). In his meaning-driven cultural framework, inspired by Clifford Geertz, Islamist radicalism is simply an expression of global antimodernism.

Bernard Lewis's (2003) position is similar, as he makes an umbilical link between radicalism and Islamic theology.[4] David Cook, in *Understanding Jihad*, dwells on this link more thoroughly, showing an organic connection between the Qur'an and jihad. Islam, in his judgment, is "rooted in . . . domination and violence" (2005:166). According to Cook, jihad is "one of the core elements of Islam" (ibid.:13) that galvanized readers of the Qur'an to conquer one territory after another. While linking conquest to the Qur'an, however, he offers the qualification that the earliest Qur'anic verses were peaceful; it was the verses reveled to the Prophet Muhammad after his migration from Mecca to Medina that preached violence and conquest. He presents a timeline of jihad that begins with Muhammad's migration to Medina and ends with 9/11 (ibid.:211), thus forging an umbroken connection between the Qur'an and 9/11. Because Cook considers the Qur'an as well as *hadīth* and the body of juridical literature to be the cause of radicalism, he predicts that the "syncretistic" Muslims from Africa and Indonesia-Malaysia will become increasingly radical as they read classical Arabic sources on jihad (ibid.:165).[5]

Central to what I term "theological-cultural theories," such as those of Gladstone, Juergensmeyer, Lewis, and Cook, is the primacy of culture or beliefs. It is within this framework that Rushdie (2005) calls Muslim radicals "Islamofascists."[6] By not simply calling them "fascists" but instead "Islamofascists"—a masterful act of naming—Rushdie underscores the primacy of their religious beliefs. To him, Islam is antimodern by definition, and hence his clarion call for Islam's Reformation and modernization. It follows from this line of argument that Islam, as Lewis (1993, 2002, 2003) and other scholars assert, is a nemesis of modernity, of secular democracy, in particular,[7] and hence a depot of violence. In this formulation, secular democracy and jihad appear as two separate—nay, foreign—domains.

Against these theories of the causes of jihad, in this chapter I offer two alternative explanations. First, I argue that it is not the seamless culture or sacred text of Islam that fosters radicalism but, on the contrary, it is the dynamics of politics, particularly the role of the state in the (mis)treatment of its citizens that sets the discourse of jihad in motion. Put differently, the idiom of jihad, rather than being the cause of radicalism, is a manifestation of an exclusivist, undemocratic politics. The Islamist radicalization in India, as exemplified in the SIMI's call for jihad, was a response to Hindutva's politics of hate against Muslims evident, inter alia, in the large-scale anti-Muslim violence during the 1980s and 1990s. Thus the SIMI's declaration of jihad did not stem from its members' reading the Qur'an but from Hindutva's violent mass mobilization against Muslims through its campaign to build the Ram temple. Second, the SIMI became radical because the Indian state failed to practice secularism. Following Sen (1998:479), by secularism I mean "symmetric treatment of different religious communities in politics and in the affairs of the state." Thus my argument that the SIMI became radical as a result of the state's failure means that the state did not protect the lives, property, and dignity of its Muslim citizens who were targeted by the Hindutva activists during riots and various institutions of the state—civil and police alike—were complicit with the rioters. Here I call for a political-anthropological approach to jihad that assigns primacy to the relational, dialectical, and political context in which the discourse of jihad gains its salience.[8]

In the first section of this chapter I show the ways in which the SIMI began to radicalize after the 1992 election of the AMU Students' Union, an election that was related to Hindutva's campaign to build the Ram temple. In the second section I demonstrate SIMI's radicalization at the national level and show that it unfolded in parallel to Hindutva's mobilization of the forces that demolished the Babri mosque. After the demolition, the SIMI announced its radicalism by exhorting Muslims to prepare for jihad and install a caliphate. In the final section I discuss the theological justifications that the SIMI offered for its radical turn.

Roots of Radicalization

Although previously the SIMI had fought the AMU Students' Union (AMUSU) elections, in 1992, for the first time, its candidate, Hafiz Sikandar Rana, a graduate of Falāḥ and its *anṣār*,[9] was elected president. A key factor in his victory was his radical resistance to Hindutva. Almost all candidates for the presidency of the AMUSU were against Hindutva, but what mattered then was not opposition per se but rather its form, packaging, and, above all, its radical nature. Rana seldom had any rival when it came to opposing Hindutva. Because I contend that the SIMI's first moment of radicalization was symbolized in Rana's victory owing mainly to his fierce resistance to Hindutva, let us begin with an account of the political context in which Rana won the 1992 AMUSU election.

Saffron Wave: Context of the Election

The 1991–92 AMUSU election was scheduled for March 1992 (*RAM* 1992:20), and the context in which it began was heavily charged with communal anger ignited by the Hindutva movement, or what Hansen calls "Saffron Wave."[10] Hindutva,[11] a cluster of Hindu organizations, known as *Sangh̲ parivār*,[12] at the ideological core of which stands RSS, a movement initiated in 1925 with the aim of fashioning India into a Hindu nation-state (Kanungo 2002:28; Ludden 1996:13). The idea of a Hindu nation[13] is the raison d'être of *Sangh̲ parivār's* ideology. Though presumably there is tension in *Sangh̲ parivār* on the issues of caste and gender, Muslims figure as the defining other of the Hindu nation.

In the mid-1980s *Sangh̲ parivār* renewed its assertion by launching a campaign to build the Ram temple in Ayodhya, UP, on the existing site of the Babri mosque, believed to be the birthplace of the god Ram.[14] The reclamation of the site of Ram's birth was for *Sangh̲ parivār*, a *dh̲arma yudh̲*, or holy war (Chaturvedi and Chaturvedi 1996:177). Started in October 1984 by the Vishwa Hindu Parishad (VHP), the temple campaign, by the late 1980s, had reached a flashpoint resulting in sharp communal antagonism, especially in UP. The worst attacks against Muslims that occurred in its aftermath was in 1987 in Meerut, a town with a sizable Muslim population near Delhi. According to an Amnesty International report, at least eighty-nine Muslims were burnt alive in the Hashimpura locality of Meerut and Maliana, a village some 10 kilometers from Meerut. The report stated that the police had killed people (*Indian Union* 1988:3–4). When the SIMI president visited the riot-torn Meerut, the district administration arrested him (*IM* [December 1997–February 1998]: 79).

In 1989 the VHP organized processions throughout India to collect sacred bricks to build the Ram temple. Chanting slogans such as "*saugandh̲ rām kī kẖātē haiñ, ham mandir vahīñ banā'engē* [we swear by Ram, we will build the temple there only]," these processions ignited some of the worst anti-Muslim riots, leaving hundreds killed. The most horrific was the riot of Bhagalpur, Bihar, which continued unabated for weeks, killing eight hundred people (Engineer 1995:173). On September 25, 1990, casting himself in the image of the god Ram, L. K. Advani, leader of the Bhartiya Janata Party (BJP), the political constituent of *Sangẖ parivār*, began *dẖarma yudẖ* (Kanungo 2002:203) by riding a chariot, *ratẖ yātra*, from Somnath in western Gujarat. The journey was scheduled to culminate in Ayodhya on October 23, to mark the beginning of the construction of the Ram temple. As Advani's *rath yātra* passed through one town after another, it sparked "violence and riots wherever it went" (Khilnani 1997:146–47). But it drew such participation from Hindus that Advani described it as "the greatest mass movement" of free India (in Kanungo 2002:204). Thousands of Ram devotees gathered in Ayodhya on October 30 to build the Ram temple. On the orders of the UP chief minister, police opened fire on the crowd, killing sixteen people (Brass 2003:117). The VHP, however, claimed that thousands of Hindus were killed. To continue the agitation, its followers carried the ashes of "martyrs" across the country before immersing them in the river. As a result of this mobilization, communal antagonism heightened. In November 1990 thirty-two towns in UP were under curfew (Hasan 1996:96). Like Advani's *rath yātra*, VHP processions also led to gory riots. Orchestrated to reap political harvest, the riots benefited the BJP. In the parliamentary elections of 1991 its number of seats rose from 86 in 1989, and from just 2 in 1984, to 118 (Davis 1996:30).[15]

The rise of the BJP as the largest opposition party in 1991 had unleashed unprecedented fear among Muslims of north India, especially in UP. Not only did the display of violence frighten Muslims, but equally threatening was the humiliation the Hindutva movement hurled upon them. For example, Sadhvi Ritambhra and Uma Bharati, two of its so-called female ascetic leaders, made umpteen diabolical speeches describing Muslims as innately intolerant, retrograde, and, above all, quislings of the Indian nation (Kakar 1996). At rallies, loudspeakers blared abusive slogans reeking of sexism and hatred against Muslims. Such slogans also appeared on walls.

> *Musalmānōn kē dō hī astẖān: pākistān yā qabristān*
> Muslims have only two places: Pakistan or the graveyard
>
> *Jab kaṭū'ē kāṭē jā'engē, tab rām rām chillā'engē*
> When the circumcised [Muslims] are killed, they will shout Ram Ram
>
> *Jab jab hindū jāgā hai, dēsh sē mullā bhāgā hai*
> Whenever Hindus have arisen, mullahs [Muslims] have fled from the country

In Aligarh, too, the temple campaign led to the worst riot in its history, even surpassing riots during Partition. In the riots of December 1990 and January 1991, according to official figures, ninety-two people were killed, and two-thirds of the victims were Muslims (Brass 2003:116). Unlike the previous riots in Aligarh, which remained limited to the town's old quarters, this time it also spilled over to the Civil Line area where AMU is located. The pro-Hindutva local newspapers, especially *Amar Ujālā*, alleged that Muslims killed seventy-four Hindus in the Nehru Medical College of AMU. The allegation, wrote the AMU vice chancellor at the time, was a lie, as no dead bodies were found (Farooqui 1998). However, clashes took place in Jamalpur, half a kilometer away from AMU. Even the Civil Line area of AMU came under curfew. In 1989 Krishna Kumar Navman, an old RSS member and a BJP leader, was elected from Aligarh to the UP Assembly. Reelected in 1991, he aided the anti-Muslim riots in many ways (Brass 2003:244). Like Cook, he held that the Qur'an preached violence against non-Muslims (ibid.:245).

Against Injustice

In an atmosphere marked by the temple campaign, the 1992 AMUSU elections took place. A few months earlier, in November 1991, the SIMI had organized a meeting in the Kennedy auditorium of AMU. Speaking on "Increasing Communalism and the Response of the Muslim Community," a former *anṣār* remarked: "Enemies of Islam should understand that India is not Andalusia from where Muslims can be driven out. . . . And now we have to show that if the process of injustice doesn't stop, then we will not tolerate it. We would rather retaliate" (*IM* 1992 [January]: 39). In February of the same year SIMI launched a campaign to regain the Babri mosque by observing February 1 as Babri mosque day. Its candidate in the AMU elections, Rana, highlighted it more than any other issue; indeed, at AMU and within the SIMI, he was the staunchest advocate of restoring the Babri mosque to Muslims.

In November 1989, when the VHP called for *shīlānyās* (laying the foundation for the Ram temple), the All-India Babri Masjid Action Committee called on Muslims to gather at Ayodhya to protest the plan. To this end, the SIMI also mobilized AMU students, and, under Rana's leadership, seventy-two students marched to Ayodhya. The SIMI's choice of seventy-two students was symbolic. In the battle of Karbala in 680 AD, the army of Imam Husain, the grandson of Muhammad and claimant to the caliphate after the death of his father, Ali, consisted of seventy-two soldiers lined up against the mighty army of Yazid. Husain lost the battle and his life. For the Shiites, however, this is a remarkable day, for it is emblematic of martyrdom and resistance against the injustice of Yazid, who, in their view, had usurped the caliphate. In an arresting replay of that event, the SIMI's choice of seventy-two students symbolized a resistance against the injustice of the state with whose support the Hindutva forces had usurped the Babri mosque.

A word about the conflict between Muslim leaders over the Babri mosque issue is in order here. In 1986, the same year the Faizabad court ordered the opening of the mosque, under the leadership of Syed Shahabuddin (a diplomat turned politician of the Janata Party), Muslims formed the Babri Masjid Movement Coordination Committee (henceforth, the Coordination Committee). According to Nazar, an Aligarh-based leader of the Babri mosque movement, three years later the Coordination Committee split. Disgruntled members formed a new group, the All-India Babri Masjid Action Committee (henceforth, Action Committee). The split occurred because the Coordination Committee vacillated on certain decisions it made but later revoked. In its Delhi conference, in 1986, the Coordination Committee took four decisions: (1) observe an all-Indian strike on February 1, 1987, marking the first anniversary of the court order to unlock the Babri mosque; (2) organize a protest rally of Muslims in Delhi the next year; (3) boycott the official celebration of Republic Day as a mark of protest; and (4) organize a march to Ayodhya, known as the "Ayodhya March," to pray in the Babri mosque (*IM* 1993 [February–March]: 32). The group implemented the first two decisions but revoked the rest. Those unhappy with the revocation—certainly the SIMI among them—sensed a far deeper reason: the Coordination Committee was not radical. The dissenters, who formed the Action Committee, believed that, rather than taking to the streets, the Coordination Committee had too much faith in the political parties that had been assuring Muslims of a settlement of the dispute. For example, they resented that the call for the Ayodhya March had been withdrawn on the advice of the then prime minister Rajiv Gandhi (members.tripod.com 2004). We return to this matter in the next section.

The Jamaat had sided with the Coordination Committee, which particularly after the split, was fairly moderate in that it seldom initiated mass actions. Indeed, the Jamaat stood against any form of agitation. Believing firmly in the political-legal system, it stated that the judgment of the Supreme Court was the best solution (*MMS* 1997:301–15). The SIMI, by contrast, backed the Action Committee.

In the AMUSU election of 1992, SIMI, as noted above, focused on the Babri mosque. Rana delivered speech after speech urging his audience to prepare to defend the mosque. He constantly invoked the Muslim "martyrs [*shahīd*]" killed by Hindutva activists and police bullets in the wake of the temple campaign. For him, the issue at stake was not simply a place of worship but was Islam itself. Other candidates also spoke of defending the mosque. What set Rana apart from them was his passionate call to Muslims to sacrifice themselves in order to retain the mosque. He also aligned the issue of the moque to the global issue of Islam. Connecting the two issues was his vehement attack on *Sangẖ parivār* and its design "to wipe out Muslims from India."

"What Has Secularism Given Us: Riots and Dishonor?"

Anjan was a student when Sikandar Rana contested the 1992 election. Before joining AMU in 1989, he was already a SIMI sympathizer. He keenly participated in SIMI election meetings. He explained to me the theme and style of mobilization, especially those of Rana:

> The election of 1992 was very interesting and emotionally charged. What should I tell you? *Dauk ṣāḥib* . . . The issues of the Babri mosque and communal riots were the most important. You would remember how insecure Muslims felt then. They were being killed everywhere. So the whole election canvasing centered on the Babri mosque. Of all the candidates, it was SIMI's who raised it in the most emotional [*jaẕbātī*] way. . . . You may know that poetry is an integral part of elections here. All candidates begin or end their speeches with Urdu couplets. Rana had the most emotional and radical [*kaṛa*] couplets. He was a great Urdu orator. He spoke with immense passion and depth. As if his voice came not from his mouth, but from deep inside.
>
> Hardly had he finished reciting the couplets when hundreds of students who listened to him would turn emotional. I attended several of his meetings. So charged I used to get that I would almost have tears in my eyes when he described the way innocent children, women, and Muslims were brutally massacred [*qaṭl-e-ʿām*] in riots . . . .
>
> And yes, I was telling you about his couplets. His favorites were:
>
> *tū pukārēgī tō ai ṣeḥn-e-ḥaram āʾeñgē*
> O' sanctuary of the mosque, if you call, we would come
> *hāñ abābīlōn kē andāz mēñ ham āʾengē*
> Yes, we would come the way divine birds did
> *lē kē āʾeñgē ham hāthōn mēñ ṣadāqat kā ʿalam*
> We would come holding the flag of truth
> *yē alag bāt hai taʿdād mēñ kam āʾeñgē*
> It is another matter that we would come in small numbers

Rana and his comrades recited the above couplets so many times that they got on the lips of many a student. However, it was not simply the number of recitations that touched so many students but the sheer passion and emotion invested in them. To amplify the power of the couplets, at certain turns during the speech SIMI activists would join both their fists, bring them close to their heart, and then raise them straight up in the air shouting "*naʿra-e-takbīr, allāh-o-akbar* [Allah is great]."

The recitation was often a performance, but equally significant were the words reverberating with memories of Islam and Qur'anic events. In Arabic and Urdu, the word *harem* in the opening line means the sanctuary of a mosque, but also refers specifically to the mosques in Mecca and Medina. In the couplets, it had thus acquired a double meaning: the Babri mosque but also the mosques in Mecca and Medina. Those responding to the call of harem would "come the way divine birds (*abābil*) did," evoking an event from the Qur'an in which birds saved Allah's house. *Abābil* is mentioned in *sūra al-fīl*, 105. When the Abraha-led army, riding elephants, came to destroy Allah's house in Mecca, Allah sent a flock of divine birds, *abābil*, to defend the mosque. All the birds carried a pebble in their beaks and two in their claws; whoever the pebble hit was destroyed. In this way Allah saved His house. By invoking this event, SIMI depicted itself as the savior of the Babri mosque. The line "We would come holding the flag of truth" implies that only those willing to march to Ayodhya to save the mosque were true Muslims—thus the cautionary end note that "we would come in small numbers" in other words, mostly SIMI activists would march to save the mosque.

Though Rana's couplets referred to the divine miracle, he focused on the earthly roles Muslims must adopt, as Husain did, to face the injustices (*ẓulm*) done to Muslims. Through his narration, Rana would re-create the gory scenes in which police and Hindutva activists killed Muslims in riots. He would describe the cries and the pleading voices of Muslims, especially those of children and women calling for help. He offered a heart-wrenching description of how "our young sisters and mothers were raped, dishonored, and then cut into pieces." In his speech, the riots of Bhagalpur became metaphors of what it meant to be a Muslim.

Having described the injustices carried out by Hindutva, police, and the administration—all of them dubbed "tyrants [*ẓālim*]"—Rana would ask the audience, his face flushed with anger, what their duty as a Muslim was. With his right open palm trembling in the air, he would tell them that the orphans, widows, and martyred called upon them to challenge the injustices (*ẓulm kā muqābla karẽñ*).

> For how long will the river of Muslims' blood flow, for how long will we allow the honor of our sisters and mothers to be looted? What has secularism given us: riots and dishonor. . . . This is the real face of secular India. Secularism and democracy in reality mean that those

> who butcher Muslims roam free. Have you ever heard of any culprit being punished?

He thundered that it was not Muslims who were under attack but Islam itself. To prove his point, Rana cited the demand of a Hindu lawyer of Rajasthan to ban the Qur'an (see Kakar 1996:177).

Unlike his rivals, Rana also connected *ẓulm* against Indian Muslims with the plight of Muslims in Palestine. In his rendition, the Palestinian issue was not a nationalist issue as portrayed by the Yasir Arafat-led movement[16] but instead was a matter of regaining the lost first *qibla* of Islam, *baitul maqdis*, namely, Jerusalem, the third most sacred site of Islam where the *aqṣā* mosque stands. The Babri mosque and the *aqsa* mosque in Jerusalem were thus portrayed as two sides of the same attack on Islam. Most of those I spoke with told me that Rana also called for jihad against *ẓulm*. A few, however, tended to refute it. Whether or not he used the word jihad in his speeches, all agreed that Rana undoubtedly called upon Muslims to save the honor of their mothers and sisters and to challenge Hindutva. They also told me that his fiery speeches generated a sense of fear among Hindu students at AMU (see chap. 4 n. 4).

Supported by hundreds of students from his alma mater, Falāḥ, and with no rival to articulate, as he did, the fear and anger that defined the mood of Muslim students in early 1992, Rana was elected president of the AMUSU by a huge margin, 1,477 votes. He polled a total of 3,798 votes (*RAM* 1992 [April]: 20). As noted this was the very first victory SIMI had scored in the AMUSU elections, and there was fervent jubilation throughout the campus.

Call for Jihad

SIMI's radicalization in response to Hindutva was not unique to AMU but became a nationwide phenomenon. In December 1991, shortly before the AMUSU elections in Bombay, SIMI held an all-India conference titled "*iqdām-e-ummat* [Action for Muslims]" (*IM* 1997 December–February 1998: 81; *JMK*:5). The conference was a watershed in that SIMI, given the epic transformation in national politics, redefined its agenda, urging Muslims to jihad in order to defend themselves against Hindutva's almost routine onslaught.

Jihad for Self-Defense

SIMI's organ, *Islamic Movement* justified the Action for Muslims conference as follows:

> The massacre of Muslims [has been] going on for the last fifty years. Life, property, honor, and dignity are being looted openly. . . . Attacks are repeatedly being organized on Islamic laws [Muslim Personal Laws (MPL)]. Hundreds of places of worship are still in the clutches of Hindus. Every effort is being made to destroy the identity of Muslims. By creating fear and insecurity among Muslims through riots, they are being forced to become assimilated into the national stream [majoritarian culture]. New conspiracies are being hatched to defile the sacred *sharia* and ban the Qur'an. . . . They [*aghyār*] have always tried not to let Muslims come out of the circle of defense and gradually push them to such a state that they are not capable even of defense and thus surrender under compulsion. The initiative taken in this direction is not hidden from a keen observer nor is the net of conspiracies that has been cast on a national . . . level after the passage [of Indian Muslims] from the slavery of the British to the slavery of Brahmanism. . . .
>
> This Muslim community [*ummat*] can achieve that objective [*islām kā ghalba*] efficiently only when it emerges from the circle of defense and takes the frontline of action [*iqdāmī mōrcha kī pōzīshan*]. This step is both a remedy for so many internal ills and a solution to external problems. (*IM* 1992 [January]: 5)

This long quote is offered to illustrate SIMI's rationalization of its radical stand. To respond to Hindutva's attacks, the Action for Muslims conference laid down three steps: (1) return to Allah (*rujūʿ ilallāh*); (2) preach Islam to nonbelievers (*daʿvat ilallah*); and (3) seek jihad in the path of Allah (*jihad fī sabīl Allāh*). The first two steps were historically available in SIMI's repertoire, but the call for jihad departed from SIMI's past agenda.

Jihad in no way constituted SIMI's action plan prior to 1991. The interviews with its first-generation members as well as its official documents (e.g., see *JMK*:4–18; and *IM* 1997 [December–February 1998]: 75–82) demonstrate that SIMI's objective was educational, and its constituency was the student community. As a student organization, it raised educational awareness, preached Islam to both Muslim and non-Muslim students, and raised moral issues such as obscenity, films, and drug use. This is not to say that it ignored international political issues. In 1980, for example, when Yasir Arafat visited Delhi, SIMI activists exhibited a black flag to protest his support of the Soviet invasion of Afghanistan.[17] A year later they marched to protest Israel's military action against Lebanon. However, politics was not central to SIMI. Before 1991 the word "jihad" was never mentioned, let alone raised as the focus of an entire conference. It was in the Action for Muslims conference that SIMI brought jihad to the topic of its agenda. Underlying its centrality, SIMI contended that "jihad is a permanent duty" (*IM* 1992 [January]: 8). By jihad it did not mean a battle against temptation of the self; SIMI stated that it meant killing the enemy (ibid.:9). Anticipating the criticism from ulema, it said that as a defense jihad required no preconditions (ibid.:10). Equally crucial in the Action for Muslims conference was the shift it made from student issues to the problems of the Muslim community at large and thereby to national politics.

Barely a year had passed since the conference when, in December 1992 the Hindutva activists demolished the Babri mosque. Swearing by the "sacred blood of martyrs" (the Muslims killed in riots sparked by the demolition), the SIMI president said that the "tyrants would surely be punished" (*IM* 1992 [December–January 1993]: 5). "To protect our chastity [and our] places of worship, and to face the tyrants," he urged Muslims to "write a new history of martyrdom and determination [*ʿazīmat*]" (ibid.:43). The theme of martyrdom grew dominant for SIMI as the killing of Muslims continued in various places (see Engineer 1995, 1995a). Particularly, gruesome were the unabated attacks by Shiv Sena Party[18] militants in Bombay that lasted for weeks during the winter of 1992–93. In an interview for *Time* magazine, the Shiv Sena leader Bal Thackeray legitimized the violence as teaching a lesson to the anti-national, treacherous Muslims. He remarked that there was "nothing wrong if they [Muslims] are treated as Jews were in Nazi Germany"[19] (in Eckert 2005:46). SIMI responded to the reality of the unveiled threat by calling for martyrdom. The joint February/March 1993 issue of *Islamic Movement* was christened the "martyrdom number." The term "martyrdom" was used in a double sense: first, the Muslims killed during riots and the demolition of the Babri mosque both symbolized martyrdom; and, second, it was meant to exhort Muslims to embrace martyrdom by combatting the combined injustice and violence of Hindutva and the police, as pictured on the cover of the issue (Figure 7). So crucial became martyrdom that SIMI's organ declared, "Of the hundreds of problems confronting Indian Muslims today, it is the lack of desire for martyrdom that is the greatest" (*IM* 1993 [February–March]: 40).

Jihad for Babri Mosque

The disinterest in martyrdom was best illustrated by the lack of enthusiasm among nearly all Muslim leaders for jihad to regain the Babri mosque. SIMI blamed them for foolishly trusting the hypocritical, and so-called secular leaders (of the non-*Sangẖ parivār*) to save the Babri mosque and for underestimating the danger Hindutva posed. It also blamed Muslim leaders for not launching a mass struggle to save the Babri mosque. The SIMI resented that Muslim leadership was in the hands of irreligious,

Figure 7. The SIMI's portrayal of the horror of anti-Muslim violence in its organ, *Islamic Movement*. From author's collection.

non-praying individuals (*IM* 1992 [December–January 1993]:10) whose "hearts were filled more with the sanctity of India's Constitution than with the greatness of the mosque" (*IM* 1993 [February–March]: 33).

I already discussed the conflict between the Coordination and Action Committees over the Babri mosque. After its demolition, the Action Committee underwent infighting. The All-India Muslim Personal Law Board, formed in 1972, took up the Babri mosque issue quite late, after both committees were discredited in the wake of the demolition (*Dawat* 1999 [October 16]: 35–43). Like the Coordination Committee and the Jamaat, the Board showed its faith in secularism and said that it would accept a court verdict over the mosque (Rahman 2004:73). Other Muslim organizations had the same faith and never advocated force to regain the Babri mosque, which all of them nonetheless regarded as belonging to Muslims.

The SIMI, however, opposed all these Muslim organizations. Right after the demolition, the cover of *Islamic Movement* (1992 [December–January 1993]) carried two photographs, one of the makeshift temple built at the demolished Babri mosque and the other of the mosque intact, before it was destroyed. The cover carried the poetic line "only the daredevil Muslims are heir to the world."[20] Later the SIMI stated that "since the mosque was demolished by force, it could only be built by force" (*IM* 2000 [October 5]). "Allah wants to punish the hands," argued the SIMI's English organ *Newsletter*, "that demolished the mosque by the hands of Muslims" (1998 [November–December]: 2). Against Hindutva's slogan, "We swear by Ram, we will only build the temple there," the SIMI's slogan read "*p̱hir gūñjēgī takbīr vahāñ, kal kẖaṛī tẖi masjid jahāñ* (*takbīr* [Allah is the greatest] will again be raised there, where the mosque stood yesterday). Another SIMI slogan that appeared on a public wall (Figure 8) and was again a ditto response to Hindutva's, read "*shirk miṭēgā tauḥīd rahēgī, mandir nahīñ vahāñ masjid banēgī* [polytheism will disappear, monotheism will prevail; not a temple, but a mosque will be built there]." Responding to the BJP's slogan that Muslims had only two places to go, Pakistan or the graveyard, SIMI issued a counter-slogan, "*musalmānōñ kē kai asthān, āḍvāniyōñ kā ēk hī asthān* [Muslims have several places, Advanis have just one]."[21]

In a widely distributed pamphlet, the SIMI also drew a blueprint of the future mosque that would replace the demolished one. The first photo in the pamphlet[22] was marked with the year 1528, when the mosque was built, and the second one with the year 1992, when "Hindu fanatics" demolished it. The third undated photo, marked with "Allah willing," pictured the future mosque. This blueprint was, again, a response to the future Ram temple that Hindutva activists distributed en mass, including in their posters (Kapur 1993).[23] Describing the restoration of the

Figure 8. The SIMI's wall slogan pledging to rebuild the Babri mosque. Photo from *Afkā r-e-millī* (November 2000): 41.

Babri mosque to the Muslim community as a "debt," the SIMI pamphlet pledged that if the SIMI could not do so itself, it would hand over the responsibility to future generations.

The determination to regain the Babri mosque was aimed at Hindutva's repeated assertion that it would build the Ram temple anyway, even if it meant flouting laws. In the same way, the SIMI also proclaimed that it would not accept the court verdict, as regaining the Babri mosque was a matter of faith, not a legal issue (*Newsletter* 1998 [November–December]: 5). To bolster its position, it quoted Prime Minister Vajpayee's statement that "the construction of the Ram temple is an unfinished national duty" (*IM* 2001 [January]: 13). SIMI's counter-position to regain the Babri mosque was starkly manifest in its characterization of the dispute. Against all Muslim organizations, which described the dispute as a test of Indian secularism, the SIMI characterized it instead as a test of "*shirk banām bābrī masjid* [polytheism versus the Babri mosque]" (*JMK*:15). In the closing months of 1998, it launched a campaign called "polytheism versus the Babri mosque," in which the standing makeshift temple in Ayodhya symbolized polytheism, and the mosque prior to its demolition epitomized monotheism. Further, the SIMI perceived that polytheism was the root of the Muslims' persecution and the basis of the Indian political system that was responsible for the Babri mosque's demolition. It therefore decided to attack the root—polytheism—rather than its branches—the demolition of the mosque or Muslims' insecurity in general (*Newsletter* 1998 [November–December]: 4).

Caliphate versus Hindu Rashtra

Because a mosque is a house of Allah, the SIMI described the makeshift temple built on the site of the demolished mosque as "filth in the house." Since the Qur'an, in SIMI's view, describes polytheism as injustice (ibid.:4), it invoked the figure of Madmud Ghaznavi, an eleventh-century Muslim ruler who demolished the idols kept in the famous temple of Somnath in 1026. Justifying its invocation of Ghaznavi, the SIMI said that today his persona taught us to "remove the filth of shirk from the Babri mosque" (*IM* 2001 [June]: 10). In contrast to Hindutva, for which Ghaznavi is a villain par excellence (Frawley 1995:141–42; see also Van der Veer 1994:149–50), the SIMI described him as a hero of iconoclasm. It brought out a poster with the slogan "*ilāhī bhēj dē mahmūd kōī* [Allah Send Us a Mahmud]." In another poster the SIMI pictured the three domes of the Babri mosque. The middle dome showed the makeshift temple, and in the center of the two other domes was a pair of eyes dripping tears. The message was clear: because of the filth symbolized by the presence of a makeshift temple in the midst of the mosque, the Babri mosque was crying for the filth to be cleared and its sanctity restored (as shown in Figure 10; see below).

Because the SIMI saw the root of the Muslims' plight grounded in polytheism—which was the basis of the Indian polity—it advanced an alternative political system based on sharia. In November 1996 it launched a nationwide campaign, "nationalism or *ḳhilāfat*? [nationalism or caliphate?]," for the revival of the caliphate.[24] The specific catalyst of the campaign was the installation of the very first Hindutva central government, led by the BJP, in May 1996. The general catalyst of the campaign, however, lay in the slogan "Hindu nation," which had long been at the core of the Hindutva movement in general and the temple campaign in particular. As early as 1989, in an interview with *Pānch Janya*, the RSS Hindi organ, a Hindu monk and BJP leader, Mahant Avaidyanath, said that "the real issue is not that of building the Ram temple but of the future of the Hindu *rāshṭra*." The SIMI's organ quoted Avaidyanath's statement with alarm, equating it to the attempts made in Spain to expel Muslims and annihilate their culture (*IM* 1994 [November]: 15).

The SIMI's call to establish the caliphate thus emerged in response to the Hindu nation's slogan. A year before the ban, the SIMI president remarked, "If someone [*Sangẖ parivār*] has the right to work for *Ram rājya*, we, too, have every right to establish *niẓām-e-musṭafā* [the caliphate]" (*Milli Gazette* 2000). The SIMI also saw the caliphate as a solution to problems generated for Muslims by the movement to build a Hindu nation, such as demolition of the Babri mosque, the loss of Muslim lives and property, the looting of their sisters' and mothers' honor, and, above all, the Muslims' very survival. In an appeal issued to *imams* of mosques and to ulema, the SIMI president urged them to join its campaign because only a caliphate could ensure the "safety and care of sacred places of worship" (*IM* 1992 [November–December]: 96).

While calling for a caliphate, the SIMI's main audience was neither the ulema nor the Muslim public, for whom, as the SIMI president noted, the goal of a caliphate was not even an article of faith, much less its core (ibid.:94, 67). Its audience was the Jamaat, which once believed in a caliphate or Islamic state but had long abandoned it. Indeed, the Jamaat had not even used the term *ḳhilāfat* for a long time. In 1971, for instance, the Jamaat *amīr*, Maulana Abullais Nadwi, used the term "Islamic system" as its message (1971:6). In his 1988 address at the Jamaat's Delhi Session, he described moral ills such as "lies, ditching, selfishness, stinginess, hatred, lack of discipline, mutual ill will, and ill-mannerism" as the mother of all problems facing the country (Nadwi 1989:8). So removed had the Jamaat become from its earlier goal of Allah's Kingdom that, in 1983, Nadwi had gone on record to say that the Jamaat was a "nonpolitical organization" (in *Qaumi Awaz*, Lucknow 1983 [June 5]: 8).

Destruction of the Mosque, the Construction of Islam

In this section I describe the theological arguments SIMI offered to legitimize its radicalization and also SIMI's substantially redefined notion of what Islam stood for in the wake of the demolition of the Babri mosque. Since I argue that jihad in particular, and Islam in general should be seen in their specific historical mooring, and not as a decontextualized abstraction, SIMI's redefinition of Islam is equally a definition of the postcolonial Indian political system and the position therein—some might call it precarious—of Muslims.

India as Dar al-ḥarb, Secularism as "Fraud"

Following the demolition of the Babri mosque, the SIMI passed a number of resolutions, the first stating that if the original site of the mosque was not returned to Muslims, they would be compelled to secure it on their own. The second resolution stated that "the illusion of the idol of secularism and democracy has been broken and we have no relation with it" (*IM* 1992 [December–January 1993]: 32). Refuting the characterization of the demolition by Muslims and secular parties as the death of secularism, the resolution declared that indeed secularism had cast off its garb and become naked (*IM* 1993 [February–March]: 31). In 1994 the SIMI President described secularism as a "fraud"[25] coined by Hindus to fool Muslims (*IM* 1994 [December–January 1995]: 11). In SIMI's characterization, the role of the Congress Party in the demolition of the Babri mosque was "highly criminal and Zionist" (ibid.:11). The non-BJP parties, such as the Congress, Janata Dal, Bahujan Samaj Party, Telgu Desam, and even the various streams of the Left, were essentially no different from the BJP. They were all clowns of the anti-Islamic political system that SIMI sarcastically described as a "secular circus" (Figure 9).

SIMI's greatest anger was, directed, however, at *Sangẖ parivār*. It compared the Sangh activists who demolished the Babri mosque to Arab polytheists and described the former as worse than the latter. Although Arab polytheists had installed idols inside the *ka'ba*, the mosque in Mecca, they never thought of demolishing it. Nor did they break the promise they made. They tortured Muslims but did not rape women. In India, by contrast, the SIMI noted, Muslim women were not only raped but the act was also filmed (*IM* 1999 [September]: 33).[26] Because all political parties failed to protect the Babri mosque and thereby broke the promise given to Muslims, SIMI declared that India was now a *dar al-ḥarb* (*IM* 1993 [February–March]: 33; also see *Dawat* 2000 [April 28]: 121–24).

SIMI's declaration of India as *dar al-ḥarb*, however, was not only based on the demolition of the Babri mosque and the killing of Muslims in riots. Omar, with whom I began this chapter, argued that India was a *dar al-ḥarb*, regardless of the *Sangẖ parivār*'s tirade against Muslims. It must be noted, however, that Omar's declaration is rooted in the solid post-demolition context discussed above. He suggested that I read Kalim Islahi's book, *dar al-Islam aur dar al-ḥarb*. Islahi was a senior Jamaat member expelled because of his radical views on jihad and the Babri mosque. After his expulsion, he drew closer to SIMI, so close, in fact, that the SIMI presented him as one of its ideologues. Islahi believed that the renunciation of the Babri mosque was "illegitimate in the eyes of sharia" (in *IM* 2001 [January]: 15). His general position about India was that she was a *dar al-ḥarb*, because her political system was based on *human laws*, not sharia (*IM* 1992 [January]: 10).

Based on this logic, the SIMI boycotted the 2004 elections, which the BJP lost. At Falāḥ, during my second visit, the public debate centered on the forthcoming polls for the Parliament. The Jamaat leaders actively participated in the electoral efforts to defeat the BJP and ensure the victory of secularism and democracy (see the next chapter). Many Jamaat leaders also visited Falāḥ for this purpose. But at Falāḥ a silent countermobilization was taking place, with SIMI activists distributing four pamphlets railing against secularism and democracy: "Boycott the Idolatrous

Figure 9. *Islamic Movement's* depiction of the Indian political system as a "secular circus." From the author's collection.

System"; "Sedition of Secularism and Secularization"; "Sedition of Democracy"; and "Chasing Away the False Ideologies."[27] The pamphlets argued that Islam stood against elections, secularism, and democracy, and two of the pamphlets were actually reproductions of articles the Jamaat had published in its organ, *Zindgī*, in the 1950s. All those pamphlets derived their source of critique of democracy and secularism from Maududi, the citations from whose writings stamped the pages of the pamphlets. As we will see in the next chapter, it was precisely those writings of Maududi that the Jamaat disowned or interpreted anew.

Caliphate as the Foundation, Jihad as the Path

In the Action for Muslims conference in Bombay, the SIMI diagnosed the cause of Muslims' suffering as the incomplete implementation of the Qur'an. Quoting *sura al-baqara*, 85, of the Qur'an, SIMI argued:

> Then is it only a part of the Book that ye believe in, and do ye reject the rest? but what is the reward for those among you who behave like this but [are a] disgrace in this life?—and on the Day of Judgment they shall be consigned to the most grievous penalty. For God is not unmindful of what ye do. (*IM* 1992 [January]: 8)[28]

The Qur'an, the SIMI argued, enjoined Muslims to make Islam prevail over other religions and systems. Quoting *sura al-ṣaff*, 9, the SIMI said that Allah gave the Qur'an and sent Muhammad to make Islam dominant. To fulfill this commandment, the SIMI argued, it was compulsory that Muslims strive to establish the caliphate as a "religious duty" (*IM* 1996 [November–December]: 9) for two reasons. First, without the caliphate, Islam could never become dominant, nor could the system of polytheism be eliminated. Second, only under a caliphate could the tenets of Islam, such as prayer or the collection of *zakāt* (Islamic tax), be truly followed. Before the abolition of the caliphate in the 1920s, the caliph appointed an imam to lead the Friday prayer. In the absence of the caliphate today, the SIMI argued, "Friday prayer cannot be performed" (ibid.:73). According to the SIMI, all schools of thought in Islam agreed that after the abolition of the caliphate, it had to be reinstalled within three days. If the three days expired, according to the SIMI, every moment afterward would be a moment of "collective sin" (ibid.:68). Highlighting the centrality of the caliphate, SIMI recounted an episode following the death of the Prophet Muhammad. Muhammad was buried two and a half days after he died, but Muhammad's companions (*saḥāba*) installed the caliphate the very day he died. The *saḥāba* had postponed Mohammad's burial, because they considered that installing the caliphate was far more important than the burial. If the caliphate was so crucial to the Prophet's companions, the SIMI reasoned, it must be equally important for Muslims today (ibid.:68).

Along with the abandoning of jihad, the renunciation of the caliphate was another basis on which SIMI mounted its critique against the Jamaat. At Falāḥ I met Baqi, a SIMI *anṣār* and an important student leader. Given the government's ban on the SIMI, he spoke cautiously:

> The Jamaat is a coward [*buzdil*]. If it truly follows Maududi, as we do, in believing that the caliphate is an obligation [*farẓ*], then why does it not courageously say it in public? When they [the Jamaat] do *da'vat* among non-Muslims, I tell you, they only talk about monotheism [*tauḥīd*], prophethood, and life hereafter (*ākḥirat*), and out of fear leave out the caliphate. The caliphate is our foundation. You read Maududi. We are not saying something new. This is there in the Qur'an. Its sura *al-ṣaff* says that Islam has come to prevail over all other religions even though polytheists may not like it. When the Prophet Muhammad gave *da'vat* the whole of Mecca went against him. Why are non-Muslims not speaking out against the Jamaat? This only means it is not doing *da'vat* in the true sense. The Jamaat is revealing only a part of Islam to non-Muslims, not the whole of it. . . . Also note why the entire media and the Hindu polytheists are up in arms against us [the SIMI]. Because we are 100 percent truthful and are presenting Islam as it is.

When I pointed out to Baqi that the Jamaat had justified its position by offering the example of Prophet Nooh, who patiently carried the message of *da'vat* for nine hundred years (see chapter 7) and yet did not think that his mission was over, Baqi countered: "Was there any TV, radio, or newspapers in his time? That time [*vo zamāna*] was very different. Moreover, his lifespan was for more than nine hundred years, ours is just sixty." "The Jamaat gives the example of the Prophet Nooh," he continued, "but what about the Prophet Muhammad, who established an Islamic state in just twenty-three years?" According to Baqi, the example of the Prophet Nooh was insincere. In his opinion, it was a "cheap tactic," to erase the very notion of the caliphate from the minds and hearts of true Muslims.

In the Action for Muslims conference, SIMI also emphasized the significance of jihad and martyrdom. When it launched the campaign for the caliphate, jihad took on a new dimension. Now jihad was not only for the defense of Muslims under attack from *Sangḥ parivār* and the police, but it was also for the establishment of the caliphate. Without jihad, *Islamic Movement* wrote, "a revival of the caliphate is not possible" (*IM* 1996 [November–December]: 9). It concluded with this prophetic saying: "A person *sans* desire for martyrdom dies in a state of hypocrisy" (*IM* 1993 [February–March]: 48).

Muhammad as Commander

In the wake of the Babri mosque's demolition, the figure of the Prophet Muhammad became a core element of the SIMI's newly constructed radical theology. As the reader will recall, in my meeting with Omar he presented Muhammad as a "prophet of wars." During our fairly long conversation I was struck most by his portrayal of Muhammad. Having studied for six years in an Islamic seminary and read a considerable volume of literature on Islam, I had never heard or read about Muhammad as a "prophet of wars" (barring the writings of some Orientalists). Astonished, I asked him who had described Muhammad in this way. Omar claimed there was widespread ignorance concerning Muhammad's life. Even renowned ulema, Omar held, deliberately did not mention this authentic saying of the Prophet—that "he is the prophet of war" (*nabiʾul malāḥim*)—as reported in the collection of *ḥadīth* by Imam Bukhari. In his view, this came about primarily because during the last century, most ulema expunged the word "jihad" from their writings and presented it as if it were a "condemned term." Omar regarded the apologetic attitude of ulema as responsible for the suppression of the Prophet's saying.

Omar pointed to the British as the main conspirators behind this suppression. To douse the fire of jihad against the colonial regime, the British bribed many ulema to write that jihad was not a part of Islam. Ulema thus suppressed the saying that Muhammad was also the "prophet of wars." To convince me further of this saying, he referred to a practice of the Prophet. Whenever Muhammad had to attend nature's call, he always carried a spear (*nēzā*). At that time, he said, humans are at their most vulnerable state. Thus, in Omar's opinion, the Prophet took along a spear to protect himself from the enemies of Islam. Upon Muhammad's death, Omar added, the Prophet had left behind nine swords, all for the purpose of defending and expanding Islam. He then narrated several other practices from Muhammad's life to prove that he was a "prophet of wars."

It should be obvious from my argument thus far that Qasim Omar's employment of a militarized language to describe Muhammad's life and his portrayal of him as a "prophet of wars" was far from a straightforward replay of an image supposedly germane to Islamic tradition and history. In many ways, it was an invention. And the political context in which this invention took place was the ascendance of virulent Hindu nationalism, particularly its declared opposition to the cultural identity and lives of Muslims. Put differently, the SIMI's portrayal of Muhammad as a prophet of war was indeed a new Muhammad fashioned under the dark shadow of anti-Muslim, masculine Hindutva. It was an obvious response to the projection of the Hindu god Ram as a combative god, "heavily armed" and "ready for war" (Kapur 1993; also see Thapar 1993). Kapur deftly

Figure 10. The SIMI's calendar with its radicalized motto. From author's collection.

describes how the image of Ram underwent an important metamorphosis during the 1980s. According to Kapur, in the hands of militant Hindu nationalists Ram was transformed from a child god of innocence and gentleness to a combative, warrior-like figure. In response to Hindutva's militarization of Ram, the SIMI discourse transformed the image of the Prophet Muhammad into a combative, warrior-like figure.

The radicalization of SIMI, as this chapter demonstrates, was best captured in an epigraph it invented to convey its motto. From 1986 to mid-1996, the year it launched the caliphate campaign, *Islamic Movement* carried no epigraphs. Afterward it began to include, in poetic prose, a five-line epigraph that in many ways became its slogan, appearing in most of its publications, including a calendar. As the quotation below shows, the second line in the epigraph describes Muhammad as "our commander."

This use of a military vocabulary fits with Omar's militarized portrayal of the Prophet Muhammad as a "prophet of wars."

Allah is Our Lord
Muhammad is Our Commander
Quran is Our Constitution
Jihad is Our Path
Shahādat [Martyrdom] is Our Desire

The next chapter discusses how the Jamaat, in marked contrast to the SIMI, negotiated with Indian secularism and democracy and offered a new interpretation of Islam characteristically different from that of SIMI.

CHAPTER 7

Negotiating the Idol

SECULARISM, DEMOCRACY, AND ALLAH'S KINGDOM

> The option elected by any religious community will be determined, of course, not by the timeless truths of scripture but by the struggle for influence among the rival bearers of the world.
>
> —ROBERT HEFNER, *Civil Islam*

> Realism and flexibility are . . . the most important features of Islamic methodology.
>
> —RACHID GHANNOUCHI, *"Participation in a non-Islamic Government"*

The February 2002 UP Assembly elections were remarkable in many ways. The BJP, which was in power in Delhi an in Lucknow, had banned the SIMI only a few months before the elections on charges of "sedition" (*Hindustan Times* 2001). To woo voters, the BJP's advertisements described SIMI as a "Pak [Pakistan]–supported anti-national organization . . . spreading terrorism," and listed the BJP's banning of SIMI as one of its achievements (*PJ* 2002 [February 18–24]: 11; see Figure 11). The advertisements projected the BJP as the defender of the Indian nation under attack from "Muslim terrorists."[1]

In this milieu, the Jamaat plunged into the elections and launched the "People's Awareness Campaign [*ʿavāmī bēdārī muhim*]." Its leaders toured every nook and cranny of UP to mobilize voters against the BJP. On January 31, the National Secretary of the Jamaat (who was also secretary general of the Mushāverat; see below) held a press conference in Aligarh. Although some members of the Jamaat resented its participation in the elections on the ground that it was a "straight deviation from the original ideology" and that Maududi had described democracy as "*shirk* [polytheism] and *ṭāġhūt* [idol],"[2] the majority welcomed the engagement. I accompanied the most vocal leader of the pro-election position to a hotel in Russellganj, the venue of the conference. Addressing reporters, the Secretary said the Jamaat had intervened in elections to "defend secularism and democracy." When a reporter asked whom the Jamaat was supporting, this was their exchange:

Figure 11. The BJP's election poster featuring the SIMI's ban. From *Pānch janya* (18–24 February 2000): 11.

SECRETARY: We are not supporting any party or candidate. We want that the parties that stand for secularism and democracy, as opposed to the fascism [of the BJP], should win. Our country [*dēsh*] and Constitution [*dastūr*] adopted the path of <u>secularism</u> and <u>democracy</u>. Now some forces are bent on tampering with them. We are against such a tampering.

REPORTER 1: Ok, we understood your point. . . . Tell us which candidates you are backing?

SECRETARY: We are not supporting any particular candidate. . . . We want that secular votes don't get divided so that secular, democratic [*jamhūriyatpasand*] parties grow stronger in UP.

REPORTER 2: Do you have any connections [*ta'alluq*] with the SIMI?

SECRETARY: No! The SIMI is independent [*āzād*]. Our own student organization is the SIO.

Although the Secretary never named the BJP, it was clear that *muhim* was directed against it. Notably, while arguing for the defense of "secularism and democracy" and the defeat of "fascism," he did not mention Islam. Without the reporters bringing it up, he clarified that the defeat of fascism was necessary not for Muslims but for the very survival of "the nation [*mulk*], the Constitution [*dastūr*], and democracy [*jamhūriyat*]." Two weeks after the conference, the Jamaat's Urdu organ, *Dawat*, published a list of candidates, instructing its members to vote for them (*Dawat* 2002 [February 13]: 4; [February 16]: 4). The list included candidates of nearly all the non-BJP parties—the Samajwadi Party, the Congress Party, the Communist Party of India (CPI), and the Communist Party of India Marxist (CPIM).[3]

An important question is whether the Secretary's call for democracy, secularism, and India's Constitution was the Jamaat's true belief or merely a tactical posture dressed up for public consumption. What is significant, in any case, is the Jamaat's participation in democracy and the recognition of its rules. Here Oliver Roy's contention seems pertinent. Disagreeing with the view that Tariq Ramadan's new theology hides the real Islamist motive, he observes, that "whether you live as an owner of the world or merely as a tenant, the important thing is to respect the terms of the lease" (2007:51). My point is that participation in the democratic processes makes actors like the Jamaat, which had less enthusiasm for democracy in the past, become democracy's avid advocate. To quote Roy again: "If we had to wait for everyone to become a democrat before creating democracy, France would still be a monarchy" (ibid.:93). But, more important, I take the Secretary's statement not as the *basis* of my argument but as a culmination of a long drawn-out *internal* process—from 1961 to 1985—within the Jamaat. To this end, I discuss at length how the illegitimacy of secularism and democracy became an issue of intense debate within the Jamaat's *shura*.

This chapter charts out the transformation of the Jamaat's ideology from Partition to the present. I show how the Jamaat, which once believed that true Muslims must establish Allah's kingdom and described any other form of government as idolatry, came to canvass for the victory of non-Muslim parties. What was *haram* and *shirk* for the Jamaat in one context became *halal* and Islamic in another. This mutation of the Jamaat, or what Crossley (2002:7) calls *movement* within a movement, indicates, I contend, that Islamism is not frozen in discourse but is dynamic. Clearly questionable is the generalization that Islam and Islamism are everywhere opposed to democracy and secularism. Indeed, today the Jamaat is an ardent defender of secularism and democracy. Far from being signs of *jāhiliyat*, secularism and democracy are now a "divine boon" for the Jamaat. Furthermore, in the course of its mutation, the obligation to establish an Islamic state strayed from its agenda. In the past, Jamaat equated Islam with an Islamic state, but now an Islamic state is just one among several aspects of Islam, not the foundation. In the changed context of postcolonial India, the Jamaat (re)interpreted Maududi's ideology and came to a new interpretation of Islam, radically different from the SIMI's.

The first section of this chapter outlines why the Jamaat initially (from Partition to the early 1960s) regarded voting in elections of secular democratic polity *haram* and banned its members from voting in elections. Boycotting elections stemmed from a mythic hope that an Islamic state was around the corner. The Jamaat's strategies for establishing an Islamic state are discussed in the second section, where we see Jamaat's shift from boycott to participation in elections and its acceptance of secularism and democracy. This shift culminated in the Jamaat's acceptance of the legitimacy of secularism and democracy, and the lifting, in the 1980s, of its voting ban on members. By the early 1960s the mythic hope for an Islamic state began to fade, and thus the Jamaat started to reconsider its position. The key reason for the erosion of mythic hope was that the Muslim public rejected its ideology. The final section describes how the Jamaat's second shift, from acceptance of secularism and democracy to passionate defense of them, was catalyzed by the rise of Hindutva since the 1980s and its onslaught on secularism and democracy. The Jamaat's monumental ideological mutations offered a sharp critique of the SIMI.

Secularism and Democracy as *Haram*

Although it is wise to doubt the theory that important social changes are usually brought about by great individuals, we should not dismiss the role of leadership as studies of social movements often do. Obsessed with "irrationalism," collective behavior theorists barely took leadership seriously. For a different reason, resource mobilization and political process theories also shunned the study of leadership. The theorists of new social movements were too preoccupied with "spontaneity" to pay attention to leadership. As Gramsci argued, however, pure spontaneity does not exist. Collective action by its very nature is based on the leadership of certain individuals who matter more than ordinary activists (Barker et al. 2001; Melucci 1996). This is certainly relevant to understand the history of the ideological transformation of a Leninist organization such as the Jamaat. My approach to understanding the Jamaat's history differs from the usual mode. The Jamaat's transformation, I believe, cannot be grasped in fixed calendrical terms (Geertz 1980), and so my use of dates and periods are descriptively suggestive, not deterministic.

Install a Hindu, not a Secular, State

The signature cause behind the Jamaat's continued opposition to secularism and democracy in post-Partition India was its belief that they were *ṭāghūt* par excellence. Equally important was the hope that *ḥukūmat-e-ilāhiya*, or Islamic revolution, was as possible in India as it was in Pakistan. In chapter 2 I dwelled on the two paths Maududi charted: one was gradual, long, and from below and the other was quick and top-down. So unflinching was the Jamaat members' conviction of a possible Islamic revolution that the Jamaat leadership dismissed any change in its ideology. In March 1948, however, the Secretary of the Jamaat, Banaras division, Hafiz Imamuddin Ramnagri, was the first to urge the leadership to redefine its ideology "under the changed circumstances" as follows:

- Change, "obligatorily," the Constitution and goal of the Jamaat (including its name). The goal of the Jamaat should be "reform of moral behavior. . . ."
- Only that portion of the Jamaat's literature should be retained that are "in tune with current situation."
- The Jamaat should not consider it a "sin [*gunāh*]" if a member leaves the party. (Ramnagri's letter quoted in Nadwi 1990:21–24)

Considering Ramnagri's proposal as almost sacrilegious, the Jamaat expelled him from the party. Abullais Nadwi, the first *amīr* of the Jamaat after Partition, stated that "we are not ready to budge from our ideology [*maslak*]" or "change our goals and principles" (1990:61). Describing Ramnagri's proposal as a sign of "fear," the Jamaat argued that if it changed so fundamentally, then what difference would remain between the Jamiatul Ulema-e-Hind and the Jamaat (Nadwi 1990:29)?[4]

Soon after Ramnagri's expulsion, in April 1949, he wrote to Nadwi that he wanted to continue his friendship with him and other party members. But because, as noted, the Jamaat regarded it a sin if a member left the party, Nadwi replied: "Your friendship can be dear to us only when you like our ideology, [our] goal . . . and work with us. However, unfortunately, if this is not the case . . . then, we do not accept your friendship even for a moment" (Nadwi 1990:34–35). Indifferent to Ramnagri's proposal, the Jamaat proceeded to follow Maududi's charted parth to Islamic revolution (see chapter 2). In pursuit of the "quick, top-down" route, Nadwi, as the Jamaat *amīr*, published a pamphlet in 1949 titled "*Kyā hindustān dunyā kā rahnumā ban saktā hai*" (hereafter, *Rahnumā*) (Can India Become the World Leader).[5] Its goal was to appeal to Hindus not to base the political system on democracy (*Rahnumā* n.d.). Almost duplicating Maududi's Pathankot speech of 1947, the pamphlet stated that India would emerge a world leader only if she became a state based on three Islamic principles: submission to God, humanism, and the sovereignty of God (as opposed to secularism, nationalism, and democracy). Stating that these Islamic principles were "your [Hindus'] own lost thing," the pamphlet stated that if Hindu leaders agreed to a religious state, "the Jamaat would offer help in such an endeavor" (ibid.:32). The pamphlet concluded:

> It is your duty [*farẓ*] to recognize, assess, and examine that [the three Islamic principles] and display the same objectivity [*bē-taʿṣṣubī*] you have adopted towards European democracy and Russian communism. We are sure that if you examine that, then you would realize that in reality only this system [Islamic] is the guarantee of your and the world's welfare. And only this way can India become a leader of the world. (ibid.:32)

However, if Hindus did not accept the Islamic system, Nadwi urged them in 1950, to install a Hindu state. He also agreed to accept, unconditionally, whatever treatment such a state would give to Muslims, including death.

> But I request them [Hindu leaders] to adopt only those principles and based on them establish whatever system of life [*niẓām-e-zindgī*] exists among them. We would prefer that [Hindu state] to the secular systems of Europe. In that [Hindu] system, if there is a provision of death for Muslims like us, we are agreed even to that. (*RIR* 1951:59)[6]

The Jamaat's campaign for a religious state, and its opposition to a secular state,[7] as stated before, was based on Maududi's strategy that, once Hindus accepted the need for a religious state, they could be convinced that Islam was preferable to secular democracy. To this end, the Jamaat proceeded to try to convince the "illustrious personalities of India" (all invariably top Congress leaders) about the viability of Islam. It gave *daʿvat* of Islam, among others, to Rajendra Prasad (1884–1963), the first president of the Indian Republic; Jawaharlal Nehru, the first prime minister of India; Pattabhi Sitaraimayya, the president of the Congress in 1948 and the governor of Madhya Pradesh; Gobind Balabh Pant, the chief minister of UP; C. Rajagopalachari, the first governor general of Independent India; and Sardar Baldev Singh, India's first defense minister (*RIR* 1951:60–62).[8]

The *daʿvat* by the Jamaat to Hindu leaders probably meant conversion to Islam, or, if they did not convert at least acceptance of the three principles of an Islamic state. In other words, even Hindus could run an Islamic state if they accepted the Islamic principles necessary to run the state. This was Maududi's innovation. When urging Hindus not to mimic Western secular democracy, in May 1947, he pleaded:

> Our real goal is *not to change the hands* that run the present system but to change the system. The objective of our endeavor is not that the [present] system continues and is run on the same principles and an easterner, and not a westerner, ran it; an Indian, not a British ran it; or

> a "Muslim," not a Hindu, ran it. For us, with a mere change of hands, nothing changes. Pork is after all pork and is by nature unholy whether a *kāfir* cooks it or a Muslim. *Rather, it is more poignant and misleading if the cook is a Muslim.* (1951:6–7, my emphasis)

Maududi used the metaphor of pork to denote a polity based against sharia, and it did not matter who governed such a polity, Hindu or Muslim. In fact, Maududi placed Muslims who would run such an anti-sharia system in quotes, "Muslim," meaning that they were not true Muslims. Clearly he was referring to the Muslim League, which Maududi believed did not have the agenda of an Islamic state. Notably Maududi's focus was on the "principles" of Islam and their disentanglement from "Muslim." In Pakistan he opposed the League leaders because they were also trying to establish an "infidelic system [*kāfirāna niẓām*]," the only difference being that it would be presided over "by an Abdullah [meaning a Muslim] rather than a Ram Prasad [meaning a Hindu]" (Maududi 2003a: 64). In India the Jamaat interpreted Maududi's words to mean that even Hindus could run an Islamic state if it were based on the principles of submission to God, humanism, and the sovereignty of God.

In the 1960s Syed Hamid Husain (1920–1985), a prominent Jamaat leader, visited AMU. A scion of a feudal family, Husain, before converting to the Jamaat, was a Communist, was Westernized, and was an avid filmgoer (*HN* 1985–86 [December–January]: 6ff.). Under the Jamaat's influence, he resigned from his job with the British Army, considering it *haram*. Because he had a Western education, the Jamaat regarded him its star preacher for AMU. In his lectures to students, Husain attacked secularism, nationalism, and democracy, presenting Islam as an alternative system based on submission to God, humanism, and the sovereignty of God. Describing Hussain's alternative as "foolish" and "reactionary," an agitated student asked Husain how an Islamic system was possible in India. Intizar, a retired AMU professor who was a student at the time and attending the lecture, told me that Husain replied, "Yes, it is [possible]. If Hindus accepted the three Islamic principles, India could become an Islamic system." When asked if he meant that Hindus had to convert to Islam, he answered no. At that, Intizar and his friends laughed at Husain's "foolishness [*bē-vaqūfī*]" and "irrationality [*pāgalpan*]."

Mimicking the Communists

The Jamaat's first path to an Islamic revolution—gradual, and from below—replicated that of the Communists, whom it condemned in public but privately admired. In a document meant only for members, the Jamaat reflected upon its strategy during the 1950s as follows:

> If we organized Muslims along the real principles of Islam and presented *da'vat* of Islam in the same way as . . . Communists were doing for . . . communism, then there was no reason why we could not get the *support of the people of this country*. . . . And we also used to say that Communists did not even comprise 1 percent of India's population but they were determined to make this country communist, whereas Muslims numbered forty-five million. If even 50 percent of them . . . preached Islam, then, *Muslims had one thousand times more of a chance than Communists had to make India an Islamic state*. (*JID* undated:7, my emphasis)

Imitating the Communists, in 1955 *Zindgī*, the Jamaat's monthly Urdu organ launched in November 1948, wrote:

> If we consider the population of the whole world . . . we can say that every sixth man is a Muslim, whereas out of three hundred men there is only one member of the Communist Party. Despite their small number, however, communism has captured one-fourth of the planet and is one of the two leading world powers. (1955 [July–August]: 66)

Dismissing the demographic fact that Muslims are a minority in India, it then concluded:

> Thus this proves that the issue of minority and majority is nonsense. What makes a movement successful is the action of its activists and the sacrifices made on the way to achieving its goal. (ibid.:67)

The model for the Jamaat, it appears, was not the Prophet Muhammad but the Communists, who were also its chief competitors. As its competitors, the Jamaat campaigned against communists by presenting Islam as a morally superior system of life (*niẓām-e-ḥayāt*) compared to communism. From its first issue, *Zindgī*, carried endless polemics—in prose and verse—against communism. By the early 1950s the Jamaat had published three Urdu booklets against communism (*Zindgī* 1951 [April–May]: 2) for an audience of Western-educated Muslim Communists. To address ulema, *Zindgī* carried a series of articles detailing how the five pillars of Islam, such as prayer (*namāz*), could enthuse Muslims to establish an Islamic system (*iqāmat-e-dīn*) (1951 [April–May]: 24). It should be noted that the Jamaat had replaced its earlier goal of *ḥukūmat-e-ilāhiya* with *iqāmat-e-dīn* in 1948, pointing out that the replacement was merely terminological. Thus the Jamaat published articles with titles like, for example, "obligation of *iqāmat-e-dīn*" (*Zindgi* 1957 [July–August]: 137), "*iqāmat-e-dīn* is an obligation" (Qadri 2000), and "Mission of Muslims" (Qadri 1999).

For non-Muslims the Jamaat published a Hindi magazine, *Ujālā*, but when it failed financially, *kānti* was launched (*RIR* 1951:60). By the end of 1951 the Jamaat had published eight books and pamphlets in Hindi and eleven in English (*Zindgī* 1951 [April–May]: 4). As the 1950s drew to a close, the Jamaat also published a Hindi translation of the Qur'an (*Zindgī* 1955 [July–August]: 113). Equipped with these assets, the Jamaat wanted to win the educated, influential classes of Hindus to its cause.

The Jamaat literature, although rich, barely had an impact. From 240 members in 1948, the Jamaat membership rose only to 981 by 1960 (see Appendix 1). Given India's population of 420 million, of which roughly 42 million were Muslim in 1961, a membership of 981 was clearly insignificant. Still, the tiny organization had great hopes. As early as 1951 *Zindgī* described how life would be better if "God-worshippers [*ḳhudāparastōn*]," as opposed to Communists, were to run the Indian state:

- Humans would not rule over humans, and humans would be God's vice regent. There would be "God's Rule [*ḳhudāī rāj*]."
- The free intermingling between sexes would be regarded as a "serious crime." "Women will remain women, and men will remain men." (*Zindgī* 1951 [January]: 35–40)

That the Islamic state was imminent may seem "foolish" and "irrational," as Intizar implied at the AMU lecture.[9] Yet, I was told by Kaif Islahi, a Rampur-based young Jamaat activist during the early 1950s, that it looked "real" to him then. In his recollection, the reality of an Islamic state lay in the "revolutionary ideology" of Maududi, whose book changed him almost magically. He thought that an Islamic state would come about through the hard work of *da'vat* and by divine miracle (*ghaibī madad*). "We had madness [*dīvāngī*] that the revolution would inevitably come." So convinced was he about the revolution that an unmarried Islahi preferred to stay alone in India rather than migrate with his parents to Pakistan.

Like other ideologies, the Jamaat ideology had its own myth. According to Georges Sorel, ideology grows out of myth and at the same time begets myth defined as "expressions of a determination to act" (in Halpern 1961:138). Myth thus propels actors into action for radical change. For Sorel, myth is neither false nor unreal bur rather is an ideology, like Marxism, imbued with an impeccable power to swing its practitioners into action.[10] Islahi, too, believed that the Jamaat was heralding an Islamic state.

Boycott of an Idolatrous System

The myth of the Islamic state went hand in hand with the Jamaat's boycott of the political system it characterized as an "idolatrous system [*ṭāghūtī niẓām*]." Five institutions, in particular, became the target of the Jamaat's boycott: the judiciary, the army, the banking system, the "Western" university, and elections. It considered the judiciary the most crucial institution of *ṭāghūt*, because it executed the anti-sharia laws. The Jamaat did not allow its members to take a dispute to court, least of all to allow them to become lawyers or judges. In 1954, when Nadwi and several other leaders were arrested, the Jamaat did not contest their arrest (*RMS*-1:103).[11] Joining the army was also considered *haram* (*Zindgī* 1951 [November–December–January 1952]; also reproduced in Hamdi 1990), as was the banking system. In chapter 2 I outlined the reasons why the Jamaat boycotted universities such as AMU, calling them "slaughterhouse[s]." Elections of secular democracy, however, were the most violent embodiment of *ṭāghūt*, according to the Jamaat.

India held its first elections to Parliament in 1951 and 1952. Abullais Nadwi had campaigned against Muslims' participation in those elections. In a pamphlet titled *The Issue of Elections and Indian Muslims,*[12] laced with verses from the Qur'an and *hadīth* and mass-distributed (within months it was reprinted)[13] before the elections, Nadwi argued why Muslims must boycott the elections:

> A Muslim believes in the *sovereignty of Allah*; that, among others, is the straight and foremost demand of his basic [belief in] *kalima*. And it is an open matter that the entire hullabaloo about elections is the spectacle [*tamāshā*] of *sovereignty of man* whose relation, howsoever stretched, in no way can be linked with the sovereignty of Allah. (Nadwi 1951:63; my emphasis)

He then issued a warning to Muslims:

> If you go into details, you will realize that in whatever form you participate in elections, you are flouting the commandments and guidance of sharia at every step. (ibid.:63)

Nadwi refused to participate even in the elections of village bodies (*panchāyat*), saying that however independent they may be, they were still a "department of an un-godly system" and Muslims' participation in then was equally "wrong" and "lethal" (*RIR* 1951:47). There was no way that Nadwi could enforce his *fatwa* on ordinary Muslims. In line with the Jamaat's pre-Partition position, however, he continued the organizational ban on its members to vote in elections. The Jamaat also boycotted all Muslim organizations, including those run by ulema of the Deoband, which did not have an Islamic state on their agenda and were enthusiastic about elections. According to Nadwi, participation by Muslim organizations in elections was "absolutely against the faith [of Islam]" (*RIR* 1951:47).

In 1950 Zahirul Hasan Lari convened a conference at Lucknow appealing to all Muslim organizations, the Jamaat included, to come together to safeguard community interests. Nadwi refused to participate, stating that the other Muslim organizations participating in the conference lacked the "fundamental perspective of Islam" and were not ready to solve Muslims' problems "by making Islam as their foundation." Nadwi's response to Lari's invitation was similar to his response to Ramnagri, the expelled Jamaat member. Just as he had refused Ramnagri's offer of friendship because the latter would not endorse the Jamaat ideology, he also refused Lari's invitation because Muslim organizations participating in the conference did not regard the political system as *ṭāghūt* (*RIR* 1951: 48–49). Those organizations, according to Maududi, were "Muslim" within quotes, or "census Muslim." The Jamaat also refused to participate in the Jaunpur Muslim Convention held after Partition. It did, however, send an observer, who remarked that although Muslim leaders conducted their other affairs in accordance with sharia, albeit only partially, in politics they always followed an anti-Islamic European model (*RIR* 1951:51). In 1961 Muslims organized another convention, which also rejected Jamaat's Islamist agenda. Later the Jamaat regretted that the convention had "secularism as its *kalima*" rather than Islam (*RMS-1*:189).

The Jamaat also boycotted the second parliamentary and Assembly elections of 1957. Electing a Parliament to legislate against divine laws, Nadwi argued, was blatant polytheism. He further said, "we consider it totally wrong that . . . India has adopted secularism." There was one visible difference, however. Unlike in 1952, in 1957 Nadwi said that he would not ask Muslims to boycott the elections (*Zindgī* 1957 [February]: 53, 62).

From Boycott to Participation in an Idolatrous System

The shift from boycott to participation was not swift and straightforward. Although the Jamaat publicly acknowledged the legitimacy of the Constitution of India, and of secularism and democracy, in private this acknowledgment was complex and punctuated with a lengthy strategy. The strategy of the Jamaat leadership was to reorient its rank and file from boycott to participation in the idolatrous system in the name of *iqāmat-e-dīn* (see below). Once the grounds for participation were set, the Jamaat leadership, with Nadwi in the forefront, shelved the goal of *iqāmat-e-dīn* and invoked it to justify participation and gradually erode the idea of *iqāmat-e-dīn*. As the following discussion indicates, the Jamaat's transformation was shot through with conflict and debate over what constituted authentic Islam.

Following the Masses

On the eve of the third parliamentary elections in 1962, the Jamaat made a dramatic turn and, before the elections, mass-distributed an Urdu pamphlet with a Leninist title in Persian, *Pas che bāyad kard?* ("What Is to Be Done?" hereafter, *Kard*). Nadwi argued that it was "tantamount to suicide" for Muslims to remain aloof, and he pleaded with Muslims to "take part in the elections" (1962:9, 25). Two factors forced the Jamaat into this shift. First, an allegation was leveled against the Jamaat that it was "communal" (*RMS-1*:185) in that it did not believe in the Indian Constitution and, ergo, refrained from participating in elections. The allegation was not unfounded, for Nadwi had previously stated that the Jamaat would not participate even in the village elections, let alone the parliamentary elections, of an ungodly state. When the Jamaat's hope reigned high in the 1950s, it dismissed this allegation, arguing that if rebellion against an anti-God state was a crime, then rebellion against God was a greater crime (*Zindgī* 1955 [September]: II). As the allegation grew fiercer, however, the Jamaat became concerned because it was leveled not only by the government[14] but even more by Muslims. The Jamiatul Ulema, among others, was the most outspoken as it described the Jamaat as "communal [*firqāparast*]" (in Rizvi 1989:155), because, by challenging the composite nationalism of the Jamiatul Ulema, it was guilty of partitioning India. Displeased with my research, a leader of the Jamiatul Ulema, in its Delhi office, asked me: "Why are you doing research on these people [the Jamaat]; they helped create Pakistan."[15] The Jamiatul Ulema described the Jamaat as "akin to Motazelite, Kharjite . . . Qadianist" and "its principles, beliefs, and practices . . . [as] opposed to Ahl-e-Sunna-o-Jamaat [majority Sunni Islam]" (*Zindgī* 1951 [June–August]: 53). In 1951 Deoband published a series of *fatwas* against the Jamaat: "Wipe Out Maududi Mischief [*fitna*]," "The Maududi Movement Is Lethal and Poisonous," "Followers of Maududi Are Deviant," and "Don't Offer Prayer behind Maududites" (ibid.:51). In 1951 the madrasa Mazāhirul Ulūm at Saharanpur expelled one of its teachers who had converted to the Jamaat under Maududi's influence (in *Zindgī* 1951 [October]: 38).

Second, and more important, the masses of Muslims and their leadership refused to heed the Jamaat's call for boycotting elections. As a result, it became isolated and demoralized. Nadwi's call for participation in the elections reflected the frustration that had gripped the Jamaat, whose activists had also begun to persuade the leadership to reconsider its position (*Dawat* 1960 [January 28]: 165). Nadwi's *Kard* was a rhetorical coup to enable the Jamaat to save face and prepare it for a radical shift. Pressured by multitudes of Muslims who believed in the "*kalima* of secularism," the Jamaat was now following them, rather than leading. Against the Jamaat's position, 42 Muslim candidates contested 35 seats in the 1952 parliamentary elections, and 23 were elected (the total number of seats was 489). In the 1957 parliamentary elections, 61 Muslims contested 46 seats, and 22 were elected. In the Assembly elections, too, Muslims massively participated. Throughout India, 617 Muslim candidates contested 416 seats for the 1952 Assembly elections, and 520 for 387 seats in the 1957 elections. In the Assembly elections for UP, 41 Muslims (9.53 percent of the total seats) were elected to the Assembly in 1952, and 38 (8.84 percent) were elected in 1957. The figures for the same period in Bihar were 22 and 25 (Krishna 1967:185–187; Blair 1973:1280).[16] As these figures show, the Muslims and their leaders obviously disavowed the Jamaat's boycott of elections in 1952 and 1957.

Fearful of further isolation from Muslims, on the eve of the third elections in 1962 the Jamaat took a new course. Nadwi contended that Muslims should participate in the elections but only to realize the Qur'anic obligation of *shahādat-e-ḥaq*, witness to the Truth (1962:34–37).[17] He proposed a national convention to map out a plan and also suggested that the convention must invite Muslims of all schools of thought (1962:23). Nadwi's 1962 pamphlet, *Kard*, was indeed a signal the Jamaat flashed to Muslims that it was now willing to cooperate with them and participate in the political process. Three political streams came together to form the All-India Muslim Majlis Mushāverat (henceforth, Mushāverat) in 1964: the Muslim League, a disgruntled section of the Jamiatual Ulema,[18] and the Jamaat (Qureshi 1971). The first two had no issue with secular democracy. The Jamaat alone opposed secularism and democracy.

The key leader around whom all Muslim organizations rallied to form the Mushāverat was Syed Mahmud (1889–1971), Nehru's contemporary at Cambridge. After Independence, he served as minister of state for external affairs. Mahmud agreed to lead the Mushāverat because, after Independence, he was disappointed with the Congress's failure to practice secularism (Makki 2003:210–12; Rizvi 1989:153). His disappointment only increased after Nehru's death in May 1964. Under his leadership, the Mushāverat stood for secularism, democracy, and national integration (Ansari 1966; Quraishi 1971:1230). Mahmud doubted that the Jamaat shared the framework of the Mushāverat, and before the Mushāverat's formation, he had asked Nadwi if the Jamaat believed in the Constitution of India and if it was opposed to secularism. In his reply, Nadwi affirmed the Jamaat's faith in the Constitution as well as in a secular state (*Radiance* 1964 [July 12]: 16).

Theological versus Demotic

By participating in the Mushāverat, the Jamaat publicly accepted secularism and the Indian Constitution, and also agreed to share a platform with the Muslim organizations it had boycotted in the past. However, it still opposed sharing a platform with Hindus. Some Hindus had also joined the Mushāverat meeting, which led Nadwi to say that "a joint platform of leaders belonging to different religions is contrary to the principles and policies of the Jamaat" (in Hussnain 1968:75–76). A writer wedded to the "original ideology" of Maududi observed that "the Jamaat's practical participation in the politics of the Mushāverat tore apart the attire of the Jamaat-e-Islami's revolutionary ideology" (Shaz 1987:39).

In preparation to participate in the Mushāverat, the Jamaat, in 1961, sent a questionnaire to fifteen ulema (including those from Deoband and Nadwa) asking if Islam allowed participation in secular-democratic elections. Of the fifteen respondents, twelve answered yes. Saeed Akbarabadi, a noted *ʿālim*, argued that Muslims should indeed strive to achieve a "truly secular-democratic" state (*JIMI* 160). The three respondents opposing participation were ardent followers of Maududi. Clearly, by asking ulema about the legitimacy of participating in elections, the Jamaat inadvertently separated the religious from the secular. Thus the Jamaat did not consider its own authority Islamic, or at least sufficiently Islamic.

The Jamaat's participation in the Mushāverat was not a cosmetic device addressed to Muslim or non-Muslim outsiders. This shift had also begun within the Jamaat. In July 1961 the *shura*, the Jamaat's most powerful decision-making body, similar to the Communist Party's Politburo, had set up a committee to determine if "the path of elections could be used for the goal of *iqāmat-e-dīn*." It proposed the following recommendations: (1) "It would be illegitimate [*nājāʾiz*] to fight elections and enter the Assembly if the purpose was only to sustain an ungodly system [*ghair- ilāhī niẓām*]"; and (2) "to make the Indian Constitution Islamic, we can participate in elections" (*JIMI* undated: 20). The committee also reported that the Jamaat could participate in elections for the above objectives only when "the condition of the country should be such that the change of public opinion for an [Islamic] system would be enough for the establishment of that system," and "public opinion has been molded to the extent that, through participation in elections, there is hope for change in the Constitution." The Jamaat's *shura* accepted both the objectives and conditions for participation, using *iqāmat-e-dīn* as a reference point. Further, participation meant that the Jamaat candidates, in principle, could contest elections.

In the same *shura* meeting, three new resolutions were introduced that did not refer to *iqāmat-e-dīn* but did relate to voting even when the Jamaat would not put up its own candidates. In the "interests of Islam and Muslims," if a Jamaat member, the resolution suggested:

- Becomes a *candidate* in the elections of an ungodly system, then "his candidacy is legitimate [*jāʾez*] *if he is not from a non-Islamic Party*."
- "*Votes* in elections under an ungodly system, then *his casting of a vote is legitimate under some conditions*."

- "*Votes* in elections of an ungodly system and *if the candidate is not from a non-Islamic party*, then his casting of a vote is legitimate." (27–28; my emphasis)[19]

With Nadwi as *amīr* and ex-officio chair of the sixteen-member *shura*, these resolutions were passed by a majority vote. However, in the 1962 elections, the Jamaat did not field its own candidates and maintained the voting ban on its members. The *shura* urged common Muslims to participate in elections but not to become "a tool of the ungodly system" (30–32).

The election issue resurfaced in the *shura* on the eve of the third parliamentary elections in 1967. In 1966 the *shura* had passed a new resolution of objective with majority votes: "considering the present system of anti-Islamic government against the Truth [*ḳhilāf-e-ḥaq*], it is legitimate to participate in elections for the vital interests of Islam and Muslims" (46). With this new objective, the *shura* decided that the Jamaat would not field its own candidates for the 1967 elections nor would it lift the voting ban on its members. However, in 1967 the *shura* approved three criteria under which members could vote.

Under the criteria in Table 3 an exception was made in the Assembly elections for the Bhopal Constituency where Aftab, a Muslim candidate, was in the fray. The *shura* argued that Aftab lived up to its criteria (60), and so for the first time the Jamaat lifted the voting ban in the 1967 Assembly elections. After this decision, Nadwi stated that the Jamaat should proceed slowly, but firmly, to lift the voting ban in the future (61–63). In 1968, taking a major leep, the *shura* went directly to the issue of lifting the ban with no reference either to *iqāmat-dīn* or to the "interests of Islam and Muslims." The following new resolution was put to vote: "The voting ban on members should be lifted, but they must abide by the criteria and limits set by the Jamaat in exercising their votes." The result was a tie. According to Article 39 (b) of the Jamaat's Constitution, if the *shura* could not pass a resolution concerning its fundamental policy by a three-fourths majority, the policy must be decided in the *majlis-e-numāindagān* (hereafter, *numāindagān*), a larger representative body consisting of fifty-eight members. Thus the resolution was sent to *numāindagān* (68), where it was defeated despite Nadwi's appeal to the contrary. The ban continued.

Meanwhile, Nadwi was removed as *amīr*.[20] Distancing himself from the Jamaat, he returned to his village in Azamgarh (Islahi 1996; *RAM* 1991 [October]: 7). Yusuf, who was Nadwi's Secretary from 1948 to 1972, was elected as the new *amīr* in 1972. In contrast to Nadwi, who was a madrasa graduate, Yusuf (1908–1991) had a modern education and was a reader in a British District Court, a post he resigned from after considering it *haram*. The conventional wisdom is that someone educated

TABLE 3
Voting Criteria for Jamaat Members

Political Conditions	*Qualities of the Candidate*	*Expectations from the Candidate*
– The threat of a party or group coming to power that is opposed to Islam and Muslims and seeks to establish a totalitarian or dictatorial regime. – The hope of a party or group coming to power that promises to protect the interests of Islam and Muslims.	– Must believe in the creed of *kalima*. – Considers legislation against Allah *haram* and does not endorse it.	– On being elected, the candidate promises to protect . . . life, property, primary religious education, personal law, Urdu, and Islamic endowments, and on these issues agrees with our stands. – Should not be from a party opposed to Islam and Muslims and does not endorse legislation against their interests. – Is expected to keep his word.

Source: *JIMI*:53–58.

in a modern environment would have embraced the change for which Nadwi had pleaded. The opposite was true, however, as Yusuf opposed lifting the voting ban.

In June 1975 Indira Gandhi declared a state of Emergency, and, using the Forty-second Amendment to the Constitution, she suspended fundamental rights and civil liberties and banned all opposition parties. Along with the RSS, she banned the Jamaat (see chapter 3). The top leaders, Yusuf included, were arrested. When Mrs. Gandhi announced the holding of parliamentary elections in early March 1977, the Jamaat had still not resumed functioning. Its *shura* met only after the results of elections that Mrs. Gandhi lost. In the elections, many of its members campaigned and voted against Mrs. Gandhi. Shams Pirzadah from Bombay, violating the Jamaat's ban on voting, was one such prominent leader (123). The Jamaat tolerated such indiscipline temporarily but reprimanded the likes of Pirzadah.

Once Mrs. Gandhi was out of power, the elections issue reappeared in the *shura*. In 1977 the *shura* sent out a questionnaire to all members asking if they were for or against voting. Of the 2,000 Jamaat members, 1,334 returned the questionnaire: 1,046 were in favor of voting and 277 were opposed.[21] Yusuf himself did not fill out the questionnaire (85). When the resolution against the ban was put to a vote in the subsequent *shura* meeting, 9 were in favor and 8 were opposed. As per Article 39 (C) of the Jamaat Constitution, in May 1977 the resolution was sent to the *numāindagān*, where it was passed with a thumping majority. Consequently Jamaat members voted in the 1977 Assembly elections. This ran counter to Maududi's 1974 edict, which had forbidden the Jamaat to participate in elections.[22] Unlike the criteria spelled out in 1967, in 1977 it was not specified that the candidate had to be a Muslim, who "must believe in the *kalima*." Nor was it required for the candidate[23] to "consider legislation against Allah *haram*." The foremost criterion was that the candidate support the "restoration of democracy." The interests of Muslims were secondary (116–18). With the ousting of the Congress in the 1977 elections, the *shura* reinforced the voting ban in February 1978, stating that because Parliament had repealed the Forty-second Amendment, there was no justification for lifting the ban (139). In May 1978 the *shura* again discussed the voting issue, but no consensus evolved. Under Article 39 (C) of the Jamaat Constitution, the resolution to lift the ban was again sent to *numāindagān* where it was defeated.

Ever since the start of the voting ban debate, many influential Jamaat members also sitting on the *shura* had hoped they would be allowed to participate in the political process. After the Emergency was lifted, the Hyderabad unit of the Jamaat had passed a resolution against the ban and appealed to the central leadership to do the same. Owing to the *shura's* continued indecision and Yusuf's diehard stance, serious discontent had accumulated. It finally imploded. Two weeks before the Maharashtra Assembly elections in February 1978, Pirzadah, who had already violated Jamaat's ban by canvassing in the 1977 parliamentary elections, resigned from the Jamaat to form the Muslim Democratic Forum. Because he had been a *shura* member and *amīr* of Maharashtra, his resignation was a serious blow to the Jamaat. In his letter to the Press, Pirzadah stated:

- The ban on voting is not only "wrong and anti-democratic" but is also an "injustice [*zeyādtī*] against [Jamaat] members."
- The Jamaat leadership is "ideologically confused and most ulema of the Jamaat are unable to find the path for the movement because of their narrow-mindedness." They want to "stick to the Jamaat's old literature." (126–27)

Pirzada's case demonstrates that the Jamaat was now also under pressure from within its own party. The democratic processes of which common Muslims were an integral part had now permeated the Jamaat. The impact of Pirzada's resignation went far beyond the frontier of Maharashtra. Violating the organizational ban, a Jamaat member in Hazaribagh (Southern Bihar) took part in canvassing and voting (*ME*:63). Abdul Hafiz Khan, a prominent member from Hyderabad, resigned from the Jamaat, and in the early 1980s established the Muslim Front. He launched an Urdu magazine, *Rahguzar*. Opposing the Jamaat's position, he held that Muslims could simultaneously believe in human and divine sovereignty. "There is no opposition between the religious idea of divine sovereignty and the political idea of democratic sovereignty" (*Rahguzar* 1986 [March]: 26, 7). Frustrated with the ban by the SIO, in the early 1980s one of its members in Patna established the Bihar Muslim Forum. He told me how frustrated he felt because of this "illogical" ban. For violating party discipline, the SIO suspended him. However, neither the SIO nor the Jamaat could suspend their own members' desire to participate.

Decentering of the State

Now under more pressure from within, the *shura* was desperate to abolish the voting ban. However, Yusuf was a formidable hurdle. The progress made during Nadwi's presidency (1961–1972) had faltered since Yusuf's ascendance. A change of guard was on the anvil, and in 1980 Yusuf was removed as *amīr* and Nadwi was reinstated. The official reason for the change was Yusuf's preoccupation with Muslim countries abroad and his neglect of the Jamaat at home (Islahi 1996). However, a Delhi-based expelled member told me that Yusuf was removed because he opposed Jamaat's "deviation from Islam."

In 1984, during Nadwi's second term, the *shura* passed a resolution to permanently lift the ban on voting. As a member of *shura*, Yusuf tried to block it. Under Article 39 (b) of the Jamaat Constitution, a new resolution was put to a vote before the eighteen-member *shura*: "The ban on Jamaat members to vote in the elections to Parliament and the Assemblies should be lifted; the *shura* will decide the criteria of how to use the votes" (*ME*:32). Led by Yusuf, six voted against and eleven in favor of the resolution (1 abstained). Describing the Jamaat's decision as tantamount to "cooperation with an idol [*ṭāghūt*]," an outraged Yusuf said that it was a show of "infidelity [*kufr*], polytheism [*shirk*], disobedience to Allah [*fisq*], everything" (*ME*: 12). He continued: "It is by order [of sharia], clearly, absolutely, perennially, eternally *haram*. Rather, it is doubly *haram*" (ibid.:9–10). Regarding the decision as a violation of monotheism (*ʿaqīda*), Ziaulhoda, a former *shura* member, resigned from the party (Akhtar et al 2003:485). So severe was the opposition that the Jamaat was on the brink of a serious split (Islahi 1996:51), but the leadership was determined to proceed with its decision. In February 1985 the *shura* allowed members to vote if a candidate met the following conditions:

- Promises, upon getting elected, that he will try his best to promote common human values; eliminate evils; pursue justice; keep a check on totalitarian tendencies; eradicate untouchability, bias against religious, linguistic, and cultural units stemming from communalism and cultural aggression; and purify national society by ridding it of corruption, evil practices [*badkārī*], gambling, lottery, alcohol, and interest;

- Sympathetizes with, and supports, the Muslims' demands for life and property, religious education, Personal Law, and language and endowments;
- Is not affiliated with a party whose ideology is "clearly against Islam and Muslims" and which intends to establish a totalitarian system in the country; and
- Is known to be a good human being who can be expected to be truthful (*ME*: 46–47; see also *RMS-2*:382–85, 481–86).

In an explanatory note, the *shura* wrote: "The above criteria also apply to *non-Muslim* candidates" (*ME*:47; my emphasis). Further, if no candidate met the necessary criteria, then the Jamaat would vote for "the less detrimental [*kam muẓir*] candidate."

In *Challenging Codes*, Melucci (1996:332–47) argues that if leaders of a movement anticipate that a decision is likely to spark conflicts, they will put off making the decision for as long as possible. The decision mechanism is also depersonalized. Both these mechanisms were at work in the issue of the voting ban. The decision to allow members to vote in elections took almost twenty-five years. And when that decision was made, the *shura*, and not the leaders, was held responsible. In his second term Nadwi declined to voice his opinion, saying that his job was simply to implement the *shura*'s decision (*ME*:14ff.). The Jamaat case reveals an additional mechanism at work: purposeful ambiguity in the decision and language. In the course of the prolonged decision-making process, the original objective of the decision was erased. In 1961, when the *shura* decided to participate in elections, the aim was to pursue *iqāmat-e-dīn* and change India's Constitution. But in the same year the objective was changed to "in the interests (positive and negative) of Islam and Muslims." In 1966 the goal was further modified: "considering the present system of government anti-Islamic and it is legitimate to participate in elections for the vital interests of Islam and Muslims." In 1961 the *shura* endorsed voting for a candidate if "he is not from a non-Islamic party." In 1967 the criterion was shifted from party to individual; the candidate himself and not his party, must be Muslim. Moreover, he must consider any legislation against Allah as *haram*.

In the decision to permanently lift the voting ban, however, no mention was made of either the original objective of *iqāmat-e-dīn* or the modified one. Also not mentioned were the criteria that the candidate must be a Muslim and must consider any legislation against Allah as *haram*. Instead it clearly stated that the candidate could be non-Muslim, as long as he was not "clearly" opposed to Islam and Muslims. Thus the criteria were so malleable that they could be interpreted to justify voting for any candidate, and this was indeed the case. As I indicated at the beginning of this chapter, in the UP Assembly elections of 2002 the Jamaat voted and canvassed for the candidates of almost every non-BJP party in order to defeat fascism. In the course of twenty-five years of belabored decision-making, through alterations, modifications, and ambiguity, the Jamaat leadership had radically changed the content of the decision.

The disappearance of *iqāmat-e-dīn* is worth some consideration. Stuart Hall (1983) discusses how black popular cultures use bodies as markers of identity. So, too, I argue, does a party in its logo, banner, flag, monogram, slogan, images, and insignia. The disappearance of *iqāmat-dīn* from the election issue broadly coincided with its disappearance from the Jamaat's Urdu organs, *Dawat* and *Zindgī*. Prior to 1985 *Dawat* carried an epigram on the front page: "Herald and Inviter of *iqāmat-e-dīn* in India" (e.g., 1979 [April]: 1). And *Zindgī*, too, carried the following on its cover: 'Inviter of . . . *iqāmat-e-dīn*' (e.g., 1978 [February–June]). Both no longer carry an epigram.

This is not to say that *iqāmat-e-dīn* has completely disappeared from Jamaat's discourse. It still exists, but its meaning has changed. Readers will recall that when Maududi founded the Jamaat, he described its goal as "*ḥukūmat-e-ilāhiya kā qeyām* [the establishment of Allah's Kingdom]." After Partition, in 1948, Jamaat replaced the pre-Partition goal with "*iqāmat-e-dīn* [the establishment of religion]." However a clarification stated: "In the Jamaat Constitution, the word for *iqāmat-e-dīn* was previously *ḥukūmat-e-ilāhiya*, which carried the same meaning as *iqāmat-e-dīn*" (*Dastūr Jamaat-e-Islami* undated:12, also see *JISS*:31, 89). Based on this clarification, the change was only in the terminology. In 1956 the Jamaat expanded the clarification: "It [Islam] should be pursued and implemented in individual, collective, and every arena of life such that the development of the individual, the construction of society, and the formation of the state all happen in accordance with this *dīn* [Islam]" (Dastūr Jamaat-e-Islami 1997:8). Clearly, in 1948 the change in goal was merely in the wording. Six years later the clarification took on ideological dimensions as well. The construction of the state lost the primacy it had had in 1948. Now the development of the individual and the construction of society took precedence over the formation of the state.

In 2002 the editor of the Jamaat's newly christened monthly Urdu organ *Zindgī-e-nau*,[24] who was also a member of the *shura*, wrote, "It [Islam] definitely provides principles for the formation of society and the state, but the state is not its [Islam's] foundation" (February:10). A shocked reader asked the editor how on earth *Zindgī-e-nau* could have published such a statement "against the Jamaat's policy." The editor reiterated, "How can the establishment of state be the foundation of the religion of Truth?" He further explained that the foundation of Islam "is monotheism, prophethood, and life hereafter." The absence of a caliphate, which, to Maududi and the Jamaat, was the foundation of Islam, is evident.

For Afsar, *amīr* of the Patna unit of the Jamaat, the disappearance of *iqāmat-e-dīn* from *Dawat* and *Zindgī* was accompanied with "things undoubtedly considered *haram*." Quoting Maududi, he said that he had declared photographs *haram*. Now the Jamaat not only published photos in its organs, but its leaders made special arrangements to have their photos published in Hindi and English newspapers. He told me that if such photo-hungry leaders ever installed a caliphate (and he seriously doubted they would), it would be a secular, Western caliphate, not an Islamic one. Afsar was concerned about the deviation of the younger generation of SIO members, most of whom, particularly those from the southern states of India, did not believe that listening to music was *haram*.

In Defense of Secularism and Democracy

The reevaluation of secularism by the Jamaat occurred simultaneously with its debate on electoral participation. Prior to the formation of the Mushāverat, in 1964, the Jamaat had accepted both secularism and democracy. By the early 1970s it had moved from mere acceptance to their defense. With the rise of virulent Hindutva since the mid-1980s, the Jamaat became one of the most ardent defenders of secularism and democracy. A remarkable feature of the second shift was its collaboration with Hindus as well as atheists. At the same time the Jamaat's defense of secular democracy also presented a critique of the SIMI.

Against Medieval Duality

Central to the second shift is the Jamaat's elemental redefinition of India. Maududi upheld the distinction between *dar al-kufr* and *dar al-Islam*. Shortly after he left for Pakistan in 1951, Maududi declared India *dar al-kufr*. He decreed that Muslims from Pakistan, *dar al-Islam*, could not marry Muslims from India, *dar al-kufr* (2001b:152–54).[25] Among others, the Deoband ulema criticized Maududi's *fatwa* (see Mian 1957).[26] To ward off the embarrassment Maududi's *fatwa* had caused, including among its own members, the Jamaat declared that it was not bound to follow his views on peripheral issues of *fiqh* (*Zindgī* 1951 [September]:

69). As the Muslims' disavowal of the Jamaat forced it to reconsider its stand on elections, the Jamaat felt compelled also to reevaluate its stand on the status of India. The *shura* fiercely debated whether India was a *dar al-Islam* or *dar al-kufr*? One *shura* member proposed:

> The style of thinking of the communist parties of India is also that they first analyze the society. We have to also decide under what conditions do we live? What is the status of the country—*dar al-Islam*, *dar al-kufr*, or some other *dār* [abode] (*ME*:26)?

No consensus evolved. Members who opposed lifting the voting ban argued that India as a whole was *ṭāġhūt*, whereas their rivals argued the opposite. According to the latter, the postcolonial state was based on fundamental rights, freedom, and democracy (*JIMI*:7). Muslims were free to form civil associations and run their own institutions, religious or otherwise. Crucial to this argument was the recognition that the Indian state was, in principle, secular. Given the secular and democratic features of the Indian Constitution, one *shura* member described democracy as "an unexpected divine boon" (*ME*:36). Another member said that "the present democratic system" was "neither openly anti-Islamic nor Islamic" (*JIMI*:7). Maulana Irham (*amīr* of the Jamaat at Falāḥ), whom we met in chapter 5, told me that because India was a democracy and Muslims enjoyed the right to practice Islam, it could no longer be described as *dar al-ḥarb*. He also called secularism "a divine boon [*neʿmat*] for Indian Muslims." In his view, India was *dar al-daʿvat*.[27]

A *shura* member from Jharkhand went even further than Irham. In an interview with me he remarked that the Indian Constitution is the best in the world and is already Islamic. It needed just one small change. If, in the Preamble, it replaced the sovereignty of people with divine sovereignty, it would then become fully Islamic. Another *shura* member, Fazlurrahman Faridi, argued that in today's world marked by international migration the concepts of *dar al-ḥarb* and *dar al-Islam* were "out of tune with reality and hence redundant" (1998:51).

The Jamaat also called into question Maududi's premise that Islam was an organic whole or system and that the state was its pivot. In chapter 3 I described how one of the leading proponents of affiliation of the Jamaat school with the government questioned Maududi's practice of boycotting the *ṭāġhūtī niẓām* based on his conceptualization of Islam as an organic whole. In his view Maududi's call for a boycott was influenced by Gandhi's call for boycotting the British imperial polity. Without naming Maududi, a *shura* member averred that it was wrong to compare a polity to a human organism; although a system might be un-Islamic on the whole, it may not be so for each and every part (*JIMI*:5–7). From the 1970s to 1980s on, therefore, the Jamaat began to grant membership to those who worked in government departments such as income tax and banking. At the Jamaat headquarters a senior Jamaat leader introduced me to one of his colleagues from Bangalore, who worked in the income tax department. Similarly the SIO was no longer disinclined to grant membership to a student of secular law.

The changing practices of the Jamaat led to a thorough critique of Maududi on several points. Some questioned him indirectly, whereas others did so directly. Rao Irfan Khan, a U.S.-based Jamaat member, pleaded to his colleagues in India not to turn Maududi into a "cult." He believed that, unlike Qutb, Maududi had more "intellectual content" and was therefore more prone to gaining cult status. He advised his party members to refer "directly" to the Qur'an rather than reading Maududi's interpretation, the *Tafhīmul Qur'an*. Unlike Maududi, he argued that Islam was not a static, and an already, crafted system but was a "changing reality" (in Siddiqi 2001:269, 266).

Defending the Divine Boon

The Jamaat's acknowledgment of secular democracy did not accord with its old literature, and so the stage was set for a revision in its ideology. By the late 1960s the Jamaat stopped denouncing secularism, in speech as well as in print (*JISS*:82). In 1970 it passed a resolution defending the "secular democratic form of government."

> The Jamaat . . . compared to other totalitarian . . . forms of government . . . wants India's secular democratic form of government to endure. We are against any change in the present form of government that curtails those liberties of the inhabitants of the country which allows them to profess and propagate their creed and change the existing system through democratic means according to that creed (*RMS*-2:44–45).

Following the passage of this resolution the Jamaat began to invoke, eulogize, and defend secularism and democracy (*JISS*:82). In 1972 the central government passed the Amendment Act, which extended the changes introduced in the 1965 Act, and aimed at further altering AMU's "minority character." Protest against the Act was wisespread, as Muslims saw it as a threat to their community identity (Graff 1990). The Jamaat stated that the 1972 Act was not a "communal [i.e., Muslim] issue" and that Muslims should be prepared for a long struggle not only for their community rights but also for the "secular democratic character of the country" (*RMS*-2:77). In the wake of the 1971 India-Pakistan War, the Jamaat urged the government to check the tendency of Hindu nationalists to portray the war as between Hindus and Muslims. Describing this portrayal as the "negation of secularism," the Jamaat pleaded with the government to "curb communal, fascist sentiments" and instead highlight the "secular character of its foreign policy" (*RMS-2*: 57–58). In 1979 Vinoba Bhave, a leader of the Bhoodan movement,[28] went on a silent fast asking Parliament to pass a law banning the slaughter of cows. Many parties agreed to Bhave's demand, but the Jamaat was unhappy with this agreement and a *Dawat* editorial grudgingly commented, "Vinoba Bhave Won, but Secularism Lost" (1979 [April 1]: 3).

The Jamaat's defense of secular democracy grew robust with the rise of Hindutva. In chapter 6 I discussed Hindutva's campaign to build the Ram temple. In 1986, with the unlocking of the Babri mosque, the Mushāverat formed the Babri Masjid Movement Coordination Committee (henceforth, Coordination Committee) under the leadership of Syed Shahabuddin, who was then the acting president of the Mushāverat. Two senior Jamaat leaders became founding members of the Coordination Committee. After the split in the Mushāverat[29] in 1968, it disappeared into near oblivion. From 1972 to 1977 the Mushāverat came under the Jamaat's control (Rizvi 1989:162), and in the mid-1980s, the Jamaat resurrected the Mushāverat to expand the Jamaat's own influence (*MMS*:334–36). In 1995 Shafi Monis, Jamaat's deputy *amīr*, became its secretary general (*RAM* 1996 [January]: 14). At the time of my fieldwork another senior Jamaat leader had replaced Monis as secretary, and Shahabuddin became its disputed president. In a controversial election, both Shahabuddin and his rival, Salim Qasmi, claimed that they were the president of the Mushāverat.[30] The Jamaat sided with Shahabuddin.

Opposed to the unlocking of the Babri mosque, the Coordination Committee, in December 1986, called for boycotting the celebration of Independence Day (see chapter 6). The Jamaat refused to go along with the Coordination Committee (*Jamaat-e-Islami Hind* n.d.:52–54). In 1989 the Coordination Committee split and a "more militant" committee (Khan 1995:110), the All-India Babari Masjid Action Committee, was formed. The Jamaat sided with the Coordination Committee, which was anything but radical. Expecting the government to be "judicious and nonpartisan," the Jamaat urged Muslims to use "peaceful, democratic, and constitutional means" to resolve the Ayodhya issue (*MMS* 1997:301–15). When Hindutva activists demolished the Babri mosque, the Jamaat's English organ, *Radiance*, wrote, "The December 6 happening was only a [single] string of the abysmal strategy aimed at subverting the Indian Constitution, democracy [and] secularism" ([December 13 1992–January 2 1993]: 5). The Jamaat *amīr* warned that "this tragedy is not only about the martyrdom of the Babri mosque"; it is also a heinous attempt on the part of fascist and narrow-minded revivalism "to damage the unity and integrity of the country" (*Dawat* 1992 [December 10]).

Anthem for Secularism

A year after the demolition of the Babri mosque, the Jamaat established the Forum for Democracy and Communal Amity (FDCA) to fight "communalism and fascism." Its objective was "to bring together *secular-minded* persons and parties to put up a united fight against the *communal political parties*" and "to strive for a strong united India based on the principles of equality of all citizens, irrespective of religion, caste, race, sex etc. . . ." (FDCA Constitution undated: 1; my emphasis). Not even once was Islam or *iqāmat-e-dīn* mentioned. These aims were not only secular but were also nationalist. During the 1999 Kargil War between India and Pakistan, hundreds of Muslim soldiers in the Indian Army were killed. Delhi's Hanifuddin was one of them. In one of its regional publications, the Jamaat reported Hanifuddin's "sacrifice for India [*waṭan*]" in glowing terms. The SIMI criticized the Jamaat's stance: "What was undesirable gradually became desirable" (*IM* 1999 [September]: 29).

The formation of the FDCA was a watershed in the Jamaat's history in that it built an institutional alliance with Hindu intellectuals-activists who opposed Hindutva. In 1964, although the Jamaat accepted secularism and the Indian Constitution, it still regarded "a joint platform of leaders belonging to different religions" as "contrary to the principles and policies of the Jamaat." In the period following the demolition of the mosque, it threw those "principles" to the wind. In the list of thirty-five lifetime members of FDCA, twenty were Hindus—four retired judges of High Courts; two academics, including the historian Romila Thapar; two journalists; one former foreign secretary; one retired general; and one sometime solicitor general of India, Soli J. Sorabjee. Among the remaining 14 Muslims, three were *shura* members and two were Jamaat sympathizers (FDCA Constitution n.d.:12, Annexure). To get a sense of the full spectrum of ideological diversity, consider two lifetime members of the FDCA: Justice V. M. Tarkunde and Swami Agnivesh. Tarkunde (d. 2004), a former judge of the Bombay High Court, was a comrade of the radical Marxist M. N. Roy. He propagated Roy's philosophy— atheistic humanism—through the magazine *Radical Humanist*. Agnivesh (b. 1939) was a saffron-robed Hindu renouncer and a leader of Arya Samaj. Previously he had propounded the idea of Vedic socialism. Thus, to defend secular democracy, the Jamaat now forged an alliance with individuals with ideologies as divergent as atheistic humanism, on the one hand, and Vedic socialism, on the other.

In 2002, in a Jamaat *ijtimāʿ*, many Hindu pontiffs (*shankarāchārya*) were invited. One of them even blew a conch and chanted "Om Om." Emphasizing religious pluralism and calling India a "bouquet of all religions," he further stated: "I went to the Jamaat office and there I also blew a conch and chanted 'Om Om.' No one prohibited me [from doing so] either there or here" (*Zindgī-e-nau* 2002 [March]: 65). I will return to this shortly. Let us first take a look at the issue of the national anthem. Like the RSS,[31] seldom did the Jamaat ardently unfurl the tricolor on Independence Day or Republic Day. Nor did it sing the national anthem, *Jana gana mana*. It considered both to be signs of *jāhiliyat*. But in 1997, in an FDCA meeting, the then Jamaat vice president Shafi Monis stood up to sing the anthem (*Milli Times* 1997 [August]: 2).

The Jamaat leadership's alliance with Hindu pontiffs and intellectuals to defend secular democracy invited extremely acrimonious reactions. Khalid Hamdi, son of Syed Hamid Ali (who briefly served as Jamaat *amīr*), ridiculed the Jamaat, rather cheaply, for its compromise. Commenting on a Congress leader's proposal that eunuchs should be brought into the mainstream, he wrote: "When at the national level, through the Forum for Democracy and Communal Amity, the Jamaat can be brought to the national mainstream, then what crime have eunuchs committed?" (Hamdi 2002:62). Most other reactions were more serious. Shocked at a Hindu pontiff blowing a conch in a Jamaat congregation and his characterization of India as a "bouquet of all religions," a Jamaat member from Meerut wrote: "The religion of Islam can never be a beauty in that bouquet, which is decorated with the different colorful flowers of polytheism, disbelief . . . atheism." Arguing that "polytheism is a great sin" and "only Islam a true religion," he concluded: "If a believer in a polytheistic religion doesn't oppose your [Jamaat's] . . . movement but rather praises it, then it has to be considered whether our . . . movement is truly the one that is derived from the Qur'an and sunna" (*Zindgī-e-nau* 2003 [March]: 67). Another member, a teacher at Falāḥ, remarked that the Jamaat was derailing from its original track: "It is not the forum [FDCA]; it is the coffin of the Jamaat-e-Islami" (*HN* 1996 [March–April]: 15). Calling Monis's singing of the anthem an act of *jāhiliyat*, a student from Falāḥ sarcastically remarked that, in order to sing the national anthem, he stood up the way that Muslims did when singing a salutational hymn to the Prophet Muhammad (*Milli Times* 1997 [August]: 2). Malik, a Delhi-based member who had resigned from the Jamaat in protest against the lifting of its ban on voting, was the most critical voice against the FDCA.

> How on earth could Islam allow voting for *ṭāġhūt*? When I joined the Jamaat, we were told to eliminate *ṭāġhūt*, secularism, democracy . . . , everything that is against the Qur'an. . . . We joined it for *iqāmat-e-dīn*. Now the Jamaat is fighting for *iqāmat-e-secular democracy*. Do you know about the forum [FDCA]? . . . What is it doing? It is fighting for the glory of secularism and democracy. You have also read Maududi. Tell me what has secularism got to do with Islam? Where is the original ideology?

Having resigned from the Jamaat, Malik joined the United Muslims of India. When I asked him if that organization stood for *iqāmat-e-dīn*, he replied no. "Then why did you leave the Jamaat?" I persisted. "If I have to work for secularism, then there are much better platforms than the Jamaat," he answered.

Critique of the SIMI

When we compare the SIMI's positions on secularism, democracy, and elections (see chapters 6) with those of the Jamaat and the long drawn-out changes in the Jamaat since Partition, it is clear how radically different, even conflicting, are the trajectories of each. It is relevant here to present the Jamaat's critique of SIMI on three issues: the caliphate, jihad, and the personality of the Prophet Muhammad.

In Chapter 6 I discussed the SIMI's 1996 campaign "Nationalism or Caliphate?" The then vice president of Jamaat, Monis, described the campaign as a "*fitna*" (*Milli Times* 1997 [November]: 4). In his magazine, *Muslim India*, Shahabuddin, the convener of the Coordination Committee and later, the president of the Jamaat-controlled Mushāverat, implied that the SIMI's slogan for a caliphate was a "mirage." The slogan of caliphate, even in a Muslim-minority country, by "Muslim fanatics," was dubious. If Muslims asked for the caliphate, he wrote, "Why shouldn't the Hindu majority of a country like India . . . dream of a Hindu State?" In his view, Islam entailed piety, not power; compassion, not coercion. The Prophet Muhammad was compassionate to humanity. Shahabuddin advised the SIMI to embrace "the principles of democracy, the goals of the welfare state, and the concept of neo-secularism (which is neither irreligious nor anti-religious)" and to stop chasing "the mirage of . . . the restoration of [a] caliphate" (*Muslim India* 1996 [February]: 51).

The Jamaat Urdu organ *Zindgī-e-nau* also criticized the SIMI because, unlike other Muslim youth who took to the path of extremism, they (i.e., SIMI members) claimed to be engaged for "purely Islamic objectives" (*Zindgī-e-nau* 1997 [August]: 5–18).[32] The organ referred to the SIMI as "some youngsters." Shahabuddin wrote a letter congratulating the editor for his insightful piece (1997 [September]: 65). The rebuttal, and Shahabuddin's endorsement of it, invited scathing criticism from the SIMI; one SIMI supporter wrote to the editor of *Zindgi-e-nau*, "You composed such an editorial about some youngsters that *even a <u>secularist</u> like Shahabuddin* became your fan; now you yourself decide to what extent your editorial *is it nearer to the Qur'an and sunna*" (1997 [December]: 67, my emphasis).

In the rebuttal the Jamaat enumerated several mistakes of which "some youngsters" were guilty, the greatest one their "flawed knowledge of the

Qur'an," "superficial . . . knowledge of life of the Prophet Muhammad," and their sheer ignorance of what sharia meant. They took sharia literally without thinking of the context and circumstances of its application (1997 [August]: 10, 17). The result of their distorted understanding of Islam, *Zindgī-e-nau* declared, was manifest in their thinking that "the basis of religion" was "the desire for martyrdom [*sharfarōshī*]." They also conflated the interests of Islam with those of Muslims, the honor of *jāhiliyat* with the demands of Islam, and the history of Muslims with the history of Islam. According to the rebuttal, even the emperor Aurangzeb was not a true representative of Islam (meaning, How can Mahmud Ghaznavi, the SIMI's hero, be a true Muslim?). The cumulative result of all the mistakes perpetrated by "some youngsters" was that they advocated a policy of "direct confrontation with the power of the time" (7). Reminding these "youngsters" of the teachings of the Islamic prophets, the rebuttal argued, had they read about the Prophets from a Qur'anic perspective, they would have known that most of them devoted their lives to preaching, persuasion, and *da'vat*, not confrontation. The Prophet Nooh continued carrying out *da'vat* for 950 years. The Prophet Jesus met the gallows while preaching. And *da'vat* alone marked the life of the Prophet Moses. Quoting several of its passages, the rebuttal argued that the Qur'an taught its believers to preach for a long time in order to change hearts.

Da'vat was required especially in India, because the majority of non-Muslims, in the Jamaat's view, did not know about Islam, much less about pure Islam. They knew Islam as a religion that created Pakistan, whose believers kept women in veils, worshiped graves, and organized *'urs* (commemoration ritual of the death date of a Sufi) much like Hindus did their *kumbh̠* (a key Hindu ritual) fare. They did not know that Muslims were the bearers of a just, humane, friendly, and balanced system of life. Hence the need for *da'vat* and not *mubārzat*, war (10). The rebuttal further explained that the use of force was illegitimate, because the Qur'an (*al-ghāshiya* 21–26) instructed Muhammad simply to preach and not act "as if he were a policeman" (13). The SIMI's call for jihad, the Jamaat urged, was not jihad but *fasād*,[33] because Allah disliked the notion of "some youngsters" becoming martyrs when they created disorder, anarchy, and injury to human life (14–15). Allah issued these sanctions precisely because He wanted Islam to be a religion of compassion. For this reason, Allah sent Muhammad as the compassion for the whole world, *raḥmatul lil 'ālamīn*. He sent Islam as a defender of the weak and old, and as torchbearer of justice (15). If Allah wanted to cast Muhammad in the image of a policeman, the rebuttal continued, He would not have said, "I have sent you as the compassion for the whole world" (16). This portrayal of Muhammad as the compassion for the world contrasted with the SIMI's portrayal of him as the "commander."

What does the Jamaat's long drawn-out process of negotiation with Indian secularism and democracy theoretically entail? Does this historical negotiation signal a metamorphosis in the discourse of Islamism? More important, what led to the transformation in the Islamist discourse? These questions are all addressed in the conclusion to this volume.

Conclusion

> After all, what is the worth of that Islam which can be followed only in a specific context and, when the circumstances change, then it is abandoned and a different ideology is adopted according to convenience?
>
> —Maududi, *Musalmān aur maujūda seyāsī kashmakash*, vol. 3

> The surpassing of a . . . tradition never takes place in the form of . . . a collapse, but in the way that river waters, having originated at a common source, spread in various directions and mingle with currents flowing . . . from other sources.
>
> —Ernesto Laclau and Chantal Mouffe, *Hegemony and Socialist Strategy*

In a searching critique of theories that gave Muslims the option of "Mecca or mechanization," Dale Eickelman questioned the dichotomy in this option. He argued that the religious (or caste) phenomena that modernization theories neatly categorized as traditional were actually "distinctly modern" (2000:122; also see Eickelman and Piscatori 1996:22–30). This book has demonstrated the modernity of Islamism and the ideology of Maududi, the Jamaat founder. It has shown that there is *movement* within the Indian Islamist movement.

Maududi did not cling to "traditions"; indeed, he ferociously attacked them under the flag of *jāhiliyat*. Recall his description of Sufism as "opium," his call for mimicking the Western educational system, and his scathing critique of ulema for remaining steeped in "blind imitation" rather than carrying out *ijtihād* (independent reasoning). So new was his Islam that the non-Islamist ulema detected rank Westernism in Maududi's thought. They likened him to the Orientalists who, as self-appointed sanitary inspectors, only saw dirt in the towns of Islam. In the words of Sufi Nazir Kashmiri, Maududi was a "Muslim Machiavelli" with "affinities to the atheist philosophers of the present age," and thus "acceptance of Maududism is no less than apostasy" (1979:57–58, 27–29). The modernity of Islamism was further manifest in the new meanings Maududi invested in prevalent words and practices like Allah, *dīn* (religion), *qaum* (nation), *ʿibādat* (worship), and *jamāʿat* or party. In chapter 2 I showed how his novel idea of Islamic history, what I call "Islamist dialectics," bore the deep imprint of Hegelian and Marxist idioms. His definition of Islam as a movement was equally modern, as were the notions of an Islamic vanguard (*jatthā*) and party, both modeled on Leninist principles. No less important were Maududi's distrust of miracles and the coming of *dajjāl*. The distrust of the divine, I pointed out, was integral to the social movements, themselves products of modernity, that sought to take hold of the future by human intervention (Bourdieu 1979; Touraine 1985).

In what follows, first I summarize the salient aspects of the Jamaat's moderation that were empirically brought out in this volume. I discuss the Jamaat's positions on secularism and democracy, the Islamic state, Aligarh Muslim University, inter- and intra-religious pluralism, and the conflict and ambiguity that accompanied the Jamaat's moderation. I also discuss the conceptual transformation of two postulates of Islamism: the blurring of the boundary between Islam and *jāhiliyat*, and the dissolution of Islam as an organic whole. In the final section I delineate the conditions under which the possibility for moderation gains salience. Comparing Muslim-majority societies such as Algeria, Egypt, and Iran, I argue that the Jamaat's moderation was set in motion by democratic processes, that indeed the Muslim public's disavowal of the Jamaat acted upon its moderation. To make this point I move from the micro world of the Jamaat to the macro coordinates of the postcolonial Indian state—the institutions of secularism and democracy. In the final section I discuss the radicalization of the SIMI, which was the result of many factors. The primary catalyst was the rise of militant Hindutva and the concomitant erosion of secular democracy. The SIMI's radicalism unfolded under national conditions where Muslims were marginalized in important arenas of public life. The SIMI's radicalization should also be seen, I suggest, as a process of democratization *within* Muslim society.

Landscape of Transformation

Before outlining the many faces of the Jamaat's moderation, it is worthwhile here to recapitulate the sine qua non of the Jamaat's ideology. The *differentia specifica* of the Jamaat was its belief that Islam obligated its followers to install an Islamic state, and that Muslims *qua* Muslims could not even breathe, let alone live, in a non-Islamic system. According to the Jamaat's founder, Maududi, India was *dar al-ḥarb*. From this perspective, he argued, secular democracy was anti-Islamic, because it empowered legislators to frame human laws in violation of sharia, the divine laws. Maududi thus issued a call to Muslims to boycott the secular democratic elections. Given his lack of authority, he could not enforce his call on the entire Muslim community, but he made it compulsory for his party members to boycott the elections. The Jamaat Constitution required its members also to shun all the prime institutions of a godless state such as the judiciary, the army, the banking, tax, and excise departments, and so on. All institutions, including the educational systems run by Muslims themselves but not serving the real objective of Islam—a pure sharia state—were simply un-Islamic.

Secularism, Democracy, and an Islamic State

The thorniest issue dominating the Jamaat agenda was therefore the illegitimacy of the secularism and democracy embodied in the Indian Constitution and the state, as that form of government challenged the very foundation of the Jamaat's ideology, namely, an Islamic state. In chapter 2 I indicated that Maududi had forbidden Jamaat members to vote in the elections of a "secular democratic" state because he considered it *haram*. Secularism and democracy were the ultimate symbols of the *ṭāghūtī niẓām* (idolatrous system). Following Partition, the Jamaat continued its opposition. In chapter 7 I discussed how, soon after Independence, the Jamaat *amīr*, Abullais Islahi Nadwi, urged the Congress not to make the state democratic and secular. So opposed was he to secular democracy that he preferred a Hindu state, even if it had a provision calling for the death of Muslims. Given this militant position, the Jamaat boycotted the first two elections, arguing that, because Muslims believed in the "sovereignty of Allah," it was against their faith in *kalima* to vote in elections that established the "sovereignty of man." Nadwi reasoned that voting meant "the flouting . . . of sharia at every step," as the elected members would frame laws against sharia. He opposed voting even in elections to the village council (*panchāyat*), for that was also a "department of the un-godly system."

Unmindful of the Jamaat's position, the Muslim populace eagerly participated in the elections. By the early 1960s the Jamaat stood discredited among the Muslim public. To gain credibility, the Jamaat helped form the Mushāverat, a coalition of Muslim organizations, and for the first time accepted secularism and the Indian Constitution. This led to a fierce debate within its *shura*, the Jamaat's most powerful decision-making body. In 1967 the Jamaat made a simple exception to the voting ban and allowed its members to vote for a Muslim candidate in Bhopal. The general ruling against voting continued, however, until Indira Gandhi declared a state of emergency and banned all parties, including the Jamaat and the RSS. In 1977, when elections were held, the Jamaat temporarily lifted the ban and allowed its members to vote (despite Maududi's directives from Pakistan to the contrary) for the "restoration of democracy." Years later, when the Jamaat permanently lifted the ban, Islamic criteria were not mentioned. From being a symbol of *ṭāghūt*, democracy had become "an unexpected divine boon." Once the Jamaat had embraced democracy, there was no going back. In the 2002 UP elections it fervently canvassed for the victory of secular democracy.

In Maududi's formulation, enshrined in the Jamaat Constitution, Islam and the state were interchangeable. In a notable invention, he defined Allah as a "political God." The Jamaat's initial opposition to the secular democratic state also lay in a mythic hope that the Islamic Revolution would soon come about. As hopes began to dwindle, the Jamaat began to revise its ideology. In 1961 it passed its first resolution to participate in the elections in order to make the Constitution of India "Islamic." The subsequent debate in the *shura* gradually erased this objective. In 1967, when it made a solitary exception to the ban, it laid down the condition that the candidate must be a believer in *kalima*, the Islamic creed. In 1977, when the ban was relaxed, there was no such religious condition and the Jamaat members voted for anyone who stood for the "restoration of democracy." In the final decision permanently lifting the ban, no mention at all was made of *iqāmat-e-dīn*. Instead, it categorically stated that Jamaat members could also vote for non-Muslim candidates.

Here it is pertinent to note the change in terminology stating the Jamaat's goal in its Constitution. When founded, *ḥukūmat-e-ilāhiya* (Allah's Kingdom) was declared its goal, but in 1948 the phrase was replaced by *iqāmat-e-dīn* (establishment of religion). A note of clarification, however, stated that the change was only in terminology. In 1956 the Jamaat expanded the note according to which the state lost the primacy it had had. In the expanded note, the growth of the individual and the construction of society preceded the formation of state. Clearly, in 1956 the change had gone beyond terminology and had taken a profound ideological turn. In 2002 the Jamaat organ, *Zindgī-e-nau,* wrote that, although Islam offered principles for the formation of a state, the state was not the foundation of Islam. It further stated that the foundation of Islam was monotheism, the prophethood, and the afterlife. The absence of a caliphate or an Islamic state, which to Maududi was the foundation, was more than evident.

The Jamaat did not accept democracy only externally; its own functioning also became democratic. Before Partition, Maududi was the unchallenged decision maker. Rather than electing members of the *shura*, he nominated them. The task of the *shura*, moreover, was to advise the *amīr* (Maududi), who was then not bound to abide by the advice. This practice continued after Partition as well, but later it changed in two ways. First, *shura* members, rather than being nominated by the *amīr*, were to be elected. Second, the *amīr* was made to accept decisions that the *shura* took by majority vote. This democratic basis of decision making became so crucial that even the Islamic creed, the *kalima*, from which, according to Maududi, the voting ban had been derived, was put to vote—a practice unknown in the history of Islam—and clinched by a majority vote. As we saw in chapter 7 the entire debate on participation in elections was carried out over two decades on the principle of a majority vote. In this respect, the issue of women's participation is important. In 1999 the Jamaat *shura*, recognizing the invisibility of women in the leadership (in 2000, of 4,776 members, 303 were women), proposed that the Jamaat *amīr* should be authorized to name 15 women to the larger body from which *shura* members were elected (*Zindgī-e-nau* 1999 [June]: 62–63). Though there are still no women in the *shura*, the proposal itself was momentous. Maududi had argued that, in Islam, women are not even allowed to vote, much less don the mantle of leadership (Ahmad 2008a).[1]

The Jamaat also changed significantly on the issue of secularism, which in the past it had condemned as *jāhiliyat*. The change was only logical, for in postcolonial India democracy was tied to secularism. I referred above to the Jamaat's first public acceptance of secularism, when, in 1970, the *shura* passed a resolution acknowledging the "secular democratic form of government." After the India-Pakistan War over the creation of Bangladesh, the Jamaat urged the Indian government not to allow the Hindu nationalists to portray the war as one between Hindus and Muslims. Calling it the "negation of secularism," the Jamaat urged the government to "curb the communal, fascist sentiments" and instead display the "secular character of its foreign policy." Likewise, when on the plea of Vinoba Bhave several political parties agreed to ban the killing of cows, the Jamaat organ grudgingly stated, "Vinoba Bhave Won, but Secularism Lost." With the rise of militant Hindutva, the Jamaat's defense of secularism took on a more robust form. After the demolition of the Babri mosque, it formed the Forum for Democracy and Communal Amity (FDCA) to defend secularism. I showed how, in the 2002 UP elections, the Jamaat campaigned to save "secularism" from the onslaught of the "fascist" BJP. Like democracy, secularism became, as a Jamaat member at Falāḥ put it, "a divine boon."

Secularization was at work in another crucial way. According to Maududi, Islam and an Islamic state were synonymous. In postcolonial India, as the Jamaat became more moderate, it reinterpreted its theology according to which the state was no longer intrinsic to Islam. Clearly it had moved away from its position that fused religion and the state. This principle of differentiation was most visible when it decided to participate in democratic politics. In 1961 the Jamaat sent a questionnaire to reputed ulema and Islamic institutions asking if sharia allowed participation in elections. In seeking validation from the religious authorities, the Jamaat inadvertently separated the religious and nonreligious domains. Obviously the Jamaat did not see itself as religious, or sufficiently religious, and hence it resorted to the ulema's opinion. In the Jamaat's everyday practices this principle of separation was even more prominent. The Jamaat leaders and activists with a madrasa background called their colleagues with a university education "secular" and even "secularist" (Ahmad 2005:294). Anyone asking a secular member a theological question would be directed to a colleague who was an *ʿālim*, a theologian. These trends were also visible in the SIO. Jamal, an SIO activist based at AMU, called for privatizing religion, because he was displeased that the SIO leadership had asked him if he prayed and why he watched films, both of which he regarded as "individual choice." The SIO, in his view, should raise sociopolitical issues of the student community rather than religious matters. He also believed that the leftist SADA was more popular than the SIO because the former raised sociopolitical issues, not religious ones. Further, he claimed that the Islamic state in the golden era was secular and that the West had actually borrowed secularism from Islam (see chapter 4).

Most dazzling, however, was the change in the revisionist reading of Maududi by Abdulhaq Ansari, a prominent member who, in 2002, became the Jamaat *amīr*. In a speech delivered at the All-India Convention of the Jamaat members in 1997, he argued against Maududi's position of opposing secularism. Describing that position as "incorrect," he contended that "certain writings" of Maududi legitimized a "secular democratic system" (1998:18). To this end, Ansari cited Maududi's response to the integration of the Hyderabad state into the Indian Union in 1948. Maududi had advised Hyderabad's Muslims to participate in the Indian polity and secure rights to their religion and culture. As a solution to the Palestinian crisis, Maududi proposed that the Christians, Muslims, and old Jews—Jews already living in what later became Israel—should come together to form a "democratic" state. In Ansari's argument, the state Maududi proposed in Palestine was not "Islamic but was secular [and] democratic" (ibid.:20).

Pluralism: Within and Without

Also linked to the Jamaat's position on secularism was the issue of AMU. Maududi had called Western Muslim colleges, including AMU, "slaughterhouse[s]" of Islam. For some Jamaat members, even Nadwa's seminary at Lucknow was a "slaughterhouse of a different kind." Because of this, students under Maududi's influence left AMU, believing that its education was un-Islamic. Alternatively, the Jamaat established its own institute, the Ṡānvī Darsgāh at Rampur. Throughout the 1950s, by rule it forbade its members and friends (*rofaqāʾ*) to study there. Under internal and external pressure, from the 1960s on the Jamaat's position underwent a radical shift so that it began to fight for what it previously had called a "slaughterhouse." In chapter 4 we saw that the SIO called upon the "true secular people and forces" to defend the Muslim character of AMU, when, in 2003, the government sought to slash the proportion of Muslims in the professional courses. The SIO's defense of AMU was a continuation of the Jamaat's shift that had begun long before. In 1965, when the government sought to erode AMU's minority character, Muslims protested this move. The Jamaat also jumped in to defend AMU's "Muslim character." In 1972, when the government passed a similar bill, the Jamaat again urged Muslims to fight for the minority character of AMU. Most significant, it argued that the issue at stake was not the Muslim character of AMU but the "secular democratic character of the country."

Soon after the Jamaat's formation, Maududi had warned Muslims either to join the organization or stand condemned like the Jews who had rejected Islam. He also warned that those leaving the Jamaat would be considered apostates. His warning stemmed from the Jamaat's claim to be the only true Islamic party. That was why its Constitution asked its members to sever ties with "transgressors [and] sinners [*fāsiqīn*]," and described the Jamiatul Ulema's alliance with the Congress as a "sin." Under Maududi's influence, Farhan Qasmi resigned from the Jamiatul Ulema, considering it a false (*bāṯil*) party. Recall, too, the refusal by the Jamaat *amīr*, Abullais Islahi Nadwi, to maintain "friendship even for a moment" with Ramnagri who had left the Jamaat. So firm was the Jamaat's belief in its monopoly of the truth that, in the 1950s, it declined to share a dais with non-Jamaat Muslims because they lacked "the fundamental perspective of Islam" and believed in the "*kalima* of secularism." With the changes that occurred from the 1960s on, the Jamaat's belief in its monopoly of the truth started to wane as it began to accept other viewpoints. Its participation in the Mushāverat was the strongest evidence of its intra-religious pluralism, as it began to accept the standpoints of Muslims as different as the Deoband ulema, the Congress, and the socialists.

The Jamaat still considered interactions with non-Muslims as "contrary to" its "principles and policies." Recall also the Jamaat's opposition to Abulkalam Azad's ecumenical approach to Islam. The acceptance of intra-religious pluralism, however, was accompanied by inter-religious pluralism, as was evident in the Jamaat's institutionalized collaboration, through the FDCA, with intellectuals of different faiths—including atheists and Communists—to defend secularism and democracy. In chapter 7 I documented that, in a Jamaat congregation, Hindu pontiffs even blew a conch and praised India as a "bouquet of all religions." Similarly, in chapter 5, I pointed out that the portion of a lesson titled "The Fair" in the Jamaat textbook *Our Book* (written in 1962), which showed a Muslim child bewildered at the offering of flowers and food to an idol, was deleted. Religious pluralism was subsequently accompanied by political pluralism. In the 2002 UP elections the Jamaat voted for the candidates of all parties, including the Communists whom Maududi had called a "plague" and had pledged to dislodge.

Myriad conflicts stamped the very lengthy process of the Jamaat's transformation toward moderation. The daily conflict the Jamaat experienced was not between Islam and the West but rather was between contending streams of its own leadership and between ordinary members. The penultimate chapter of the book shows the forms and magnitude of the conflict within the Jamaat over the issue of voting in elections. The fierce conflicts that took place questioned the very coherence and monochromatism of Islamism. When the final decision to lift the voting ban was taken, the former *amīr*, Yusuf, equated it with "polytheism" and called it "doubly *haram*." Ziaulhoda, who resigned from the party, argued that, far from eliminating *bāṭil*, the Jamaat was now perpetuating it. The conflict within the Jamaat revealed that there was not one Islam, as the opposing streams accused each other of betraying true Islam. Though expressed in ideological language, I also showed how the conflict was punctuated by regional and linguistic factors.

In chapter 5 I demonstrated the raging conflict between the SIO and the SIMI, a radical splinter group of the Jamaat, over the definition of true Islam. Chapter 3 depicted how the administration and teachers of the Jamaat school conflicted over whether the school should become affiliated with the UP government and what the criteria should be for appointing a teacher. Chapter 4 examined the contrasting worldviews of two SIO activists on various issues ranging from growing a beard and talking to veiled or unveiled girls to music, entertainment, and watching films. I also showed the SIO leadership's ambiguity toward Jamal, who resisted organizational rules and watched films and dance, and listened to Western music. In his view, "entertainment is part of Islam."

Conceptual Transformations

The transformation of the Jamaat occurred concomitantly with a transformation in several conceptual premises of Islamism. Here let us examine the transformation of two such premises: the boundary between Islam and *jāhiliyat*, and the conceptualization of Islam as an indivisible organic whole. A basic premise of the Jamaat's ideology was that India, as Maududi stated, was *dar al-kufr*, and hence the need to transform it into *dar al-Islam* by establishing Allah's Kingdom. Maududi drew an ineradicable boundary between *dar al-Islam* and *dar al-kufr*: in the former Islam ruled, and in the latter *jāhiliyat*. Further, Islam and *jāhiliyat* could never coexist. Recall Maududi's judgment that for Muslims even to breathe under *dar al-kufr* (because its state was not based on sharia) was illegitimate, unless they fought to convert it into *dar al-Islam*. Having migrated to Pakistan, in 1951, he reiterated his position when he said that Muslims of Pakistan could no longer marry Muslims in India, because the latter was *dar al-kufr*. The Jamaat's boycott of elections in Independent India was based on the same premise.

From the 1960s on, however, as the debate on elections started within the *shura*, the premise of an ineradicable boundary between *dar al-Islam* and *dar al-kufr* began to blur. The Indian democratic system was, as one *shura* member put it in the early 1970s, "neither openly anti-Islamic" nor "Islamic." Two decades later another *shura* member argued that the distinction ulema maintained between *dar al-Islam* and *dar al-kufr* was "out of tune with reality and hence redundant." What, then, was India's status? The Jamaat argued that India was *dar al-daʿvat*, the land of propagation. The Indian Constitution was secular, a "divine boon" in the words of one Jamaat member, as Muslims enjoyed the right to live their religion. It is more than evident that what led to the blurring of the boundary was the secular democratic character of the state. In the words of another *shura* member from Jharkhand, the Indian Constitution was the best in the world and already Islamic. The only problem, he told me, was that it affirmed its sovereignty to people. If the sovereignty to people was replaced with sovereignty to God, then the Constitution would become fully Islamic.

According to Maududi's formulation, which Nadwi also upheld initially, Islam was an organic totality in perpetual conflict with *jāhiliyat*, which was also an organic totality. As an organic totality, moreover, its parts could not be separated from one another. The Islamist totality was to be pursued in its entirety. The Jamaat thus opposed *jāhiliyat* in its totality—from the boycott of the parliamentary or Assembly elections and admission to AMU to village council elections. To Nadwi, let us recall, the village council was also a department of the un-godly system, and so was AMU because its objective was not to work for the establishment of Allah's Kingdom. One of the first signs of the dissolution of the Islamist totality was the abolition, in 1957, of the ban on Jamaat "friends" to study at AMU. Some years later, the ban on Jamaat members was also abolished (see chapters 2 and 4). Logically AMU was no longer part of the *jāhiliyat*. Recall the argument of a *shura* member that it was wrong to compare a polity with a human organism, and that although a system might be un-Islamic on the whole, it may not necessarily be true for each and every part. The most striking example of the dissolution of the Islamist totality, however, was the removal of the state from the center of the Jamaat's agenda, an act that also entailed recognition, though gradual, of the legitimacy of the Indian state. It was for that reason that the Jamaat school began to seek affiliation with the government (see chapter 3). Also, the Jamaat no longer refused membership to Muslims who worked in government banking or insurance companies, which earlier were regarded as *haram* professions. In fact, as discussed in chapter 7, the Jamaat even positively reported the "sacrifice for India" by a Muslim soldier killed during the 1999 Kargil war. In the Jamaat's previous formulation, it was illegitimate for a Muslim to be part of an army of a non-Muslim state (*qitāl fi ghair sabīlillāh*).

The Condition of Transformation

Thus far I have summarized the salient dimensions of the Jamaat's transformation. To turn to my main argument, I discuss the condition that made the discourse of the Jamaat's moderation possible, looking at several factors that I contend were responsible for it. First, the Muslim masses disavowed the Jamaat's ideology. The basis of this disavowal was what I call an "ideological dissonance" between the Jamaat agenda and the political aspirations of the Muslim public. This dissonance worked on the Jamaat to refashion its ideology. In contrast to the Jamaat, most Muslims, including ulema, did not believe that secular democracy violated their faith in *kalima*; rather, they valued it.[2] I have discussed how the Jamiatul Ulema, the largest organization of ulema, regarded secularism as a "golden principle" (Siddiqi undated:2), and a "pious objective" (Miftahi 1995:69). The Jamiatul Ulema's leader, Husian Ahmad Madni (2002), played a particularly pivotal role in offering an Islamic rationale for, and securing, secular democracy. More important, secular democracy had the seal of legitimacy from Abulkalam Azad, an Islamic scholar and a key leader of the Congress. In free India, secular democracy had thus become the language of Muslim politics across all groups (see the introduction and chapter 7). Another level of ideological dissonance was the incongruence between the Muslim public's desires and those of the Jamaat. Chapter 3 documents how the Jammat school in Aligarh *shahr*, the Green School, changed under pressure from Muslim society, which was the Jamaat's main constituency. Whereas the Jamaat wanted to produce activists or workers for its organization, the ordinary Muslims wanted their children to become government servants and to be economically successful. In the Jamaat's ideology, AMU may have been a slaughterhouse, but for *shahr* Muslims it was an ideal destination; hence their desire to have their children educated there. This ideological dissonance impelled the Jamaat to refashion its educational ideology.

Second, but equally important, was the ability of the Jamaat's leadership to transform its ideology in the midst of complex sociopolitical and religious forces. Having already discussed the leadership's role[3] (see chapter 7) and the Muslim opposition to the Jamaat (see chapters 2 and 7), I focus here on the structure of the state. My reason for doing so is that although ethnography offers a rich approach to understanding the specifics of a movement, it is "hardly sufficient" for illuminating the larger political field in which the movement works (Camaroff and Camaroff 2003; Edelman 2001; also see Burawoy 2000). It is true that social movements aim at influencing the practices and ideology of the state, but the opposite is no less true. The practices and structure of the state equally shape the trajectory of social movements (Goldstone 2003). Whether or not and how much the movement activists in a given polity will become moderate or militant depends not only on their own desire but equally on the state's willingness to change as well as the contours of the state's structure. This insight about the centrality of the state in unraveling the dynamics of social movements is central to the "political process" approach of social movement studies (see McAdam 1982).

Democratic State and Moderation

My argument that the state's secular democratic structure catalyzed the Jamaat's moderation becomes clearer when we ask a comparative question: Why do Islamists become radical? I answer this question by examining the causes of radicalism in Muslim-majority societies. In *Why Muslims Rebel*, Hafez (2003) addresses the causes of radicalization in Algeria and Egypt, and concludes that Islamists turned radical when the states denied them participation in the political process. Hafez further stresses that the states' repressive policies—denial of the right to criticize the government, restriction of the press, a near ban on all public protest, and persecution of Islamists—unleashed radicalization. In Algeria, between 1992 and 1993, 166 Islamists were sentenced to death. In February and March 1995 state forces killed 396 Islamists. By 1996, 43,737 suspected Algerians were jailed. The situation in Egypt was similar. Between 1992 and 1997 state authorities arrested around 50,000 dissidents, and killed about 500 Islamists (2003:78–81, 85–87). To quote Hafez, "exclusionary and repressive political environments force Islamists to undergo a near universal process of radicalization" (ibid.:22). Hafez's argument is similar to Bayat's (1998), who asks: Why did Iran, in the late 1970s, with its "repressive political system," undergo a revolution even though at the time there was no Islamist movement, whereas Egypt, in the 1980s and 1990s, with a "more liberal political system," saw no revolution even though it had one of the oldest Islamist movements? His answer is that, unlike Iran, Egypt's political system was less repressive, as it gave some freedom to opposition parties, and the country had a fairly independent "civil society."

Hafez occasionally refers to "democracy," but he hesitates to make it central to his analysis. Likewise, Bayat refers to "civil society" and "degrees of political control" in his argument, but he is also reluctant to use the term "democracy." Clearly, however, Hafez's "exclusionary and repressive political environments" are, in fact, undemocratic state structures. Similarly, Bayat's argument that Egypt had a civil society and Iran did not as an explanation for the moderation of Islamism in the former is an argument for democracy. Following Kumar (1993) and Walzer (1991; cf. Kamali 2001; and Sivan 1992), I believe that civil society cannot be entirely detached from democracy. In other words, one can justifiably interpret both Hafez's and Bayat's arguments as meaning that the more democratic a state, the less likely Islamist movements will become radical.

Because my argument is built around the democratic secular state, I should define "democratic" and "secular" in the Indian context. Unlike an exclusionary and repressive state, a democratic state structure is based on the participation of all segments of the population, among others, through periodic elections to form a government, and the state guarantees political freedom, including a free press, the right to protest against state policies, and legal checks against the state's abuse of laws. A democratic state entails a civil society independent of state control. By "secular," I mean that the state does not represent any religion, treats all religions equally, and does not forbid citizens from participating in politics on religious grounds, as it does, for example, in Iran.

Unlike Algeria, Egypt, and Iran, the Indian state was *inclusionary*, in principle. The Jamaat was entitled to participate in the democratic processes, and because the state was secular, it placed no restrictions on the Jamaat to do so. But given the Jamaat's peculiar ideology—that a state based on "human" rather than "divine" sovereignty was *ṭāġhūt*—it imposed a ban on its members to vote in or contest elections. Participation in elections, according to the Jamaat *amīr*, violated Muslims' belief in monotheism and flouted sharia at every step. Recall the Jamaat's characterization of AMU as a "slaughterhouse." Although the Jamaat's moderation had begun in the late 1950s, when it abolished the ban on its "friends" to study at AMU, the hallmark of its ideology was the opposition to and boycott of secularism and democracy. India's democratic processes made the Jamaat moderate its position even on secularism and democracy.

When the Muslim public and its organizations rejected the Jamaat's call, in 1951, to boycott elections, the Jamaat stopped appealing for a boycott. This retreat in itself was a result of democracy, as masses of Muslims and their leaders had voted in and contested the elections despite the Jamaat's call to the contrary. In the 1952 parliamentary elections, 42 Muslim candidates contested 35 seats. The number increased in the 1957 election, with 61 Muslims contesting 46 seats (the total numbers of seats were 489 and 494 in 1952 and 1957, respectively). In the Assembly elections too, Muslims participated massively. Throughout India, 617 Muslim candidates contested 416 seats for the 1952 Assembly elections, and 520 contested for 387 seats in the 1957 elections (see chapter 7). Clearly the Jamaat was isolated. By 1960 many Jamaat activists began pressuring the leadership to participate in the elections. Obviously the activists themselves were pressured from the democratic environment where most Muslims were participating in the elections. Owing to this dual pressure from within its own party and from ordinary Muslims, on the eve of the third general elections in 1962 the Jamaat *amīr*, Nadwi, argued that Muslims should not shun the elections, but he exhorted them to participate only to pursue *iqāmat-e-dīn*. The exhortation was rhetoric aimed at orienting the Jamaat for a larger change in the long run. It became clear only a few years later when, to win the Muslim public to its side, the Jamaat participated in the formation of the Mushāverat and committed itself to secularism and the Indian Constitution.

It is instructive that the first resolution to revise the position on boycotting the elections was placed in the Jammat *shura* precisely on the eve of the third parliamentary elections in 1961. All subsequent debates were also connected to the timing of elections. Under pressure from the Muslim public and its own party members, the Jamaat was on an irreversible path to moderation. In the elections of 1967 the moderation found expression when the Jamaat allowed its members to vote for a Muslim candidate. In the course of the debate within its *shura* on the elections, meanwhile, the Jamaat had acknowledged, in 1970, the legitimacy of both secularism and democracy. But a section of the Jamaat desired a far more drastic change, the magnitude of which the leadership probably failed to anticipate. As a result, discontent within the Jamaat began to well up. It imploded in 1977, when a top national leader from Bombay, Shams Pirzada, resigned from the Jamaat, describing its voting ban as "anti-democratic" and "unjust." He formed his own party, the Muslim Democratic Forum, to take part in the political process. Pirzada's resignation blazed a trail as more members resigned from the Jamaat. Abdul Hafiz Khan from Hyderabad also resigned and formed the Muslims Front. In Patna, an SIO member was expelled because he believed that the ban on voting was "illogical," and he formed the Bihar Muslim Forum. The implosion of discontent over the "illogical" ban on participating in the democratic process was the main catalyst that later led to a series of transformations; the most telling, of course, was the permanent lifting of the ban. With the rise of Hindutva, the Jamaat's acceptance and defense of secular democracy only intensified.

The Jamaat's mutation, far from being unique, is analogous to that of the Communist Party of India (CPI). To quote a Jamaat *shura* member from

Kerala, a bastion of the Left, "the Communists call the present government bourgeoisie, which is infidelic [*kāfirāna*] in our language" (*ME*:17). Having made the comparison, he argued that if the Communists could participate in the bourgeoisie system, why not the Jamaat? The CPI decried democracy as a bourgeois idea but later embraced it (Banerjee 1996, Schwartz 1955), as did the Jamaat. Following the split in the 1960s, when the Communist Party of India, Marxist Leninist (CPIML) was formed, it, too, rejected democracy as the "hoax of parliamentarism" and believed in "an immediate revolution . . . through [a] revolutionary people's war" (in Franda 1969:806). In the early 1990s we, the activists of the student wing of the CPIML, debated ad nauseam whether combining democratic and armed paths was true to the revolutionary credo. By the late 1990s the Liberation Group had embraced democracy and almost renounced violence.

Like the CPIML, also known as Naxalites, the Jamaat did not suffer violent repression by the state. Since Partition, the Jamaat was banned twice. In 1975 Indira Gandhi outlawed all the opposition parties, including the Jamaat, and across the nation the Jamaat's top leaders were arrested. When I spoke with some of them, none told me that he had been beaten or tortured. Rather, they were treated with respect. The false charge against the Jamaat was that its leaders spoke of "overthrowing the government" (in Naim 1979:11). In fact, one Jamaat member testifies in a memoir of the Emergency that he wrote, that the police in Delhi were embarrassed that they had arrested the Jamaat leaders there because the police knew they were innocent (Naim 1979).[4] A story I heard during my fieldwork had it that an adviser, probably a Muslim, to Mrs. Gandhi persuaded her not to ban the Jamaat, stating that it was peaceful and harmless. She reacted by saying that the Jamaat did not believe in the Indian Constitution. The advisoer argued that long ago it had publicly accepted the Constitution. "It is too late," was Mrs. Gandhi's reply. When the adviser persisted in his argument, she said that she needed to ban it for "balance," meaning that in order to ban the RSS, a Muslim party also had to be banned.

The same policy of "balance," as the Jamaat itself noted (*Radiance* 1993 [December 13–January 2]:18; *MMS*:196), was adopted in 1992, when, after the demolition of the Babri mosque, the Congress government banned both the RSS and the Jamaat. The government banned it because its then *amīr*, Sirajul Hasan, had said that "the separation of Kashmir from India was inevitable" (*Radiance* 1993 [December 13–January 2, 1994]: 15). Later the Supreme Court struck down the ban, because the government could not substantiate its charge (*Afkār-e-millī* 1993 [March]: 31–35). Obviously the government ban had more to do with the strange logic of balance and less with its targeting of the Jamaat.

The local police knew the logic of balance well. In the Aligarh *shahr*, the head of the police station asked a senior Jamaat member to send one or two of his colleagues to the police station as a mark of obeying an order "from above." Because the police chief knew the Jamaat members, he found the government allegations baseless. In Rampur, when the police came to arrest an elderly Jamaat member, his son (also a Jamaat member) offered himself for arrest. The police jokingly told him to wait. He waited and waited, but the police never returned. Like their counterparts in Aligarh, the police in Rampur obeyed the order "from above" by making a few token arrests.

The Erosion of Secular Democracy and Radicalization

My argument so far that secular democracy catalyzed the moderation of the Jamaat, one may point out, fails to explain the radicalization of the SIMI. But far from weakening my argument, I hold that the SIMI's radicalization strengthens my contention. In chapter 6 I showed that the SIMI radicalized in response to the Saffron wave; that is, the SIMI began to radicalize with the rise of Hindutva following the Ayodhya campaign that left a trail of brutal violence throughout India, costing thousands of lives (mostly Muslims) and leading to the demolition of the Babri mosque. Until the late 1980s the SIMI's prime concern was moral and educational. Neither jihad nor a caliphate were on its agenda (see the 2003 interview of its founding president, Siddiqi). The SIMI's radicalization from the 1990s on—centered around the Babri mosque—was expressed in three issues: the call for jihad, the declaration of India as *dar al-ḥarb*, and the installation of the caliphate. All these matters were intimately linked to state practices.

As discussed earlier, the SIMI candidate in the AMUSU elections, Hafiz Sikandar Rana, spoke against the *ẓulm* (oppression) of the police, the Hindutva activists, and the administration, all of whom he held responsible for the killing of Muslims in riots unleashed in the wake of the Ayodhya campaign. Rana drew a heart-wrenching picture of how "our young sisters and mothers were raped, dishonored, and then cut into pieces." Tremendous insecurity plagued the Muslims, which the SIMI described at its Action for Muslims conference at Bombay and it called for jihad. This call only intensified afterward. Upon his release in 2004, Qasim Omar, the SIMI president, jailed for his alleged role in inciting violence and national treason, continued to stress the need for jihad. He told me: "We have been regularly killed in riots. . . . Muslims were massacred in Gujarat [in 2002]. What do you expect us to do? We must wage jihad to defend ourselves." It scarcely requires reflection to see that the state's failure to protect the lives, dignity, and property of its citizens led to the call for jihad. But more than its failure to protect, the state, especially the police, sided with the rioters (Brass 2003; Roy 2002).

The erosion of secularism was manifest in the state's involvement at various levels in the anti-Muslim riots. Thus my argument is also a critique of Varshney's (1997, 2002, 2002a) studies of Hindu-Muslim violence. Inspired by Robert Putnam's work on Italy, Varshney's thesis that the inter-religious associational networks are a bulwark against violence bypasses the state's role in producing and prolonging violence, directly or indirectly. Even if we accept that inter-religious civic networks are an antidote to communal violence, it still does not tell us how the state itself is a key player in forging or dismantling these networks. As in his critique of Putnam, Hefner (2000; also see Tarrow 1996) rightly argues that an uncivil state barely facilitates the civil associations required for a robust democracy. It is important to point out that much of the writings on violence in India, including Varshney's, often treat Hindus and Muslims as ethnic units equally capable of violence. This is simply incorrect. As a minority, Muslims have more often been victims rather than perpetrators of violence (Brass 2002, 2003). My description of Muslims as a minority is not merely in the numerical sense. I am also referring to the sheer lack of accessibility Muslims have to state resources and institutions. As the history of recurring riots in postcolonial India suggests, the state has often aided the perpetrators of violence. The state's bias against Muslims was evident, above all, in not protecting the Babri mosque, which had become a litmus test of secularism. After Hindutva activists demolished the mosque in complicity with state authorities, the SIMI noted that the "illusion" of secularism and democracy had burst and it had "no relation with it [secularism and democracy]." *Islamic Movement*, the SIMI's organ, published an angry statement:

> Today it is being stated that though the tragedy of the demolition has shaken the foundation, it has not destroyed the structure of secularism. However, I ask: Where is secularism? Is this democracy to demolish the places of worship of the minorities? Is this justice . . . that when Muslims protest against the unlawful demolition and injustice done to them, bullets are pierced into their chests; and the chastity of their mothers and sisters looted and video filmed? Are these the composite civilizational . . . traditions of Ram and Sita, Nanak and Chishti that [Muslim] women are paraded naked in a procession? (*IM* 1993 [February–March]: 41)

Following the demolition of the Babri mosque, the SIMI called secularism a "fraud" crafted to fool Muslims. It reminded all the non-BJP parties of their promise to protect the mosque. Since they had failed to keep their promise, it declared India *dar al-ḥarb*. Contending that democracy has been more harmful than beneficial to Muslims, it appealed to Muslims to boycott elections. The elected representatives, SIMI observed, had helped perpetuate injustice against Muslims. Like the Jamaat before and soon after Independence, SIMI declared that Indian polity was *bāṭil*, anti-Islamic. The link between the state's failure to be secular and SIMI's characterization of India as *dar al-ḥarb* is tightly linked. Similarly SIMI's call for a caliphate was mirrored in its reaction to the *Sangh parivār's* campaign to convert India into a Hindu nation. Let us recall the statement of the SIMI president: "If someone [the RSS] has the right to work for *Ram rājya* [the Hindu nation], we, too have every right to establish *niẓām-e-muṣṭafā* [a Caliphate]." More important, the SIMI saw the caliphate as a way to solve the problems that the Hindutva movement, in SIMI's view, had generated for Muslims: the demolition of the Babri mosque, loss of Muslim lives, the looting of their sisters and mothers' honor, destruction of their property, and, above all, the very survival of Muslims. It is relevant here to remember that the frequent anti-Muslim riots were crucial to the formation of Islamist student organizations during the late 1960s and 1970s (see chapter 4).

SIMI's portrayal of the Prophet Muhammad as a "prophet of wars" and as a "commander" took place precisely in a context where virulent Hindu nationalism threatened the lives and identity of Indian Muslims. In chapter 6 I discussed the employment by Qasim Omar of a militant language to describe Muhammad. SIMI's militant portrayal of Muhammad, I pointed out, was a new Muhammad fashioned under the dark shadow of anti-Muslim, masculine Hindutva. It was an obvious response to the projection of the god Rama as a combative god; "heavily armed" and "ready for war" (Kapur 1993; also see Thapar 1993). Kapur describes how the image of Ram underwent a metamorphosis. In the hands of Hindu nationalists, Ram was transformed from a child god of gentleness to a combative, warrior-like figure. In response to the militarization of Ram, in SIMI's discourse the image of Muhammad was likewise transformed into a combative, warrior-like image.

The point is that Hindutva's agenda of the Hindu state and its fierce anti-Muslim nature spurred SIMI's radicalization. Worth noting is that over fifteen percent of its total members came, according to an *anṣār* of SIMI, only from the state of Maharashtra where the Shiv Sena, a constituent of the *Sangh parivār*, had been in power and involved in one of the worst riots ever in Bombay. This also explains SIMI's diatribe against polytheism and Hindutva.[5] As long as the Nehruvian project of a plural, non-monopolistic, secular, and democratic India (Khilnani 1997) was hegemonic, Islamist radicalization was almost nonexistent. Even a party as rigid as the Jamaat underwent moderation. This is not to say that the Congress was divinely secular. The state under its dispensation also practiced communal policies, but its communalism was *pragmatic*. By contrast, the communalism of the *Sangẖ parivār* was *programmatic* (Vanaik 2001:58) or, to quote Sumit Sarkar (1993) and Amartya Sen (1993), it was "fascism." Undoubtedly the BJP came to power through democracy. It was not democracy as Nehru envisioned it, however, but a masculine, exclusivist majoritarianism masquerading as democracy (Basu et al. 1993:1). Anguished at his colleagues' prejudices toward Muslims in the garb of democracy, Nehru wrote, "If that is called democracy, then I say: to hell with such a democracy" (1993:139). It is precisely against Hindutva's version of democracy that Michael Mann draws our attention to in *The Dark Side of Democracy* (2005; also see Appadurai 2006). Mann shows how democracy has been used to legitimize some of the worst acts of violence, including ethnic cleansing.

Democracy, it follows, is not the naked game of numerical superiority. Nor is it merely about reasoned discussion, a notion central to the theory of deliberative democracy inspired by Habarmas (Guttmann and Thompson 2004). Surely it is vital, probably indispensable. The model of deliberative democracy is useful in that it invalidates the hegemonic idea of aggregative democracy. But with Iris Young (2000), we ought to go a step further and question the purpose of deliberation. In her view, it is also a tool to include the disadvantaged. In Young's formulation, justice, beyond its formal compass, is integral to democracy (also see Sen 1992). Arend Lijphart (1996) similarly argues that power sharing between different groups is essential for a healthy democracy. Nehru's democracy, in principle, stood for empowerment of the excluded classes and the minorities. That it did not deliver is subject to debate. Jaffrelot (2001), for instance, shows the marginalization of Muslims in postcolonial India and their status as second-class citizens. Many government reports have also shown that in various fields—education, economics, business, government services, and politics—Muslims lag astonishingly far behind other disprivileged groups. The report of the Sachar Committee (Government of India 2006), set up by the Congress-led government in 2005, once again demonstrates the grotesque marginalization of Muslims. The arena where their percentage exceeded their demographic size was prison. Hearsay had it that the Sachar Committee, perhaps under duress, scrapped this finding from its report.

This argument that the erosion of secular democracy led to SIMI's radicalization does not only mean that state authorities discriminated against Muslims. From a different understanding of democracy, such as that advanced by Iris Young and Arend Lijphart, the failure of democracy is also evident in the abysmally low presence of Muslims in public life. It is in the midst and because of this marginalization that the SIMI's radical discourse blossomed. *Islamic Movement* published a special issue after the demolition of the Babri mosque, in which, while calling for jihad to regain the Babri mosque, SIMI lamented how Muslims were rendered to the periphery of society. "The topmost leader of the Independence movement, Maulana Abulkalam Azad," wrote *Islamic Movement,* "was given the insignificant ministry of education" (*IM* 1993 [January–March]: 31). It added, sarcastically, that as if Maulana Azad (d. 1958) did not deserve Bharat Ratna (the Indian government's highest civilian award) when alive, he was sent the award by post, meaning after his death. Maulana Azad was awarded the Bharat Ratna, posthumously, in 1992. Furthermore, *Islamic Movement* poignantly observed the Muslims' pitiable economic condition and their negligible presence in the army, the police, civil services, and the like (ibid.:35). By the erosion of secularism I also mean what Jeffery et al. (2004:36) call "banal Hinduism," the ways in which Hinduism becomes normalized in everyday life (for example, in schools), whereas other religions traditions such as Islam are routinely marginalized (also see Benei 2001; and Osella and Osella 2007).

As stated, the Muslims' marginalization preceded the rise of Hindutva. But with the onset of Hindutva even discussions of Muslim minority became taboo. The Hindutva agenda did not include the marginalization of Muslims. Muslims instead appeared as an object of ridicule, scorn, and, above all, as the nation's quislings. K. R. Malkani, a Hindutva ideologue, asked Muslims to meet in a conference and apologize to Hindus for the crimes "Muslim invaders did to this country [read Hindus]" (1986:8). Muslims' marginalization did not concern him. Not the state, but Muslims themselves and their religion were responsible for sweeping Muslims to the side. Malkani argued, "The Muslim not only has less money, he has more mouths to feed thanks to his polygamy and extra-allergy to family planning" (ibid.:9). The radicalization of SIMI, as has amply been shown, cannot be detached from the process (and consequences thereof) through which Hindu nationalism pulverized democracy to stigmatize and exclude Muslims. In Hindutva activists' hands, democracy indeed became a high-tech theater of entertainment and violence against Muslims. In the post-demolition riots, Muslim women were raped and filmed in Gujarat. In 2002 Muslims were massacred under the aegis of a democratically elected state in Gujarat. Clearly the resolve of Qasim Omar, SIMI's national president, for jihad is solidly linked to the world's largest democracy turning into a theater of entertainment and violence against Muslims. Troubling though it may seem, John Keane's question is pertinent:

> What will prosperity remember democracies for? Propping up dictators and having tea with totalitarians? . . . Or the napalm bombs they dropped on innocent civilians . . . and the nuclear explosions they first

> triggered? Or will posterity recall how democracies turned rapes and murders into light entertainment? How should democracies today come to terms with all this violence, all this hypocrisy? Should they not feel ashamed of what we . . . have done to ourselves and to others in the name of democracy? (2004:208–9)

Two additional factors contributed to the radicalization of SIMI. Like radicals of other ideologies, its members were young. SIMI was an organization of youth. Muslims above the age of thirty were not eligible for membership (*Dastūr Student Islamic Movement of India* 1993:6). The youthfulness, or what the Jamaat called emotionalism (*jaẕbātiyat*), played an important role in its radicalism. Although SIO members were also under thirty, the SIO was under the tutelage of the Jamaat, which, as a party of the middle-aged and the elderly (mostly the latter), controlled its activities. The SIMI was independent. Finally, in accord with media reports (see Yeshwantrao 2003, 2003a) a few of the Jamaat members, as well as retired SIMI members, told me, often in a whisper, that lately SIMI had developed hideous links with jihad organizations in Pakistan. Based on the whispers, SIMI, unknowingly or not, was playing into the hands of the Pakistani Jamaat and Pakistan's Inter-Services Intelligence (ISI), which aimed to destabilize India to take revenge for the 1971 war. SIMI's cross-border links unleashed an internal conflict, as those opposing the links resigned (*IM* 1995 [January]: 85) or were expelled from the party. In the mid-1990s *Islamic Movement* published the names of expelled members. After the ban on SIMI, Sayeed Khan, the former president of SIMI's Mumbai unit who opposed the cross-border connections, formed Muslim Youth for India, known as MY India (Rediff.com 2003). The aim of this group was to counter SIMI's takeover of Islam for anti-national objectives. Khan told the media, "I love my religion but I will not let my country disintegrate" (*The Telegraph* 2004). Many of its retired members also told me that SIMI's call for jihad was both un-Islamic and against the interests of *mulk* (the nation).[6]

Radicalization and Democratization

The radicalization of SIMI also reflected complex internal dynamics, symbolizing the democratization of Islam and Muslim society from within. The discourse of radicalization, I submit, should also be understood in relation to the yearning for democratic rights among SIMI activists from a stratum I call the "Islamist class." They were largely urban. Their parents, certainly their fathers, had both a madrasa and a modern education. Their educational capital, including their familiarity with Maududi's writings critical of "traditional" ulema, enabled them to question rather than obey the authority of elders. Moreover, because most SIMI activists came from well-off families, they paid for their education. As such, their dreams were different. They did not want to become *mu'azzin*, imams, or booksellers. Their desire was to obtain a modern education and join AMU from where they also learned the repertoires of protests and strikes.

As chapter 5 documented, in 1990 SIMI staged a strike at Falāḥ, a Jamaat madrasa, when Mubarak, a teacher, found a student cheating during an exam and slapped him in front of everyone. Later the administration expelled some six to ten SIMI student leaders who had organized the strike. During the 2004 India-Pakistan cricket series, hostel wardens had seized thirteen radios from students. The hostel rules forbade students to have radios and to listen to cricket commentaries. Those whose sets were seized belonged to both the SIMI and the SIO. But it was a SIMI activist who broke the warden's locked almirah to get the radios. Several other defiant episodes were staged by the SIMI. On the Falāḥ campus, SIMI indeed was synonymous with resistance, against both the Falāḥ administration and Hindutva.

These acts of protests by SIMI exhibit a yearning for rights. Obviously both the protest and the strike belong to what Charles Tilly calls the "repertoire of collective action" bequeathed by modernity. Less obvious is that protests such as SIMI's were not defensive but were an "offensive pursuit of new rights and advantages" (Tilly 1984:304). SIMI's claim for rights against the gerontocratic authorities of Falāḥ is novel in the context of Indian madrasas. The discourse of rights is nearly foreign to most non-Jamaat madrasas, because they draw their finances from the community's charity and endowments. Their education is free. Most students in these madrasas come from poor, rural families. The discourse there is thus the discourse of obligation and duties. Students are taught to obey their teachers, for to disobey their authority is to disobey Islam itself.

By contrast, SIMI's discourse was of democratic rights that was made possible by the larger transformation in postcolonial political formation. Initially democracy worked along the lines of what Rudolph and Rudolph (1987) call "command politics." Based on patron-client ties, the elites commanded the "masses" to act. The Congress, for example, cultivated relationships with the Jamiatul Ulema with the result that the eminent Jamiatul Ulema leader Asad Madni was made a Member of Parliament for eighteen years. The shift from command to demand politics, or "plebeianization" of democracy in Hansen's (1999) words, occurred with the rise of social strata from below. SIMI activists belonged to one such stratum, the one I call the "Islamist class," that democratization had unleashed.

Along with the plebeianization of democracy, Islam was also plebeianized. The established centers of Islamic learning headed by the gerontocratic ulema had lost the monopoly on defining Islam. The new social stratum from which SIMI activists came sought to have its own definition of Islam. In many ways, it was a great reversal of roles. If during much of the modern period the gerontocratic ulema had told the laity what Islam meant, now it was the young activists of SIMI who instructed ulema about true Islam. When the students at Deoband organized the 1968 strike, the gerontocratic ulema called it anti-sharia. In contrast, the SIMI regarded the strike as a true act of Islam. Likewise, none of the ulema considered the establishment of a caliphate in India as an obligation for Muslims. Nor did they regard jihad as an article of faith, much less a foundation. While calling for a caliphate and jihad, SIMI thus criticized ulema for having abandoned "true" Islam. In chapter 6 we saw that Qasim Omar criticized the entire stratum of ulema who, in his view, had not only given up on jihad but presented it as a "condemned word." SIMI's call for jihad thus symbolizes the demonopolization of religious authorities. No established institutions–not Deoband, nor Nadwa in Lucknow, including the Jamaat—endorsed SIMI's jihad. Yet, the SIMI claimed that its call for jihad was Islamic. This claim for true Islam did not emanate from a painstaking study of canonical Islamic texts. SIMI members were well below the age of thirty. Under the flag of "true" Islam, SIMI thus subverted the authorities of the gerontocratic ulema who had spent their entire lives studying Islam. SIMI's contesting of the established authorities testifies to Devji's (2005) argument that the discourse of jihad signals the democratization of Islam.

This language of democratization typically marked the conflict-ridden interaction between SIO and SIMI over the issue of who controlled Falāḥ's Old Boys' Association (OBA). According to the SIO, since SIMI had taken over the OBA to spread its "obnoxious" ideology, it launched a parallel alumni union. After the showdown between SIO and SIMI in 1999, the vice chancellor of Falāḥ proposed a settlement that both the SIO and the SIMI should have an equal representation in the OBA's leadership. SIMI rejected the proposal because it was "undemocratic" to give a share of 50 percent to the SIO, which enjoyed the support of less than 20 percent of alumni. After SIMI's rejection, a new committee was set up to resolve the conflict. SIO offered a formula at whose heart lay a change in the very procedure of elections. It suggested that the general members of the OBA should first elect a Council, which would then elect a *shura* and its officers. The aim of the SIO's formula was to block SIMI's candidates from getting elected as officers. It sought to do so by having a Council, which, SIO thought, would be easier to manage than a crowd of hundreds that had been directly electing its officers thus far. However, the SIO framed its argument in the language of democracy, invoking the idea of a reasoned debate, integral to the notion of deliberative democracy. The SIO argued that the Council was a necessity for a reasoned debate, as an immature crowd of two hundred had the tendency, especially with SIMI's encouragement, to become unreasonable. SIMI rejected this formula as well. In the SIO's proposal, SIMI saw a design of what it called "disenfranchising a large number of alumni" on the flimsy grounds that "they were immature." Clearly Islamist radicalization is at once a motor and consequence of Islam's democratization.

Finally, I return to the question with which this book began: Why did the Jamaat accept its ideological transformation privately but often disown it in public? The answer to this dilemma lies in the Jamaat's attempt to meet conflicting demands made by different audiences. While the Muslim public and their leaders pressured the Jamaat to recast its ideology, the SIMI criticized the Jamaat for deviating from the "original ideology." The Jamaat vice president reflected this dilemma when he said: "Ordinary Muslims [*lōg*] urged the Jamaat to change, but when the Jamaat changed there were internal allegations that "we [the Jamaat] are deviating from our original line" (*Taḥrīk-e-Islāmī* . . . undated:24). This does not mean, however, as SIMI President Qasim Omar claimed, that it was only the Jamaat that changed. Both the Jamaat and the SIMI changed, albeit along markedly divergent paths. And so, too, did the culture of Indian politics change.

Appendix 1

TABLE 4
Organizational Strength of the Jamaat from 1941 to 2000

	1941	*1947*	*1948*	*1960*	*1978*	*1990*	*2000*
Members (*Arkān*)	75	999	240	981	2,400	3,871*	4,776**
Sympathizers (*Muttafeqīn*)	—	—	—	4,000	—	—	—
Workers (*Kārkun*)	—	—	—	—	—	14,475	270,246
Under influence (*Muta'ṡṡerīn*)	—	—	—	15,000	—	—	—
Associates (*Mu'āwenīn;* for non-Muslims)	—	—	—	—	—	3,006	2,769

Source: The sources of figures for 1941, 1947, 1948, 1960, 1978, 1990, and 2000 are, respectively, *Rūdād jamā'at-e-islāmī hind*, vol. 1 (2000:4); Agwani (1986:61); Agwani (1986:61); Dawat, *Ijtimā'* Number (1960:213); *JIMI* (undated:185); Dawat (1991 [November 7]: 165); and data provided by the Jamaat headquarters.

—Data not available.

*Of which 181 were women.

**Of which 303 were women.

The terms for different levels of affiliates changed over time. A cadre was called a member (*rukn*, pl. *arkān*). This term has remained since its inception until today. The second tier of affiliates was variously called, at different times, *muttafiq*, *hamdard*, or "under influence." Notably only the first level of affiliates had the right to take part in organizational decision-making processes. The category of *mu'āvenīn* for non-Muslims was a new addition, perhaps introduced at the turn of the century.

Appendix 2

TABLE 5
Organizational Strength of the SIO from 1983 to 2001

	1983	*1986*	*1993*	*1998*	*2001*
Members	2,692	3,098	1,118	2,736	3,049
Associates	—	—	27,589	49,580	40,546
Sympathizers (non-Muslims)	—	345	—	—	—

Source: *Tīn sālāripōrṭ* . . . (Undated: 4) and data given to me by the SIO Headquarters.
—Data not available.

Appendix 3

TABLE 6
Organizational Strength of the SIMI from 1977 to 1996

	1977	*1979*	*1981*	*1996*	*2001*
Assistant (*Anṣār*)	132	440	461	413*	—
Fellow (*Ikḥvān*)	5,000	26,000	40,000	—	—

Source: Dawat (1982 April 14: 116) and Inṣāf (1998 May: 17)
—Data not Available.
*Male 359, female 54.

Initially, the SIMI had two-tiered membership. While the cadres were called "members," the second level of affiliates was known as "associates." In the early 1980s, the core cadres began to be called *anṣār* after the Qura'nic phrase *kūnū anṣārallāh* which also appears on its logo. The second tier of affiliate was named *member*. Later, the term *member* was replaced with *ikḥvān,* an Arabic term meaning "fellow." It is not clear when exactly the replacement took place. According to a SIMI activist, it happened in the early 1990s. The reason for the replacement of both terms was that they did not foster commitment among the activists the way the Arabic terms did later. A few years before the ban, the SIMI added a third tier of affiliates called *'aivān*.

Notes

Introduction

1. The most recurring phrase in Maududi's prose is "Islamic state." He also frequently uses *Ḳhudā kī bādshāhat*, Allah's Kingdom (1942:87; 1941a), and "Kingdom of God" (1951:30).

2. To be fair to Roy, he does dwell on the "inadequacies" but does not tie them to his definition.

3. We need to differentiate Islamism from communalism. Unlike Islamism, communalism lacks an alternative *Weltanschauung*. Although it uses religious symbols, it does so mainly to share power within a polity on whose codes both ego and alter ego broadly agree. Communalism may manifest in separatism, as in the case of the Muslim League's call for Pakistan. However, the League did not want an alternative sharia state. The "other" of communalism is thus particular. In contrast, Islamists do not want to share "un-Islamic power" but to dethrone it. For Islamists, it is "us" versus "the rest"; their adversary is general, not specific. Finally, they have internal "other," sects and groups that do not share their "infallible truth" (Gupta 1993: also see Ahmad 1997).

4. The interface between democracy and Muslim movements has not been sufficiently explored. The rich volume edited by Kohli (2001) on India's democracy does not address this interface. The contribution of Muslims as co-makers of Indian democracy is seldom noted (e.g., in Brown 1994; Kaviraj 2003; Khilnani 1992; and Roy 2005). Muslims appear as mere consumers of democracy, and presumably a democracy not of their own making.

5. One might argue that I am downplaying the theological factors. One may ask: Do the radical writings of Maududi or others not foster a particular orientation among their readers? And if the political is so important, why is radicalization articulated in the language of Islamic culture, not Marxism? To answer the first question, Maududi's *Al-jihad fil Islam*, published in 1927, has been reprinted continuously since then, and Islamists, not to mention others, have been reading this and similar books all along. Why did they not become get radicalized in the 1950s or 1960s (also see chap. 6 n. 5)? Regarding the second question, I do not distinguish sharply between the cultural and the political. That an actor speaks a distinct language is subject to its credibility in a specific context. Some current Islamists were Communists, even Naxalites, in the past (Ahmad 2005), and in its heyday communism was their language of politics. With its decline, religion (Islam) became their language instead. At AMU the space for radical student politics, previously occupied by Communists, was taken over by SIMI from the 1980s on. Roy (1994) makes a similar point about Afghanistan. It is noteworthy that, in the 1980s, a former SIMI activist, Moazzam Beg, contested elections for the UP Assembly from the Jan Sangh, a Hindu party.

6. Van der Veer (1994:196) explains the marginalization of Muslims as a result of anthropologists' desire to contribute to "understanding of what is understood to be the 'dominant' culture of the majority." Anthropologists, he continues, "thereby unwittingly support Hindu nationalism."

7. Likewise, a Pakistani Urdu-English dictionary (undated) calls Hindustan "the country of Hindus."

8. Tocqueville, too, held that the Qura'nic emphasis on faith rather than splendid deeds made Islam fanatical and inhospitable to democracy (Kelly 1995). Also see Dumont 1970; and Weiner 1987.

9. Curiously the broadside against secularism as an "alien cultural ideology" is rarely extended to democracy. Has democracy gone "native" because it supports the majority rule? See Jaffrelot 2000.

10. My use of the term "minority" follows Azad's (2006:292) for whom it was not just a numerical category. He theorized that "minority" represented a weaker group in relation to a powerful one. I use the term as a cultural collectivity lacking in or denied access to resources and a share in power.

11. Christians, Parsis, Sikhs, and the untouchable (now Dalits) also fell under the category of "minority."

12. A view of secularism as an all-encompassing philosophy, rather than a political mechanism, is shared by its critics such as Asad as well as its diehard French defenders; see Roy 2007: 107.

13. In the Indian Constitution, secularism entered only in 1976. In the French Constitution, *laïcité* did not enter until 1946 (Roy 2007:17).

14. Asad regards Europe as secular. As such, he reproduces the secularization thesis. Far from religion being inconsequential, the post-Enlightenment Europe indeed saw "the expansion of religious activity" (Van der Veer 2001:22), even "religious revival" (van Rooden 2003:119). As late as 1998 Gerd Ludemann was removed as a professor of theology at the University of Göttingen because he ceased to be a Christian (Bowden 2005). In Holland, only in the 1960s did the state-recognized religious "pillars," which also included trade unions, wither away (Poeisz 1967; Van der Veer 2006). For Dutch Muslims, the state may remain Christian in many ways. Weeks before and after Christmas, the streets constantly remind one of the Christian holiday. The Muslim festival Eid, however, passes without notice in the public square.

15. Asad writes, "It is when something is described as belonging to 'religion' and it can be claimed that it does not that the secular emerges" (2003:237).

16. There is no such corresponding phrase for Hindus who stood with the Congress. They were "naturally" nationalist. On the politics of this phrase, see Hasan 1992 and Pandey 1999.

17. The following was noted at a conference in 1972: "We have lost everything—the government, our honor, property, and . . . Urdu . . . —and if attempts are made to take away from us our religion and the personal law given by God himself, we shall be left with nothing to fall back upon" (in Noorani 2003:155).

18. By Muslim politics, I mean a politics to which Islamic idiom is crucial but which has an aim that differs from Islamism's (cf. Eickelman and Piscatori 1996:

ix). Scores of Muslims also belonged to Communist parties. Since Islam was not their idiom, they fall outside the pale of Muslim politics.

19. They included Majlis Ahrar, Anjuman Watan, All-India Momin Conference, Khudai Khidmatgar, Muslim Majlis, and the Independent Party, formed, respectively, in 1929, 1932, 1925, 1924, 1924, and 1937 (Adrawi 1988:339–41). None of them had an Islamist agenda; see Smith 1946.

20. In Madni's (2002) reading, Syed Ahmad Khan and Mohammad Ali Jauhar held a similar view.

21. On Azad, see Hameed 1998, and Hasan 1992. Also see Robinson's (1989) elegant review essay.

22. In 1813 Shah Abdulaziz declared India as *dar al-ḥarb*. His followers fruitlessly waged jihad against the British (Faruqi 1963; Rizvi 1970; cf. Masud 2005; and Metcalf 1982).

23. For a fuller treatment of this theme, see Ahmad 2009.

24. As noted, this book draws on social movement literature. However, I find it inattentive to the role of ideology (see Buechler 2000; Diani and Eyerman 1992; Jasper 1997; and MacAdam et al. 1988). The Frame Theory of Benford and Snow (2000; Snow and Benford 1992) takes ideas seriously. But, as Oliver and Johnston (2000) note, framing is a social-psychological, linguistic process unable to address the deeper meanings of ideology rooted in the longer tradition of political studies. I use "ideology" to mean a worldview, a "conceptual organization of society" (Malesevik 2002:104) and a "system of ideas which couple understandings of how the world works with ethical, moral and normative principles that guide personal and collective action" (Oliver and Johnston 2000:44). For an overview of literature on ideology, see Cash 1996; Lewins 1989; Purvis et al. 1993; Therborn 1980; Thompson 1990; and Zizek 1992.

25. On the interaction between the West and India, also see Mehta 1999 and Viswanathan 1989.

Chapter 1. Doing Fieldwork in Times of War

1. For a contrasting tale by an Indian anthropologist, see Chakravarti 1979.

2. My account of anthropology, based on the works mentioned in the next paragraph, may seem homogenizing. One may argue that the discipline has diverse traditions, including the tradition of "anthropology at home" (Jackson 1987; Peirano 1998). Both points are valid. However, as Thomas (1991) contends, the depiction of other cultures as "other" continues to have canonical status in anthropology. Even "anthropology at home" has not fully escaped it (di Leonardo 1998).

3. In 2003 two SIMI activists, one being a U.S. national of Indian origin, were sentenced to five years in prison for "destroying Indian nationalism" (Indiainfo .com 2003).

4. On the history of Aligarh, see Siddiqi 1981 and Mann 1992: chap. 1.

5. Maheshwari does not state if the data about the population below the poverty line concerned Muslims alone, nor does he mention the year of the data.

6. On caste among Muslims, see Ahmed 1973, on caste among Aligarh Muslims, see Mann 1992 and Ahmad 2003a.

7. Previously they were known as *qasāī, julāhā, lōhār, bhishtī, hajām/nāī, and faqīr*, respectively. Unlike in the past, their current names are considered respectful.

8. On the conspiracy theory about 9/11, see Ahmad 2004.

9. For a rich social-historical account of Azamgarh, particularly Mubarakpur, see Pandey 1988.

10. References in the bibliography marked with an asterisk (*) are documents meant "only for Jamaat members." These documents concern the debates on the participation in the parliamentary elections within the *shura*, the supreme body of the Jamaat. Many Jamaat members urged me to consult these documents but refused my request to borrow them. Strangely, all the documents were available in the Jamaat library except one, which I obtained from a former Jamaat member.

11. On the Jamaat's changing terms for its different categories of affiliates, see the note in Appendix 1.

12. Later Soz moved to Delhi's Jamia Millia Islamia to become a lecturer of Urdu. During the late 1960s he disappeared. It is believed that he is dead.

13. In one oral account, a missionary *ʿālim* of the Ahl-e-hadīth sect from Bengal came to the *shahr* to propagate his sect's ideology. Following his lecture, two families converted to the Ahl-e-hadīth. One was Sultan's family on his mother's side. Given his family's high status, many Qureshi families also converted. At the time of my fieldwork, according to one estimate, 25 percent of the Qureshi families belonged to the Ahl-e-hadīth. However, over 50 percent of the women in the Ahl-e-hadīth families remained Barēlvī, as they visited the tombs of Sufis and saints.

14. Asri was expelled, because he used an Ahl-e-hadīth mosque to propagate the Jamaat's ideology. The case is controversial and is interpreted differently by the Jamaat (Rauf 2001) and the Ahl-e-hadīth (Azad 1990; Qasoori 1990). Abulkalam Azad, then India's education minister, arbitrated in the case and delivered his judgment, in the Jamaat's account unjustly and in the Ahl-e-hadīth's justly, for Asri's expulsion.

Chapter 2. Contextualizing the Formation and Ideology of Islamism

1. A journalist described the Jamaat as "a party of some well-dressed, well-fed booksellers" (in Agwani 1986:108), a description invoked by the Jamaat critics I met.

2. On caste associations, see Aloysius 1997 and Rudolph 1960; on linguistic and religious associations, see Ornisi 2002 and Pandey 1990.

3. This obviously draws on Anderson 1991.

4. Earlier a province of the Mughal Empire, in the 1720s Nizamul Mulk Asaf Jah took control of it and established a state known as Hyderabad. Jah's successors were called Nizams (Khalidi 2004).

5. The British divided India into "British India," which was under British control, and "Princely India," which had dominion status (Khalidi 2004; Markovitz 2002).

6. Ahmad probably does not spell Mr. Mhew's name correctly. In his personal accounts, Maududi (1971; 1979) mentions the Urdu name, *madrasa fauqaniā*, and omits the fact that it was not a "traditional" madrasa.

7. For a Deoband scholar, the new syllabus replacing the *dars-e-niẓāmī* syllabus was a British conspiracy to erase Islam (Alqasmi undated: 8).

8. See the introduction, note 22.

9. The AIPWA's iconoclasm is illustrated by the short story *Vision of Paradise*. In it, Zaheer has a hypocritical cleric fall asleep over the Qur'an and dream of making love with a heavenly virgin. When he awakens, presumably he has ejaculated on the holy book (Coppola 1988). For more on the AIPWA, see Russell 1992.

10. By the early 1930s the *Communist Manifesto* and *Capital* were available in Urdu (Daudi 2001).

11. By "master ideology," I mean the dominant principles and idioms of (re)organizing the state and society. I am reluctant to use the term "master frame"—in vogue in social movement studies (Benford and Snow 2000; Snow and Benford 1992; Snow et al. 1986)—because as Oliver and Johnston (2000) argue, it resonates more with linguistic studies of interactions than with ideology which is rooted in political dynamics. See the introduction, note 24.

12. I am thankful to Muhammad Khalid Masud for pointing this out to me. I was unable to find Maududi's biography of Gandhi. It is worth noting that in the regional congress of the Jamaat, held in Patna in April 1947, Gandhi had participated and remarked "I listended to your [Amin Ahsan Islahi's] speech carefully and I am very happy" (in *Rūdād jamā'at-e-islāmī* 1967: 239; also see Monis 2001:59).

13. Based on Gandhi's philosophy, the plan was conceived as India's indigenous system of free and compulsory education; see Mujeeb 1972.

14. A Sanskrit song written by Bankim Chatterjee, Muslims consider it un-Islamic; see Ahmad 1999a.

15. The Pakistani Jamaat interprets Maududi's formulas as a demand for a separate state (Ahmad in Maududi 1981:474), when, in fact, he desired only "cultural autonomy." Pakistani scholars, like Indian scholars aligned to "nationalist" thought, also take Iqbal's speech of 1930 as an endorsement for Pakistan. He, too, wanted autonomy within a federation (Hasan 1987; Naim 1999; Zakaria 1994).

16. Scholars across the national divide—(Agwani 1986; Jalal 1995; Ahmad 1967; and Sardar 2003)—hold that Maududi opposed Pakistan. This view persists despite Maududi's signed clarification to the contrary (*Tarjumān Qur'an*, 2003 [October]: 114, and 2003a:73).

17. Nasr writes that *Tafhīmul Qur'an* is a political interpretation of the Qur'an (1996:61). Regarded as the magnum opus by Islamists, the Deoband ulema decreed that it was "dangerous" (Zakaria 1976:30), that reading it or listening to it was "categorically *haram*" (Qasmi 2001:108–9) and that it was "a complete storehouse of distortions" whose "status is that of a religious novel" (Kashmiri 1979:93).

18. Abul Hasan Ali, rector of the Nadwa who resigned from the Jamaat, wrote that Maududi's claim implied that he was the first person to lift the veil on the real meanings of those terms. Arguing that their correct meanings existed throughout history, he noted that Maududi's claim also challenged the caliber of the whole *ummat* (Ali 1980:34). Nomani, whom we met before, accused him of "politically

interpreting" the Qur'an, adding that it also raised doubts if other words of the Qur'an were correctly understood. In his view, the book opened the "door for sedition [*fitna*]," offered "legitimacy for the atheists," and shook "the very foundation of Islam." It is instructive to note Maududi's response. When Nomani asked him if none before him understood their real meanings, Maududi said that Ibn Taimiyah (d. 1328) nearly did but even he could not get them right (1998:94, 84, 88, 90). See also Qureshi 1987; and Sambhali 1993a.

19. Mashriqi, a materialist, held Darwin, Bacon, Hobbs, and Machiavelli in high esteem. He wrote a materialist interpretation of the Qur'an, and he did not believe in Satan, the angels, or life hereafter. Opposed to the League's two-nation theory, he professed Hindu-Muslim unity. After 1945 Mashriqi drifted toward the League (Makki 2003; Muhammad 1973; Smith 1946).

20. On his expositions on rituals, see Maududi 2001 [1934]: 46–73.

21. For more on what Maududi meant by Islam, see his *Towards Understanding Islam* (1981a [1940]).

22. For the Deoband ulema, Maududi's usage of "leader" was "horrifying," as it "smears the spirit of Islam" and wrongly presented "Islam as a political movement" (Sambhali 1993b:24). Maududi also rejected the consensus that the prophets were above human frailty, arguing that they "also took wrong decisions . . . committed mistakes and they were even punished [by God]" (in Qureshi 1987:260). To the Deoband ulema, Maududi's view was "madness" challenging the very faith in Islam (ibid.: 257–64).

23. I owe this information to the sociologist Anand Kumar.

24. According to an Ahl-e-hadīth scholar, the notion of Allah's vice regent is *shirk*, polytheism. Because Allah is omnipotent, He does not need a deputy to execute His wish (Ansari 1988:11ff.).

25. It was delivered as a lecture in February 1941, at Islamia College, Peshawar. Such colleges were "Western" because, in their curricula, Islam figured as an appendix (Husain 1999:24).

26. According to an Ahl-e-sunnat scholar, such practices are truly Islamic. Maududi called them "polytheistic" for he had "the sword of *takfīr* [to declare a Muslim *kafir*] in his hand" and his pen moved in "vagrancy like a dead-drunkard's" (Qadri 1965:62, 83).

27. On the last page of *Kashmakash*, vol. 2 (reprinted in 1944), there is a list of the Jamaat's publications (without authors' names) one of which is titled "Hegel, Marx, and Islam." One wonders: was Maududi its author?

28. In a footnote, Maududi explained that Hegel called God "world spirit, world reason, absolute spirit," and "absolute idea." Further, as history evolved so did God (Maududi 1999a: 265).

29. It is not my concern here if Maududi's view of Hegel or Marx was correct. For example, Mueller (1958) says that the dialectics attributed to Hegel was a Marxian vulgarization.

30. Maududi uses *haq* and Islamic revolution synonymously. He also interchanges *bāṭil*, *jāhiliyat,* and *ghair-Islam*.

31. The quote comes from an article-length editorial note Maududi wrote for the readers of *Tarjumān* to contextualize an article (written by Manazir Ahsan Gilani) on the political life of Imam Hanifa.

32. This refers to French Minister Paul Reynaud, who after the German invasion of France had said, "Only a miracle can save France now. And I believe in miracles" (Maududi 1941:57 n. 1).

33. I am thankful to Muhammad Khalid Masud for clarifying this distinction.

34. In 1939 Maududi visited Mewat where the Tablīghī jamāʿat was active. Although he praised its efforts to eradicate "ancient *jāhiliyat*," he did not find it relevant to his project (*Tarjumān* 1939 [October]: 59–71).

35. Inspired by the Russian Revolution, Ubaidullah Sindhi (d. 1944) preached communism: The Qur'an," he wrote, "is the program of an international revolution" (in Azmi 1999:111).

36. The Jews stood condemned because they rejected Islam after Muhammad presented it to them.

37. Maududi's alternative was a "theo-democratic state" (1999 [1946]: 297). He called it a "theocracy" in that the sources of laws would be the Qur'an and *hadīth* and sovereignty would be Allah's. Unlike Christian theocracy, however, the priestly class would not monopolize it. An executive chosen by *religiously qualified* Muslims would supervise the executions of laws. See Maududi (1980 [1939]:24ff.).

38. On organizational resemblance between the Communist Party and the Jamaat, see Ahmad 2003.

39. On Azad's ecumenism, see Imam (n.d.). For a critique by a Jamaat member, see Khan 1995.

40. Like AMU, such colleges were "Western" because they taught Western social and natural sciences. They had only one subject on Islam, called Islamic theology; see Husain 1999:24.

41. A *shura* is an advisory body. As the Jamaat *amīr*, Maududi nominated its members. The task of the *shura* was to advise the *amīr*, who was not constitutionally bound to accept it. Indeed, he opposed the checks that "Western-style democratic parties" had against their presidents (*Tarjumān* 1941 [June–August]: 471). After Partition, the role of the *shura* and *amīr* remained virtually the same (*Zindgī* 1950 [November]: 43). From the 1960s on, it changed in two ways. First, *shura* members began to be elected. Second, the *amīr* was constitutionally made to accept the decision of the *shura* taken by a majority vote (see chapter 7).

42. On the cover of *Taʿlīmāt*, Maududi figures as its author. However, matters from page 107 though 116 are not his but are reports of the Jamaat's post-Partition meetings.

43. On the relationship between sports, ideology, and race, see Gilroy 2000.

44. In 1954 Maududi reiterated his position that he would have no objection if India became a Hindu state, promulgated Manu's laws, and treated Muslims like untouchables; see Usmani 1975.

Chapter 3. Educating the Children

1. On the distinctiveness of the Jamaat's syllabus, see Ahmad 2005a:chap. 3.

2. AMU offers education from nursery school up to doctoral programs. In the 1970s it had six schools: four in the Civil Line and two in the *shahr*. The admission to all AMU schools was open only for classes 1 and 6.

3. The name change of the Jamaat school in 1972 is at odds with the changes the Jamaat introduced only after the Emergency imposed in 1975. The deletion of "Jamaat-e-Islami" from the names of almost all institutions of the Jamaat, including its schools, occurred after the Emergency. Since then, the Jamaat decided not to run its institutions under its own name. It founded various Trusts and Boards. Thus, in Aligarh, "Jamaat-e-Islami" was dropped from the name of its research institute. It was renamed "Idāra-e-taḥqīq-o-tasnīf-e-Islami" (Islahi 1999:38). Constitutionally, its link with the Jamaat was also severed (*RMS-2* 1989:260). Similarly "Darsgah Jamaa-e-Islami" of Rampur was renamed "Darsgah-e-Islami." The names of the Jamaat schools in the post-Emergency period, taken from a list provided by the Jamaat headquarters, were, for example, Iqra School, An-noor Public School and Jamiatul Islamia, all in UP.

With the Emergency, the Jamaat office and library in the *shahr*, then housed inside the Green School, were sealed, and a teacher who was a Jamaat member staying there was arrested. The school was also shut down. Jamaat members in both the Civil Line and the *shahr* were jailed, including the school manager, Sultan. After several petitions, the government allowed a partial reopening of the school two weeks after it was sealed. The Jamaat office remained sealed for four months and reopened only in October of the same year. For months, the school remained under government surveillance.

4. This practice is common for schools of other ideologies as well.

5. Soon after joining the Green School, Aurangzeb left it to become an administrator at Nisvān College, a Jamaat madrasa for women (see below). Though no longer in the school, as a Jamaat member he was an influential participant in the debate.

6. In UP, only in the 1980s did the madrasa students become eligible for admission to AMU. However, they could gain admission *only* in Arabic, Persian, Urdu, and Theology (see chapter 5).

7. As a confederation of Muslim organizations, including the Jamaat, the Deeni Talimi Council (DTC), formed in 1959, opposed the "Hinduization" of education in government schools for several reasons. Many courses in the syllabi of the UP government were contrary to Muslims' beliefs; they were replete with the teachings of Hindu mythology and idols. On accepting any of it, the DTC argued, "Muslim children can no longer remain Muslim and monotheist" (in Hasan undated: 3). Further, the teaching of Urdu was practically blocked in all the government schools. Non-familiarity with Urdu, the DTC contended, implied abandoning Islam (ibid.:4).

8. By the early 1990s Jamaat textbooks began to carry photos of living beings (Mahmood 1994:238). Book covers were also made more attractive.

9. The distinction between "ideologue" and "professional" teachers is derived from Thapan 1991.

10. For an introductory account of AIMC, see Alam 2002, its founder.

11. In the case of female alumni, either parent was present during the interviews.

12. No modern subjects such as physics, biology, geography, and history were taught there. Grades 1 to 5 were called *taḥtānīya*, and grades 6 to 8 were termed *fauqānīya*. Grades from 9 on were known as *ʿalīya* (higher). In *ʿalīya*, students had two options: *farsi munshī* or *maulvī*. The former was a specialization in Persian language and literature, and the latter in Arabic and Islam.

13. As pointed out earlier, the Jamaat had promulgated a rule that it would not admit children to its schools unless their guardians submitted in writing that they had given their wards "to serve Islam according to the ideology of the Jamaat." Now the Green School even admitted students whose father, like Zahid, was a member of the BJP.

14. Varshney (2002:7) ranks Aligarh fifth in his list of the eight most riot-prone cities of India.

15. The term *qaum* had multiple meanings. It referred to Muslims in relation to Hindus but also differentiated one Muslim *birādrī* from another. Mann's (1992) observation is similar.

Chapter 4. Mobilizing the Young

1. The formation of the Jamaat's student organizations, which started at state levels, gathered momentum during the late 1960s and 1970s. Ḥalqa-e-ṭalba-e-Islami of Patna was one such organization. A major factor for the formation of these regional organizations was the rise of communal violence since the mid-1960s (Akhtar Undated). At the Jamaat's initiative, in March 1976, a national student organization was formed at Aligarh, but because this was the period of Emergency, it was unnamed. After the Emergency, in April 1977, it was christened the Student Islamic Movement of India (SIMI). The Jamaat officially extended its "moral support" to the SIMI (*RMS*-2:176). Because the Jamaat later had serious differences with the SIMI, in 1982 the Jamaat formed its own official student organization, the SIO. For details, see Ahmad 2005a:chap. 5). For the SIO-Jamaat's version of this contentious history, see SIO 1991, 1998; and Monis 2001; for the SIMI's version, see Salfi undated.

2. The data are for the year 2000. For source, see note 4.

3. The boarding houses at AMU were called 'halls'. Each hall had many hostels. I use hostel in the sense of hall. Most hostels were based on campus.

4. The data given by the Public Relations Office of AMU did not mention the religious breakup. It was believed, however, that of the six thousand students in the faculties of engineering, medicine, architecture, management, and so on, known as the professional courses, 50 percent were Hindus. Their percentage in the faculties of arts and social sciences was far lower. In one estimate, there were at least five thousand Hindu students. According to Maheshwari (2001: 188), Hindus constituted 26 percent of the student population.

5. Respectively, the student wings of the Communist Party of India, the Communist Party of India (Marxist), and the Communist Party of India (Marxist-Leninist). By the 1990s the AISF and SFI, previously quite influential, had become almost defunct. In the 1990s the AISA grew influential. In 1999 one of its sympathizers, representing the Forum for Democratic Rights (FDR), was elected president of the Union. When the Vice Chancellor, dissolved the Union, the AISA also disintegrated.

6. In 1948 the government tried to secularize AMU and BHU by dropping, respectively, the words "Hindu" and "Muslim." AMU agreed to this move, but BHU rejected it (Ray 1977).

7. To ensure anonymity, I provide no reference, an approach I follow in subsequent chapters.

8. This echoes Maududi (1996a), who characterized literature as legitimate, illegitimate, and Islamic.

9. The Arabic film *Baḥib al-sima* (I Love Cinema), made in 2004 and directed by Osama Fawzi, depicts a similar attitude toward cinema among Egyptian Christians during the 1960s.

Chapter 5. Defining Islam

1. The varying accounts put the figure at seven, eight, and nine.

2. Unaffiliated with the SIMI, the Kashmiri student was charged on the assumption that as a Kashmiri he must have had links with the militant outfits.

3. My entry in the debate on democracy relates to the body of works inspired by what Hefner calls an "anthropological turn" (2000:5). Key works in this tradition include Heffner 2000; and Putnam 1993, 1995, 2000.

4. On Falāḥ's history, see Ahmad 2005a:chap. 3. In 2002 the Jamaat had 234 madrasas of different levels throughout India. This does not include non-madrasa institutions such as nursery schools (67), primary schools (277), colleges (32), technical schools (6), and adult educational centers (288). Many of these institutions are in the South, particularly in Kerala. In UP, there were 110 educational institutions, and the Uttar Pradesh Falāḥ-e-ʿām Society (UPFS) ran all of them. The Jamaat headquarters provided these figures.

5. At the time of my fieldwork, female students numbered 2,940, of which 490 lived in the campus hostels. A study of Jamaat's educational system for girls is needed.

6. Officially the youngest hosteller would be eleven years old. Given the common practice of reducing the actual age in north India, however, the youngest hosteller was likely thirteen.

7. Reliable statistics on madrasas is not available. In 1985 their number was estimated to be 2,890. In 1992 Agwani (1992:355) estimated 8,000 belonging to the Deoband sect alone. In 1995 the Human Resources Development Ministry estimated the number at 12,000. In the mid-1990s the Registrar, Arabi-Farsi Examination Board, Allahabad, stated that in UP alone there were 10,000 madrasas (Fahimuddin 1998:5). In 2002 the Home Ministry gave the figure of 31,857 (Sikand 2005). These statistics, however, must be taken with a grain of salt. Since the mid-1990s, when madrasas became a hot issue, statistics on them also became politicized. The nearly threefold increase in the number of madrasas in a span of seven years, as the government's statistics suggests, seems somewhat suspicious. The precise definition of a madrasa is also unclear. All institutions teaching Islam are usually called a madrasa. Thus *maktab*, largely secular schools offering elementary education, are also numbered among the madrasas. My use of the term refers to institutions offering Islamic education at the secondary or tertiary level or both.

8. Fahimuddin included girl's madrasas. Neither he nor Sikand clarify what they mean by "poor families."

9. See the World Bank web site provided in the bibliography.

10. Compiled based on a list of members published by the Jamaat headquarters. Members' names include their locations. The predominantly urban location of the Jamaat members does not mean that they were born there. Although the rural-urban distinction is useful, one should view it as a continuum (Sharma and Gupta 1991). On the rural-urban nexus in Africa, see Geschiere and Gugler 1998.

11. Falāḥ had its own local Jamaat unit separate from the Bilariaganj unit. Of the twenty-six members (*arkān*) at the Falāḥ unit, twenty-two were teachers and four were non-teaching employees. The latter were all educated. Of the twenty-one uneducated fourth-grade-level employees, such as peons, drivers, cleaners, or gatekeepers, none was a Jamaat member. Zahir Madni explained that none of these employees was a Jamaat member because they were either uneducated or only nominally educated. Of the seventy-five founding members of the Jamaat in 1941, thirty-seven held a bachelor's degree or higher (from the modern educational system), sixteen were pass outs from madrasas, eight were practitioners of oriental medicine (*ṭib*), and thirteen were matriculates or below (Jamaat-e-Islami Pakistan Web site 2001).

12. The students of Nadwa and Deoband were also eligible to take those courses, but very few of them entered AMU.

13. Another degree after the *fazīlat*, the *takhaṣṣuṣ* (specialization), required writing a thesis with a supervisor. On average, one student opted for specialization every three years.

14. At Nadwa in Lucknow, as well as at Ahl-e-hadīth madrasa in Varansi, there was no room for student politics. Barring the Jamaat, the Ahl-e-sunnat sect, in 1992, was the first to form its own student organization in Aligarh, the Muslim Student Organization (MSO), to counter, inter alia, the SIMI's influence at AMU. MSO, however, was active only at AMU and called itself "nonpolitical."

15. This is also true in the case of student activists in the United States; see Lipset 1971.

16. Three SIMI presidents were reelected for second terms. My figure of thirteen counts them as one.

17. The acronym SIMI became popular thanks to its usage by the media after the government banned the organization. The SIMI members themselves called their organization SIM, pronounced as three independent letters.

18. The text in Urdu reads: "*sab sē baṛā jihād ẓālim ḥukmarān kē sāmnē ḥaq bāt kahnā hai.*"

19. In Urdu the slogans read as follows: "*Jang kā nām suntē hī kāfir bhāg khaṛā hōtā hai*" and "*Jihād sē mohabbat ʿain ʿibādat hai.*" In Arabic the slogan reads "*foreẓa al-jihād ʿalā kulle muslim.*"

20. SIMI and SIO activists did not distinguish between the Jamaat and the SIO, and nor would I.

21. In sharia sexual intercourse between two persons of the opposite sex outside wedlock, with or without mutual consent, is defined as rape.

22. This quotation and the one preceding it is from Asim's book. To protect his and Rahmani's anonymity I cannot name their books.

23. The Constitution of the Anjuman lists four objectives: (1) to organize alumni for the pursuit of Falāḥ's goals; (2) to make their talents useful for those

objectives; (3) to cooperate with Falāḥ's authorities in its development; and (4) to establish relations with other institutions to pursue Falāḥ's goals (*Dastūr Anjuman* undated:1).

24. Jurgen Habermas, among others, is a major proponent of this model. See Ferree et al. 2002:300–6.

25. In 1914 the Nadwa witnessed a strike (see *Al-Hilal* 1914 [March 4–11]: 2–4).

Chapter 6. Invoking Jihad

1. See, for example, *Amar Ujālā*, April 12 and May 6, 2002; *Hindustan Times* 2001a; and *The Pioneer* 2001a.

2. My argument goes against the popular notion that Hindutva is a reaction to Islamic fundamentalism. For example, consider this quote from Amit Chaudhary's *Freedom Song*: "The heart of the parrot of Hindu fundamentalism beats in the giant of Muslim fundamentalism. Kill the giant, and you will have killed the parrot" (in Dev 2004:78). I thank Ward Berenschot for this reference.

3. Recently, Indian journalists have often used this quote, for example, Goradia and Phanda 2005.

4. See the popular works of Cox and Marks 2003; Spencer 2002, 2004; Schwartz 2003; and Timmerman 2003. See, too, the and academic works of Johnson 1997; and Tibi 2002.

5. Cook's argument is based on two unsubstantiated premises. First, he assumes that *reading* leads to *action*. Second, as Asad perceptively notes in a related context, such an argument assigns "a magical quality" to Islamic texts for "they are said to be both essentially univocal . . . and infectious" (2003:11). Cook also views the Qur'an as a text with meaning. However, as A. Neuwirth argues, many Muslims believe that not only is the meaning of the Qur'an pious but that the very recitation of the Qur'an is an act of piety (ibid.:56).

6. Recently George W. Bush (2006) used the term "Islamofascism."

7. See, for instance, Dumont 1970; Fukuyama 1992; Lambton 1988; and Weiner 1987.

8. In this respect I find Asad's (2003:21–22) call for an anthropology of secularism instructive. As he notes, anthropology has devoted itself to the study of religion but has neglected secularism. If jihad is taken as a subject of religion, however, as is usually the case, then anthropology has also not given sufficient attention to it. Its understanding has often been, to borrow a term Naim (1999:195–96) uses in relation to the Western study of Islam, "textualized" rather than anthropologically "contextualized."

9. On the SIMI's multitiered membership, see the note in Appendix 3. In 1981, as the archival sources record, the SIMI had 461 *anṣār* and 40,000 members (*Dawat* 1982 [April 14]: 116). In 1996 the number of *anṣār* declined to 413, of which 359 were male and 51 were female (*Inṣāf* 1998 [May]: 17). SIMI's Constitution included the clause that, after thirty years, members were to retire from the organization (*Dastūr SIMI* 1993).

10. This phrase is borrowed from Hansen 1999.

11. In addition to Hindu fundamentalism, scholars (e.g., Sarkar 1993; and Sen 1993) have also used communal fascism to refer to Hindutva. I use the terms "Hindu nationalism," (Sangẖ parivār) and "Hindutva" interchangeably. "Hindutva" is an emic term coined by an ideologue of Hindu nationalism, V. D. Savarkar, in a tract bearing the same name.

12. The cluster is called *parivār* (family) and is prefixed with *Sangh*, the last word of the name RSS, to show the control that the latter commands over the former (Metcalf and Metcalf 2002). Its main constituents are the BJP, Vishwa Hindu Parishad (VHP), Bajrang Dal (BD), Akhil Bhartiya Vidyarthi Parishad (ABVP), Seva Bharti, Kalyan Ashram, and the Shiv Sena (Noorani 2000).

13. Over time different political parties have used different terms to convey the goal of the Hindu nation; for example, Ram *rājya,* Ram's rule; *dẖarm rājya,* rule of religion; and *bharatiya maryādā,* Indian/Hindu conduct of life were used, respectively, by the Ram Rajya Parishad, the Jan Sangh, and the Swatantra Party (Ahmad 1999a:17).

14. For an excellent account of the campaign, see Van der Veer 1987; see, also, 1994b.

15. My description of the Ayodhya campaign, as Appiah notes in a different context, is "bound to spend some of its time telling readers that something he or she already knows" (1992:xi). This exercise is necessary, however, as I do not assume that South Asianists are my only audience.

16. The Palestinian Liberation Organization (PLO), led by Yaser Arafat, saw the question of Palestine as an issue of Arab nationalism (Kepel 2002:151).

17. Notably both Islamists and the Naxalites opposed the Russian invasion of Afghanistan. They also jointly protested Russian "social imperialism"; see Ahmad 2005.

18. On the Shiv Sena, see Gupta 1982 and Hansen 2001.

19. Because of the Shiv Sena's fascistic command in Maharashtra, over 15 percent of the SIMI members came from that state. It was impossible for me to obtain the regional breakdown of SIMI membership. During my fieldwork an underground SIMI activist confirmed my hunch regarding the regional dimension of radicalization early on in the field.

20. The line in Urdu reads: *ʿālam hai faqat mōmin-e-jā ñbāz kī mīraṡ.*

21. This slogan is pictured on the cover of the August 1998 issue of *Islamic Movement*, and the first is pictured on the cover of the January 1999 issue.

22. This pamphlet is in my possession.

23. Kapur (1993:76) reproduces this map in her article.

24. For a brief commentary on this subject, see Ahmad 1997.

25. Compare SIMI's description of secularism as "fraud" to *Sangẖ parivār's* characterization of it as "pseudo." Whereas, for *Sangẖ parivār*, "pseudo" secularism means the appeasement of Muslims, for the SIMI it means the Indian state's failure to be truly secular as it failed to protect the Babri mosque and the lives and property of Muslims.

26. This refers to riots in Gujarat, where women were raped and filmed. See Engineer 1995a:202.

27. In Urdu the titles read, respectively, *Nizam-e-ṯāghūt se Bara'at*, *fitna-e-sekūlarizm-o-sekularāizēshan*, *fitna-e-jamhūriyat*, and *naẕariyāt-e-bāṭila kā*

ta'āqub. Except for the third one, published by Shahada in Thane, the remaining three were published by Darul Islam in Delhi.

28. The translation is that of Abdullah Yusuf Ali (2004).

Chapter 7. Negotiating the Idol

1. Many SIMI activists laughed at their numerical canonization by the media. They claimed that the core members, *ansars*, did not exceed 1,000. See Appendix 3.

2. For lack of a better English term, I use idol as an equivalent to *ṭāghūt*. To Maududi, *ṭāghūt* is the ultimate of three stages of transgression against Allah's laws. When a Muslim obeys Allah in principle but disobeys Him in practice, it is the stage of *fisq*. In the stage of *kufr*, he no longer believes in obedience to Allah and does whatever he desires. In the final stage, "not only does he rebel against God, denying Him and His right to lay down the law for man but also begins to make his own law prevail in the land." A Muslim can never be a Muslim "in the real sense unless he repudiates *ṭāghūt*" (Maududi 2000:96, n. 1). Maududi links the transgression of belief in Allah with political authority. Thus, quoting Qur'anic verses, he writes, "In all these three verses, *'ibādat* [worship] of *ṭāghūt* means bondage to any or all of what the latter term stands for, that is, every state or authority or leadership, etc., which in transgression against God, makes its own word prevail in the land" (2000:75). This reading of *ṭāghūt* also informs Maududi's translation of the Qur'an (2001:153–54). See also Maududi (1991a: 182–83) and ODI (2003:310).

3. Whereas the first list of candidates published in *Dawat* (2002 [February 13]) was issued under the banner of the All-India Muslim Majlis Mushāverat (henceforth, Mushāverat), the second one in the subsequent issue was under the banner of Jamaat (*Dawat* 2002 [February 16]: 4). The name of the CPIM candidate appeared in the first list, but that of the CPI figured in a different list issued by the Mushāverat and published in *Rashtriya Sahara* (2002 [February 15]).

4. The material for this section is drawn from Nadwi's book (1990).

5. First carried in two installments in *Zindgī* (1948 [December]: 36–43; 1949 [January]: 23–29), these articles were later revised and published as a pamphlet.

6. The Jamaat-e-Islami Kashmir, outside the purview of this study, made a similar plea (Bhat 1970:37).

7. In 1952 Nadwi (1953) addressed a gathering of Muslims and Hindus in Hyderabad and called on the latter to build an Indian state on a religious, rather than Western or secular, basis.

8. In a rally at Trafalgar Square, on August 13, 1995, the UK's Hizb al Tahrir called on the whole nation to embrace Islam and urged John Major to lead the way (Taji-Farouki 1996:ix). After the Islamic Revolution in Iran, Khomeini wrote to the then USSR premier to embrace Islam (Kramer 1997).

9. Another Muslim critic said: "This organization [the Jamaat] lives in a fool's paradise" (in Bhat 1970:38).

10. When I discussed the "irrationality" of the Jamaat with a JNU Professor, who was himself a card-holding Communist, he sympathized with the Jamaat. In the early 1960s a colleague advised him to buy a flat in Delhi. Disgusted with

such "bourgeoisie" advice, he said, "Why should I buy private property. In a few years or so, when the Revolution comes, it will be abolished."

Maududi also saw the Revolution knocking at the door. In 1977 Hasnain Syed (b. 1917), one of his earliest comrades who remained in India, sent him a letter expressing his desire to see him. Maududi replied that he would invite him once the Islamic Revolution had come, which he believed would happen "in his own life time." Only a year later Syed sent him a second letter saying that he wanted to meet him soon, for they were both getting old. In response, Maududi said that he should indeed come soon, for he did not know when the Revolution would arrive (*RAM* 1991 [January]: 14).

11. The proceedings of the Jamaat's *shura* do not mention the reason for their arrest.

12. The pamphlet is a compilation of editorials Nadwi wrote for *Zindgī* (1950 [December]: 2–8, 3842; 1951 [January]: 2–11, [February]: 2–7, [March]: 2ff., [April–May]: 2ff., [October]: 2–8, 43–45).

13. One thousand copies were published in April 1951 (Nadwi 1951:I), and the publication was reprinted in 1952 (Shakir 1970a:33 n. 8).

14. In a letter to K. N. Katju, Minister of Home Affairs, in 1953, Rajendra Prasad, President of India, noted that the Jamaat wanted an Islamic state in India (Hasan 1997:202).

15. See also Ahmad 1969; Hyder 1974; *JIMI* (undated: 77); Nizami 1975; *RMS-1* 1962:184–85; Sampradāiktā Virōdhī Committee (undated); Shakir 1970, 1970a; and Usmani 1975.

16. To the best of my knowledge, no data are available on the number of Muslims who voted in the first two parliamentary and Assembly elections; see also Krishna 1967:185.

17. In a 1946 lecture Maududi used the term *shahādat-e-ḥaq* in the sense of an Islamic state (2000a).

18. Soon the Jamiatul Ulema left the Mushāvrat (Rizvi 1989).

19. All subsequent page numbers without an author are from *JIMI*.

20. The Jamaat literature does not discuss why Yusuf replaced Nadwi as *amīr*.

21. Eleven did not clearly state their opinion. The major argument against lifting the ban was that voting in the elections of a secular democratic state violated the monotheistic creed. Opinions diverged along regional and linguistic lines. Most members from the southern states such as Andhra Pradesh, Karnataka, and Kerala did not think that voting violated their belief in monotheism. Of those who did, almost half were from UP, 130 out of 277 (*JIMI*:174).

22. In a letter to Yusuf, dated January 28, 1974, Maududi reiterated his position that participation in the elections of a secular state was "illegitimate [*nājā'iz*]." The Jamaat could take part, he said, only when there was sufficient hope that, through elections, it could change the government. He did not see such a hope for long (Maududi's letter quoted in Hamdi 1990:120–21).

23. Although throughout the discussion the Jamaat refers to candidates using "he," obviously candidates were also women.

24. From its beginning in 1948 until August 1984, *Zindgī* was published from Rampur, the Jamaat's second headquarters after Malihabad. When it shifted

to Delhi, on technical requirements for registration, its name was changed to *Zindgī-e-nau*.

25. Imam Hanifa (d. 765) held that a territory would be called *dar al-Islam* if Muslims there enjoyed religious liberty and security. For divergent theological positions on this issue, see Khan 1997:321–34.

26. I thank Zafrul Islam Khan, editor of *Milli Gazette*, for this reference.

27. Wahiduddin Khan, a noted Islamic scholar who left the Jamaat in the 1960s, told me that it was he who coined the term *dar al-daʿvat*.

28. The Bhoodan movement aimed at gifting land to the poor, see Oommen 1972.

29. The UP unit of the Mushāvrat split to form a separate party, Muslim Majlis; see Quraishi 1971.

30. On this conflict, see *Qaumi Tanzeem*, Patna 2000 [July 14]: 3.

31. For the RSS, the existing tricolor flag is not representative of the Indian (i.e., Hindu) nation. It had its own saffron flag (*bhagvā jhanḍā*), the "embodiment of God." Hedgewar, founder of the RSS, directed its activists only to "worship" the saffron flag. It had hoisted the tricolor only twice in its history: first, in an effort to lift the ban which the government had clamped on it following Ghandhi's assassination, and, second in 2002, when the BJP was in power. It should also be noted that the RSS does not believe in the Indian Constitution. Golwalkar, the RSS ideologue, said, "It [the Constitution of India] has absolutely nothing which can be called *our own*" (in Parsa 2002; my emphasis).

32. All subsequent page numbers without an author are from *Zindgī-e-nau*'s 1997 issues.

33. In Urdu-Hindi, *fasād* also means "riots."

Conclusion

1. On the "woman question" and the Jamaat, see Ahmad 2008a.

2. Maududi noted with a sense of anguish that those who primarily resisted the Jamaat were Muslims, especially those of the "religious class [ulema]" (in *Rudaad* . . . 1966:64).

3. On the diasporic elements of the Jamaat's leadership in moderating its ideology, see Ahmad 2005.

4. In 1953 some Jamaat leaders were arrested; but it is not clear why. A memoir of a jailed leader does not record torture but rather mentions that he was treated well in jail; see Khan 1995. During the India-Pakistan wars of 1965 and 1971, some Jamaat members were arrested under the Defense of India Rules Act. In the Jamaat's own account, none of them was tortured (*MMS*:163–69).

5. A young lawyer, my neighbor in the *shahr*, asked me if I had read SIMI's organ, *Islamic Movement*. When I replied yes, he asked if I owned them. When I said that I did, he advised me to destroy them as he had done soon after the ban on SIMI. A SIMI supporter, he appreciated its courage to speak out against the *zulm* done to Muslims. Lamenting the closure of *Islamic Movement*, he urged me to read *Ahvāl-e-mishan*, a magazine of the Bahujan Sevak Sangh (BSS), a militant offshoot of the Bahujan Samaj Party: "What SIMI did before the ban, the BSS is

doing now." He showed me some issues that were anti-Hindutva. For example, the magazine idolized the Mughal ruler Aurangzeb and carried a special editorial "Jai Aurangzeb [Victory to Aurangzeb]." Its slogan read "Jai Ambedkar, Jai Periyar, Jai Aurangzeb." Further, it ran a front-page story describing L. K. Advani as "the ring leader of the Hindu terrorism" (*Aḥwāl-e-mishon* 2002 [January]: 6, 10, 1).

6. Although I do not focus on SIMI's transnational dimension, I have touched on it in chapter 6 where SIMI linked the Babri mosque with the Palestinian issue (also see Ahmad 2005). A less acknowledged aspect of transnationalism, however, is how a distinctly national issue becomes transnationalized. As discussed in chapter 1, after 9/11 the BJP *transnationalized* SIMI's radicalization to serve a specific *national* aim. I thank Faisal Devji for drawing my attention to this point.

Glossary of Urdu-Hindi Terms

ʿālim. Islamic scholar, trained for several years in a religious seminary.
amīr. Literally, leader; in the Jamaat's vocabulary the president of its organization at the local, regional, or national level.
ahl-e-hadīth. A sect hostile to Sufism and to "popular" Islam; its followers do not abidb by the four schools of law.
anṣār. The core members of SIMI; also see Appendix 3.
bāṭil. False or non-Islamic religions; in the Jamaat's vocabulary, an anti-Islamic polity.
bhāī. Literally, brother; suffixed with the name of an elder to show respect.
birādrī. Caste-like institution among Muslims.
chanda. Monetary contribution.
chungī. Literally, tax; government schools are called *chungī* schools in Aligarh; tea stalls are also called *chungī*.
dar al-islam. Land of Islam; in Jamaat's vocabulary, a land where a sharia-based state prevails.
dar al-ḥarb. Land of unbelief; the opposite of *dar al-islam*.
dīt. Monetary compensation paid to the nearest kin of a murder victim.
ḍauk ṣāḥib. A respectful term of address, used in Aligarh Muslim University and in the *shahr*.
duʿā. Supplication, prayer to God.
fatwa. Religious opinion, or decree.
fiqh. Islamic jurisprudence/laws.
fitna. Sedition, disorder.
hadīth. Sayings and traditions of the Prophet Muhammad.
hamdard. Sympathizer.
haram. Religiously forbidden.
halal. Religiously approved.
ijtimāʿ. Religious congregation, usually inside but also outside a mosque; periodic congress of the Jamaat.
ijtihād. Interpretation of Islamic law based on analogy and reasoning which, in Islamic jurisprudence, is often contrasted to *taqlīd* (based on imitation).
iḳhvān. Second-rank member of SIMI; also see Appendix 3.
imam. One who leads a prayer, also a leader.
ʿizzat. Dignity.
jāmeʿ masjid. Central mosque where the Friday prayer is offered.
jāʾiz. Legitimate; antonym, *nājāʾiz*.
jāhiliyat. Usually, pre-Islamic Arab beliefs and practices; in the Jamaat's vocabulary, an anti-Islamic polity.
kāfir. Disbeliever; plural, *kuffār*.
kārkun. Activist/worker.
kalima. An Arabic phrase recited as a declaration of belief to become a Muslim.

kārobārī. Commercial, money-oriented.
kurta. A knee-high, loose upper garment for men.
madrasa. An Islamic seminary.
maktab. An elementary school, religious or secular; pl., *makātib*.
masjid. Mosque; *jāmeʿ masjid*, where Friday prayer is also offered.
mohalla. Locality, neighborhood.
mujāhid. One who does jihad.
murīd. Disciple of a *pīr*, Sufi master.
mushrik. One who believes in or practices polytheism.
niẓām. System.
pān. Betel leaves Indians chew.
qaṣāṣ. Sharia provision for killing a murderer who has committed a murder.
qaum. Community; used in the sense of a religious community as well as caste/ *birādrī*; adj., *qaumi*.
rajam. Stoning to death a married person guilty of adultery.
rāmpurī ṭōpī. Thick cap that covers the entire head; it cannot be folded.
rūdād. Proceedings.
rukn. Member; pl., *arkān*.
shahr. Town; the old part of Aligarh, in contrast to its Civil Line, is known as *shahr*.
shirk. Polytheism.
shura. Central leadership body of the Jamaat, similar to the Communist Party Politburo.
sunna. Historically established customs, normative precedents, conduct typically based on the Prophet's example.
tablīghī jamāʿat. A purificatory movement launched by a Deoband *ʿālim*, Maulānā Ilyas, in the 1930s; popularly known as *jamāʿat*.
ṭāghūt. Literally, idol; in the vocabulary of the Jamaat, a secular-democratic polity.
tauḥīd. Monotheism.
ulema. Plural of *ʿālim*.
zāt-birādrī. See *birādrī*.
ẓulm. Injustice, tyranny.

Bibliography

Primary

Urdu

journals and newspapers

Afkār-e-millī Delhi
Aḥāl-e-mishan Delhi (in Hindi)
Al-Falāḥ Annual magazine of Jāmiʿatul Falāḥ
Al-ḥasanāt Rampur
Al-hilāl Calcutta
Al-jamʿiyat Delhi, Jamiatul Ulema-e-hind's organ, special issue of 1995 to mark its Twenty-Fifth General Congress
Al-maʿārif Lahore
Amar ujālā Agra, Aligarh edition (in Hindi)
Dawat Delhi, biweekly organ of the Jamaat
Fikr-o-naẓar Aligarh
Friday Special Delhi
Islamic Movement Delhi, monthly organ of SIMI
Ḥayāt-e-nau Organ of the Old Boys' Association of the Jāmiʿatul Falāḥ
Inṣāf Burma
Ḳhabarnāma Newletter of Tanẓīm Ṯalaba-e-qadīm, Jāmiʿatul Falāḥ
Kirneñ Rampur, annual magazine of Darsgāh Jamaat-e-islāmī
Milli Times Delhi
Mīzān Patna
Pānch Janya Delhi, organ of the RSS (in Hindi)
Qaumi Awaz Lucknow
Qaumi Tanzeem Patna
Rāsḥtriya Sahārā Delhi
Rafīq-e-manzil Delhi, Monthly organ of the SIO
Rahguzar Hyderabad
Samkālīn Janmat Patna
Tahẕīb al-aḳhlāq Aligarh
Tarjumānul Qur'an Organ of the Jamaat before Partition, now Pakistani Jamaat's
Zindgī Rampur (1948–1984), monthly organ of the Jamaat
Zindgī-e-nau Delhi, monthly organ of the Jamaat (1984 on)

documents and reports

Dastūr anjuman ṯalaba-e-qadīm. Undated. Azamgarh.
Dastūr Jāmiʿatul Falāḥ. Undated; enforced from January 1997.
Dastūr-e-jamāʿat-e-islāmī hind. Undated. Rampur: maktabā jamāʿat-e-islāmī hind.
Dastūr-e-jamāʿat-e-islāmī hind. 1997. New Delhi: jamāʿat-e-islāmī hind. Amended until April 1995 and enforced on April 13, 1956.

Dastūr Student Islamic Movement of India. 1993. New Delhi: SIMI Headquarters. 5th ed. Adopted on April 25, 1977.

Fihrist-e-arkān (FA). 1974, 1981, 1986, 1989, 2002. Delhi: jamāʿat-e-islāmī hind.

Fihrist-e-fāreghīn/fāreghāt, 1967–2001. 2001. Azamgarh: Jāmiʿatul Falāḥ.

Idāra-e-taṣnīf jamāʿat-e-islāmī hind: ēk taʿārruf. 1981. Aligarh: idāra-e-taṣnīf jamāʿat-e-islāmī hind.

Istūḍent islāmik aurganāizēshan āf inḍiyā manzil ba manzil. 1991. New Delhi: Student Islamic Organization of India.

Istūḍent islāmik aurganāizēshan manzil ba manzil. 1998. New Delhi: Student Islamic Organization of India.

Jamāʿat-e-islāmī kā chahār sāla prōgirām, 1968–1972. 1969. Delhi: jamāʿat-e-islāmī hind.

Jamāʿat-e-islāmī hind kē satāīs sāl. Undated. Delhi: jamāʿat-e-islāmī hind.

Jamāʿat-e-islāmī hind: April 1986 tā December 1989. Undated. Delhi: markazī maktaba islāmī.

Jamāʿat-e-islāmī hind aur masʾala-e-intikhābāt: markazī majlis-e-shura kī 1961 tā 1979 kī rūdād kā khulāṣa. Undated. Delhi: jamāʿat-e-islāmī hind.*

Jamāʿat kī daʿvat, uskā naṣbul . . . ʿain lāʿeḥa-e-ʿamal, unmēn tarmīm aur iẓāfē . . . Undated. New Delhi, Headquarters: jamāʿat-e-islāmī hind.*

Jāmiʿatul falāḥ. 2001. *Niṣāb-e-taʿlīm*. Azamgarh.

Jehd-e-musalsal kē pachīs sāl. Undated. Delhi: Student Islamic Movement of India.

Maqālāt-o-mokhtaṣar rūdād ijtimāʿ bhōpāl munʿaqeda May 26–30, 1978. Undated. Delhi: jamāʿat-e-islāmī hind.*

Markazī majlis-e-shura jamāʿat-e-islāmī hind kī qaraīrdādēñ, July 15, 1961 tā July 7, 1997. 1997. New Delhi: shoʿba-e-tanẓīm, jamāʿat-e-islāmī hind.

Masʾala-e-elekshan aur markazī majlis-e-shura jamāʿat-e-islāmī hind. 1986. Delhi: shoʿba-e-tanẓīm, jamāʿat-e-islāmī hind.*

Rūdāde ijtimāʿ rāmpūr jamāʿat-e-islāmī hind-1951. 1951. Delhi: jamāʿat-e-islāmī hind.

Rūdād jamāʿat-e-islāmī hind. Vol. 3. 1966. Delhi: markazī maktaba islamī.

Rūdād jamāʿat-e-islāmī hind. Vol. 5. 1967. Delhi: markazī maktaba islamī.

Rūdād jamāʿat-e-islāmī hind. Vol. 1. 2000. New Delhi: markazī maktaba islamī pablisharz.

Rūdād majlis-e-shura, jamāʿat-e-islāmī hind, August 1948 tā July 1966. 1966. Delhi: shoʿba-e-tanẓīm, jamāʿat-e-islāmī hind.

Rūdād majlis-e-shura, jamāʿat-e-islāmī hind, May 1967 tā May 1989. 1989. Delhi: shoʿba-e-tanẓīm, jamāʿat-e-islāmī hind.

Taḥrīk-e-islāmī, mushkilāt-o-masāʾel: ʿalīgaṛh mē munʿaqid IIFSO sēminār kī rūdād. Undated. Aligarh. Compiled by Anjum Naim.

Tīn sāla ripōrṭ pēshkarda General Secretary SIO ba mauqaʿ-e-pahlī kul hind Conference 1986, Bangalore. Undated. SIO.

ARTICLES, BOOKS, AND PAMPHLETS

Ahmad, Ashfaq. 1990. "Afzal Hussain." *Ḥijāb* (August–September): 149–68.

———. 1997. "Jamāʿat-e-islāmī hind kī taʿlīmī kāvishēn." *Rafīq-e-manzil* (May–June): 55–60.

Ahmad, Iqbal. 2003. "Savāneḥī ḳhāka." *In* Ahmad Ali Akhtar et al. (eds).

Ahmad, Israr. 1990. "Afzal ḥusain ṣāhib aur nayā niẓām-e-taʿlīm." *Rafīq-e-manzil* (September): 31–54.

Ahmad, Khurshid. 1997. "Dēoband kī taʿlīmī taḥrīk." *Rafīq-e-manzil* (May–June): 19–22.

Ahmad, Syed Shakil. 1981. "Maulānā saiyad abul āʿlā maudūdī." *jamāʿat-e-islāmī hind Souvenir*. Published to mark the Sixth All-India Congress in Hyderabad. Deluxe Printers.

Akhtar, Ahmad Ali et al. (eds.). 2003. *Naẓr-e-ẓiāulhodā*. Patna: majlis-e-rofaqā'-e-qadīm, ḥalqa-e-ṭalaba islāmī Bihar.

Akhtar, Javed. Undated. *Ḥalqa-e-ṭalaba islāmī, bihār: ek taʿārruf*. Bihar: maṭbūʿāt ḥalqa-e-ṭalaba islāmī.

Ali, Abul Hasan. 1980. *ʿAṣr-e ḥāẓir mēñ dīn kī tafhīm-o-tashrīḥ*. Lucknow: dār-e-ʿarafāt.

———. 2000. *Purānē cherāgh*. Vol. 2. Lucknow: maktaba firdaus.

———. 2000a. *Karvān-e-zindgī*. Lucknow: maktaba-e-islām.

Ali, Jawed. 1979. "Kab ruk sakēgā rōke merā qāflā javān hai." *Rafīq* (February 15): 3–8.

Ali, Syed. 1980. *ʿAllāma iqbāl aur maudūdī*. Delhi: markazī maktaba islāmī.

Alqasmi, S. A. Shamon. Undated. *Dō bhāī: Abulʿālā maudūdī aur imām ḳhomainī*. Deoband: shaiḳhul islām Academy.

Ansari, Abdulhaq. 1998. *Sekūlarizm, jamhūriyat aur intiḳhābāt*. New Delhi: markazī maktaba islāmī pablisharz.

Anṣārī, Muhammad Sabahuddin. 1981. *Kyā Insān ḳhalīfatullāh hai?* New Delhi: maktaba alfauzān.

Azad, Abulkalam. 1990 [1954]. "Masjid ahl-e-hadīth māler kōtlā kī imāmat kā moʿāmla." *In* H. A. Khan ed.

Azmi, Altaf Ahmad. 1999. *Aḥyā-e-millat aur dīnī jamāʿatēn*. Aligarh: idāra-e-taḥqīqāt-o-ishāʿat-e-ʿulūm-e-Qur'an.

Baghpati, Mateen Tariq. 1979. *Maulānā maudūdī aur fikrī inqilāb*. Delhi: markazī maktaba islāmī.

Dogar, Rafīq. 1980. "Tafhīmul Qur'an kyōn?" *Al-ḥasanāt*, 257–62.

Hamdi, Khalid (ed.). 1990. *Niẓām-e-jāhiliyat sē taʿāvun*. New Delhi: Idāra-e-shahādat-e-haq.

———. 2002. "Hijrōn kō qaumī dhārē mē lānē kē liyē qarārdād." *Allāh kī pukār* (June): 62.

Husain, Mohammad. 1999. *Sayyad maudūdī kē taʿlīmī naẓaryāt*. New Delhi: markazī maktaba islāmī pablisharz.

Islahi, Sultan Ahmad. 1996. *Maulānā Abullaiṡ nadvī: shaḳhsiyat kē chand numāyān pahlū*. Aligarh: idāra-e-ʿilm-o-adab.

Islahi, Zafrul Islam. 1999. "Maulānā ṣadruddīn Iṣlāḥī marḥūm." *Fikr-o-naẓar* 35(4): 35–52.

Kashmiri, Sufi Nazir Ahmad. 1979. *Jamāʿat-e-islāmī kē dīn kā ḳhulāsa*. Srinagar: Islamic Publications.

Khairabadi, Mael. 1990. "Afzal Husain." *Ḥijāb*. (August–September): 86–112.
———. 1990. "Markazī darsgāh jamāʿat-e-islāmī hind, Rampur." *Ḥijāb* (August–September): 122–32.
Khan, Hakim Ajmal (ed.). 1990. *Jamāʿat-e-islāmī kō pahchāniyē*. Delhi: dār al-kitāb.
Khan, Hakim Ubaidullah. 1984. 'Jamāʿat sē ʿalāhedgī kā sabab'. *In* Abdul Quddus Rumi (ed.). *Maudūdiyāt bēnaqāb: āpbītī kī ṛaushnī mēñ*. Agra: Sohaib Brothers.
Khan, Inamurrahman. 1995. *Zindāñ kā dāʿī*. Delhi: markazī maktaba islāmī pablisharz.
Maherulqadri. 1990. "Chand noqūsh-e-zindgī." *In* Yusuf bhaṭ (ed.), *Maulānā maudūdī Apnōñ aur dūsrōn kī naẕar mēn*. Delhi: markazī maktaba islāmī.
Mian, Muhammad. 1957. *Dō ẕarūrī masʾalē*. Deoband: idāra-e-nashr-o-ishāʿat dar al-ulūm Deoband.
Maududi, Syed Abul Ala. 1937. *Musalmān aur maujūda seyāsī kashmakash*. Vol. 1 Pathankot: maktaba jamāʿat-e-islāmī.
———. 1938. *Musalmān aur maujūda seyāsi kashmakash*. Vol. 2. Pathankot: maktaba jamāʿat-e-islāmī.
———. 1940. "Tajdīd-o-aḥyā-e-dīn." *Tarjumānul Qur'an* (November–December): 265–346.
———. 1941. "Islāmī ḥukūmat kis ṯaraḥ qā'em hōtī hai." *Tarjumānul Qur'an* (February–March): 47–83.
———. 1941a. "Islām aur jāhiliyat." *Tarjumānul Qur'an* (April): 102–28.
———. 1942. *Musalmān aur maujūda seyāsī kashmakash*. Vol. 3. Pathankot: daftar resāla Tarjumānul Quran.
———. 1944. *Rūdād-e-jamāʿat-e-islāmī*. Vol. 2. Pathankot, dar al-islām: maktaba jamāʿat-e-islāmī.
———. 1951. *Jamāʿat islāmī kī daʿvat*. Rāmpūr: maktaba jamāʿat-e-islāmī hind.
———. 1953 [1940]. *Parda*. Delhi: markazī maktaba islāmī.
———. 1959. *Tanqīhāt*. Delhi: markazī maktaba islāmī.
———. 1962. *Masʾala-e-qaumiyat*. Delhi: markazī maktaba islāmī.
———. 1963. "Sinēmā." *In Taḥrīk-e-islāmī*. Compiled by Khurshid Ahmad Lahore: idāra chirāgh-e-rāh Karachi.
———. 1971. "Main Ābul āʿlā maudūdī hūñ." *Zindgī* (January): 21–30.
———. 1972 (1941). *Islāmī ḥukūmat kis ṯaraḥ qāʾem hotī hai*. Delhi: markazī maktaba islāmī.
———. 1977. *Islāmī tahẕīb aur uskē uṣūl-o-mabādī*. Delhi: markazī maktaba islāmī.
———. 1979. "Maulānā maudūdī kī ḳhudnavisht ḥālāt-e-zindgī." *Zindgī* (November/December–January): 24–38.
———. 1979a [1941]. *Qur'an kī chār bunyādī iṣtelāḥēn*. Delhi: markazī maktaba islāmī.
———. 1980 [1939]. *Islām kā naẕarya-e-seyāsī*. Delhi: markazī maktaba islāmī.
———. 1981. *Taḥrīk-e-āzadī-e-hind aur musalmān*. Lahore: Islamic Publications. Compiled and edited by Khurshid Ahmad.
———. 1991. *Taʿlīmāt*. Rev. ed. Delhi: markazī maktaba islāmī.

———. 1991a. *Islāmī reyāsat*. Edited by Khurshid Ahmad. Delhi: Islamic Book Foundation.

———. 1992 [1919]. *Pandit madan mōhan mālvīya*. Patna: Khudabakhsh Oriental Public Library (in Hindi).

———. 1992a. [1960]. *Islām bīsvīn ṣadī mēn*. Rampur: Saeed Publications.

———. 1996. *Khuṭba-e-madrās*. Delhi: markazī maktaba islāmī pablisharz.

———. 1996a. *Islāmī adab*. Delhi: markazī Maktab islāmī

———. 1997 [1943]. *Dīn-e-haq*. Lahore: Islamic Publications.

———. 1999. *Rasā'el-o-masā'el*. Vol.1. New Delhi: markazī maktaba islāmī pablisharz.

———. 1999a. *Tafhīimāt*. Vol. 2. Delhi: markazī maktaba islāmī pablisharz.

———. 1999b. *Salāmtī kā rāsta*. Lahore: Islamic Publications.

———. 2000a. *Shahādat-e-haq*. Lahore: Islamic Publications.

———. 2001. *Tafhīmāt*. Vol. 1. New Delhi: markazī maktaba islāmī pablisharz.

———. 2001a. *Tarjumā Qur'an majid*. New Delhi: markazī maktaba islāmī pablisharz.

———. 2001b. *Rasā'el-o-masā'el*. Vol. 2. New Delhi: markazī maktaba islāmī pablisharz.

———. 2003 [1927]. *Al-jihād fīl islām*. markazī maktaba islāmī pablisharz.

———. 2003a. *Taḥrik-e-islāmī kā ā'inda lā'eḥa-e-ʿamal*. Lahore: Islamic Publications.

Miftahi, Ahsan. 1995. "Qaumi itteḥād kā naẓarya aur Jamiʿatul ʿolamāʾ-e-hind." *Al-jamʿiyat* (October 27): 69–70.

Monis, Shafi. 2001. *Mokhtaṣar tārikh: jamāʿat-e-islāmī hind*. New Delhi: markazī maktaba islāmī pablisharz.

Nadwi, Abul Lais Islahi. Undated. *Kyā hindustān dunyā kā rahnumā ban saktā hai?* Malihabad: jamāʿat-e-islāmī hind.

———. 1951. *Mas'ala-e-intikhābāt aur musalmānān-e-hind*. Vol.1. Rampur: maktaba jamāʿat-e-islāmī hind.

———. 1953. *Bhārat kī naī taʿmīr aur ham*. Delhi: markazī maktaba jamāʿat-e-islāmī hind.

———. 1962. *Pas che bāyad kard?* Delhi: jamāʿat-e-islāmī hind.

———. 1989. *Mulk-o-millat kē masā'el aur musalmānōñ kī zimmēdāriyāñ*. Delhi: markazī maktaba islāmī.

———. 1990. *Tashkil-e-jamāʿat-e-Islamī hind: kyōn aur kaisē?* Delhi: markazī maktaba islāmī.

Naim, Intizar. 1990. "Qā'em afẓal ḥusain." *Rafīq-e-manzil* (August–September): 71–82.

Naim, Intizar. 1979. *Jab dār-e-zindān khulā*. Delhi: Gulsetān.

Niazi, Kausar. 1973. *Jamāʿat-e-islāmī ʿavāmī ʿadālat mēñ*. Lahore: qaumi kutubkhāna.

Nomani, Manzoor. 1998. *Maulāna maudūdī kē sāth mērī refāqat kī sarguzashta aur ab mērā mauqif*. Lucknow: Al-furqān Book Depot.

Qadri, Arshadul. 1965. *Jamāʿat-e-islāmī*. Delhi: maktaba jamiʿā nūr.

Qadri, Syed Urooj Ahmad. 1999. *Ummat-e-muslema kā naṣbul ʿain*. Delhi: markazī maktaba islāmī pablisharz.

———. 2000. *Iqāmat-e-dīn farẓ hai*. New Delhi: markazī maktaba islāmī pablisharz.

Qasmi, Mohammad Sajid Qureshi. 2001. *Tafhīmul Qur'an mēñ aḥādiṡ-e-sharīfa sē bē-eʿtemādī aur bāibil par eʿtemād*. Barialy: Kutubḳhāna tafsīrul Qur'an.

Qasoori, Maulānā Mohiuddin. 1990 [1954]. "Masjid ahl-e-hadīth malerkōṭlā kī imāmat." *In* H. A. Khan (ed.).

Qureshi, Ishtiaq Hasan. 2001. "Maulānā maudūdī kī seyāsat qayām-e-pākistān sē pahlē." *In* Mujiburrahman Shami (ed.).

Qureshi, Izharul Haq. 1987. *Maudūdī ṣāhib kā aṣlī chehra: qur'ān-o-sunnat kī raushnī mē*. Udgir: Anjuman ḥemāyat-e-islām.

Rafīq-e-Manzil. 1999. "Shaḳhsiyāt: ḍākṭar faẓlurraḥmān farīdī." (September): 21–22.

Rahman, Hakim Zillur. 1995. "Jamʿīatul ʿolamā'-e-hind aur uskā ṭarz-e-fikr." *Al-jamʿiyat*. Special issue. October 27: 78–80.

Rahmani, Abdus Samad. Undated. *Jamāʿat-e-islāmī per tabṣera*. Vol. 1. Delhi: Al-jamiat Book Depot.

———. 1955. *Jamāʿat-e-islāmī kā dīnī ruḳh*. Vol. 4. Delhi: Al-jamiat Book Depot.

Rauf, A. 2001. "Taḥrik-e-islāmī kā mard-e-mujāhid maulānā amīn aṣrī." *Zindgī-e-nau*. November: 34–49.

Salfi, Abdul Aziz. Undated. *ʿAks-e-rāh*. Delhi: Student Islamic Movement of India, Department of Publications.

Salim, Syed Mohammad. 1991. *Islāmī tarbiyat yā darsgāh kī hamniṣābī sargarmiyāñ*. Delhi: markazī maktaba islāmī.

Sambhali, Abdul Khaliq. 1993. *Maudūdiyat ēk taʿārruf*. Deoband: dar al-ʿulūm.

———. 1993a. *Maudūdiyat* 1. Deoband: dar al-ʿulūm

———. 1993b. *Maudūdiyat* 2. Deoband: dar al-ʿulūm.

Sampradāiktā Virōdhī Committee. Undated. *Jamāʿat-e-islāmī kā ḥaqīqī kirdār*. Delhi.

Sayeed, A. A. 1998. *Bisvīn ṣadī kā qāʾed-e-āʿlā: maulānā abul āʿlā maudūdī*. Hyderabad: idāra-e-shān.

Shaami, Mujiburrahman. 2001. "Kiran sē āftāb tak." *In* M. Shami (ed.).

Shaami, Mujiburrahman (ed.). 2001. *Ēk shaḳhs, ēk kārvān*. New Delhi: markazī maktaba islāmī pablisharz.

Shamshuddin, Mufti. 1990. "Āh Marhūm afẓal husain ṣāhib." *Ḥijāb* (August–September): 61–67.

Shaz, Rashid. 1987. *Ġhalba-e-islām*. Aligarh: Institute of Ummah Affairs.

Siddiqi, Adil. Undated. *Jamʿiatul ʿolamā-e-hind āīna-e-aiyyām mēñ*. New Delhi: jamʿiatul ʿolamā-e-hind, Publicity Division.

Siddiqi, Muhammad Nejatullah. 2000. *Islām, mashīyat aur adab*: *Ḳhuṭūṭ kē āʾīne mē*. Aligarh: Educational Book House.

Tahir, Mohammd Yaqub. Undated. *Jamāʿat-e-islāmī par ilzāmāt kā Jāʾezā*. Sargodha (Pakistan): idāra-e-adab-e-islāmī.

Yusuf, Hafiz Salahuddin. 1991. "Sanitary inspectors, mustashreqīn aur maulānā maudūdī." *In* Hafiz Salahuddin Yusuf (ed.), *Ḳhilāfat-o-mulūkiyat kī sharʿī ḥaiṣiyat*. Delhi: maktaba tarjumān.

Zakaria, Mohammad. 1976. *Fitna-e-maudūiyat*. Sahārnpūr: kutubk̤hāna ishāʿatul ulūm.

English

JOURNALS AND NEWSPAPERS

Frontline Madras
Hindustan Times Delhi
The Message Aligarh, SIO's wall magazine
Milli Gazette Delhi
Muslim India Delhi
Newsletter Delhi, SIMI's newsletter
The Pioneer Delhi
Radiance Viewsweekly Weekly organ of the Jamaat, Delhi
Secular Democracy Delhi
Times of India Delhi

DOCUMENTS AND REPORTS

Constitution of Forum for Democracy and Communal Amity. 2000. Delhi: Publicity Department of the FDCA.

Constitution of SIO (Amended up to September 2000). Undated. New Delhi: SIO Headquarters.

Jāmiʿatul Falāḥ. Undated. Jāmiʿatul Falāḥ: *A Brief Introduction*. Azamagarh.

Three-Year Progress Organizational Report by General Secretary, SIO, The First All-India Conference (December 26–28, 1986, at Bangalore. Undated. SIO.

WEB SITES

Hindustan Times. 2001. "Six Sedition Cases against SIMI Members." www.hindustantimes.com/nonfram/290901/detcit06.asp. Accessed on 29/9/2001.

———. 2001a. "Govt Has Proof of SIMI, Bin Laden Links: Home Secy."
www.hindustantimes.com/nonfram/290901/detnat08.asp Accessed on 29/9/2001.

Indiainfo.com. 2003. "SIMI Activists Get 5 Yrs under POTA, 7 for Sedition." http://servlet.indiainfo.com/indiainfo/printer. Accessed on 9/18/2003.

Islamic Foundation for Education and Welfare (IFEW). "Qazi Ashfaq Ahmad: Insight." http://www.ifew.com/insight/authors/ashfaq.html. Accessed on 13/6/2002.

Jamaat-e-Islami Pakistan. 2001. "The Profile of the Founding 75 Members." http://www.jamaat.org/overview/profile.html. Accessed on 31/8/2001.

Milli Gazette. 2000. "Media Is Tarnishing SIMI Image." http://milligazette.com/Archives/01-10-2000/Art17.htm. Accessed on 10/12/2002.

The Pioneer. 2001. "SIMI Ban Soon, Says Advani." www.dailypioneer.com/secon2.asp?cat=\story2&d=FRONT_PAGE. Accessed on 19/8/2001.

———. 2001a. "Long Overdue Ban." www.dailypioneer.com/secon3.asp?cat=\edit1&d=EDIT. Accessed on 29/9/2001.

Rediff.com. 2001. "Mulayam Seeks an All-Party Meet on SIMI Ban." http://www.rediff.com/news/2001/sep/28simi1.htm. Accessed on 2/11/2004.

Rediff.com. 2003. "Militancy Destroyed SIMI." http://www.rediff.com/news/2003/sep/25vijay.htm. Accessed on 10/7/2003.

Siddiqi, Ahmadullah. 2003. "The SIMI I Founded was Completely Different." http://www.rediff.com/news/2003/sep/02inter.htm. Accessed on 9/30/2003.

The Telegraph. 2004. "Jihad to Put Country First." http://www.telegraphindia.com/1030606/asp/nation/story_2041569.asp. Accessed on 7/8/2004.

Yashwantrao, Nitin. 2003. "SIMI Story: A Movement Turns Deviant—Part 1." http://timesofindia.indiatimes.com/articleshow/46898860.cms. Accessed on 3/4/2005.

———. 2003. "Government Must Have Talks with Muslim Youth—Part 2." http://timesofindia.indiatimes.com/cms.dll/htmll/uncomp/articleshow?msid=47200284. Accessed on 29/3/2003.

ARTICLES AND BOOKS

Ansari, Abdulhaq. 2003. "Maududi's Contribution to Theology." *The Muslim World* 93 (July/October): 521–31.

Faridi, Fazlurrahman. 1998. *Living as a Muslim in a Plural Society*. Chennai: Islamic Foundation Trust.

Maududi, Syed Abul Ala. 1981a. [1940]. *Towards Understanding Islam*. Translated by Khurshid Ahmad. Rev. ed. Delhi: Markazi Maktaba Islami.

———. 1987. *Let Us Be Muslims: New English Version of* Khutbat. Edited by Khurram Murad. Delhi: Markazi Maktaba Islami.

———. 1992b [1946]. *Witnesses unto Mankind: The Purpose and Duty of the Muslim Ummah*. Edited and translated by Khurram Murad. Delhi: Markazi Maktaba Islami.

———. 2000. *Four Basic Quranic Terms*. Translated by Abu Asad. New Delhi: Markazi Maktaba Islami Publishers.

Nadwi, Maulana Abul Lais. 1971. *The Future of India and the Message of Jamaat-e-Islami Hind*. Delhi: Markazi Maktaba Jamaat-e-Islami Hind.

Rao, K. S. Ramakrishna. Undated. *Muhammad: The Prophet of Islam*. Madras: Islamic Foundation Trust.

SECONDARY

Urdu

Abrar, Rahat. 1997. "UP rābṭa kamīṭī." *Rafīq-e-manzil* (May–June): 74–75.

Adrawi, Aseer. 1988. *Taḥrīk-e-āzādī aur musalmān*. Deoband: dar al-muṣannefīn.

Alam, Manzoor. 2002. *Nuqūsh-e-kārvān*. New Delhi: All-India Milli Council.

Anjuman Ṭalaba-e-qadīm (ed.). 1992. *ʿAllāma ḥamīduddīn farāḥī ḥayāt-o-afkār*. Azamgarh: dā'era-e-ḥamīdiya.

Anjum, Ghulam Yahya. 2002. "ʿArabī aur fārsī bōrḍ uttar pardēsh aur uskā jadīd niṣāb." *Tahẕīb al-akhlāq* 21 (1): 21–25.

Anṣārī, Qamruddin. 1966. *Muslim majlis mushāverat keyā hai?* Allahabad: muslim majlis mushāverat.

Azad, Abulkalam. 1913. "Maghrib-e-aqsā." *Al-hilāl* (July 2).

———. 2006. *Ḳhuṭbāt-e-āzād*. Compiled by Malik Ram. 3rd ed. Delhi: Sahitya Academy.

Dastūr jamʿiatul ʿolamā-e-hind. Accepted in the General Session, April 16–18, 1949, Lucknow. Undated. Delhi: jamʿiatul ʿolamā-e-hind, Publicity Division.

Daudi, Zohra. 2001. *Manzil-e-gurēzāñ*. Vol. 2. Karachi: al-banōriyā Press.

Ghazali, Muzaffar Husain. 1992. "Maulāna ḥamīduddīn farāḥī kē taʿlīmī afkār." *In* Anjuman ṭalaba-e-qadīm (ed.).

Hasan, M. Undated. *Dīnī taʿlīmī kāunsil, uttar pardēsh: maqāsid, ṭarīqa-e-kār, ḳhidmāt aur manṣūba*. Lucknow: Dīnī Taʿlīmī Council.

Imam, Syed Fazl. Undated. "maulāna abulkalām āzād aur vaḥdat-e-adyān." *Nuqūsh* 142: 140–47.

Indian Union Muslim League. Undated. 1988. *Mēraṭh fasād par Amnesty International kī ripōrṭ 1987*. New Delhi: shoʿba-e-nashr-o-ishāʿat, Indian Union Muslim League.

Islahi, Zafrul Islam. 1992. "Maulāna ḥamiduddīn farahī." *In* Anjuman Ṭalaba-e-qadīm (ed.).

Khan, Nadir A. 1987. *Urdū ṣaḥāfat kī tārīḳh*. Aligarh: Educational Book House.

Khurshid, Abdussalam.1963. *Ṣaḥāfat pāk-o-hind mēn*. Lahore: majlis taraqqī-e-adab.

Madni, Syed Husain Ahmad. 2002 [1938]. *Islām aur muttaḥeda qaumīyat*. New Delhi: Al-jamiat Book Depot.

Makki, Mokhtar Ahmad. 2003. *Taḥrīk-e-āzādī aur hindustānī musalmān*. New Delhi: qāzī pablisharz.

Masud, Muhammad Khalid. 2005. "Shāh ʿabdulʿazīz mohaddiṡ dehlavī (1746–1824)." *Al-maʿārif* 41 (10–12): 34–63.

Nadwi, Syed Sulaiman. 1999. *Ḥayāt-e-shiblī*. Azamagarh: matbaʿ maʿārif.

Nomani, Haidar Ali. 1999. *Jang-e-āzādī mēñ musalmānōñ kī qurbāniyāñ*. Translated into Urdu by Mohammad Diler Azad. Ambedkarnagar: Danish Book Depot.

Nomani, Shibli. 1999. *Maqālāt-e-shiblī, maẕhabī*. Vol. 1. Azamgarh: dar al-muṣannefīn.

Rizvi, Syed Aminul Hasan. 1989. "Muslim majlis mushāverat." *Afkār-e-millī* (September): 153–63.

Saif, Qazi Mohammad Aslam. 1996. *Taḥrīk ahl-e-hadīth tarīḳh kē āīnē mēñ*. Delhi: al-kitāb International.

Sen, Arindam. 1994. "Bangāl kā Punarjāgaraṇ: ēk punarvichār." *Samkālīn Janmat* (May 1–15): 9–13 (in Hindi).

Taban, Ghulam Rabbani. 1994. *Sheʿriyāt sē siyāsat tak*. Translated from English by Ajmal Ajmali. Delhi: Maktaba Jamia.

Tayyib, Qari. Undated. *Dar al-ʿolūm dēoband kī estrāik 1389 hijrī par ẕimmedārān-e-madāris-e-dīniyā kē taʾaṡṡurāt aur ghair-estrāikī ṭalabā kā iẕhār-e-barāʾat*. Dar al-ʿolūm dēoband: shoʿba-e-tanẓīm.

Thanvi, Maulāna Ashraf Ali. Undated. *Ashraful javāb*. Dēoband: kutubḳhāna-e-naʿīmiya.

Urdu-English Dictionary. Undated. Lahore: Ferozsons.

Zilli, Ishtiaq A. 1992. "Ḳhutba-e-istaqbāliya." *In* Anjuman ṭalaba-e-qadīm, ed.

English

Abu-Lughod, Lila. 1991. "Writing against Culture." *In* Richard Fox (ed.), *Recapturing Anthropology: Working in the Present*. Santa Fe, N.M.: School of American Research Press.

Adams, Charles J. 1966. "The ideology of Mawlana Mawdudi." *In* D. E. Smith (ed.), *South Asian Politics and Religion*. Princeton, N.J.: Princeton University Press.

Agwani, Mohammad Shafiq. 1986. *Islamic Fundamentalism in India*. Chandigarh: Twenty-first Century Indian Society.

———. 1992. "Muslim Denominational Institutions and Communalism." *In* Pramod Kumar (ed.), *Towards Understanding Communalism*. Chandigarh: Centre for Research in Rural and Industrial Development.

Ahmad, Aziz. 1967. *Islamic Modernism in India and Pakistan, 1857–1964*. London: Oxford University Press.

———. 1970. "India and Pakistan." *In* P. M. Holt, Ann K. S. Lambton and Bernard Lewis (eds.), *The Cambridge History of Islam*. Vol. 2A. Cambridge: Cambridge University Press.

Ahmad, Irfan. 1997. "A New Agenda for Muslim Radicals." *Times of India* (Delhi), April 1, editorial page.

———. 1999. "RSS versus the Jamaat." *World Focus* 20 (4): 16–19.

———. 1999a. "Contextualizing *Vande Matram*." *Manushi. A Journal about Women and Society* 111:29–30.

———. 2002. "Timothy McVeighs of the Orient." *Economic and Political Weekly* 37 (15): 1399–1400.

———. 2003. "'Ninety-nine Percent Individuals of this *qaum* are Ignorant of Islam, Ninety-five Percent are Deviant . . .': Discourse of Purity and Purity of Discourse." Paper presented at the Dutch Anthropological Association Conference, Leiden.

———. 2003a. "A Different Jihad: Dalit Muslims' Challenge to Ashraf Hegemony." *Economic and Political Weekly* 38 (46): 4886–91.

———. 2004. "The Jewish Hand: The Response of the Jamaat-e-Islami Hind." *In* Peter Van der Veer and Shoma Munshi (eds.), *Media, War, and Terrorism*. London: RoutledgeCurzon.

———. 2005. "Between Moderation and Radicalization: Transnational Interactions of Jamaat-e-Islami of India." *Global Networks: A Journal of Transnational Affairs* 5 (3): 279–99.

———. 2005a. "From Islamism to Post-Islamism: The Transformation of the Jamaat-e-Islami in North India." Ph. D. dissertation, University of Amsterdam.

———. 2006. "The State in Islamist Thought." *ISIM Review* 18 (fall): 12–13.

———. 2008. "Power, Purity and the Vanguard: Educational Ideology of the Jamaat-e-Islami of India." *In* Jamal Malik (ed.), *Madrasas in South Asia*. London: Routledge.

———. 2008a. "Cracks in the 'Mightiest Fortress': Jamaat-e-Islami's Changing Discourse on Women." *Modern Asian Studies*. 42 (2–3): 549–75.

———. 2009. "Genealogy of the Islamic State: Reflections on Maududi's Political Thought and Islamism." *Journal of the Royal Anthropological Institute* (NS) 15: S145–62. Annual Special Fifth Volume: *Islam, Politics, and Modernity: Anthropological Perspectives.*

Ahmad, Mumtaz. 1991. "Islamic Fundamentalism in South Asia: The Jamaat-e-Islami and Tablighi Jamaat of South Asia." *In* Martin E. Marty and S. Appleby (eds.), *Fundamentalisms Observed*. Chicago: University of Chicago Press.

Ahmad, Nafees. 1969. "Reactionary Politics of Jamaat-e-Islami." *Mainstream* (June 21): 16–17.

Ahmad, Rizwan. 2008. "Scripting a New Identity: The Battle for Devanagari in Nineteenth-Century India." *Journal of Pragmatics* 40:1163–83.

Ahmed, Imtiaz (ed.). 1973. *Caste and Social Stratification among Muslims in India*. Delhi: Manohar.

Akbar, M. J. 1985. *India: The Seige Within—Challenges to a Nation's Unity*. London: Penguin.

Alavi, Hamza. 1988. "Pakistan and Islam: Ethnicity and Ideology." *In* Fred Halliday and Hamza Alavi (eds.), *State and Ideology in the Middle East and Pakistan*. London: McMillan.

Ali, Abdullah Yusuf. 2004. "SoundVision.com: Translation of the Quran." http://www.soundvision.com. Accessed on 11/26/2004.

Almond, Ian. 2004. " 'The Madness of Islam': Foucault's Occident and the Revolution in Iran." *Radical Philosophy* 128: 12–22.

Aloysius, G. 1997. *Nationalism without a Nation in India*. New Delhi: Oxford University Press.

Anderson, Benedict. 1991. *Imagined Communities*. London: Verso.

Appadurai, Arjun. 1986. "Theory in Anthropology: Center and Periphery." *Comparative Studies in Society and History* 28 (2): 356–61.

———. 2006. *Fear of Small Numbers*. Durham, N.C.: Duke University Press.

Appiah, Kwame Anthony. 1992. *In My Father's House: Africa in the Philosophy of Culture*. New York: Oxford University Press.

Archer, Robin. 2001. "Secularism and Sectarianism in India and the West: What Are the Real Lessons of American History?" *Economy and Society* 30 (3): 273–87.

Armstrong, Charles. 2003. *Romantic Organicism: From Idealist Origin to Ambivalent Afterlife*. London: Palgrave Macmillan.

Asad, Talal. 1986. *The Idea of an Anthropology of Islam*. Occasional Papers series. Washington, D.C.: Georgetown University, Center for Contemporary Arab Studies.

———. 1993. *Genealogies of Religion: Discipline and Reasons of Power in Christianity and Islam*. Baltimore, Md.: John Hopkins University Press.

———. 2003. *Formations of the Secular: Christianity, Islam, Modernity*. Stanford: Stanford University Press.

Austin, Granville. 1999. *The Indian Constitution: Cornerstone of a Nation*. Delhi: Oxford University Press.

Bader, Veit. 2007. *Secularism or Democracy? Associational Governance of Religious Diversity*. Amsterdam: Amsterdam University Press.

Baird, Robert D. (ed.). 1991. *Religion in Modern India*. 2nd rev. ed. Delhi: Manohar.

Banerjee, Sumanta. 1996. "Strategy, Tactics and Forms of Political Participation among Left Parties." *In* T. V. Sathyamurthy (ed.), *Class Formation and Political Transformation in Post-Colonial India*. Delhi: Oxford University Press.

Bajpai, Rochna. 2002. "The Conceptual Vocabulary of Secularism and Minority Rights in India." *Journal of Political Ideologies* 7 (2): 179–97.

Balasubramanian, M. 1980. *Nehru: A Study in Secularism*. New Delhi: Uppal.

Balibar, Étienne. 2007. "Secularism Has Become Another Religion." http://kafila.org/2007/10/02/%E2%80%98secularism-has-become-another-religion%E2%80%. Accessed on 2/2/2008.

Barker, Colin, et al. 2001. "Leadership Matters: An Introduction." *In* Colin Barker et al. (eds.), *Leadership and Social Movement*. Manchester: Manchester University Press.

Barlas, Asma. 1995. *Democracy, Nationalism, and Communalism: The Colonial Legacy in South Asia*. Boulder, Colo.: Westview.

Basu, Tapan, et al. 1993. *Khaki Shorts and Saffron Flags: A Critique of Hindu Right*. Delhi: Orient Longman.

Baumann, Gerd. 1996. *Contesting Culture: Discourses of Identity in Multi-Ethnic London*. Cambridge: Cambridge University Press.

Bayat, Asef. 1996. "The Coming of a Post-Islamist Society." *Critique* (Fall): 43–52.

———. 1998. "Revolution without Movement, Movement without Revolution: Comparing Islamic Activism in Iran and Egypt." *Comparative Studies in Society and History* 40 (1): 136–69.

———. 2007. *Making Islam Democratic: Social Movements and the Post-Islamist Turn*. Stanford: Stanford University Press.

Beattie, John. 1964. *Other Cultures: Aims, Methods, and Achievements in Social Anthropology*. London: Routledge and Kegan Paul.

Benford, Robert D., and David A. Snow. 2000. "Framing Process and Social Movements: An Overview and Assessment." *Annual Review of Sociology* 26:611–39.

Benei, Veronique. 2001. "Teaching Nationalism in Maharashtra School." *In*. C. J. Fuller and Veronique Benei (eds.), *The Everyday State and Society in Modern India*. London: Hurst.

Bhargava, Rajeev (ed.). 1998. *Secularism and Its Critics*. New Delhi: Oxford University Press.

———. 1998. "What Is Secularism For?" *In* Rajeev Bhargava (ed.).

Bhat, Ayesha. 1970. "Jamaat-e-Islami and the Indian Muslims." *Secular Democracy* (September): 37–38.

Bhatt, Chetan. 1997. *Liberation and Purity*. London: University College London Press.

Blair, Harry W. 1973. "Minority Electoral Politics in a North Indian State: Aggregate Data Analysis and the Muslim Community in Bihar, 1952–72." *American Political Science Review* 67 (4): 1275–87.

Bose, Sugata, and Ayesha Jalal. 1997. *Modern South Asia: History, Culture, and Political Economy*. London: Routledge.

Bowden, John. 2005. "Secular Values and the Process of Secularization." http://www.islamonline.net/. Accessed on 10/25/2006.

Bowen, John R. 2007. *Why the French Don't Like Headscarves: Islam, the State and Public Sphere*. Princeton, N.J.: Princeton University Press.

Bourdieu, Pierre. 1979. "The Disenchantment of the World." *In Algeria 1960*. New York: Cambridge University Press.

———. 1997. "Forms of Capital." *In* A. H. Halsey et al. (eds.), *Education: Culture, Economy and Society*. Oxford: Oxford University Press.

———. 2003. "Participant Objectivation." *Journal of Royal Anthropological Institute* (n.s.). 9:281–94.

Brass, Paul R. 1994. *The Politics of India since Independence*. New Cambridge History of India 5. 2nd ed. Cambridge: Cambridge University Press.

———. 2002. "The Gujarat Pogrom of 2002." *Items and Issues* 4 (1): 1, 5–9.

———. 2003. *The Production of Hindu-Muslim Violence in Contemporary India*. Seattle: University of Washington Press.

Breckenridge, Carol A., and Peter Van der Veer (eds.). 1993. *Orientalism and the Post-Colonial Predicament: Perspectives on South Asia*. Philadelphia: University of Pennsylvania Press.

Brennan, Lance. 1996. "The State and Communal Violence in UP." *In* John McGuire et al. (eds.), *Politics of Violence: From Ayodhya to Behrampada*. New Delhi: Sage.

Brown, Judith. 1994. *Modern India: The Origins of an Asian Democracy*. 2nd ed. Oxford: Oxford University Press.

Brown, Wendy. 2006. *Regulating Aversion: Tolerance in the Age of Identity and Empire*. Princeton. N.J.: Princeton University Press.

Buechler, Steven M. 2000. *Social Movements in Advanced Capitalism: The Political Economy and Cultural Construction of Social Activism*. New York: Oxford University Press.

Burawoy, Michael. 2000. "Introduction." *In* Michael Burawoy et al. (eds.), *Global Ethnography: Forces, Connections and Imaginations in a Postmodern World*. Berkeley: University of California Press.

Burgat, Franciois. 2003. *Face to Face with Political Islam*. London: I. B. Tauris.

Burke, Edmund, III. 1988. "Islam and Social Movements: Methodological Reflections." *In* Edmund Burke III et al. (eds.), *Islam, Politics, and Social Movements*. Berkeley: University of California Press.

Bush, George W. 2006. "President Bush and Secretary of State Rice Discuss the Middle East Crisis." http://www.whitehouse.gov/news/releases/2006/08/20060807.html. Accessed on 9/11/2006.

Camaroff, Jean, and John Camaroff. 2003. "Ethnography on an Awkward Scale: Postcolonial Anthropology and Violence of Abstraction." *Ethnography* 4 (2): 147–79.

Casanova, Jose. 1994. *Public Religions in the Modern World*. Chicago: University of Chicago Press.

———. 2001. "Civil Society and Religion: Retrospective Reflections on Catholicism and Prospective Reflections on Islam." *Social Research* 68 (4): 1041–80.

Cash, John Daniel. 1996. *Identity, Ideology, and Conflict: The Structuration of Politics in Northern Island*. Cambridge: Cambridge University Press.

Chakravarti, Anand. 1979. "Experience of an Encapsulated Observer." *In* M .N. Srinivas et al. (eds.), *The Fieldworker and the Field: Problems and Challenges in Sociological Investigation*. Delhi: Oxford University Press.

Chatterjee, Partha. 1995. "History and Nationalization of Hinduism." *In* Vasudha Dalmia and Heinrich von Stietencron (eds.), *Representing Hinduism*. New Delhi: Sage.

Chaturvedi, Jayati, and Gyaneshwar Chaturvedi. 1996. "Dharm Yudhya: Communal Violence, Riots, and Public Space in Ayodhya and Agra." *In* Paul Brass (ed.), *Riots and Pogroms*. London: Macmillan.

Chandra, Bipan, et al. 1989. *India's Struggle for Independence*. New Delhi: Penguine.

Cook, David. 2005. *Understanding Jihad*. Berkeley: University of California Press.

Copland, Ian. 1998. "The Further Shores of Partition: Ethnic Cleansing in Rajasthan 1947." *Past and Present* 160, August: 203–39.

———. 2001. *India: 1885–1947*. Seminar Studies in History series. Harlow: Longman.

Coppola, Carlo. 1988. "All India Progressive Writers' Association: The Early Phases." *In* C. Coppola (ed.), *Marxist Influences and South Asian Literature*. Delhi: Channakya.

Cox, Caroline, and John Marks. 2003. *The "West," Islam, and Islamism: Is Ideological Islam Compatible with Liberal Democracy*. London: Civitas.

Crehan, Kate. 2002. *Gramsci, Culture, and Anthropology*. London: Pluto.

Crossley, Nick. 2002. *Making Sense of Social Movements*. Buckingham: Open University Press.

Dahl, Robert A. 2001. *On Democracy*. New Delhi: East West Press.

Davis, Richard H. 1996. "The Iconography of Ram's Chariot." *In* David Ludden (ed.).

Davutoglu, Ahmet. 1994. *Alternative Paradigms: The Impact of Islamic and Western Weltanschauungs on Political Theory*. Lanham, Md.: University Press of America.

Dev, Nirendra. 2004. *Godhra, A Journey to Mayhem*. New Delhi: Samskriti.

Devji, Faisal. 2005. *Landscapes of Jihad: Militancy, Morality, Modernity*. Ithaca, N.Y.: Cornell University Press.

Di Leonardo, Micaela. 1998. *Exotic at Home: Anthropologies, Others, American Modernity*. Chicago: University of Chicago Press.

Diani, Mario, and Ron Eyerman (eds.). 1992. *Studying Collective Action*. London: Sage.

Donnan, Hastings (ed.). 2002. *Interpreting Islam*. New Delhi: Vistaar.

Dumont, Louis. 1970. *Religion, Politics, and History in India*. Paris: Mouton.

———. 1988 [1970]. *Homo Hierarchicus*. New Delhi: Oxford University Press.

Eckert, Julia. 2005. "Whose State Is It? Hindu-Nationalist Violence and Populism in India." *In* Kalus Schlichte (ed.), *The Dynamics of States: The Formation and the Crises of State Domination*. Hampshire: Ashgate.

Edelman, Marc. 2001. "Social Movements: Changing Paradigms and Forms of Politics." *Annual Review of Anthropology* 30:285–317.

Eickelman, Dale F. 1982. "The Study of Islam in Local Contexts." *Contributions to Asian Studies* 17:1–16.

———. 2000. "Islam and the Languages of Modernity." *Daedalus* 129 (1): 119–35.

Eickelman, Dale F., and James Piscatori. 1996. *Muslim Politics*. Princeton, N.J.: Princeton University Press.

El Fadl, Khaled Abou, et al. 2004. *Islam and the Challenge of Democracy*. Princeton, N.J.: Princeton University Press.

El-Zein, Abdul Hamid. 1977. "Beyond Ideology and Theology: The Search for the Anthropology of Islam." *Annual Review of Anthropology* 6:227–54.

Engineer, Asghar Ali. 1995. *Lifting the Veil: Communal Violence and Communal Harmony in Contemporary India*. New Delhi: Sangam Books.

———. 1995a. *Communalism in India: A Historical and Empirical Study*. Delhi: Vikas.

———. 2006. "Introduction." *In* Asghar Ali Engineer (ed.), *They Too Fought for India's Freedom: The Role of Minorities*. Gurgaon: Hope India.

Esposito, John L. (ed.), 1983. *Voices of Resurgent Islam*. New York: Oxford University Press.

———. 2000. "Introduction: Islam and Secularism in the Twenty-First Century." *In* John L. Esposito and Azzam Tamimi (eds.),

Esposito, John L., and John O. Voll. 1996. *Islam and Democracy*. New York: Oxford University Press.

Esposito, John L., and Azzam Tamimi (eds.). 2000. *Islam and Secularism in the Middle East*. London: Hurst.

Euben, Roxanne L. 1999. *Enemy in the Mirror: Islamic Fundamentalism and the Limits of Modern Rationalism*. Princeton, N.J.: Princeton University Press.

Fahimuddin. 1998. *Evaluation of Madrasa Modernization Program in Uttar Pradesh*. Lucknow: Giri Institute of Development Studies.

Farooqi, M. N. 1998. *My Days at Aligarh*. Delhi: Idarah-e-adbiyat.

Faruqi, Zeyaul Hasan. 1963. *The Deoband School the Demand for Pakistan*. Bombay: Asia.

Ferree, Myra Marx et al 2002. "Four Models of the Public Sphere in Modern Democracies." *Theory and Society* 31:289–324.

Ferguson, James. 1999 *Expectations of Modernity: Myths and Meanings of Urban Life on the Zambian Copperbelt*. Berkeley: University of California Press.

Fiedl, John. 2003. *Social Capital*. Key Ideas series. London: Routledge.

Filali-Ansary, Abdou. 1996. "The Challenge of Secularization: Islam and Liberal Democracy." *Journal of Democracy* 7 (2): 76–80.

Foucault, Michael. 1982. "Afterword: The Subject and Power." *In* Hubert Dreyfus and Paul Rabinow (eds.), *Michael Foucault: Beyond Structuralism and Hermeneutics*. Chicago: University of Chicago Press.

1996. "What Is Critique?" *In* James Schmidt (ed.), *What Is Enlightenment?* Berkeley: University of California Press.

———. 1999. *Religion and Culture*. Edited by R. Carrette. New York: Routledge.

Franda, Marcus F. 1969. "India's Third Communist Party." *Asian Survey* 9 (11): 797–817.

Franzosi, R. 2001. "Strikes: Sociological Aspects." *International Encyclopedia of Social and Behavioral Sciences*. Amsterdam: Elsevier.

Frawley, David. 1995. *Arise Arjuna: Hinduism and the Modern World*. New Delhi: Voice of India.

Friedman, Jonathan. 1987. "Beyond Otherness or the Spectacularization of Anthropology." *Telos* 71:161–70.

Friedmann, Yohanan. 1971. "The Attitude of the Jamiatul Ulema-e-Hind to the Indian National Movement and the Establishment of Pakistan." *Asian and African Studies*. 7:157–80.

———. 1976. "The Jamiatul Ulema-e-Hind in the Wake of Partition." *Asian and African Studies* 11 (2): 181–211.

Fukuyama, Francis. 1992. *The End of History and the Last Man*. New York: Avon.

Gaborieau, Marc. 1985. "From Al-Beruni to Jinnah: Idiom, Ritual, and Ideology of the Hindu-Muslim Confrontation in South Asia." *Anthropology Today* 1 (3): 7–14.

Geertz, Clifford. 1980. *Nagara: The Theater State in Nineteenth-Century Bali*. Princeton, N.J.: Princeton University Press.

Gellner, Ernest. 1981. *Muslim Society*. Cambridge: Cambridge University Press.

———. 1992. *Postmodernism, Reason, and Religion*. London: Routledge.

———. 1994. *Conditions of Liberty: Civil Society and Its Rivals*. London: Hamish Hamilton.

Geschiere, Peter, and Joseph Gugler. 1998. "The Urban-Rural Connection: Changing Issues of Belonging and Identification." *Africa* 68 (3): 309–19.

Ghannouchi, Rashid. 1998. "Participation in a non-Islamic Government." *In* Charles Kurzman (ed.), *Liberal Islam: A Sourcebook*. Oxford: Oxford University Press.

Gill, Anthony. 2008. *The Political Origins of Religious Liberty*. Cambridge: Cambridge University Press.

Ghosh, Partha S. 1999. *BJP and the Evolution of Hindu Nationalism: From Periphery to Center*. Delhi: Manohar.

Ghosh, Sunit. 1998. *Modern History of the Indian Press*. New Delhi: Cosmo.

Giddens, Anthony. 1985. *The Nation-State and Violence*. Cambridge: Polity.

Gilroy, Paul. 2000. *Between Camps: Race, Identity, and Nationalism at the End of the Color Line*. London: Penguin.

Goldstone, Jack A. 2003. "Introduction: Bridging Institutionalized and Non-Institutionalized Politics." *In* Jack A. Goldstone (ed.), *States, Parties, and Social Movements*. Cambridge: Cambridge University Press.

Gopal, S. 1996. "Nehru, Religion, and Secularism." *In* R. Champakalakshmi and S. Gopal (eds.), *Tradition, Dissent, and Ideology: Essays in Honor of Romila Thapar*. Delhi: Oxford University Press.

Goodwin, Jeff, and James M. Jasper. 1999. "Caught in a Winding, Snarling Vine: The Structural Bias of the Political Process Theory." *Sociological Forum* 14 (1): 27–54.

Goradia, Prafull, and K. R. Phanda. 2005. "Ignoble War, Noble Claims." *The Pioneer*, New Delhi. http://www.dailypioneer.com/displayit1.asp?pathit=/archives2/aug2705/books/book1.txt, Accessed on 9/15/2005.

Gosse, Edmund. 1925 [1907]. *Father and Son: A Study of Two Temperaments*. London: Heinemann.

Government of India. 2006. *Social, Economic, and Educational Status of the Muslim Community of India: A Report*. New Delhi: Government of India.

Graff, Violette. 1990. "Aligarh's Long Quest for 'Minority' Status: AMU (Amendment) Act, 1981." *Economic and Political Weekly* (August 11): 1771–81.

Graham, Bruce. 1990. *Hindu Nationalism and Indian Politics: The Origins and Development of the Bharatiya Jana Sangh*. Cambridge: Cambridge University Press.

Gupta, Akhil, and James Ferguson. 1992. "Beyond 'Culture': Space, Identity and the Politics of Difference." *Cultural Anthropology* 7 (1): 6–23.

Gupta, Dipankar. 1982. *Nativism in a Metropolis. The Shiv Sena in Bombay*. New Delhi: Manohar.

———. 1993. "Review Article: Between General and Particular 'Others': Some Observations on Fundamentalism." *Contributions to Indian Sociology* (n.s.). 27 (1): 119–37.

Guttmann, Amy, and Dennis Thompson. 2004. *Why Deliberative Democracy?* Princeton, N.J.: Princeton University Press.

Habermas, Jurgen. 1989. *The Structural Transformation of the Public Sphere*. Translated by Thomas Berger. Cambridge: Polity.

Habib, Irfan. 1998. *Indian People in the Struggle for Freedom*. New Delhi: Sahmat.

Hafez, Mohammed H. 2003. *Why Muslims Rebel*. Boulder, Colo.: Lynne Rienner.

Hall, Stuart. 1983. "What Is This 'Black' in Black Popular Culture?" *In* Gina Dent (ed.), *Black Popular Culture*. New York: New Press.

Halpern, Ben. 1961. "'Myth' and 'Ideology' in Modern Usage." *Theory and Society* 1 (2): 129–49.

Hameed, Syeda Saiyidain. 1998. *Islamic Seal on India's Independence*. New Delhi: Oxford University Press.

Hamid, Saiyid, et al. Undated. *Center for Promotion of Educational Cultural Advancement of Muslims in India: A Review of Its Progress and a Proposed Plan of Action*. Aligarh: Aligrah Muslim University Press.

Hansen, Thomas Blom. 1999. *The Saffron Wave: Democracy and Hindu Nationalism in Modern India*. Princeton, N.J.: Princeton University Press.

———. 2001. *Wages of Violence: Naming and Identity in Postcolonial Bombay*. Princeton, N.J.: Princeton University Press.

Hardy, Peter. 1972. *The Muslims of British India*. Cambridge: Cambridge University Press.

Harvey, David. 1989. *The Condition of Postmodernity: An Inquiry into the Origins of Cultural Change*. Cambridge: Blackwell.

Hasan, Mohammad. 1987. *A New Approach to Iqbal*. New Delhi: Government of India, Publication Division.

Hasan, Mushirul. 1979. *Nationalism and Communal Politics in India, 1916–1928*. Delhi: Manohar.

———. 1988. "The Muslim Mass Contacts Campaign: Analysis of a Strategy of Political Mobilization." *In* Richard Sisson and Stanley Wolpert (eds.),

———. 1991. *Nationalism and Communal Politics in India, 1885–1930*. Delhi: Manohar.

———. 1992. *Islam and Indian Nationalism: Reflections on Abul Kalam Azad*. Delhi: Manohar.

———. 1997. *The Legacy of a Divided Nation: Indian Muslims since Independence*. London: Hurst.

Hasan, Zoya. 1996. "Communal Mobilization and Changing Majority in Uttar Pradesh." *In* David Ludden (ed.).

———. 2000. "Religion and Politics in a Secular State: Law, Community and Gender." *In* Z. Hasan (ed.), *Politics and State in India*. New Delhi: Sage.

Hassner, Pierre. 1987. "Georg W. F. Hegel." *In* Leo Strauss and Joseph Cropsey (eds.), *History of Political Philosophy*. 3rd ed. Chicago: University of Chicago Press.

Hefner, Robert W. 2000. *Civil Islam: Muslims and Democratization in Indonesia*. Princeton, N.J.: Princeton University Press.

Hobsbawm, Eric. 1983. "Introduction: Inventing Traditions." *In* Eric Hobsbawm and Terence Ranger (eds.), *The Invention of Tradition*. Cambridge: Cambridge University Press.

Hunter, W. W. 1871. *The Indian Musalmans: Are They Bound in Conscience to Rebel against the Queen?* London: Trubner.

Huntington, Samuel P. 1996. *The Clash of Civilizations and the Remaking of World Order*. New York: Simon and Schuster.

Huq, Mushirul. 1970. *Muslim Politics in Modern India, 1857–1947*. Meerut: Meenakshi Prakashan.

Hussain, Asaf, et al. (eds.). 1984. *Orientalism, Islam, and Islamists*. Brattleboro, VT: Amana Books.

Hussnain, S. E. 1968. *Indian Muslims: Challenge and Continuity*. Bombay: Lalvani.

Hyder, G. 1974. *Politics of Jamaat-e-Islami Hind*. New Delhi: Communist Party of India.

International Crisis Group. 2005. *Understanding Islamism*. Middle East/North Africa Report No. 37. Brussels. International Crisis Group.

Jackson, Anthony (ed.). 1987. *Anthropology at Home*. London: Tavistock.

Jaffrelot, Christophe. 2000. "Hindu Nationalism and Democracy." *In* Francine Frankel et al. (eds.), *Transforming India: Social and Political Dynamics of Democracy*. New Delhi: Oxford University Press.

———. 2001. "The Rise of Hindu Nationalism and the Marginalization of Muslims in India Today." *In* Amrit Shastri and A. J. Wilson (eds.), *The Postcolonial States of South Asia*. London: Curzon.

Jalal, Ayesha. 1995. "Conjuring Pakistan: History as Official Imagining." *International Journal of Middle East Studies* 27 (1): 73–89.

Jasper, James J. 1997. *The Art of Moral Protest*. Chicago: University of Chicago Press.

Jeffery, R., P. Jeffery, and C. Jeffrey. 2004. "Islamization, Gentrification and Domestication: 'A Girls' Islamic Course' and Rural Muslims in Western Uttar Pradesh." *Modern Asian Studies* 38 (1): 1–53.

Jha, Shefali. 2002. "Secularism in the Constituent Assembly Debates, 1946–1950." *Economic and Political Weekly* (July 27): 3175–80.

Johnson, James Turner. 1997. *The Holy War Idea in the Western and Islamic Traditions*. University Park: Pennsylvania State University Press.

Jones, Kenneth W. 1991. "Politicized Hinduism: The Ideology and Program of the Hindu Mahasabha." *In* Robert D. Baird (ed.).

Juergensmeyer, Mark. 2000. *Terror in the Mind of God: The Global Rise of Religious Violence*. Rev. ed. with a new preface. Berkeley: University of California Press.

———. 2002. "Global Antimodernism." *In* Dominic Sachsenmaire et al. (eds.), *Reflections on Multiple Modernities: European, Chinese, and Other Interpretations*. Leiden: Brill.

Kakar, Sudhir. 1996. *The Colors of Violence: Cultural Identities, Religion, and Conflict*. Chicago: University of Chicago Press.

Kamali, Masoud. 2001. "Civil Society and Islam: A Sociological Perspective." *Archives Europeenes de Sociologie* 42:457–82.

Kanaungo, Pralay. 2002. *RSS's Tryst with Politics*. Delhi: Manohar.

Kapur, Anuradha. 1993. "Deity to Crusader: The Changing Iconography of Ram." *In* G. Pandey (ed.), *Hindus and Others: The Question of Identity in India Today*. New Delhi: Viking.

Kates, Gary. 1989. "Jews into Frenchmen: Nationality and Representation in Revolutionary France." *Social Research* 56 (1): 213–32.

Kaviraj, Sudipta. 1999. "The Modern State in India." *In* Zoya Hasan (ed.), *Politics and State in India*. New Delhi: Sage.

Kean, Webb. 2003. "Self-Interpretation, Agency, and the Objects of Anthropology: Reflections on a Geneaology." *Comparative Studies in Society and History* 45 (2): 222–48.

Keane, John. 2004. *Violence and Democracy*. Cambridge: Cambridge University Press.

Kelidar, A. 1981. "Ayatollah Khomeini's Concept of Islamic Government." *In* A Cudsi and A. E. H. Dessouki (eds.), *Islam and Power*. London: Croom Helm.

Kelly, Christopher. 1995. "Civil and Uncivil Religions: Tocqueville on Hinduism and Islam." *History of European Ideas* 20 (4–6): 845–50.

Kepel, Gilles. 1985. *The Prophet and the Pharaoh: Muslim Extremism in Egypt*. London: Al-saqi Books.

———. 1994. *The Revenge of God: The Resurgence of Islam, Christianity, and Judaism in the Modern World*. University Park: Pennsylvania State University Press.

———. 2002. *Jihad: The Trail of Political Islam*. London: I.B. Tauris.

———. 2003. *Muslim Extremism in Egypt: The Prophet and the Pharaoh*. Berkeley: University of California Press.

Khalidi, Omar. 2003. "Maulana Maududi and the Future Political Order in British India." *The Muslim World* 93 (July/October): 415–27.

———. 2004. *Between Muslim Nationalists and Nationalist Muslims: Maududi's Thoughts on Indian Muslims*. New Delhi: Institute of Objective Studies.

Khan, Zafrul Islam. 1995. "Shahabuddins: Leave Babri Alone." *Muslim and Arab Perspective* 2 (4–7): 110.

———. 1997. *Hijrah in Islam*. London: Muslim Institute.

Khilnani, Sunil. 1992. "India's Democratic Career." *In* John Dunn (ed.), *Democracy: The Unfinished Journey*. Oxford: Oxford University Press.

———. 1997. *The Idea of India*. New Delhi: Penguin.

Kohli, Atul, (ed.). 2001. *The Success of India's Democracy*. Cambridge: Cambridge University Press

Kramer, Martin, (ed.). 1997. *The Islamist Debate*. Moshe Dayan Center for Middle Eastern and African Studies. Dayan Center Papers 120. Tel Aviv: Tel Aviv University Press.

Krishna, Gopal. 1967. "Electoral Participation and Political Integration." *Economic and Political Weekly* (February): 179–90.

———. 1972. "Piety and Politics in Indian Islam." *Contributions to Indian Sociology* (n.s.): 143–71.

Kumar, Krishan. 1993. "Civil Society: An Inquiry into the Usefulness of an Historical Term." *British Journal of Sociology* 44 (3): 375–95.

Kurzman, Charles. 2003. "The Poststructuralist Consensus in Social Movement Theory." *In* Jeff Goodwin and James M. Jasper (eds.), *Rethinking Social Movements*. Lanham, Md.: Rowman and Littlefield

———. 2004. "Conclusion." *In* Quintan Wiktorowicz (ed.).

Laclau, Ernesto, and Chantal Mouffe. 2001. *Hegemony and Socialist Strategy: Towards a Radical Democratic Politics*. 2nd ed. London: Verso.

Lambton, A. K. S. 1988. "Introduction." *In* K. Ferdinand et al. (eds.), *Islam: State and Society*. London: Curzon.

Lawrence, Bruce B. 1987. "Muslim Fundamentalist Movements: Reflections towards a New Approach." *In* B. F. Stowasser (ed.), *The Islamic Impulse*. London: Croom Helm.

———. 1995. *Defenders of God: The Fundamentalist Revolt against the Modern Age*. Columbia: University of South Carolina Press.

Lee, Robert D. 1997. *Overcoming Tradition and Modernity: The Search for Islamic Authenticity*. Oxford: Westview.

Lelyveld, D. 1978. *Aligarh's First Generation: Muslim Solidarity in British India*. Princeton, N.J.: Princeton University Press.

Lenin, V. 1. 1970. *What Is to Be Done?* Translated from the Russian and edited by S. Utechin. London: Panther.

Lewins, F. 1989. "Recasting the Concept of Ideology: A Content Approach." *British Journal of Sociology* 40 (4): 678–93.

Lewis, Bernard. 1988. *The Political Language of Islam*. Chicago: University of Chicago Press.

———. 1993. *Islam and the West*. Oxford: Oxford University Press.

———. 1996. "A Historical View: Islam and Liberal Democracy." *Journal of Democracy* 7 (2): 52–63.

———. 2002. *What Went Wrong?* Oxford: Oxford University Press.

———. 2003. *The Crisis of Islam*. London: Weidenfeld and Nicolson.

Lijphart, Arend. 1996. "The Puzzle of Indian Democracy: A Consociational Interpretation." *American Political Science Review* 90 (2): 258–68.
Lippmann, Walker. 2005. *The Stakes of Diplomacy*. Kessinger.
Lipset, Martin. 1971. *Rebellion in the University*. Boston: Little, Brown.
Ludden, David (ed.). 1996. *Contesting the Nation: Religion, Community, and the Politics of Democracy in India*. Philadelphia: University of Pennsylvania Press.
———. 1996. "Introduction." *In* David Ludden (ed.).
Luker, Kristin. 1984. *Abortion and the Politics of Motherhood*. Berkeley: University of California Press.
MacKenzie, Ian, and Sinisa Malesevick (eds.). 2002. *Ideology after Poststructuralism*. London: Pluto.
Madan, T. N. 1987. "Secularism in Its Place." *Journal of Asian Studies* 46 (4): 747–59.
———. 1993. "Whither Indian Secularism?" *Modern Asian Studies* 27 (3): 667–97.
———. 1997. *Modern Myths, Locked Minds*. New Delhi: Oxford University Press.
———. 1998. "Composite Culture: Inadequacy of Secular Response." *Times of India*, April 4.
Mahajan, Gurpreet. 2003. "Secularism." *In* Veena Das (ed.), *The Oxford Indian Companion to Sociology and Social Anthropology*. Vol. 1. New Delhi: Oxford University Press.
Maheshwari, Anil. 2001. *Aligarh Muslim University: Perfect Past and Precarious Present*. New Delhi: UBSPD.
Mahmood, Saba. 2004. "Is Liberalism Islam's Only Answer?" *In* Khaled Abou El Fadl (ed.).
Mahmood, Siddiq. 1994. "Jamaat-e-Islami Hind and Its Contribution to Education: A Critical Study." Ph.d. thesis, Martahwada University, Aurangabad.
Majumdar, R. C. (ed.). 1960. *The Delhi Sultanate*. Bombay: Bhartiya Vidya Bhavan.
Malesevick, Sinisa. 2002. "Rehabilitating Ideology after Poststructuralism." *In* Ian MacKenzie and Sinisa Malesevick (eds.).
Malik, Hafeez. 1980. *Moslem Nationalism in India and Pakistan*. Lahore: People's Publishing House.
Malkani, K. R. 1986. "K. R. Malkani." *In* Ameenul Hasan Rizvi (ed.), *The Dialogue between Hindus and Muslims*. New Delhi: Crescent.
Mann, E. A. 1992. *Boundaries and Identities: Muslims, Work, and Status in Aligarh*. New Delhi: Sage.
Mann, Michael. 2005. *The Dark Side of Democracy: Explaining Ethnic Cleansing*. Cambridge: Cambridge University Press.
Marcus, George E. 1995. "Ethnography in/of the World System: The Emergence of Multi-sited Ethnography." *Annual Review of Anthropology* 24: 95–117.
Marcus, George E., and Michael M. J. Fischer. 1986. *Anthropology as Cultural Critique: An Experimental Moment in the Human Sciences*. Chicago: University of Chicago Press.
Markovitz, Claude. 2002 [1994]. *A History of Modern India, 1480–1950*. Translated by Nisha George and Maggy Hendry. London: Anthem.

Martins, E. C. de Rezende. 2001. "Political Parties, History of." *In* Neil J. Smelser et al. (eds.), *International Encyclopedia of Social and Behavioral Sciences*. Amsterdam: Elsevier.

Marty, M. E., and S. R. Appleby (eds.). 1991–1995. *The Fundamentalism Project*. 5 vols. Chicago: University of Chicago Press.

McAdam, Doug. 1982. *Political Process and Development of Black Insurgency, 1930–70*. Chicago: University of Chicago Press.

McAdam, Doug, et al. 1988. "Social Movements." *In* Neil J. Smelser (ed.), *A Handbook of Sociology*. Newbury Park, Calif.: Sage.

McAdam, Doug, et al. 1996. "Introduction: Opportunities: Mobilizing Structures and and Framing Processes—Towards a Synthetic, Comparative Perspective on Social Movements." *In* Doug McAdam et al. (eds.), *Comparative Perspectives on Social Movements: Political Opportunities, Mobilizing Structures, and Cultural Framings*. Cambridge: Cambridge University Press.

McDonough, Sheila. 1991. "Shibli Numani: A Conservative Vision of Revitalized Islam." *In* Rober D. Baird (ed.).

McLane, John R. 1988. "The Early Congress, Hindu Populism, and the Wider Society." *In* Richard Sisson and Staley Wolpert (eds.).

Mehta, Pratap Bhanu. 2004. "Why the BJP Is Calm: What Would a Hindu State Do That the Secular State Has Not Done Already?" *Telegraph*, March 4.

Mehta, Uday Singh. 1999. *Liberalism and Empire: A Study in Nineteenth-Century Liberal Thought*. Chicago: University of Chicago Press.

Meier, Heinrich. 2002. "What Is Political Theology?" *Interpretation: A Journal of Political Philosophy* 30 (1): 79–91.

Melucci, Alberto. 1996. *Challenging Codes: Collective Action in the Information Age*. Cambridge: Cambridge University Press.

Members.tripod.com. 2004. "Muslims Should Blame Themselves."
members.tripod.com/~babrimasjid/blame.htm. Accessed on 7/23/2004.

Metcalf, Barbara D. 1982. *Islamic Revival in British India: Deoband, 1860–1900*. Princeton, N.J.: Princeton University Press.

———. 1990. *Perfecting Women: Maulana Ashraf Ali Thanvi's Bahishto Zewar, A Partial Translation with Commentary*. Berkeley: University of California Press.

———. 1995. "Too Little and Too Much: Reflections on Muslims in the History of India." *Journal of Asian Studies* 54 (4): 951–67.

Metcalf, Barbara D., and Thomas R. Metcalf. 2002. *A Concise History of India*. Cambridge: Cambridge University Press.

Middle East Quarterly. 1999. "Is Islam a Threat—A Debate?" December 6 (4): 29–40.

Minault, Gail. 1982. *The Khilafat Movement: Religious Symbolism and Political Mobilization in India*. New York: Columbia University Press.

Mitra, Subrata Kumar. 1991. "Desecularizing the State: Religion and Politics in India after Independence." *Comparative Studies in Society and History* 33 (4): 755–77.

Moghissi, Haideh. 1999. *Feminism and Islamic Fundamentalism: The Limits of Postmodern Analysis*. London: Zed.

Monsma, Stephen V., and Chrisopher Soper. 1997. *The Challenge of Pluralism: Church and State in Five Democracies*. Lanham, Md.: Rowan and Littlefield.

Morris, Aldon D., and Carol M. Muller (eds.). 1992. *Frontiers in Social Movement Theory*. New Haven, Conn.: Yale University Press.

Mufti, Aamir. 2000. "The Aura of Authenticity." *Social Text* 18 (3): 87–103.

———. 2000a. "Auerbach in Istanbul: Edward Said, Secular Criticism, and the Question of Minority Culture." *In* Paul A. Bove (ed.), *Edward Said and the Work of the Critic: Speaking Truth to Power*. Durham, N.C.: Duke University Press.

———. 2007. *Enlightenment in the Colony: The Jewish Question and the Crisis of Postcolonial Culture*. Princeton, N.J.: Princeton University Press.

Mueller, Carol McClurg. 1992. "Building Social Movement Theory." *In* Aldon D. Morris and Carol M. Muller (eds.).

Mueller, Gustav E. 1958. "The Hegel Legend of 'Thesis-Antithesis-Synthesis'." *Journal of the History of Ideas* 19 (3): 411–14.

Muhammad, Shan. 1973. *Khaksar Movement in India*. Meerut: Meenakshi Prakashan.

Mujeeb, Mohammad. 1972. *Dr. Zakir Husain*. New Delhi: National Book Trust.

Naim, Chaudhri Mohammed. 1999. *Ambiguities of Heritage*. Karachi: City Press.

Nandy, Ashis 1985. "An Anti-Secularist Manifesto." *Seminar* (October) 314:14–24.

———. 1991. "Hinduism versus Hindutva: The Inevitability of a Confrontation." *Times of India*, February 18, editorial page.

———. 1998. "The Politics of Secularism and the Recovery of Religious Toleration." *In* Rajeev Bhargava (ed.).

———. 2002. *Time Warps: Silent and Evasive Pasts in Indian Politics and Religion*. London: Hurst.

Nasr, Syed Vali Reza. 1994. *The Vanguard of Islamic Revolution: The Jamaat-e-Islami of Pakistan*. Berkeley: University of California Press.

———. 1994a. "Maududi and the Jamaat-e-Islami: The Origins, Theory, and Practice of Islamic Revivalism." *In* Ali Rehnema (ed.), *Pioneers of Islamic Revival*. London: Zed Books.

———. 1996. *Maududi and the Making of Islamic Revivalism*. New York: Oxford University Press.

Needham, Anuradha Dingwaney, and Rajeswari Sundar Rajan (eds.). 2007. *The Crisis of Secularism in India*. Durham, N.C.: Duke University Press.

Negt, O., and Alexander Kluge. 1993. *Public Sphere and Experience: Towards an Analysis of Bourgeois and Proletarian Public Sphere*. Minneapolis: University of Minnesota Press.

Nehru, Jawaharlal. 1993. "China, Pakistan and Communalism." *In* S Gopal (ed.), *Selected Works of Jawaharlal Nehru*, vol. 15, part 1, 2nd series. New Delhi: Oxford University Press.

Nizami, Z. A. 1975. *Jamaat-e-Islami: Spearhead of Communalism*. New Delhi: Ministry of Information and Broadcasting, Government of India.

Noorani, A. G. 2000. *The RSS and the BJP: A Division of Labor*. Delhi: Leftword.

———. 2003. *The Muslims of India: A Documentary Record*. New Delhi: Oxford University Press.

Oliver, Pamela E. and Hank Johnston. 2000. "What a Good Idea! Ideologies and Frames in Social Movement Research." *Mobilization* 5 (1): 37–54.

Oommen, T. K. 1972. *Charisma, Stability, and Change: An Analysis of Bhoodan-Gramdan Movement in India*. New Delhi: Thompson.

Orsini, Francesca. 2002. *The Hindi Public Sphere, 1920–40: Language and Literature in the Age of Nationalism*. Oxford: Oxford University Press.

Osella, Caroline, and Filippo Osella. 2007. "Muslim Style in South India." *Fashion Theory* 11 (2–3): 233–52.

The Oxford Dictionary of Islam. 2003. Edited by John Esposito. Oxford: Oxford University Press.

Pandey, Gyanendra. 1988. "'Encounters and Calamities': The History of a North Indian *Qasba* in the Nineteenth Century." *In* R. Guha and G. Spivak (eds.), *Selected Subaltern Studies*. Oxford: Oxford University Press

———. 1990. *The Construction of Coomunalism in Colonial North India*. New Delhi: Oxford University Press.

———. 1993. "Which of US Are Hindus." *In* G. Pandey (ed.), *Hindus and Others*. New Delhi: Viking.

———. 1998. "Beyond Majorities and Minorities." *Times of India*, February 17, editorial page.

———. 1999. "Can a Muslim Be an Indian?" *Comparative Studies in Society and History* 41 (4): 608–29.

Parsa, V. 2002. "RSS Breaks New Ground, Hoists Tricolor for 2nd Time since Independence." www.tehelka.com/cahnnels/currentaffairs/2002/jan/27/printable/ca012/02rsspr.htm. Accessed on 2/2/2002.

Parekh, Bhikhu. 1995. "Ethnocentrity of the Nationalist Discourse." *Nations and Nationalism* 1 (1): 25–52.

———. 1998. "Cultural Diversity and Liberal Democracy." *In* Gurpreet Mahajan (ed.), *Democracy, Difference, and Social Justice*. New Delhi: Oxford University Press.

———. 2000. *Rethinking Multiculturalism: Cultural Diversity and Political Theory*. London: Palgrave.

Peirano, Mariza G. S. 1998. "When Anthropology is at Home: The Different Contexts of a Single Discipline." *Annual Review of Anthropology* 27:105–28.

Pels, Peter, and Oscar Salemink. 1994. "Five Theses on Ethnography as Colonial Practice." *History and Anthropology* 8 (4): 1–34.

Poeisz, Joseph J. 1967. "God's People on the Way." *In* Michel van der Plas and Henk Suer (eds.), *Those Dutch Catholics*. London: Geoffrey Chapman.

Puri, Balraj. 2003. "Iqbal and the Idea of Pakistan." *Economic and Political Weekly* (February 1): 490–93.

Purvis, Trevor, and Alan Hunt. 1993. "Discourse, Ideology, Discourse, Ideology, Discourse, Ideology . . ." *British Journal of Sociology* 44 (3): 473–99.

Putnam, Robert D. 1993. *Making Democracy Work: Civic Traditions in Modern Italy*. Princeton, N.J.: Princeton University Press.

———. 1995. "Bowling Alone: America's Declining Social Capital." *Journal of Democracy* 6 (1): 65–77.

———. 2000. *Bowling Alone: The Collapse and Revival of American Community*. New York: Simon and Schuster.

Qureshi, Ishtiaq Husain. 1962. *The Muslim Community of Indo-Pakistan Subcontinent, 610–1947*. Mouton: The Hague.

Quraishi, Z. M. 1971. "Emergence and Eclipse of Muslim Majlis-e-Mushawarat." *Economic and Political Weekly* (June 19): 1229–34.

Rahman, Fazlur. 1958. "Muslim Modernism in the Indo-Pakistan Sub-Continent." *Bulletin of the School of Oriental and African Studies* 21 (1/3): 82–99.

Rahman, Ubiadur. 2004. *Understanding the Muslim Leadership in India*. New Delhi: Global Media Publications.

Ramakers, J. J. M. 1996. "Parallel Processes: The Emancipation of Jews and Catholics in the Netherlands, 1795/96–1848." *Studia Rosenthaliana* 30 (1): 33–40.

Ray, Anil Baran. 1977. *Student and Politics in India: The Role of Caste, Language, and Region in an Indian University*. Delhi: Manohar.

Rizvi, S. A. A. 1970. "The Breakdown of Traditional Society." *In* P. M. Holt et al. (eds), *The Cambridge History of Islam*, vol. 2A. Cambridge: Cambridge University Press.

Robinson, Francis. 1979. "Islam and Muslim Separatism." *In* David Taylor and Malcolm Yaap (eds.). *Political Identity in South Asia*. London: Curzon.

———. 1989. "Congress Muslims and Indian Nationalism." *Modern Asian Studies* 23 (3): 609–19.

Roy, Arunhdhati. 2002. "The Holy Name of Liberty." *New Statesman* (June 10): 24–26.

Roy, Oliver. 1994. *The Failure of Political Islam*. Translated by Carol Volk. London: I.B. Tauris.

———. 2007. *Secularism Confronts Islam*. Translated by George Holoch. New York: Columbia University Press.

Roy, Ramashray. 2005. *Democracy in India: Form and Substance*. New Delhi: Shipra.

Rudolph, Lloyd, and Susan Rudolph. 1960. "The Political Role of India's Caste Associations." *Pacific Affairs* 33 (1): 5–22.

———. 1987. *In Pursuit of Lakshmi: The Political Economy of the Indian State*. Chicago: University of Chicago Press.

———. 2000. "Living with Difference in India." *The Political Quarterly* 71 (3): 20–38.

Rushdie, Salman. 2005. "Muslims Unite! A New Reformation Will Bring Your Faith into the Modern Era." http://www.timesonline.co.uk/article/0,,1072-1729998,00.html. Accessed on 8/19/2005.

Russel, Ralph. 1992. *The Pursuit of Urdu Literature: A Select History*. London: Zed.

Said, Edward. 1995. *Orientalism*. 2nd ed. London: Penguin.

Samad, Yunas. 1995. *A Nation in Turmoil: Nationalism and Ethnicity in Pakistan, 1937–58*. Delhi: Sage.

Sanyal, Usha. 1999. *Devotional Islam and Politics in British India: Ahmad Riza Khan Barelwi and His Movement, 1870–1920*. Delhi: Oxford University Press.

Saran, Shankar. 2002. "Madrasa Business in Terrorism." *World Focus* (January): 23–27.

Sardar, Ziauddin. 2003. "Maulana Syed Abul-Ala Maududi." *New Statesman* (July 14): 28–29.

Sarkar, Sumit. 1993. "The Fascism of the Sangh Parivar." *Economic and Political Weekly* 28 (5): 163–67.

———. 2001. "Indian Democracy: The Historical Inheritance." *In* Atul Kohli (ed.).

Savarkar, V. D. 1989. *Hindutva*. Bombay: Veer Savarkar Prakashan.

Sayyid, Bobby. 1997. *A Fundamental Fear: Eurocentrism and the Emergence of Islamism*. London: Zed.

Schmitt, Carl. 1996. *The Concept of the Political*. Translated with an introduction by George Schwab. Chicago: University of Chicago Press.

Schneider, Jane, ed. 1998. *Italy's "Southern Questions": Orientalism in One Country*. New York: Berg.

Schwartz, Morton. 1955. "The Wavering 'Line' of Indian Communism." *Political Science Quarterly* 70 (4): 552–72.

Schwartz, Stephen. 2003. *The Two Faces of Islam: Saudi Fundamentalism and Its Role in Terrorism*. Reprint. New York: Anchor Books.

Schwedler, Jillian. 2006. *Faith in Moderation: Islamist Parties in Jordan and Yemen*. Cambridge: Cambridge University Press.

Sen, Amartya. 1992. *Inequality Examined*. Cambridge, Mass.: Harvard University Press.

———. 1993. "The Threats to Indian Secularism." *New York Review of Books*, April 8, 26–32.

———. 1998. "Secularism and Its Discontents." *In* Rajeev Bhargava (ed.).

Shakir, Moin. 1970. "Maulana Maudoodi and Socialism." *Mainstream* (January 3): 13–14.

———. 1970a. "The Theory and Practice of Jamaat-e-Islami Hind." *Secular Democracy* (May): 29–33.

———. 1983. *From Khilafat to Partition*. Rev. ed. Delhi: Ajanta.

Sharma, K. L., and Dipnakar Gupta (eds.). 1991. *Country-Town Nexus: Studies in Social Transformation in Contemporary India*. Jaipur: Rawat.

Shepard, William E. 2003. "Sayyid Qutb's Doctrine of Jihad." *International Journal of Middle East Studies* 35:521–45.

Siddiqi, Jamal Muhammad. 1981. *Aligarh District: A Historical Survey (from Ancient Times to 1803 AD)*. Delhi: Munshiram Manoharlal.

Sikand, Yoginder. 2005. *Bastions of Believers: Madrasas and Islamic Education in India*. Delhi: Penguin.

Sisson, Richard, and Stanley Wolpert (eds.). 1988. *Congress and Indian Nationalism: The Pre-Independence Phase*. Berkeley: University of California Press.

Sivan, Emmanuel. 1990. *Radical Islam: Medieval Theology and Modern Politics*. Enl. ed. New Haven, Conn.: Yale University Press.

———. 1992. "The Islamic Resurgence: The Civil Society Strikes Back." *In* Lawrence Kaplan (ed.), *Fundamentalism in Comparative Perspective*. Amherst: University of Massachusetts Press.

———. 2003. "The Clash within Islam." *Survival* 45 (1): 25–44.
Smith, Christian. 1996. "Correcting a Curious Neglect, or Bringing Religion Back in." *In* Christian Smith (ed.), *Disruptive Religion: The Force of Faith in Social Movement Activism*. New York: Routledge.
Smith, Wilfred C. 1946. *Modern Islam in India*. 2nd rev. ed. Delhi: Usha.
———. 1957. *Islam in Modern History*. New York: Mentor Books.
Snow, David A., and Robert D. Benford. 1992. "Master Frames and Cycles of Protest." *In* Aldon D. Morris and Carol M. Muller (eds), *Frontiers in Social Movement Theory*. New Haven, Conn.: Yale University Press.
Snow, David A., et al. 1986. "Frame Alignment Process, Micromobilization and Movement Participation." *American Sociological Review* 51:464–81.
Spencer, Robert. 2002. *Islam Unveiled: Disturbing Questions about the World's Fastest Growing Faith*. San Francisco: Encounter Books.
———. 2004. *Onward Muslim Soldiers: How Jihad Still Threatens America and the West*. Washington, D.C.: Regnery.
Stauth, Georg. 1991. "Revolution in Spiritless Times: An Essay on Michel Foucault's Enquiries into the Iranian Revolution." *International Sociology* 6 (3): 259–80.
Swidler, A. 1986. "Culture in Action: Symbols and Strategies." *American Sociological Review* 51:273–86.
Taji-Farouki, Suha. 1996. *A Fundamental Quest: Hizb al Tahrir and the Search for the Islamic Caliphate*. London: Grey Seal.
Tambiah, Stanley J. 1998. "The Crisis of Secularism in India." *In* Rajeev Bhargava (ed.).
Tamimi, Azzam. 2000. "The Origin of Arab Secularism." *In* John L. Esposito and Azzam Tamimi (eds.).
Tarrow, Sidney. 1994. *Power in Movement*. Cambridge: Cambridge University Press.
———. 1996. "Making Social Science Work across Space and Time: A Critical Reflection on Robert Putnam's Making Democracy Work." *American Political Science Review* 90 (2): 389–97.
———. 1998. *Power in Movement*. 2nd ed. Cambridge: Cambridge University Press.
Thapan, Meenakshi. 1991. *Life at School: An Ethnographic Study*. Delhi: Oxford University Press.
Thapar, Romila. 1993. "A Historical Perspective on the Story of Rama." *In* S. Gopal (ed.), *Anatomy of a Confrontation: The Rise of Communal Politics in India*. London: Zed.
Therborn, Goran. 1980. *The Ideology of Power and Power of Ideology*. London: Verso, NLB.
Thomas, Nicholas. 1991. "Against Ethnography." *Cultural Anthropology* 6 (3): 306–32.
Thompson, John. 1990. *Ideology and Modern Culture*. Stanford: Stanford University Press.
Tibi, Bassam. 1990. *Islam and the Cultural Accommodation of Change*. Boulder, Colo.: Westview.

———. 1999. "The Fundamentalist Challenge to the Secular Order in the Middle East." *Fletcher Forum of World Affairs* 23 (1): 191–210.

———. 1995. "Islamic Dream of Semimodernity." *India International Center Quarterly* (spring): 78–87.

———. 2002. "War and Peace in Islam." *In* Sohail H. Hashmi (ed.), *Islamic Political Ethics*. Princeton, N.J.: Princeton University Press.

Tilly, Charles. 1984. "Social Movement and National Politics." *In* Charles Bright et al. (eds.), *State Making and Social Movements*. Ann Arbor: University of Michigan Press.

———. 1995. *Popular Contention in Great Britain, 1758–1834*. Cambridge, Mass.: Harvard University Press.

———. 2002. *Stories, Identities, and Political Change*. Lanham, Md.: Rowman and Littlefield.

———. 2004. "Foreword." *In* Quintan Wiktorowicz (ed.).

Timmerman, K. R. 2003. *Preachers of Hate: Islam and the War on America*. New York: Crown Forum.

Touraine, Alain. 1981. *The Voice and the Eye: An Analysis of Social Movements*. Cambridge: Cambridge University Press.

———. 1985. "An Introduction to the Study of Social Movements." *Social Research*. 54 (4): 749–87.

Turner, Bryan S. 1984. "Orientalism and the Problem of Civil Society in Islam." *In* Asaf Hussain et al. (eds.).

———. 1984a. "Gustave E. Von Grunebaum and the Mimesis of Islam." *In* A. Hussain et al. (eds.).

———. 2002. "Soverignty and Emergency: Political Theology, Islam, and American Conservatism." *Theory, Culture and Society* 19 (4): 103–19.

———. 2002a. "Orientalism, or the Politics of the Text." *In* Hastings Donnan (ed.).

Tyabji, Badruddin. 1971. *The Self in Secularism*. New Delhi: Orient Longman.

Usmani, S. H. 1975. "Jamaat-e-Islami: Muslim Counterpart of RSS." *Secular Democracy* (August): 75–85.

Vanaik, Achin. 2001. "The New Indian Right." *New Left Review* (May–June): 43–67.

Van der Veer, Peter. 1987. "'God Must Be Liberated!': A Hindu Liberation Movement in Ayodhya." *Modern Asian Studies* 21 (2): 283–301.

———. 1988. *Gods on Earth: The Management of Religious Experience and Identity in a North Indian Pilgrimage Center*. London: Athlone Press.

———. 1993. "The Foreign Hand: Orientalist Discourse in Sociology and Communalism." *In* Carol A. Breckenridge and Peter Van der Veer (eds.).

———. 1994. *Religious Nationalism: Hindus and Muslims in India*. New Delhi: Oxford University Press.

———. 1994a. "Hindu Nationalism and the Discourse of Modernity: The Vishwa Hindu Parishad." *In* M. Marty, and S. Appleby (eds.), *Accounting for Fundamentalisms*. Chicago: University of Chicago Press.

———. 2001. *Imperial Encounters: Religion and Modernity in India and Britain*. Princeton, N.J.: Princeton University Press.

———. 2006. "Pim Fortuyn, Theo van Gogh, and the Politics of Tolerance in the Netherlands." *Public Culture* 18 (1): 111–24.

———. Forthcoming. *Secularism in India.*

Van Rooden, Peter. 2003. "Long-term Religious Developments in the Netherlands, c. 1750–2000." *In* Hugh McLeod and Werner Ustorf (eds.), *The Decline of Christendom in Western Europe, 1750–200.* Cambridge: Cambridge University Press.

Varshney, Ashutosh. 1997. "Postmodernism, Civic Engagements, and Ethnic Conflicts: A Passage to India." *Comparative Politics* 30 (1): 1–20.

———. 2002. *Ethnic Conflict and Civic Life: Hindus and Muslims in India.* New Delhi: Oxford University Press.

———. 2002a. "Understanding Gujarat Violence." *Items and Issues* 4 (1): 1–5.

Viswanathan, Gauri. 1989. *Masks of Conquest: Literary Study and British Rule in India.* New York: Columbia University Press.

Vohra, Ranbir. 1997. *The Making of India: A Historical Survey.* Armonk, N.Y.: M. E. Sharpe.

Walzer, Michael. 1991. "The Idea of Civil Society." *Dissent* (Spring): 293–304.

Warren, Mark. E. 1999. "Democratic Theory and Trust." *In* Mark E. Warren (ed.), *Democracy and Trust.* Cambridge: Cambridge University Press.

Weiner, Myron. 1987. "Political Change: Asia, Africa, and the Middle East." *In* Myron Weiner and Samuel Huntington (eds.), *Understanding Political Development.* Boston: Little, Brown.

Wiktorowicz, Quintan (ed.). 2004. *Islamic Activism: A Social Movement Theory Approach.* Bloomington: Indiana University Press.

Wiktorowicz, Quintan. 2004. "Introduction." *In* Quintan Witorowicz (ed.).

Wolin, R. 1990. "Carl Schmitt, Political Existentialism, and the State." *Theory and Society* 19 (4): 389–416.

World Bank Website. 2004. "WD1-2004 table 2.5 Poverty." http://www.worldbank.org/data/wdi2004/pdfs/table2-5.pdf. Accessed on 5/10/2004.

Wright, Theodore P. Jr. 1966. "Muslim Education in India at the Crossroads: The Case of Aligarh." *Pacific Affairs* 39 (1–2): 50–63.

Young, Iris Marion. 2000. *Inclusion and Democracy.* New York: Oxford University Press.

Zaidi, Ali Jawad. 1993. *A History of Urdu Literature.* Delhi: Sahitya Academy.

Zakaria, Rafiq. 1994. *Iqbal: The Poet and the Politician.* Delhi: Penguin.

———. 1995. The *Widening Divide: An Insight into Hindu-Muslim Relations.* Delhi: Penguin.

Zamindar, Vazira. 2007. *The Long Partition and the Making of Modern South Asia.* New York: Columbia University Press.

Žižek, Slavoj (ed.). 1994. *Mapping Ideology.* London: Verso.

Index

Abdulaziz, Shah, 53, 247n22
Abu-Lughod, Lila, 35
Adams, Charles, 50
Advani, L. K., 35, 168, 177, 261n5
Afghanistan, 26, 32, 111, 117, 245; operation "infinite justice," "enduring freedom" and bombing of, 35; protest by Islamists and Naxalites against the Soviet invasion of, 257n17; Soviet invasion of, 174
Agnivesh, Swami, 212
Ahl-e-hadīth, 23, 40, 47, 85, 88, 91,100, 132; eastern UP as stronghold of, 140; expulsion from Deoband of students belonging to, 143; Falāh and, 143; introduction in Aligarh (*shahr*) of, 248n13; Jamaat and, 47; madrasa at Varanasi of, 23, 255n14; notion of Allah's vice regent and, 250n24
Ahl-e-sunnah-o-Jamaat (known as Barēlvīs), 23, 32, 40, 67, 85, 100, 132, 250n26, 255n14; Ahl-e-hadīth and, 248n13; polytheism and, 67, 143–44
Ahmad, Qazi Ashfaq (Jamaat leader), 47
Ahrar (Majlis), 247n19
Al-banna, Hasan, 139
Al-beruni, 24
Algeria, 218, 228; causes of radicalization in Egypt and, 227; the state repression against Islamists in Egypt and, 227
Al-Jihad fil Islam (Maududi), 245n5
Ali, Abul Hasan (Nadwi; rector of Nadwa): critique of Maududi by, 249n18; resignation from Jamaat by, 72
Ali, Nawab Amir, 51
Ali, Syed Hamid (Jamaat leader), 213
Aligarh, xii, 1, 4, 27, 31, 34, 35–46, 50–52, 74, 88–90, 93, 98, 103–05, 116, 118, 121, 128, 133, 135, 150, 154, 163, 169–70, 188, 226, 231, 252n3, 253nn1 and 14, 255n14; BJP in, 169; bombing of Afghanistan and public mood in, 111; caste/*birādrī* among Muslims of, 39, 248n6; expansion of Jamaat in, 46–48; history of, 247n4; internet cafés in, 121–22; Jamaat's research institute at, 93, 128; marriage in, 40; *numā'ish* (exhibition) in, 133; power failure in, 46; Rābṭā Committee formed in, 103; sect-based identities in, 34, 40; SIMI activists in, 163; soil of, 98; temple campaign and riots in, 169. *See also* Civil Line (Aligarh); *Shahr* (Aligarh)
Aligarh Muslim University (AMU), 4, 12, 27, 31, 37, 39–41, 44, 45–47, 51, 66, 75, 83, 85, 87, 88–99, 101–02, 105–07, 109–17, 119–22, 124–25, 133, 142, 154, 159, 169, 171, 194, 196–97, 210, 218, 222–23, 225–26, 228, 237, 251n2, 255nn12 and 14; anti-nationals and, 36; Banaras Hindu University and, 253n6; boycott by the Jamaat of institutions such as, 75–77; as breeding ground of terrorism, 36; *chungī* at, 134; dance party at, 129; defence by the Jamaat of, 126; as embodiment of Muslim culture, 43; the government's attempt to secularize, 125–26; Hindu students at, 173, 253n4; as an institution of *jāhiliyat*, 50; Kennedy auditorium of, 169; Maududi's lecture at, 69; media's vilification of, 36; as the microcosm of Indian Muslims, 43; Muslim character of, 125; radical politics at, 245n5; recognition of madrasa degrees by, 142–43, 252n6; Shamshad market at, 134; as "slaughterhouse," 75, 251n40; western culture at, 75
Aligarh Muslim University Student Union (AMUSU), 145; 1991–92 elections of, 167; SIMI and the elections of, 170–73; use of poetry in the elections of, 171; victory of the SIMI candidate in the elections of, 173
Aligarh Public School, 105
Allah, 74, 89, 103, 114, 125, 132, 145, 172, 174, 177, 183, 187, 215, 217; deputy/vice regent of, 66, 77, 250n24; disobedience to, 205; legislation against, 204, 206–07; meaning of, 65–66;